Stretching to Soar

A Yearlong Journey in the Walk of Faith

-a devotional-

Chad Hawkes

Hawkeye Press
Second Edition

Preface

I began the writing process for this book on January 1st, 2014, after the Lord prompted me to write down the things He has shown me in His Word over the years. I had just expected to write everyday for a year, but I did not imagine that it would come to this, an actual book with over three hundred pages. It took me fourteen months to finish the actual writing of the book, and many more to finish the editing.

I had no idea what it took to write and publish a book; I was only trying to be obedient to what I heard from the Lord. It is finally in 2017 that I see this book being published and I am ecstatic, especially when reading through it a few times, seeing what God has shown me then and what He has shown me since. It is truly remarkable what God does to and through a person in the course of a year, let alone a lifetime if we are but able to see it!

This book is intended for people in all stages of the Christian walk, hopefully appealing and connecting with those who are new to the faith, and those who have walked for years with Christ. Some of you may be offended by parts of my writing and if that is the case, I pray it is the Holy Spirit prompting you to repentance or to look at the Word of God in a different light. My goal is not to offend, but to proclaim truth.

I was twenty-three years old for the majority of this book and now I am twenty-six. Many things have happened since the writings stored within this devotional and I wrote them with the mindset and spiritual insight from the Lord at that time. Even as I am writing this, I pray for you who will read it, that it may truly bless you as it has blessed me in writing and rereading it. Compare everything contained in these pages with the Holy Scriptures to see whether it is true or false. The Scriptures are our highest authority as followers of Christ and I pray my words do not contradict it. If they do, then disregard them. Peace be with you.

Chad Hawkes

June 10, 2017

"Forget the former things; do not dwell on the past. See, I am doing a new thing! Now it springs up; do you not perceive it? I am making a way in the desert and streams in the wasteland" – Isaiah 43:18-19

It is a new year. New things. New. Different. Better? People like to make New Year's resolutions to give themselves something to aspire to, to aim for, and to push towards. But why? Because they do not like themselves as they are in their present state. They want to change themselves because they are sick of who they are now and desire to be better. Whether that is to lose weight or quit smoking or get a new job, they want to be better in some way.

But why do we not desire this new year to give life to those around us? Why not desire to shine light in the darkness and love the unlovable? Why not? "See, I am doing a new thing!...I am making a way in the desert and streams in the wasteland." The Lord through Isaiah teaches us that there is life and fruitfulness amidst the places that look dead and dark, we have only to perceive it, to open our eyes and heart to not dwell on the past, but to see that a new thing is happening and it is not as it was before.

"Therefore, if anyone is in Christ he is a new creation: the old has gone, the new has come!" (2 Corinthians 5:17). New, as in, not old, as in better. At least we hope it is better, for that is why most people choose new things because they believe it will be better than the old things. We are a new creation. We do not need to live like we used to before we were made new in Christ because the old is gone. The old, last year, is over with and this new year is upon us. Are we going to perceive it? Are we going to expect a better year, a year where we walk in closer intimacy with the Lord every day and not just a few days a week? "I am making a way in the desert." We must follow the way that He is making for us, for He is the Way, the Truth, and the Life. We must follow Him. If you are going to make any New Year's resolution this year, may it be something that will impact every other area of your life for the better. Make a resolution to follow the Lord intently and stick with it. He desires and longs for intimacy with you, and He desires for you to desire Him. Yearn for Him. He will not disappoint you and it will be the best year of your life.

January 2

"In the same way, count yourselves dead to sin but alive to God in Christ Jesus" –
Romans 6:11

Keeping with the theme of newness from yesterday, God sent Jesus Christ to do a new thing that has never been done before; He sent His one and only Son to die on the cross for the forgiveness of our sins. "God made him who had no sin to be sin for us, so that in him we might become the righteousness of God" (2 Corinthians 5:21). He had to do something new because the old way of things did not release people from sin and bondage.

"The law is only a shadow of the good things that are coming—not the realities themselves. For this reason it can never, by the same sacrifices repeated endlessly year after year, make perfect those who draw near to worship" (Hebrews 10:1). The old covenant, the law, was only a foreshadowing of what God intended for His people ever since Adam and Eve fell in the garden. He knew that something must be done, and He realized that He had to send his Son to free his beloved people and to draw them in intimacy with Himself.

Since "we died with Christ, we believe we will also live with him" (6:8). Because Jesus bore our iniquities on the cross and because He rose from the dead on the third day, the old self is done away with "because anyone who has died has been freed from sin" (6:7). We are free for the first time in our lives, free from ourselves, free from sin and death if the Lord Jesus Christ is our Savior and Lord. We are no longer slaves to sin but are now slaves to God! "You have been set free from sin and have become slaves of righteousness" (6:18).

Wait, so we went from slavery to slavery? Does that not mean we are still in bondage? By no means! "You are slaves to the one whom you obey" (6:16). We no longer have to obey our flesh and the sinful nature, but we can now obey Christ and offer ourselves and "the parts of [our] body to him as instruments of righteousness" (6:13). We are alive in Christ Jesus! This is good news! What do people usually do with good news? They spread it! They tell people because they want them to experience the good news as well! We are alive because of the work Christ did. We can freely obey Him and not the flesh and our old way of life, for we are made new in Christ! What habits from your old self can now be disbanded? What new habits should you be taking up because of your being alive in Christ? Be a slave to God and His ways, not to sin and its ways. God leads to life because He is Life.

"Be joyful always; pray continually; give thanks in all circumstances, for this is God's will for you in Christ Jesus" – 1 Thessalonians 5:16-18

At this point in my life, I am an underemployed twenty-three year old college graduate that shovels snow and throws salt by hand. I do not have a social life because I am in bed by 7pm. Lately I have been getting up at 2am, 7 days a week, and working in the freezing cold, this morning at -10 degrees, and throwing between 500-1200 lbs of salt each morning. How can I heed the commands of Paul to be always joyful, always praying, and always giving thanks, while working in those miserable conditions day in and day out? How is it possible?

Well to start off, Paul also has gone through some miserable situations himself, much more miserable than anything I have gone through in my work (see 2 Corinthians 11:23-29), and yet he was one who spoke of being joyful constantly and rejoicing in the Lord! (Philippians 4:4). Secondly, since God is speaking through Paul here, we know that it is possible, for "what is impossible with men is possible with God" (Luke 18:27).

I admit, it is incredibly difficult to be joyful and thankful while working when it is 0 degrees with a -20 degree wind chill and snow blowing in your face. But hey, I get to go in the truck every now and then with the heat on and thaw out. I have water and a banana to nourish me. I have a job and the ability to make money. I have strength enough to shovel heavy snow and to throw a half ton of salt. I know the circumstances may look bleak, but there is always something to be thankful for because things could always be worse. We can continually look for the little things that come our way and be thankful and joyful for them.

Working in the morning, in the darkest of night, with the stars far above me, is one of the best conditions for praying always. I don't have to talk to other people, it's just me and my shovel and God and I can openly talk to Him about anything and everything. Thanking Him for the beautiful night sky, for my wonderful girlfriend, for friends and family, and for His Word. Praying for the sanctification of His church throughout the world, to worship Him in spirit and in truth, for His return, and any other random (even though it's not random) prayer that comes up. This is why I do not mind the work that I do, it gives me hours with the Lord to pray things out, receive revelation, and to be in His creation. I still need to work on the being joyful part, but it is a process, a process that can come to fruition. My brothers, you now see that you can "be joyful always; pray continually: [and] give thanks in all circumstances." This is God's will for us. It is indeed possible. Believe it and live it in the power of the Holy Spirit that dwells within you.

"So do not fear, for I am with you; do not be dismayed, for I am your God. I will strengthen you and help you; I will uphold you with my righteous right hand" – Isaiah 41:10

When I was ten years old, my dad and my brother and I were in a life threatening car accident. My dad only came out with a broken ankle, my brother with a broken leg and later had some liver problems and I had a ruptured diaphragm. I was in the hospital for over a week and I forget how long my brother was, but we could not eat for quite some time. We had to have feeding tubes inserted into us and we could not even drink water. We were in ICU with braces on our necks stuck in the bed 24/7. We were utterly helpless, not being able to do anything for awhile, yet here we are, over thirteen years later, able to run and jump and eat and live life to the fullest!

This was all possible because of the Lord God and His presence in our lives. This passage from Isaiah was to His people Israel, which now in the new covenant, is to those who believe in the Lord Jesus Christ. Us. The most common command in all the Scriptures is in this verse, "Do not fear." Why would that be mentioned so often in the Bible? Because people get afraid! Afraid of losing their jobs. Afraid of being rejected. Afraid of losing a loved one. People get afraid and yet, throughout the Word of God, He continually tells us not to be afraid.

Luckily I got in that car accident when I was young and naive and did not have a care in the world. I did not fear dying then because I did not have any goals and dreams in life so far, so I did not feel like I would be "missing out" on so much. My parents, through the Lord's grace and guidance, did not fear for us either, for they lived out 1 Peter 5:7, "Cast all your anxiety on him because he cares for you." But how can we live not fearing life and the things that become of it? "So do not fear, *for I am with you.*" The Lord is with us. This is what we need to remember when the troubles of life come upon us and everything looks helpless and bleak, for the Lord God "will never leave you nor forsake you" (Deuteronomy 31:6). He will help and strengthen us. He will uphold us. He will never leave us. How awesome is that! The Creator of the whole universe and all of creation, the Lord of Hosts, the Beginning and the End, will never leave us! It is quite encouraging that He will never leave us, even though we are stupid and selfish and ignorant and prideful at times. He still chooses to keep His promise to us all those years ago and love on us and extend to us mercy and kindness. We are not helpless in hopeless situations, but we are dependent on the One who is always with us. Know that in those times, it is the Lord that is holding you, as He was holding me and my family thirteen years ago. Welcome His loving and caring arms.

"Be imitators of God, therefore, as dearly loved children, and live a life of love, just as Christ loves us and gave himself up for us as a fragrant offering and sacrifice to God" - Ephesians 5:1-2

When we were growing up as babies and children, we had no idea how to act or behave, so we imitate those around us because they are doing it, so it must be what we should be doing as well. That is also how many of us, myself definitely included, got in trouble with our parents and at school, because we saw one of our friends doing something that should not be done, but we did not know that so we committed the heinous act thinking it was alright because someone in our life was also doing it.

There is a saying that imitation is the highest form of flattery, and I believe that to be true. When we imitate someone, it is because we desire to be like them, whether they be a celebrity or a mentor or a parent. But what a lot of people do not realize is that they do not necessarily look at the actions of the people they are imitating and judge whether or not their actions are right or not, they do them anyways because those they look up to are doing it.

My brothers, we must be wiser than that! We must "Be imitators of God" and not of people in the media, for they are fallen beings that do not entrust their lives to the Maker of all things. They do not live by the standards of God, but by their own whims and desires and of the world. We are to "live a life of love" in our imitation of God because "God is love" (1 John 4:8). And our right imitation of God is flattering to Him because Christ's example for us was a "fragrant offering and sacrifice to God", meaning, that it was pleasing to Him and His senses. To imitate God we must "forgive each other, *just as* in Christ God forgave you...and live a life of love, *just as* Christ loved us." (4:32,5:2, emphasis added). That is one reason why God sent Jesus to us, so that we can see in person how God lives and acts and speaks. He set for us an example that we are to follow as followers of Him. "*As I have loved you*, so you must love one another" (John 13:34, emphasis added). "Whoever claims to live in him must walk *as Jesus did*" (1 John 2:6, emphasis added). We must continually read the Gospels so we can learn and be reminded of how Jesus really did live on earth, for He was God incarnate, "For God was pleased to have all his fullness dwell in him" (Colossians 1:19). So what can you do to imitate God today? You can forgive your coworker or your friend for hurting you all those years ago and be released from that bondage. You can show mercy to those who badly need it and can never catch a break in life. You can love the unlovable by spending time with them and listening. The options are endless. Choose to be imitators of God today and please Him.

"Be kind and compassionate to one another, forgiving each other, just as in Christ God forgave you" – Ephesians 4:32

     I am in a serious relationship at this point right now with a lovely lady. We enjoy each other and have lots of fun together. We firmly believe that God has brought us together to jointly go through life and experience it together under His ultimate authority. We try and support one another in our needs and love with the Lord's love, but it is not always a walk in the park. There are obstacles that need to be addressed and issues that cannot be averted. Words are said with logic and emotion in order to get our point across so that they can see the concern as we do.

     We mess up. We fail. As my pastor Rob says, "If you have a pulse, you have issues." And boy do we have issues, issues from someone in the past that have not been resolved or gone over that affect how we relate to other people. We are human. But thank goodness, or more properly, thank God who is good, that He sent His Son Jesus Christ to come down and die, bearing all our iniquities and shame, so that we may be forgiven before our Father in heaven. Because we have messed up with God, He has forgiven us through His Son's death and resurrection, so that we "shall be as white as snow" (Isaiah 1:18). And as we learned from yesterday and with today's verse, as we have been forgiven, so we must also forgive one another.

     In our little spat today, me and my girlfriend talked things through and we forgave each other because we know we are messed up people, no matter how hard we try and do as they want and need us to, we still screw it up. We said that we will make an effort once more to love as they need to be loved and to respect as they need to be respected. We will continue to forgive one another because I am sure we will make the same mistakes over and over again. But in time, we will overcome by the blood of the Lamb and will be better able to treat each other as they need best. We have to keep our eyes fixed upon our Savior in these times where we have been hurt by someone dear to us and have the desire to hold on to our anger and begrudgingly treat them as they deserve.

     But did God treat us as we deserve? Thank goodness no! I do not want to imagine the hell that would be. At the end of the parable of the unmerciful servant, after Jesus said that the master found out mercy was not given from the one whom he had just shown mercy, he had him tortured and said "This is how my heavenly Father will treat each of you unless you forgive your brother from your heart" (Matthew 18:35). Forgive those who have hurt you as Christ did. It will bring freedom into your life and relationships.

"One thing I ask of the Lord, this is what I seek: that I may dwell in the house of the Lord all the days of my life, to gaze upon the beauty of the Lord and to seek him in his temple" – Psalm 27:4

Being in nature is one of the things in life that brings me great joy and peace. Whether I be on the beach lying in the sand and listening to the waves crashing onto the shore, or walking through a tall grass field of rolling hills, or hiking up a grandeur mountain and seeing the world from a whole different perspective, it makes me happy. It is just me and creation. I am free to think and speak aloud and sit in silence, thanking the Lord for the breathtaking world He has created for us to enjoy and to get away from technology and civilization.

I desired to be a wilderness man growing up, leading and teaching people about the great outdoors and how to enjoy it. David also got to enjoy the beautiful works of the Lord as a shepherd and as he was running from Saul and during his adventures. But David desired something greater than the Lord's wondrous creation; He desired to dwell with God and to be in His presence.

David said "One thing I ask of the Lord." What would you ask for? A million dollars? A dream car? Your own country? Or would you truly reflect on what life really is about and give the humbling and right response that David did, the one answer that trumps all the others? "That I may dwell in the house of the Lord all the days of my life, to gaze upon the beauty of the Lord and to seek him in his temple." That is the right answer. The best answer. Nothing is greater than to be in the presence of the Lord and David knows that. From all his trials and tribulations, his victories and failures, David knows that being with God is the greatest thing that he could ever desire. He would love nothing more than to be in the house of God.

I pray that I could desire nothing more than to dwell in the house of my Father and to seek Him and His beauty. I pray this for all of us, for Jesus echoes this longing that He wants for us, saying, "But seek first his kingdom and his righteousness, and all these things will be given to you as well" (Matthew 6:33). When we seek God for who He is and yearn to be with Him and not just for what He can give us, we then reach a turning point in our lives towards maturity and a deeper walk in faith. Oh brothers, how I long to come to that point, where I desire to be in the presence of the Lord more than I desire to be loved by someone close, or to be in the midst of nature, gazing at its beauty. May the Lord be those things for us. May He become the desire of our hearts more than anything.

"Train yourself to be godly. For physical training is of some value, but godliness has value for all things, holding promise for both the present life and the life to come" – 1 Timothy 4:7-8

All throughout my life, I have played sports. Soccer, football, basketball, baseball, softball, you name it; I have played it (except cricket, even though it looks fun). In high school though, I played football and baseball for my school. I trained for football every day of the week, lifting weights, sprinting and exercises, eating lots of food, all so I could be get stronger and become a better football player for my team and be superior to my opponents. It paid off too, as one of our sayings was that "hard work pays off".

Yes, as Paul says, "physical training is of some value", as I know full well, he also tells us to "train yourself to be godly... [For] godliness has value for all things." Training requires discipline, and I know that when many of you hear the word discipline, you view it in negative light, as in something that you *have* to do and not something that you *want* to do. But in the New Testament, discipline is a good thing, for Paul elsewhere calls for us to "Run in such a way as the get the prize. Everyone who competes in the games goes into strict training...Therefore I do not run like a man running aimlessly...No, I beat my body and make it my slave" (1 Corinthians 9:24-27). Here, he compares training for the games to training for his work as an apostle of Christ.

Training to be godly, like physical training, takes work, but what does it look like? 1: Reading the Word. In Paul's second letter to Timothy he says that "All Scripture is God-breathed and is useful for teaching, rebuking, correcting and training in righteousness, so that the man of God may be thoroughly equipped for every good work" (2 Timothy 3:16-17). You want to be godly? Read and know the Word given to us to do our jobs as followers of Christ. 2: Be rooted in prayer. Jesus was a man of prayer and communion with His Father. If the Son of God needed to pray to God, how much more do we need to make time to spend with Him and be equipped and refreshed? 3: Desire God. Yearn His presence. "As the deer pants for streams of water, so my soul pants for you, O God. My soul thirsts for God, for the Living God. When can I go and meet with God?" (Psalm 42:1-2). Having a thirst for God is a key to living a godly life because the more time we spend with Him and the more His Spirit dwells in us, the more like Him we become. These are but a few tools on how to live a godly life in Christ Jesus. They are mere stepping stones to the life of faith that He calls us to. Start practicing them if you do not already, and if you already do, continue to do so and never stop. The Lord is pleased with you as His child.

"Do not be anxious about anything, but in everything, by prayer and petition, with thanksgiving, present your requests to God. And the peace of God, which transcends all understanding, will guard your hearts and minds in Christ Jesus" – Philippians 4:6-7

Today, I am traveling to Boston by plane for an interview with the TSA out there. My first flight arrives to Cleveland late, missing my connecting flight, so now I have to wait four hours for the next flight to Boston. I know it is not the worst thing in the world, but it still irritated me a bit because I was planning on getting there around 1:30 so I could have lunch, take a nap, and possibly explore a little. I do not get to Boston until 5:30, to my place of lodging until 6:30, so all I have time for now is dinner and then nothing really.

Things like this do not usually get me anxious, but it did this time probably because I wanted to settle down and relax before my interview tomorrow. I finally got to as I ate dinner and watched Chuck on Netflix. The anxiety left me at the Cleveland airport as I remembered this verse and meditated on it, knowing that the peace of God will come over me and calm my nerves. It is hard not to be anxious about anything because there are so many things going on around us and they can all go wrong. Yet, we are commanded not to, but "in everything, by prayer and petition, with thanksgiving, present your requests to God."

Those steps are crucial to having no anxiety about anything. First off, we need to talk to God about it. We need to pray to Him about the thing we are worried about, by coming before Him in earnestness, telling Him what it is that we want, which in this case is to be not worried about something. This must be done in thanksgiving though, giving thanks to Him for all the wondrous things He already has done in your life and for the situation you are in and how you can bring Him glory through it. "And he will be their peace" (Micah 5:5). "For he himself is our peace" (Ephesians 2:14).

Jesus is our peace, for His Spirit dwells within us. We do not seek the peace that God gives us, but Himself because He is our peace! How cool is that! It all seems to be coming back to seeking God, to "seek first his kingdom and his righteousness" (Matthew 6:33). His peace will flow over us like a river, calming our spirits because we know that He is in control because He is the Sovereign Lord. "Who of you by worrying can add a single hour to his life" (Matthew 6:27)? Anxiety gets us nowhere, so let us give up our cares to the Lord and be careless in the care of God, who alone can take them away as we look onto Him.

"He must become greater; I must become less" - John 3:30

The Lord of the Rings is by far my favorite set of movies that have ever existed. In the trilogy, the relationship between Frodo and Sam is one of the most heartfelt connections that help make the movies great. Frodo is Sam's master and friend and they journey together all way from the Shire to Mordor. Throughout the films, Sam knows without a doubt that the story that they have fallen into is not about him, but about how he can help Frodo destroy the One Ring and save all of Middle Earth. He knows that if Frodo is going to complete the task, then Sam has to be behind him in the background.

I know it is not the best example of what I am trying to get at, but I really wanted to introduce my passion for *The Lord of the Rings* right here because when I first read this verse, I thought of it. It was John the Baptist who said this after hearing from his disciples that many people were going to Jesus and not to him anymore. He was thrilled because of it, knowing that he had helped prepare the way for the Lord as the prophet Isaiah had foretold, "A voice of one calling in the desert, 'Prepare the way of the Lord, make straight paths for him'" (Isaiah 40:3). He knew that he completed the job God had assigned for him and he knew that it never was about him, but Jesus.

We are all given roles by God on this earth because we are all part of his plan and are one body in Christ. "But in fact God has arranged the parts in the body, every one of them, just as he wanted them to be. If they were all one part, where would the body be? As it is, there are many parts, but one body" (1 Corinthians 12:18-20). Some people are meant to have the hero roles in the story, while others are meant to have support roles. We have to know our place in God's story to be the best we can be for His glory. Once we know our position, then we are in the right place, able to see more clearly and better able to help others and fulfill our roles.

John's role was to prepare the way for Jesus' coming. Jonathon's role was to support David in spite of his father wanting to kill him. Paul's role was to preach the Gospel to the Gentiles. In all these stories, these men greatly impacted the people around them so that God might become greater and that they might become less because they knew their part. What is your part in God's epic story? What has He been telling you to do to fulfill your role? Do you have to humble yourself and know that it is not about you, but about God? Do you have to get out of the way so that God may work through you and through others as well? My good friend Gabriel used to say, "It does not matter who gets the credit, as long as God does."

"For God so loved the world that he gave..." – John 3:16

I am sure that many of us have loved people and things in our lives: food, clothes, cars, money, family, friends, pets and the list goes on and on. We love these things so much that we gather more of them and hold on to them to keep them for ourselves and our enjoyment and pleasure. The objects we like are the objects that we do not like to give away, such as food from our favorite dish because we fear there will not be enough left for seconds, or money because it is our hard-earned money that we can use on ourselves and do what we want with it.

"For we so loved the world that we *kept*." That seems a bit off from how it should be, I think more along the lines of "For God so loved the world that he *gave*..." God so loved the world that He created, the people He made, "that he *gave* his one and only Son." So is God saying that love is about *giving*, not *getting?* I think we Americans and even believers have it wrong then. We love Christmas and our birthdays because I feel that we love getting things more than we love giving. When I was in elementary school, when it was our birthday, we were the ones coming to school with cupcakes and cookies, not other people for us. Where between then and now did things get reversed?

I know this is not a perfect illustration, but you get the point. God loves us so stinking much, that He gave us His only Son, His only Son. He gave us what He loves the most, His Son, so ultimately, Himself, so that we may believe and be saved. And He willingly sent Jesus to suffer and die and rise again, knowing full well that many would not accept Him. That is what love is; giving when it hurts, and knowing that you will still be rejected. Oh how I long to be an example of that kind of love! To love realizing that I may not get any love in return (from people anyways) and knowing that my God in heaven will always love me and be pleased with me for trying to represent His selfless, sacrificial, and giving love, for "God is love" (1 John 4:8), and "since God so loved us, we also ought to love one another" (1 John 4:11). Now that you know these things, what can you do to be more loving as God is loving? Can you give to your friend who is short on rent this month, not expecting to get repaid? Can you make time to give a listening ear to your hurting neighbor even though you have to study for a test tomorrow? Can you give of yourself, so that others may live? That is what God did for us, He gave so that "[we] may have life, and have it to the full" (John 10:10). Take time today and pray about how you can give in a way that it hurts, as a Relient K song has it, "Give until there's nothing left." May it be so amongst us brothers.

"Trust in the Lord with all your heart and lean not on your own understanding; in all your ways acknowledge him, and he will make your paths straight" – Proverbs 3:5-6

One of the most widely known verses in the entire Bible, next to yesterday's verse, probably because it sums up a lot of truth for Christian living. It gives us an action on our part and the result of that action, leading to a righteous life. The verse is popular in its simplicity on the surface, as is John 3:16, but once you dig deeper, it gets more complex, but it should never lose its simplicity.

"Trust[ing] in the Lord" seems like a simple task, but it involves all of our being. To trust in God means to give all areas of our lives and selves to Him, believing they are in better hands than our own because He created us and knows what our purpose is. He is Sovereign and in control, so why not entrust Him with the features of my life?

To "lean not on your own understanding" signifies that our understanding is not good enough to lean on, and that is the truth! It is not good enough to rest our whole weight on as leaning implies because we are broken people with broken reasoning. "For my thoughts are not your thoughts, neither are your ways my ways, declares the Lord" (Isaiah 55:8). Let us lean on Him who understands all things.

"In all your ways acknowledge him" is often overlooked, or at least, often not discussed when talking about this verse. Sure, many of us acknowledge God on Sundays and in times of crisis, but we are told to acknowledge Him, or to recognize Him, in all our ways, from beginning to end. To come to Him when everything is going great and to acknowledge that He is the one that made it great, and to come to Him in the mundane because God is there as well, you have only to seek Him.

"And he will make your paths straight" is a conditional promise if you do the three things listed beforehand. Trusting in Him, leaning on Him and acknowledging Him in all things. When traversing through the wilderness and mountains, a straight path can mean the difference between life and death. So when God says that He will straighten our paths, He will remove the obstacles that get in our way or at least give us the ability to get over the obstacles with His strength. He will help throw off the things that hinder us from completing His goals. May we be working to accomplish His purposes in us, making His influence over every area of our life greater and greater as we learn to lean and trust and acknowledge Him as Lord of our lives. To God be the glory, forever and ever. Amen.

"Your attitude should be the same as that of Christ Jesus: Who, being in very nature God, did not consider equality with God something to be grasped, but made himself nothing, taking the very nature of a servant, being made in human likeness" – Philippians 2:5-7

From the time we are young, the world, and even our parents tell us to make something of ourselves. They tell us to dream big, work hard and make a fortune so we can live the American dream of comfort and luxury. But it is just that, a dream, a castle in the sky. We do what we are told. We go to college and get a degree and then work underemployed at a job that has absolutely nothing to do with our schoolwork, being bored out of our minds day in and day out. We continually try and puff ourselves up to look good in the eyes of others.

My brothers, this should not be the way of life for those of us who believe! Where in the Bible does it tell us to go and make something of ourselves? I have looked and cannot find where. This is where our culture has seeped into our Christian mindsets and has placed itself on the seat of God in our lives, dictating our actions and thoughts. "But [Jesus] made himself nothing, taking the very nature of a servant." Here we are told to make ourselves nothing, not something, because "[our] attitude should be the same as that of Christ Jesus."

God has already made us something, a child made in His image, with gifts and talents that we did not deserve, but are given out of grace because He loves us and desires us to use them to complete His works. By making ourselves nothing, by emptying ourselves, we help eliminate pride in our lives and we can begin to walk the path of humility as our Savior did. He had everything in the world because He created it, but He emptied himself and took the form of a servant. Jesus had every right in the world to use all His power and glory so that He would not have to suffer the agony of carrying everyone's sins on the cross, but He "humbled himself and became obedient to death" (2:8).

He did it all out of obedience to His Father and love for the people He created. He gave up His rights so that we may die to sin and have life in Christ! "The Son of Man did not come to be served, but to serve…" (Matthew 20:28), and servants give up their rights so that others may have them, like soldiers who give up certain rights so that the people they are fighting for can have them. What rights do you need to give up for the sake of those around you? The right to be right in a conversation? The right to pay back someone for the wrong done to you, even if it is small? Dwell on it, pray about it, so you may best serve the people around you and live selflessly.

"Am I now trying to win the approval of men, or of God? Or am I trying to please men? If I were still trying to please men, I would not be a servant of Christ" – Galatians 1:10

A Man and his son were once going with their Donkey to market. As they were walking along by its side a countryman passed them and said: "You fools, what is a Donkey for but to ride upon?" So the Man put the Boy on the Donkey and they went on their way. But soon they passed a group of men, one of whom said: "See that lazy youngster, he lets his father walk while he rides." So the Man ordered his Boy to get off, and got on himself. But they hadn't gone far when they passed two women, one of whom said to the other: "Shame on that lazy lout to let his poor little son trudge along." Well, the Man didn't know what to do, but at last he took his Boy up before him on the Donkey. By this time they had come to the town, and the passers-by began to jeer and point at them. The Man stopped and asked what they were scoffing at. The men said: "Aren't you ashamed of yourself for overloading that poor donkey with you and your hulking son?" The Man and Boy got off and tried to think what to do. They thought and they thought, till at last they cut down a pole, tied the donkey's feet to it, and raised the pole and the donkey to their shoulders. They went along amid the laughter of all who met them till they came to Market Bridge, when the Donkey, getting one of his feet loose, kicked out and caused the Boy to drop his end of the pole. In the struggle the Donkey fell over the bridge, and his fore-feet being tied together he was drowned. "That will teach you," said an old man who had followed them: "Please all, and you will please none."

This is *The Man, The Boy, and The Donkey*, from *Aesop's Fables*. It is a silly story, but with an excellent point that helps explain our verse. Paul knew full well that when you please men or the world, you cannot truly please God because "No one can serve two masters. Either he will hate the one and love the other, or he will be devoted to the one and despise the other" (Matthew 6:24). When you try to serve God and what He wants of you, it will most likely conflict with what man wants of you. Simple as that. "We must obey God rather than men!" (Acts 5:29). God's values must be higher on our priority list than the world's values, and we must choose God when the two values clash. My brothers, seek God's approval for the things that you do. If you continually strive and seek to please everyone around you, you will end up like the Man and the Boy, going every which way and losing the Donkey in the end. Think about your actions and your motives behind them. Are they so man may be pleased, or God? Learn to seek God's approval in your life, not the world's.

"Pride goes before destruction; a haughty spirit before a fall" – Proverbs 16:18

I am one to believe that pride was the sin that caused the fall of mankind in the Garden because the devil, Lucifer, succumbed to it when he tried to make himself higher than God (see Isaiah 14:12-14) and then persuaded Adam and Eve to eat the fruit of the Tree of Knowledge of Good and Evil, saying that "you will be like God" (Genesis 3:5). Both Adam and Eve and the devil fell because of pride. Both were in God's presence when they fell, so what hope does that give to us?

"Pride gets no pleasure out of having something, only out of having more of it than the next man... It is the comparison that makes you proud: the pleasure of being above the rest. Once the element of competition is gone, pride is gone" –C.S. Lewis in *Mere Christianity*. That explains why the devil fell, because according to tradition, he was the highest of all angels, having literally everything, but he saw what God had and wanted more than Him, to be above Him, and thus kicking himself out of heaven.

I feel that pride is one of the most dangerous sins, especially in today's society because it is so materialistic and a meritocracy, that it is about what I have and what I have achieved. But when push comes to shove, there will always be someone who has more than you and is better than you at something. Always. When we begin to compare ourselves to others, we will find those that we are "better than" and so self-righteousness begins to get a foothold in us. I am prone to this and it is one of my biggest stumbling blocks that the Lord is working to rid me of. This is why we must "Set [our] minds on things above, not on earthly things" (Colossians 3:2), for when we compare ourselves to Christ, we will always fall short because He is faultless, and the closer we get to light of Christ, the larger our shadow becomes because we see all our imperfections compared to His perfection.

My brothers, as the devil attacked Adam and Eve in the Garden, so he attacks us now. We must "Be self-controlled and alert. Your enemy the devil prowls around like a roaring lion looking for someone to devour. Resist him" (1 Peter 5:8-9). "Resist the devil, and he will flee from you" (James 4:7). Is pride a problem for you? If you do not know, ask someone you trust to tell you the truth about yourself. We must be watchful for the enemy's attacks and where you are at now because "if you think you are standing firm, be careful that you don't fall!" (1 Corinthians 10:12). Know your weaknesses, for that is where your armor is weak and are most prone to assault. Make sure you are standing on the Rock that is Christ and His teachings. All other ground is sinking sand.

"But the fruit of the Spirit is love, joy, peace, patience, kindness, goodness, faithfulness, gentleness and self-control. Against such things there is no law" – Galatians 5:22-23

There is a story of a young man from a small town who was mean and cruel-hearted. Until one day, he discovered that he had a hidden gift; he found out that he could fly! At first he did not know what to do with his newfound ability, but later learned how to use it to help others and he became good at it. People admired the change that took about this man and he was no longer known as being malicious and self-serving; he was different now. He delighted in helping his town and he and everyone loved that he had changed for the better.

Yes, this is a simple story that I made up for this devotional, and in fact, I am quite proud of it, even though it is short, but I hope the point of it is found in the discerning. I understand why Jesus wrote in parables because people like listening to stories, it draws them in more than merely making a point plainly, and they reveal truth to those who are looking for it. That is why Jesus said "You will be ever hearing, but never understanding...this people's heart has become calloused; they hardly hear with their ears" (Matthew 13:14-15).

The point of the story here is to show how big of an impact something in someone's life is and how it may change them and those around them. For the man it was flying, for us it is the indwelling of the Holy Spirit. The key word here is *change*. Change must come about. If the man found he could fly, and still lived his life as if he could not, how could that be and what good is that? He is forever changed. So it is with those who have the Holy Spirit living inside of them; we must be changed and not live life as we have before, but live in accordance with the Spirit that is making us holy!

Brothers, "love, joy, peace, patience, kindness, goodness, faithfulness, gentleness and self-control" are fruit of the Spirit. Fruit, not fruits. One fruit. If we have the Spirit within us, these fruit must be evident in our lives, all of them, changing us for God's glory and the good of those around us. "Since we live by the Spirit..." (5:25) implies that we do have this Spirit within us, thus allowing us to have these godly fruit be manifested in our lives! "Those who belong to Christ Jesus have crucified the sinful nature with its passions and desires" (5:24). We cannot be living with the old fruit in our lives that lead to death. People who know us ought to see the change that the Holy Spirit brings in us. Do they? Is your life characterized by the Holy Spirit's fruit? If it is not, ask the Lord to have it be so! May the Spirit dwell in you richly, leading you to godliness and righteousness in Christ.

January 17

"My soul finds rest in God alone; my salvation comes from him. He alone is my rock and my salvation; he is my fortress, I will never be shaken" – Psalm 62:1-2

This past weekend I traveled to Boston for a job interview and let's just say that things did not really go as scheduled. First off, I missed my connecting flight from Cleveland, making me wait another four hours. Secondly, on the flight back going through D.C., my connecting flight back home was delayed, then delayed a little more due to there being no crew, and they finally cancelled my flight after delaying it five hours, forcing us to stay at a hotel for the night and leave for Chicago then home in the morning. Needless to say, I was not in the best frame of mind, at least during the Cleveland wait.

But then this verse came to mind so I decided to read it and other psalms, along with Philippians 4:6-7 (as mentioned on January 9) to calm my nerves because for some odd reason, I was stressing out and I hardly ever stress out, especially while traveling. And it worked! I had an immense sense of peace come over me that can only be explained by it being the Lord. He was the place where my soul could find rest.

My brothers, I do not know how I can push the importance of the truth in this psalm. "My soul finds rest in God alone...He alone is my rock and my salvation." We have searched and searched for different ways in order to find rest for our souls, like losing ourselves in a TV show or movie or sitting in with a few cold beers. There are others, but I know for certain that these are only temporary fixes, while resting in God's presence is truly rejuvenating and brings us peace. Side note, I am not bashing on movies and beer, but they should not be the source of our rest, God is.

He is the one that we come to when we are weary, for "[He] will give you rest...and you will find rest for your souls" (Matthew 11:28-29). He is the fortress that we run to and are safe and can sleep in safety because "He alone is [our] rock and [our] salvation." He saves us from troubles and prevents them from taking control of our lives. He will not allow us to be shaken because we are on the Rock. Are you wearied from worrying or from your job or your family? Are these things causing you to run to worldly ways to try and find a moment's rest, when you know that you need to come to God whose arms are wide open waiting to hold you so you can fall asleep in His arms like the child that you are? "Come to me, all you who are weary and burdened, and I will give you rest" (Matthew 11:28). Welcome the warm invitation that the Savior of the world gives to you in your tiredness. You will find rest for your souls.

"But God chose the foolish things of the world to shame the wise; God chose the weak things of the world to shame the strong" – 1 Corinthians 1:27

The Lord of the Rings is full of kings and armies and elves and dwarves and orcs and wizards and magic. It is filled with powerful beings that use their might and strength to accomplish the goals at hand. And yet, the fate of all Middle-Earth lies in the hands of two young hobbits, Frodo and Sam. They are Halflings, people that are around three and a half feet tall with big, hairy feet and curly hair that must trek all the way to Mount Doom to destroy the One Ring and defeat Sauron for good.

Sounds quite foolish does it not, to leave the fate of an entire world to two Halflings that are weak and know nothing of war or fighting, journeying in lands they have never been to? I would say so! But that is how J.R.R. Tolkien decided to play out one of the most read books of all time. And that is how our walk with Christ is, because we are the fools, we are the weak ones through which He desired to complete His work and take care of His possessions.

The thing is though, Frodo and Sam did destroy the One Ring and wipe out the evil in Middle-Earth. "[God] chose the lowly things of this world and the despised things—and the things that are not—to nullify the things that are" (1:28). He chose us to carry out His mission for the world, which is redemption through the death and resurrection of Christ Jesus. Christ's completed work on the cross seems like the ultimate display of foolishness because who in their right mind would see it as wisdom to crucify the believed Savior of the world in order to save them from death? It does not seem like the best plan to me, but it worked. Boy did it work.

"As the heavens are higher than the earth, so are my ways higher than your ways and my thoughts than your thoughts" (Isaiah 55:9). And that is why it is said "For the message of the cross is foolishness to those who are perishing, but to us who are being saved it is the power of God...has not God made foolish the wisdom of the world?" (1:18,20). It may seem irrational and unwise to us, but it saves us. The Lord is Sovereign and knows what He is doing even when we do not. Are you willing to accept the "foolishness" that Christ offers? He offers you Himself because He loves you in your idiocy and can redeem you through it for His purposes. The world does not know what wisdom is because true wisdom cannot be found apart from God who sees the beginning and the end. May we walk in the Lord's wisdom. Amen.

"Better a patient man than a warrior, a man who controls his temper than one who takes a city" – Proverbs 16:32

At church this morning, my pastor talked about having our actual theology match up with our spoken theology, or in more common terms, having what we do (actual) match up with what we say (spoken), or even more so, practicing what we preach. He was talking about Romans 8:31 which says "If God is for us, who can be against us?" in accordance to if our actual theology is lining up with our spoken theology about God being for us; if we live our lives according to that truth.

But today is about the above verse, about patience and how I know many of us, myself most definitely included, preach it and yet we fall by the wayside in applying it to our lives on a day to day basis. Being a patient man here is correlated to being a man who controls his temper and how it is better to be that man than to be a conquering warrior that destroys. It also rolls along the lines of "Everyone should be quick to listen, slow to speak, and slow to become angry, for man's anger does not bring about the righteous life that God desires" (James 1:19-20).

This reference in James gives us a great way to apply patience in our everyday relationships with people. When someone says something that kind of irks you, do not speak and defend yourself right away, but stop and be "slow to speak" and "quick to listen" so that you will not become angry and thus not live the life that God desires of you. I know when I have gotten in fights with my girlfriend and not applied this passage, anger comes from both directions and no one is seeing and speaking from a godly perspective, but when I have practiced these verses, I am able to stop and think more clearly on how what I would say would affect her and her response.

Patience is highly praised throughout all the Scriptures: "A patient man has great understanding, but a quick tempered man displays folly" (Proverbs 14:29). "A man's wisdom gives him patience; it is to his glory to overlook an offense" (Proverbs 19:11). "Be completely humble and gentle; be patient, bearing with one another in love" (Ephesians 4:2). The list goes on and on my friends, teaching us to be patient as our Lord is patient with us (see 2 Peter 3:9). Brothers, if we have learned anything by now, it is this: if our Lord Jesus Christ did it and he commands us to do it in His Word, then we should also do it! It is that simple. Be patient with others, as I know you would want them to be patient with you.

"Because those who are led by the Spirit of God are sons of God" – Romans 8:14

Have you ever wanted something so badly that you would use whatever kind of rationale necessary to convince yourself that you "need" this thing? Or if you believe that the Holy Spirit is telling you to get this particular item and your mind is set on it, then you ask your friend who knows much about these type of items and you find out that the thing that the Spirit is "telling" you is really a piece of junk with many malfunctions? It was only you telling yourself these things because you really wanted it. Being led by the Spirit and hearing its voice takes practice and discipline.

I have mentioned the fruit of the Holy Spirit earlier, which are traits that are characterized by a Spirit-filled life, but now I will be speaking of characteristics of the Spirit itself. The quality I am focusing on is the Holy Spirit's leadership in our lives and hearing its voice so we can be led. "Those who live according to the sinful nature have their minds set on what that nature desires; but those who live in accordance with the Spirit have their minds set on what the Spirit desires" (8:5). We have to distinguish between the flesh (sinful nature) and the Spirit within us, as the two are at war. The flesh is self-centered and self-focused, while the Spirit is God-centered and other-focused.

But we have to listen to the Spirit's leading. "My sheep listen to my voice; I know them, and they follow me" (John 10:27). The Spirit is speaking to us, we only have to quiet ourselves and our surroundings and listen to it. The flesh is what gets in the way of us hearing the Holy Spirit. We need to learn to discern between the voice of the Spirit and the voice of the flesh. The flesh's voice will tell us to do things that are contradictory to God and His desires for us, while the Spirit's voice will lead us to do things that are characterized by the fruit of the Spirit (love, joy, peace, etc.).

Elijah heard the voice of the Lord as a still small voice, after the wind and the earthquake and the fire. God still speaks in a still small voice today, and distractions are all around us to hinder us from hearing Him and to hear our flesh and the world instead. Paul was "compelled by the Spirit" (Acts 20:22) to go to Jerusalem, even though others "through the Spirit they urged Paul not to" (Acts 21:4). Paul was correct in doing so, knowing that the others just warned him not to go because of the dangers awaiting him there. My brothers, we need to train ourselves to be led by the Holy Spirit and to hear His voice. Clear yourself of distractions and go to a quiet room and close your eyes. Silence yourself before the Lord and allow Him to speak. Align the Scriptures with what He says to help make sure it is the Lord. May His peace surround you as you hear His voice.

"Whoever finds his life will lose it, and whoever loses his life for my sake will find it" – Matthew 10:39

As far back as I can tell, people have been trying to discover their identity and who they are. I believe this has become even more prevalent nowadays in this "find yourself" culture where they say that you have to find yourself in order to get things done and to be beneficial in the world. Even Christian parents teach their children that they need to discover who they are in this world before they can accomplish things. Self-discovery is not inheritably bad, but too much of it is.

But why brothers? Why do we have these ideas to "find your life" thrust upon us? I believe it is because we are a selfish culture that likes to focus on ourselves. I thus believe that we have a skewed view of all of this and today's verse may help us to get away from that mentality.

Peter and some of the other disciples were fishermen by trade. They did not choose it, but they grew up with it because most likely their fathers were fishermen. That was their life. They did not find it, but when Jesus came along and said "Come, follow me" (4:19), they threw what was their only known way of life away and "At once they left their nets and followed him" (4:20). They took hold of the second part of our verse, "Whoever loses his life for my sake will find it." They have a new life that was given them because they lost who they were for Jesus' sake and He gave them new identities, for "I will make you fishers of men" (4:19).

There are countless other stories throughout the Bible where people gave up who they found themselves out to be, their lives, and gave it all to God and He in turn gave them the lives that He had for them. We need to spend less time "finding ourselves" and more time finding God and losing ourselves in Him, who alone came so that we may have life. Paul, before his conversion, thought he had found himself, but later declared, "I consider everything a loss compared to the surpassing greatness of knowing Christ Jesus my Lord, for whose sake I have lost all things. I consider them rubbish, that I may gain Christ" (Philippians 3:8). Rubbish here in Greek is referred to as dung, or refuse. What life Paul thought he had was poop compared to Christ, for which he gladly lost all things. Have you lost your life in Christ? Only then do you truly find your life, because He is the giver of all life and has a purpose for each and every one of you. Come to Him. Seek Him. Lose yourself in Him. He will unravel your identity before you as His child made in His image. All for the glory of the Lord.

January 22

"So I strive always to keep my conscience clear before God and man" – Acts 24:16

When I was quite young, probably before I was even ten years old, I went to my neighbors to feed and let out their dogs while they were away. So while I am wondering through the house, spending some time with the dogs and making my appearance, I found a tootsie roll on my friends' dresser and ate it. My mother was with me too, and she said, "What are you eating?" I said, "Gum..." "Where did you get that?" she replied. "Umm...here." I said. And needless to say, she was not happy, and myself knowing that I lied and stole, so she made me humble myself, buy a pack of gum, and personally give it to the family when they came back, even though I did not even take any gum.

That was not a fun time for me. My guilty conscience was having a heyday with it, making me feel bad over and over for lying and stealing, even something as little as a tootsie roll. But it was a sin nonetheless and I tried to cover it up, making it worse. Later in life did I come to learn that it was the devil who kept on accusing me and having me try and feel bad continuously, even after making restitution.

This is why Paul and others speak of having a clear conscience constantly: "My conscience is clear, but that does not make me innocent. It is the Lord who judges me" (1 Corinthians 4:4). "We are sure that we have a clear conscience and desire to live honorably in every way" (Hebrews 13:18). "Our conscience testifies that we have conducted ourselves in the world, especially in our relations with you, in the holiness and sincerity that are from God" (2 Corinthians 1:12). "Keeping a clear conscience, so that those who speak maliciously against your good behavior in Christ may be ashamed of their slander" (1 Peter 3:16).

Paul was able to live his life with a clear conscience because he knew that Christ had forgiven him and released him from guilt and that it is Christ who judges him, not people. Paul had a clear view of right and wrong, which allowed him to be somewhat guided by his conscience, which is a good indicator of how the Lord has worked in our lives. If you are hearing a voice inside you accusing you of past sins that you know you have given up to God in honest forgiveness and repentance, do not give in to it. Do not live with that guilt within you. Know where the voice comes from and that it is not the truth, but lies, "for he [the devil] is a liar and the father of lies" (John 8:44). Know the Lord's voice as we talked about recently and how he welcomes you and encourages you to do His good works in the world around you. He does not accuse you; He loves you and desires for you walk in Him and His confidence because He never leaves you. May you walk with a conscience of uprightness, knowing that you did what was right in the Lord's eyes.

"We live by faith, not by sight" – 2 Corinthians 5:7

As I have mentioned before, I am in the interview process with the TSA for a job out in Boston. I originally applied near the end of August, and now, exactly five months later, I still do not have the job. Their timing of things is not aligned with what I perceived they would be. They are on their own time table without relaying much information to me at all, irritating me at times. But even now, I believe that I will receive the job quite soon and then I can move to Boston to be closer to my girlfriend, Lord willing.

It is hard to believe in something that has not come to fruition yet. My girlfriend is taking this waiting process really hard, causing her to doubt our relationship at times, which then makes it hard on me to try and encourage her about us and how God has blessed us and will believe He will continue to do so. It is hard for me as well. I have been checking out apartments in Boston to rent, but they keep on renting them to others because they cannot wait too long on me since I do not have the job yet, even though they expressed interest to rent it to me.

It is like this in our relationship with Christ. He is on His own watch and we are called to "Wait for the Lord; be strong and take heart and wait for the Lord" (Psalm 27:14). I do believe that God did tell me all those months ago that I will get a job in Boston. I had no idea how long the process of doing that would be, so I believed I would get one soon. Then the weeks and months passed and still no job and I began to lose heart. But now, I am getting so close I can taste it even though I do not have it yet. I still believe that the Lord will provide for me even though I do not see anything.

"We live by faith, not by sight" is one of the hardest things for us to do because we love to see where we are going and by what means. We love knowing things and often when we do not know something, we get anxious and fret. But yet we are called to walk in the faith of Jesus Christ, "So we fix our eyes not on what is seen, but on what is unseen. For what is seen is temporary, but what is unseen is eternal" (4:18). Seeing with our physical eyes limits us only to what we can see, keeping the focus on ourselves and what we can do, and takes our eyes off Christ and what He is doing in the unseen realm, or in the present state. "But hope that is seen is no hope at all...if we hope for what we do not yet have, we wait for it patiently" (Romans 8:24-25). May our hope be in Christ, who sees the beginning from the end and will provide for His children who wait on Him. "Hope does not disappoint us" (Romans 5:5). The Lord does not disappoint us brothers. May we walk in faith in Him, no matter what we see around us, because there is more to this world than meets the eye.

January 24

"Then you will know the truth, and the truth will set you free" – John 8:32

What is truth? The world outside of the three monotheistic religions does not really know what truth is because all their truths are relative, meaning that what you believe is true is true for you and what I believe is true is true for me. There are no absolute truths in the world to them so they have no moral code and thus they claim no responsibility for their actions.

But as Christians, as followers of Christ, we know that there is an absolute truth; that God created the heavens and the earth and that He sent His only son Jesus to bear the world's iniquities and to suffer and die and rise again so that we may have forgiveness of sins and be free from sin and death and be able to live eternally with Christ on high. This was all done because God loved us so much that He could not bear to have His creation wallow in their sins and be enslaved to death. He wants us to live a life of love, not selfishness.

These are absolute truths my brothers, whether you believe them or not. This is the truth that will set you free. This is the Gospel that Jesus proclaimed and lived while on earth so that we will not be in bondage to the devil and his schemes. Before we say yes to Jesus Christ, that He is our Lord and Savior and so much more, we are servants of the devil because "everyone who sins is a slave to sin" (8:34) and "you are slaves to the one whom you obey" (Romans 6:16). But when you do accept Christ, you accept the truth "and the truth will set you free." The Word then says that "You have been set free from sin and have become slaves of righteousness" (Romans 6:18).

But I thought we were now free? Yes, we are now "free from the law of sin and death" (Romans 8:2), however, slavery in Christ gives us more freedom than we could ever ask for! Because we are free in Christ, we are free to obey Him and all that He asks of us. Before that, we had to obey the devil and now we do not have to! Since we are slaves of righteousness, we are free to love other people as God loves and we do not have to show "love", but in the back of our mind our motives are selfish and for our gain and not theirs. The truth we received in Christ not only frees us from fear and lying, but allows us to live with hope. When we tell the truth to others (not only God's truth, but truth in general), we feel liberated because we are hiding nothing. Mark Twain said, "If you tell the truth, you don't have to remember anything." There is so much freedom in the truth my brothers. I pray that you can live in it and walk in it through Christ. Be free to live for Him. There is so much more that He has yet to show you as the Spirit "will teach you all things" (14:26).

"Do not merely listen to the word, and so deceive yourselves. Do what it says" –
James 1:22

When you were growing up, you were under your parents' authority. They told you what to do because they love you and care for you and know what is best for you, even if you think they are wrong. When they told you of a chore to do, they did not just want you to hear the command and then go mosey off as if it did not happen, but they wanted you to complete the task as you have been told because by merely listening to it, nothing happens. It must be obeyed.

Back on January 8 we talked about training yourself to be godly, while reading and knowing the Word of God was numero uno on the list. This is going to be further discussed today. The Bible does tell us over and over from the beginning to the end to know and live out the Word of God, maybe not directly, but it is strongly implied. Starting with the verse above, how can we do what it says if you do not know what it says? It must be read in order to know what is in there and so we can obey it. "Walk in the way that the Lord your God has commanded you" (Deuteronomy 5:33). How can we walk in the Lord's way without knowing what He has commanded us to do?

"Do not let this Book of the Law depart from your mouth; meditate on it day and night" (Joshua 1:8). The Scriptures must be meditated on to know what is in them. We have been told that "Whoever claims to live in him must walk as Jesus did" (1 John 2:6). How can we begin to know how to walk in our Savior's footsteps without knowing how our Savior lived as declared in the Gospels? "Do not merely listen to the word, and so deceive yourselves. Do what it says."

Do what the Word says so that we are not deceived brothers, for the devil wants us to be deceived so that we do not walk in the Lord's ways but in his. The Lord has us obey His commandments which give us life and peace, while the devil wishes us to obey him so that we may be dazed and confused. "Anyone who listens to the word but does not do what it says is like a man who looks at his face in a mirror and after looking at himself, goes away and immediately forgets what he looks like" (1:13-24). The mirror (God's Word) shows us our true self and when we look away, we forget what our true self is, so we are deceived, thinking we are something we are not. May we be "the man who looks intently into the perfect law that gives freedom...not forgetting what he has heard, but [does] it" (1:25). Know and live the Word my brothers. The Lord commands us and it will benefit our walk with Him more than you can even imagine!

"The Lord, the Lord, the compassionate and gracious God, slow to anger, abounding in love and faithfulness, maintaining love to thousands, and forgiving wickedness, rebellion and sin" – Exodus 34:6-7

When people, both Christians and non-Christians alike, think of the God of the Old Testament, they tend to think of a completely different God than that of the New Testament. They see a God of wrath and judgment and condemnation. They see a God who is ever-angry with the Israelites for their foolishness and rebellion to God. They see a God who destroys nations all so that His people may possess the Promised Land.

What is wrong with this picture my brothers? Not only that we believers sometimes view God this way, but that we forget our theology about God, in this case, the immutability of God. This is where God is unchanging in his character, will, and covenant promises. "I the Lord do not change" (Malachi 3:6) helps to throw away the notions that these people have about the God of the Old and New Testaments, in which He is the same.

In this passage, The Lord is described as "compassionate and gracious", meaning that here in the OT, God shows compassion and grace to His people, which is how he treated the Israelites in their desert wanderings. They were hungry and He fed them manna and quail (Exodus 16). They were thirsty and He gave them water to drink from a rock (Exodus 17). "[Their] clothes did not wear out and [their] feet did not swell during these forty years" (Deuteronomy 8:4). If God was not "slow to anger, abounding in love and faithfulness", then He would not allow His people to enter the Promised Land, but He did despite their disobedience and wickedness, just not in the way they would have wanted. In fact, "not one of the men who saw my glory and the miraculous signs I performed in Egypt and in the desert but who disobeyed me and tested me ten times – not one of them will ever see the land I promised on oath to their forefathers...But because my servant Caleb has a different spirit and follows me wholeheartedly, I will bring him into the land he went to, and his descendants will inherit it" (Numbers 14:22-24), because "he does not leave the guilty unpunished" (34:7).

The Lord thus maintains His love and forgives His people, ultimately in the revelation of His son Jesus Christ, who is God incarnate. Jesus is the same God as seen here in Exodus, forgiving them of their rebellion against Him and forgiving us of ours. We deserve death like many of the Israelites did, but because of God's great love for us, He keeps His covenant with His people so that we may have eternal life through Him. God is the same yesterday, today, and forevermore! May we depend on Him who is always faithful.

"Carry each other's burdens, and in this way you will fulfill the law of Christ" – Galatians 6:2

Have you ever been in a situation where you felt so burdened and weighed down by your surroundings, and then at the most opportune time, someone came and helped you in your time of need, relieving you immensely? How did you feel after this person came to your rescue? Overjoyed? Thankful? And rightly so. It always does feel good to be relieved of a burden because it allows us to focus again and not on what is weighing us down.

In its original context to the Galatians, Paul is speaking about helping your brother who has fallen and to aid them in overcoming sin, but I will be speaking also of physically helping out your brothers, which is oft overlooked today. We see a fellow believer in pain and we stand idly by telling them "I will pray for you" and then do nothing! We do not even pray for the Kingdom to come upon them! We lie to their faces. And this is why I do see prayer as one of the ways we can help bear each other's burdens, as unto Christ.

"And we ought to lay down our lives for our brothers. If anyone has material possessions and sees his brother in need but has no pity on him, how can the love of God be in him?" (1 John 3:16-17). Our love for the body of Christ and for others must be shown, otherwise, do we even have the love of Christ in us? Do you see someone stuck in the ditch? Help them out. Is your friend low on rent this month? Help them out. You see people in need all around you and if you do not, then open your eyes! The world needs your help; it needs God's love to be manifested through you, His chosen vessel.

This works on both ends of the spectrum though. If you are one in need of help, accept it! Do not be just another proud Christian that says "I can do it myself. I do not need your help." Accept the help offered to you my brothers. It may be God working through them to lend you a hand. Receiving help is just as good as giving it. Remove the selfishness that surrounds your American spirit and embrace the spirit of Christ! Do not take away the opportunity for someone to earn treasures in heaven (see Matthew 10:42). I feel like I could write an entire sermon on the subject of helping out your brothers. In doing these things, in bearing our brothers' burdens, "[we] will fulfill the law of Christ." This law is love. If we are not walking in love, we are not obeying God. Simple as that. "Let us not love with words or tongue but with actions and truth" (1 John 3:18). May we carry each other's burdens, as I have said before and will continue to say many times, "Whatever you did for one of the least of these brothers of mine, you did for me" (Matthew 25:40).

"Let everything that has breath praise the Lord" – Psalm 150:6

I am one who occasionally thinks that thanking God and praising God are relatively the same thing. They are close, but they are not the same. I see thanking God as thanking Him for what He has done for us, i.e. thanking Him for a beautiful day so I could go outside for a lovely hike and enjoy His creation; while praising God I see as praising Him for who He is and exalting His character and person i.e. praising Him for being high above every other name on heaven and earth.

The idea for this came as I was listening to a sermon at work this morning on praise and how praise is one of the things that is done on earth that is also done by the angels in heaven. "Holy, holy, holy is the Lord God Almighty, who was, and is, and is to come" (Revelation 4:8) cries the four living creatures day and night in heaven, and so also we should be crying out. We tend to get so caught up in what is going on about us, whether it be school or relationships or work or worries of the present situation, that it controls our thoughts, and then we have a propensity to forget to take time and praise the Lord for who He is right now!

What I have learned in my few years of life is that praising the Lord takes our eyes off ourselves and onto Him, which is how life should always be. The Psalms are absolutely filled with praise to God for all the marvelous works He has done. "I praise you because I am fearfully and wonderfully made" (139:14). "Praise the Lord, O my soul; all my inmost being, praise his holy name" (103:1). "Praise be to the Lord, to God our Savior, who daily bears our burdens" (68:19). "The Lord lives! Praise be to my Rock! Exalted be God my Savior!" (18:46). I hope you get the point.

"Let everything that has breath praise the Lord." Not "Let everyone who is having a good day" or "Let everyone who has everything put together." Let *everything that has breath* praise the Lord my brothers! He is worthy of the highest praises and He deserves it all! "For from him and through him and to him are all things. To him be the glory forever! Amen" (Romans 11:36). I urge you to give the Lord praise all throughout your day for who He is, proclaiming His wonders, whether you feel like it or not. Praise His holy name.

Praise God, from whom all blessings flow;
Praise Him, all creatures here below;
Praise Him above, ye heavenly hosts;
Praise Father, Son, and Holy Ghost. Amen.

"Now my heart is troubled, and what shall I say? 'Father, save me from this hour'? No, it was for this very reason I came to this hour. Father, glorify your name!" – John 12:27-28

In these last days of Christianity, I have begun to notice more and more that we Western believers have become so fixated on what we are feeling. "I feel like eating ice cream and watching movies all day because I am feeling down and out." "That person made me feel mad, so I burst at them in anger." "It did not feel like God wanted me to go there and forgive my friend." Then we follow these feelings.

Yes, God gave us feelings because we are human, but He also gave us a brain and His indwelling Spirit. When Jesus said these words, He had feelings; feelings of worry and despair as He looked ahead to what was about to come of Him: suffering, crucifixion, carrying the world's sins and being separated from His Father. But one thing that makes Jesus great is that He did not dwell on His feelings and succumb to them. Instead, He obeyed God.

And that is how we should react to our feelings brothers, especially when they try and guide us to disobey our heavenly Father. We should be guided by obedience to God as the early Christians and people in the East are, and not by our feelings as we in the West are. Our culture has impacted us in this sense more than we have impacted it. "What do you feel?" they ask us. "How does that make you feel?" they say. We must obey God first and foremost.

Does your love for God depend on your feelings or obedience? If it is feelings, then you are living in disobedience already. "This is how we know that we love the children of God: by loving God and carrying out his commands" (1 John 5:2). We must follow God's commands whether you feel like it or not. Do not feel like praying? Pray anyways. Do not feel like reading the Bible? Read it anyways. Do not feel like loving people? Love them anyways. When you do these things and much more when you do not feel like it, you are becoming more like Christ. Feelings change all the time, but obedience to God should never change. "But I tell you: love your enemies" (Matthew 5:44). I do not believe you will ever come to the point where you feel like loving your enemies. Obey first, and the feelings of love and other godly attributes will follow. May the Lord bless you and keep you and guide you into all things in Him, and that you may obey Him despite how you are feeling. To Him be the glory forever and ever. Amen.

"I am the good shepherd. The good shepherd lays down his life for the sheep"
– John 10:11

Sheep are not the most intelligent animals out there; in fact, they are not very bright at all and only tend to rely on a few basic natural instincts and need a leader to follow. When one sheep goes, the rest follow, whether it is somewhere good or bad. They also have poor depth perception and do not like to go where they cannot see. They have excellent hearing but loud noises make them nervous, so the shepherd speaks to them in a calming voice.

If you did not already know, we are the sheep. We are the ones that do not like to go where we cannot see and need a leader to follow. It is a wonderful thing then that Jesus says "I am the good shepherd." Ahhh. Sigh of relief. It is great to know that we have the best leader in the world to follow, Jesus Christ, who "makes me lie down in green pastures, he leads me besides quiet waters, he restores my soul" (Psalm 23:2-3). We are in the most caring hands possible as our Shepherd provides for our needs.

"The good shepherd lays down his life for the sheep." Jesus cares about us so much that He was willing to lay down his life so that we may have it, and he has "authority to take it up again" (10:18). We the sheep cannot protect ourselves, we are practically defenseless. But "the Chief Shepherd" (1 Peter 5:4) loves the sheep because they are His; He owns them and stays with them day and night unlike the hired hand that "cares nothing for the sheep" (10:13) and scatters off. When we are with our Shepherd who never leaves us, we can honestly say "I will fear no evil, for you are with me; your rod and your staff, they comfort me" (Psalm 23:4).

As Jesus Christ is our Good Shepherd, so are we to "Be shepherds of God's flock that is under your care...being examples to the flock" (1 Peter 5:2-3). Jesus is our example in everything. As He leads us and cares for us, so are we to lead and care for others who need it. As "the good shepherd lays down his life for the sheep", so are we to lay down our lives for our brothers, giving ourselves so that God may be glorified and that we may represent Him wholly and truthfully. "Greater love has no one than this, that he lay down his life for his friends" (15:13). Thank the Lord your God today for taking care of you and providing for you out of His great love for you. He is the greatest leader the world has ever and will ever know. May we follow the Good Shepherd wholeheartedly all the rest of our days, and lead others in doing the same.

"Shout for joy to the Lord, all the earth. Worship the Lord with gladness; come before him with joyful songs" – Psalm 100:1-2

Worship (of the musical kind) last night was probably the most Spirit and truth-filled night of singing out to the Lord that I have had in two years. I entered the throne room of heaven and cried out to the King of kings, not caring what I sounded or looked like. Actually, it was a worship-filled day for me, belting out in the car and at work. The most profound sense of peace I have felt in a really long time rushed over me like a wave.

That is the best I could describe it. For you who have experienced such grace and peace in the Lord's presence, you know what I am talking about. The Holy Spirit brings so much clarity to you in those times because we are offering ourselves up wholly to God, without hindrance, as it should always be. Jesus says that "the true worshipers will worship the Father in spirit and truth, for they are the kind of worshipers the Father seeks. God is spirit, and his worshipers must worship in spirit and in truth" (John 4:23-24). May we worship our Father in heaven in spirit and in truth. God is spirit. Jesus is truth.

This worship is not strictly referring to musical worship as I am focusing on, but it still applies to today's verse. I want to focus firmly on worshiping in the form of playing instruments and singing because music is such a powerful tool that affects the mind and the heart, evoking emotion. The Psalms are just that, songs and praises to the Lord to be sung and played with musical instruments. Playing music stirs something within us. "Whenever the spirit from God came upon Saul, David would take his harp and play. Then relief would come to Saul; he would feel better, and the evil spirit would leave him" (1 Samuel 16:23).

"Shout for joy to the Lord, all the earth. Worship the Lord with gladness; come before him with joyful songs." Worship should be joyful and it should produce good fruit and have us walk closer to the Lord. Celebrate the Lord in song! The Israelites "[Sang] to the Lord a new song" (96:1) whenever the Lord did something new to celebrate the occasion. The Lord does new things all the time for us! He is continually blessing us in new ways and His faithfulness never fails us. Do not forget my brothers to shout out your praises to Him who is worthy of it all, "For the Lord is good and his love endures forever" (100:5). You have to make time to worship God, it will not just "happen", you will find something else to do. Rid yourselves of distractions and hindrances and come before His glorious throne in humility and love for Him who is above every other name.

"Love is patient…" – 1 Corinthians 13:4

It is a new month! And the month of February is usually seen as the love month, so what better way to kick it off than to be talking about love? I could find none. Actually, for the first half of this month, I am going to be discussing 1 Corinthians 13:4-8 and the topic of love and what it looks like for us to love.

"Love is patient" is how this passage begins. Now we talked about patience once before on January 19 in Proverbs, and so hopefully you have somewhat of an understanding of what that looks like. "God is love" (1 John 4:8) and patience is part of the fruit of the Spirit (Galatians 5:22), so then love is patient. But what does patience in love look like? How can we be patient in love towards the people around us?

"The Lord is not slow in keeping his promise, as some understand slowness. He is patient with you, not wanting anyone to perish, but everyone to come to repentance" (2 Peter 3:9). Looks like God is patient with us, and thank goodness He is because if He was not, He could have extended His wrath upon us all before we had the chance to be saved by His death and resurrection! We often forget that God is outside of time and is not bound by it; He is omnipresent. "With the Lord a day is like a thousand years, and a thousand years are like a day" (2 Peter 3:8). Is it coincidence that this verse immediately precedes the above verse? Not at all; I do not believe in coincidences. As Albert Einstein said, "Coincidence is God's way of remaining anonymous."

"Love is patient." Your best friend your whole life continuously messes up and commits the same sin against you over and over again. They say they will change their ways. You have believed them because you love them and live out this dialogue between Peter and Jesus, "'Lord, how many times shall I forgive my brother when he sins against me? Up to seven times?' Jesus answered, 'I tell you, not seven times, but seventy-seven times'" (Matthew 18:21-22). That is a lot of times to forgive someone, but Jesus calls us to because He has forgiven them and to be patient with them as He has graciously been patient with us. Oh what wonderful news that is brothers! Patience is a beautiful and wonderful thing in the hands of the Lord. May we walk in patience day in and day out, no matter the circumstances, trusting that the Lord's work is being done and that when we are patient with people, we are showing them love.

"Love is kind..." – 1 Corinthians 13:4

I believe as men in this day and age we shy away from calling one another kind or nice because it gives off a wimpy or unmanly connotation. But what does kindness mean? To be kind as love is kind is to be good-natured and courteous to one another, desiring to treat them in a mild and calming spirit because that is how we have we been treated through Christ.

This is also the last of the positive characteristics of what love does do while tomorrow will start on what love does not do. Paul elsewhere speaks of what it is to be kind; "Be kind and compassionate to one another, forgiving each other, just as in Christ God forgave you" (Ephesians 4:32). Here it is linked with compassion and forgiveness. Paul also said "And the Lord's servant must not quarrel; instead, he must be kind to everyone, able to teach, not resentful" (2 Timothy 2:24). Here it is linked to not quarreling, so in effect, being kind to each other is to not fight back with them and to be good and generous with them as you also would want to be treated.

"Love is kind." Showing kindness and being kind and courteous to one another is also a part of the fruit of the Spirit. But how can one be kind and forgiving to someone who absolutely hates them and delights in fighting with them and hurting them? By showing them love! "Love your enemies, do good to those who hate you, bless those who curse you, pray for those who mistreat you" (Luke 6:27-28). Our Lord Jesus Christ commands us, it is not a suggestion, to "do good to those who hate you." That is how we can show kindness to them, as God has also shown us kindness and done good to us, His enemies: "While we were still sinners, Christ died for us" (Romans 5:8).

I can honestly say that displaying kindness and doing good to those around us is what Paul means when he says that "love is kind." God is the ultimate example of what showing kindness looks like. It is undeserving, as we do not deserve it. It gives without limit, as God's grace and kindness to us never ends. It is unconditional kindness, at all times it is to be given. The one who shows kindness is the better person and understands how they have been given kindness in their time of need. "Make sure that nobody pays back wrong for wrong, but always try to be kind to each other and to everyone else" (1 Thessalonians 5:15). God is love my brothers, which means He shows kindness. May we follow in His footsteps by doing good for the others benefit and not our own.

February 3

"[Love] does not envy" – 1 Corinthians 13:4

We move towards the negatives of what love does not do in this passage. "It does not envy." When I hear the word envy, I think of desiring something that I do not have, but it means much more than that. Here, it is used in the negative form of having zeal against a person and what they have, or coveting it, as it says here, "You want something but don't get it. You kill and covet, but you cannot have what you want. You quarrel and fight" (James 4:2).

Envy is one of the seven deadly sins from which many other sins are birthed, "For where you have envy and selfish ambition, there you find disorder and every evil practice" (James 3:16). Those who are envious begrudge the happiness of others and wish that for themselves, but since they cannot have it, they show disgust and hatred towards them that do. After Joseph told his dream to his brothers and already knowing how much their father loved him more than them, they envied him greatly and so sold him into slavery (see Genesis 37).

If we are walking in the path of love, we would not have these envious desires towards those in our lives. It is not only hurtful to them, but hurtful to us because "A heart at peace gives life to the body, but envy rots the bones" (Proverbs 14:30). But we should be striving to what Paul tells us is a good way to combat envious thoughts; "Rejoice with those who rejoice; mourn with those who mourn" (Romans 12:15). When we are happy and joyful for what the Lord has done in our brother's life, we will not envy their happiness but we will be able to enjoy them and praise our Father in heaven for the goodness He has shown!

The poet Dante described envy as "a desire to deprive other men of theirs." I believe that sums it up pretty well. "[Love] does not envy." If you are desiring to be an imitator of God and to walk in His ways, stay clear of envy, even though it is quite subtle in today's society and you can do it without even realizing it. When you see one of your friends succeed and do better in school or sports and the workplace than you and you faintly feel resentment towards them because you know you worked hard and still did not do as good as them, that faint reaction is envy. Do not feed it, but come before the Lord for forgiveness and ask Him to lead you into all truth and to be grateful and content with where He has you right now. "If one part is honored, every part rejoices with it" (12:26). Rejoice with your brothers and thank your Father in heaven for blessing them with success, as you would want them to do the same when a blessing of achievement comes your way.

February 4

"[Love] does not boast" – 1 Corinthians 13:4

Here is another negative characteristic of someone who does not practice love. "It does not boast." To boast in this passage means to brag or to point to oneself. In essence, love does not show off. Oh my how this is a blow to our culture once again! We in the West love to show off, whether what we have done or what we have so we can be compared to others because we love comparison only when we are compared to someone below us so that we are seen as more superior.

And that is what Paul is preaching against here; the type of boasting that the Corinthian church was actively participating in by claiming that they were superior because of the gifts and riches they have been given or because of something they have accomplished that makes them look better than someone else, much like that of the Pharisees; "Be careful not to do your 'acts of righteousness' before men, to be seen by them. If you do, you will have no reward from your Father in heaven" (Matthew 6:1).

Why is God against showing off? Because it points others to us and raises ourselves up usually while tearing others down and because it is selfishness at its core. I have been quite guilty of this my brothers and still am from time to time because of the abilities I have been given and I do like the attention. Pray for me to be released from this bondage of self so I may be for Christ getting all the attention. We like to brag about ourselves, but I urge you to shy from doing so and to brag about Christ instead!

"[Love] does not boast." Love focuses on other people and never on self. "But 'Let him who boasts boast in the Lord'" (2 Corinthians 10:17). Christ should always be the center of who gets the attention. As I have said before, "It doesn't matter who gets the credit as long as God does." Not only that, but no one really likes to be around someone who brags about themselves all the time because they think they are better than us.

I will not boast in anything
No gifts, no power, no wisdom
But I will boast in Jesus Christ
His death and resurrection.

May that be how we are living our lives, for the praise and glory of our Lord Jesus Christ and declaring His victory over sin and death as we are now walking in freedom and life!

February 5

"[Love] is not proud" - 1 Corinthians 13:4

Gorelal was a famous sculptor. His sculptures looked like real ones. One day he saw a dream that after fifteen days, the demon of Death would come to take him. Gorelal prepared nine statues of himself and when on the 15th day he heard the Demon of Death coming, he took his place between the statues. The Demon could not recognize him and was astonished to see ten Gorelals instead of one. He rushed back to the God of death and told the matter. The God of death got annoyed and set out to take Gorelal himself. Gorelal was alert and stood motionless. The God of Death initially got perplexed. But he thought for a moment. He said, "Gorelal, these sculptures would have been perfect but for one mistake." Gorelal was unable to suffer the least blemish in his work. He came out and asked, "Where is the fault?" God of Death caught him and said, "HERE". The statues were faultless but Gorelal was caught because of his pride.

A simple short story (author unknown) on what pride does to a person, it makes them fall as we have seen before. Being proud is somewhat linked to being boastful, but it is different and it is also not linked with walking in love. It is like having a big head and being puffed up. Paul says earlier in his letter that "Knowledge puffs up, but love builds up. The man who thinks he knows something does not yet know as he ought to know. But the man who loves God is known by God" (8:2-3). Many believe that if we have a superior knowledge of something, then we have the right to be puffed up, but it says here that "love builds up", not knowledge.

Love builds one another up, not tears them down as pride does. Why do we continually think that because we know something more than someone else or of the sort that we have the right to look down on people and place ourselves above them because of our "superiority"? We have all been given grace and mercy from God above and so we are all on a level playing field. Yes, we all have different gifts, but "Do not think of yourself more highly than you ought, but rather think of yourself with sober judgment, in accordance with the measure of faith God has given you" (Romans 12:3). God is the one who appointed us different gifts and abilities all to a different measure, so there is no basis for pride or self-righteousness. One who is prideful is the object of its own love. William Penn said it well, "A proud man then is a kind of glutton upon himself; for he is never satisfied with loving and admiring himself; whilst nothing else, with him, is worthy either of love or care." Walking in love is loving God first and foremost and loving others, not ourselves. Are you willing to live outside of yourself for the sake of Christ and others? Live in such a way of humility and love as your Savior did and does day after day.

February 6

"[Love] is not rude" – 1 Corinthians 13:5

"[Love] is not rude." Rude is not a word that we read of often in the Bible, in fact, this is the only English occurrence of the word in the entire Holy Scriptures. When I think of this word, I think of not showing proper manners in relations to others, i.e. I have been invited to my neighbors for dinner and I was quite rude with them on their choice of food and the manner that they presented it, thus distancing myself from them personally and communicatively.

I guess we can say then that love has good manners because when one is rude towards others, they are then inconsiderate towards them and not thinking of how we can help them. Rudeness is rooted in selfishness, as are the majority of sins, if not all of them. When you speak or act rudely, you are communicating that it is all about you, which I am sure we know by now that love is definitely not about us, but about the other.

Love acts properly in all circumstances and does not belittle those who are beneath them, but treats them with proper respect and dignity despite who they are or where they are or what they have done. The same is true for treating your superiors with the respect that they deserve because of their position, whether they are your boss or parents or government leaders. When we are walking in love, we will watch what we say and not use coarse language or have a perverse tongue or speak indecently because that is rude and tends to put down those we are speaking to, when we are told that we should be "Speaking the truth in love" (Ephesians 4:15).

It is like when we catch a brother in sin, "[We] who are spiritual should restore him gently" (Galatians 6:1), not abrasively and with rudeness and indecency towards them, but with "Gentleness and respect, keeping a clear conscience, so that those who speak maliciously against your good behavior in Christ may be ashamed of their slander" (1 Peter 3:15-16). Those who walk in Christ's love walk in integrity and need not walk in fear of being exposed. And get this brothers, not being rude does not mean that we are not living with integrity because "we are not telling them what we really think or feel." It is love which dismisses these minor trivialities that we may have against someone. It is love that looks over that which is meaningless. Act in a way today that is proper towards those in your life, as you would like it for them to act in a proper way towards you.

"[Love] is not self-seeking" – 1 Corinthians 13:5

This is where our culture is in the wrong once again. They tend to believe that love is about them and what they want and desire, but we have firmly established this far that love is not *selfish*, but *selfless*. What society thinks is love is more like lust, which demands and puts itself as number one, while love is ready to sacrifice and puts the other person and their desires and wants before their own, more often than not at their expense.

Paul states earlier in his letter that "Nobody should seek his own good, but the good of others" (10:24), and thus promoting love. While Jesus walked on this earth, He was not seeking to do his own bidding, otherwise I highly doubt that He would have gone the route that He did, but in fact He said "I have come down from heaven not to do my will but to do the will of him who sent me" (John 6:38). Jesus was seeking to please His Father in heaven above pleasing Himself and getting His way. That is the way of love my friends.

We know for certain that love is not self-seeking, not only because it says so here, but because Jesus' life is the prime example of it. If love was all about the self, then why would "Greater love has no one than this, that he lay down his life for his friends" (John 15:13)? If love was all about me and what I wanted and preserving myself and that my way be done, then why would the greatest form of love be the utter giving up of oneself for the sake of others?

Repetition is a wonderful means of getting the point across, as I am sure you have noticed by now how I like to write, by constantly repeating the same things so it will be ingrained into your mind and heart so that in turn you will speak them, "For out of the overflow of the heart the mouth speaks." (Matthew 12:34). Love gives up the right to be right in an argument. Love gives up things so others can have them, and I believe that is why love and sacrifice are closely linked as we see soldiers and police officers and the like give up certain things so that the public may have them. "[Love] is not self-seeking." I cannot emphasize this enough brothers. In what areas have we been seeking to please ourselves in with disregard to how those in our lives are treated? Remove yourself from the picture. Keep your eyes on the Lord and seek first His kingdom. Everything else will follow. God will take care of you, so there is no need to worry about yourself. Here is a way: Stop praying so much for yourself and begin to ask unselfish things.

February 8

"[Love] is not easily angered" – 1 Corinthians 13:5

As a member of the body of Christ, I have noticed within the church that we tend to get angry rather quickly at the most minuscule of things. Whether it is during a sports game or a friend of yours did something you did not like, you get angry without much trouble or effort. This is not right, but why does it happen? (And do not say that because we are sinners, we are more than that).

I believe one of the reasons for this quick burst of anger is that we take a part of our identity from the object of which we are angry. We cannot separate ourselves from it because we have invested mentally into it. But "[Love] is not easily angered" says Paul, yet we as the church, who should be the representation of Christ's love to the world, are getting angry swiftly for no good reason (yes, I said no good reason; excuses are just to make yourself feel better). We know that James tells us that "Everyone should be quick to listen, slow to speak, and slow to become angry, for man's anger does not bring about the righteous life that God desires" (James 1:19-20).

When we become followers of Christ, we are not automatically sanctified to perfection and our emotions are not instantaneously in check, but they should be going that direction. "Do not let the sun go down while you are still angry, and do not give the devil a foothold" (Ephesians 4:26-27). When we get angry, we are giving the enemy a chance to come in and get a good footing on us, thus giving him ample opportunities to attack us even more. Do not let that happen brothers. Do not let anger get the best of you. Give it up when it comes and restrain yourself, as we know that self-control is part of the fruit of the Spirit (see Galatians 5:23).

"[Love] is not easily angered." I hope we know by now that "The Lord is slow to anger, abounding in love" (Numbers 14:18), and so shall we be! Love loves to forgive and show mercy. Love loves to overlook mistakes against them. Love in this verse looks at things with a sober mind, and though they may be hurt by someone, they are to control their passions and subdue their feelings and rid themselves of their temper because that is how love walks and does not give way to outbursts of feelings. Love first looks at Christ, thinking and praying calmly and patiently, and then acts out of a right mind and heart because of Christ within him. Take time to come before the Lord when these feelings of anger come forth, and may He guide you in the path of peace bringing forth reconciliation through His sanctifying Holy Spirit.

"[Love] keeps no record of wrongs" – 1 Corinthians 13:5

Have you ever been wronged? Of course you have, unless you live by yourself in the middle of nowhere and have no human interaction whatsoever. In *The Lord of the Rings,* Sam has been wronged by Frodo on more than one occasion. Frodo rejected Sam and their friendship and told him to go home and even tried to kill him once. But Sam loved Frodo as himself and knew that he was not in his right mind because he was being influenced by the power of the One Ring. If Sam had counted Frodo's wrongs against him, he would not be the selfless, loving friend that he has been for him his whole life. It is because of Sam's love for Frodo and willingness to look past his sins that he was able to destroy the ring of power and save Middle-Earth.

"[Love] keeps no record of wrongs." Do you remember a time when someone you trust and you believed to have forgiven you of your sins against them, and then one day they brought some of them back up to the surface? This shows that they have not truly forgiven you because they still have it in the forefront of their mind. Or in other words, they have been keeping a tally of all the wrongs you have done to them, even though they were "forgiven" awhile ago. This is not how you walk in love. This is how you walk in the way of the world.

"He who covers over an offense promotes love, but whoever repeats the matter separates close friends" (Proverbs 17:9). Here it says that in order to encourage love, you should cover over a wrong against you, and when it says "repeats the matter", i.e. bringing up the wrong again, that helps cause divisions among the brethren, something not of God. There are more verses on this matter: "Hatred stirs up dissension, but love covers over all wrongs" (Proverbs 10:12). "Surely then you will count my steps but not keep track of my sin" (Job 14:16). "Above all, love each other deeply, because love covers a multitude of sins" (1 Peter 4:8).

The world keeps track of your sins. Love, aka God, does not. So much more shall we then not keep tabs on the sins done against us! When we are walking in the way of love, we walk in the way of Christ, and thank goodness that He is "not counting men's sins against them" (2 Corinthians 5:19). We are called to be like Christ in every way, not just in the ways that are convenient or easy. Yes, forgetting the wrongs done to you may not be simple, but it must be done in order to live a Christ-like life. I pray that we as the bride of Christ may represent Him fully to the world as an agent of love and forgiveness.

"Love does not delight in evil but rejoices with the truth" – 1 Corinthians 13:6

This is the last in the list of the negative characteristics of what love is not. This is a strong one as well because it says that "love does not delight in evil." That is a scary thing to see someone that delights or rejoices in evil done to others. It is quite sad though because if Paul said that love did not do that, then he must have seen those in the Corinthian church doing it to one another.

When this is the case, people are taking pleasure in it when they see others being committed for a crime or guilty of a sin. We believers are no exception of this, as we too sometimes rejoice when we see an enemy having evil be done unto them instead of praying for them and forgiving them of their wrongs. "You are not a God who takes pleasure in evil" (Psalm 5:4). So then why should we take pleasure in evil? We shall not. We shall "hate what is evil" (Romans 12:9).

And we shall "rejoice in the truth." We shall take pleasure in what is right and good and just. When we know the truth and speak the truth, "the truth will set you free" (John 8:32) because truth has nothing to hide. We should enjoy the truth in others and delighting to see them walk in goodness and righteousness and pray for God to "Sanctify them by the truth; your word is truth" (John 17:17). That is what love does. Love does not hide and love loves seeing the good in others and not when they stumble because they want all to walk in uprightness as Jesus Christ our Lord has and called us to through the indwelling of His Spirit that continually makes us holy.

"Love does not delight in evil but rejoices with the truth." How are you viewing the people around you when they stumble and fall? Are you enjoying it? Are you proud that they have fallen? If so, repent and confess to Jesus of your sin and walk in the way of love and rejoice in their virtues. Exalt the truth that is Christ and His death, resurrection and ascension. Rejoice in His grace for us and that He loves us enough to not accept our sin, but to cleanse us and that He "sent his Son as an atoning sacrifice for our sins" (1 John 4:10). I pray for myself and all of you today, that we may walk in the path of love that Jesus Christ has set before us in His Word and in His life, and that we may have a proper prospective on the events around us and see them as He does. Grace and peace to you all. Amen.

"[Love] always protects" – 1 Corinthians 13:7

This is an interesting one to tackle. When I think of this, I think of a father protecting his children, not only in a physical capacity, but in a spiritual and emotional one as well. In the ESV and NKJV however, it has it as "love bears all things." The Greek word used literally means "to cover." I then understand why the NIV says that "[love] always protects" because when you cover something, you are protecting it from the elements and, as mentioned a couple days ago, that "love covers a multitude of sins" (1 Peter 4:8).

God throughout the Old Testament displayed this characteristic of love to the Israelites: "He protected us on our entire journey and among all the nations through which we traveled" (Joshua 24:17). "He will cover you with his feathers, and under his wings you will find refuge" (Psalm 91:4). And in the New Testament: "While I was with them, I protected them and kept them safe by that name you gave me" (John 17:12). God delights in protecting His children so that they may live and glorify His great name!

"[Love] always protects" or love covers. When we walk in love, we are willing to cover over peoples' faults because we know that God has forgiven them and looks over our faults and has forgiven us. When we love in this way, we desire to find the good in others and do not want them to be covered with guilt and shame or embarrassed publicly, but we want them to feel loved and to believe that they are more than what wrongs they have done or the quirks of their personalities.

Christ's love for us should be the compelling force for us to love as He does. "My prayer is not that you take them out of the world but that you protect them from the evil one" (John 17:15). This attribute of love delights in protecting those we love, i.e. not putting someone in a situation where they may be more susceptible to be tempted and sin, and thus putting a stumbling block in their path. The one who loves sees where someone is weak and helps to strengthen them and encourage them that Christ is strong even when they are not and that they must run from sin as Joseph did (see Genesis 39). Are you walking in this trait of love, of protection? Do you find joy in helping others stay on the right path? This part of love along with the next three, are all action verbs, meaning they are something that love does because love is not passive, but active. Are you actively loving your neighbors? Are you desiring to walk in the footsteps of Christ Jesus? Follow His feet; they will lead to life and peace.

February 12

"[Love] always trusts" – 1 Corinthians 13:7

Trusting someone is hard to do. "Why should I trust them? What have they done to deserve my trust? They hurt me repeatedly and tore me down; there is no way I can trust them!" These are thoughts that I know go into peoples' minds when the idea of trust comes up. It is hard to trust another person that is not us. We know what we believe and are capable of (for the most part), but another person? Can we trust what they say about a situation?

I believe we have to trust them when they say something because they are a person capable of trust and we would want them to trust us if we told them something. Unless it is a blatant lie that goes against everything that is true and that we know and believe to be true, we should trust because "[love] always trusts." This comes to say that love is not suspicious of the ones they love because then you will look at them with cynical and incredulous eyes, you will only see the bad and dark things of them and miss the wonderful and good things that they do and are!

Love longs to look for the good in others and to rejoice with them in that. If we cannot trust our brothers and sisters in Christ, we would greatly be hindering the work of the Lord! When you love someone, you trust them. We love God right? So do you trust God and the promises He makes in His Word? Are you suspicious of His actions and undermining His authority and sovereignty? I sure hope not because if so, then I would question your love for Him. When you trust someone, you believe in them. "You will keep in perfect peace him whose mind is steadfast, because he trusts in you. Trust in the Lord forever, for the Lord, the Lord, is the Rock eternal" (Isaiah 26:3-4). We know that "God is love" (1 John 4:8) and God does entrust us with the work of His ministry because "We are therefore Christ's ambassadors, as though God were making his appeal through us" (2 Corinthians 5:20).

God trusts us enough to carry on the work of proclaiming the Gospel to the entire world. God trusts us enough even though we have failed Him countless times and do not deserve to be trusted. What better way to make someone trustworthy than to trust them? That is love. He shows us the perfect love that we can only dream of attaining someday; the day I long for when I see Him face to face in glory! But until that day, we are being sanctified through His Spirit to love as He loves and to walk as He walks. I urge you brothers to trust one another in love, as your Father in heaven trusts you and as you trust Him. Give them the benefit of a doubt.

"[Love] always hopes" - 1 Corinthians 13:7

Hope is something that we hear a lot of these days. "I hope you have a good day." "I hope I do well on my test." "I hope for the best to come out of this situation." But what is hope as in this passage and elsewhere in Scripture? Hope has nothing to do with what we possess or what we can do for ourselves, but it has everything with who God is and what He has done and the promises He has made. We have hope that He will do what He said He would do.

This kind of hope is a hope in the unseen. "But hope that is seen is no hope at all. Who hopes for what he already has?" (Romans 8:24). This hope of ours is in Christ Jesus and no one or nothing else. We hope that God will fulfill His word in us, that we will see him face to face and that the Holy Spirit He placed within us "is a deposit guaranteeing our inheritance until the redemption of those who are God's possession" (Ephesians 1:14) as "we wait eagerly for our adoption as sons, the redemption of our bodies" (Romans 8:23) and since we have not yet been redeemed in this way, "we wait for it patiently" (Romans 8:25).

"[Love] always hopes." Love and hope are connected. If you love someone, you hope for the best in them, not the worst. You can see the potential in them and help them reach it. Do we love others this way? Do we love Christ this way? We know that Christ is sovereign, but do we have hope that He can redeem the worst of sinners and turn their lives around? I sure hope so because we were the worst of sinners before we were called to God! He redeemed us and forgave our iniquities by His precious blood, so why not hope and believe that He can do the same for others?

"And hope does not disappoint us" (Romans 5:5). Hope is the faith that is based on God's love for us that is shown through His indwelling Holy Spirit and His death and resurrection. Hope without faith is hopeless. Hope without love is hopeless. Hope needs faith and love in order to be hope. "The faith and love that spring from the hope that is stored up for you in heaven" (Colossians 1:5). When we are walking in the way of God's love, we walk in the hope that our work for His kingdom is not in vain, but that we "store up for [ourselves] treasures in heaven" (Matthew 6:20) and are bringing praises to His name and will be rewarded on that Day. "May he strengthen your hearts so that you will be blameless and holy in the presence of our God and Father when our Lord Jesus comes with all his holy ones" (1 Thessalonians 3:13). Yes Father, may we walk in that hope.

"[Love] always perseveres" – 1 Corinthians 13:7

The last of the "always" statements of what love does. This attribute is a favorite of mine and this word is a favorite of many as it comes with lasting and enduring connotations. Perseverance. Why do we love the idea of perseverance? Is it that we love the notion of immortality and foreverness? Or do we love that it means no matter what may be going on in the present moment, we can persevere? Or is it something more?

This belief of persevering is usually linked to prayer, especially in the New Testament: "They all joined together constantly in prayer" (Acts 1:14). "Devote yourselves to prayer" (Colossians 4:2). But it is also associated with suffering and persecution: "You know that the testing of your faith develops perseverance. Perseverance must finish its work so that you may be mature and complete, not lacking anything" (James 1:3-4). "Wait for the Lord; be strong and take heart and wait for the Lord" (Psalm 27:14). In order to persevere, one must always wait, so that is why patience and perseverance are related and are both part of what love is.

"[Love] always perseveres." Even through the deadliest of storms and the darkest of nights, it perseveres. True love that is, love that is represented by God to us through His prophets and presence in the Old Testament and Christ and the apostles and the Holy Spirit through the New. That love, shown to us, is the same enduring, steadfast love that we need to be showing to the world around us because the world's notion of love is shaky like a shack built with its foundations in the sand. But our love (hopefully) is built deep into the Rock that is Christ, enduring through the ages and whatever may come our way.

The love that Christ represents stays with you, much like what was said to Joshua from Moses, "The Lord himself goes before you and will be with you; he will never leave you nor forsake you" (Deuteronomy 31:8). May the love that is in us because of the Spirit be manifested in its enduring nature in our relationship to the Father and to our friends and family and neighbors in the world around us. "Therefore, my dear brothers, stand firm. Let nothing move you" (15:58). Let nothing move us and the way we love You Father and the people You have put in our lives. May we be like the trees that may seem to have moved because of the wind and the storm, but are just as strong and continuing as ever because of our roots in You that grow deeper day after day. You are too kind Father. We love you. Amen.

"Love never fails" - 1 Corinthians 13:8

This is the last day in the love series of 1 Corinthians 13 and no doubt it culminates with the greatest attribute of "love never fails." To bring all this month so far into context, Paul talks about spiritual gifts before and after this love section, but in comparison to love or if you possess those gifts without love, "[You] are nothing...[you] gain nothing" (13:2-3).

Love surpasses all other gifts because "love never fails" and other gifts do and will cease (see 13:8-10). As Jesus Culture's *One Thing Remains* goes, "Your love never fails, it never gives up, it never runs out on me." How encouraging this verse is! God's love for us never ever fails, meaning that it never ends and nothing, "neither death nor life, neither angels nor demons, neither the present nor the future, nor any powers, neither height nor depth, nor anything else in all creation, will be able to separate us from the love of God that is in Christ Jesus our Lord" (Romans 8:38-39).

Our world may be crumbling around us. Wars may be ravaging the earth. Our friends and family may hate us, but we can be assured that God will still love us and that is so encouraging! It makes all the junk and rubbish that happens to us on a daily basis not seem so terrifying and life-threatening as it does in the moment because we know that Jesus Christ loves us so much and is there with us every step of the way. As A.W. Tozer said, "When I understand that everything happening to me is to make me more Christ-like, it resolves a great deal of anxiety." Is that not the truth my friends! Everything that happens to us in this life is to make us more like Christ who is Love, so we may be walking more and more in love.

"Love never fails." It is through this love that the world will recognize us as Christ-followers. "By this [love] all men will know that you are my disciples, if you love one another" (John 13:35). Love is eternal and it is love that will still be the basic attitude of ours when we are in heaven. "I have loved you with an everlasting love" (Jeremiah 31:3). I hope to someday grasp this truth more fully because it is such a hopeful truth that should guide how we perceive situations and walk throughout our days. When we hear that His love never fails, we should rejoice because we know without a doubt that He fulfills what He has promised and will bring us home into His glory! Brothers, I pray this love over all of you, that you may bask in its fullness and walk in Christ's love and manifest that love to a dying and dark world that so desperately needs to see and experience it.

"Then God said, 'Take your son, your only son Isaac, whom you love, and go to the region of Moriah. Sacrifice him there as a burnt offering on one of the mountains I will tell you about'" – Genesis 22:2

That would be one of the worst things to ever have been told to do, especially after all that Abraham has been through up to this point. He moved from his homeland to an unknown land; was given a covenant by God that he would be the father of many nations; he had a barren wife, so the promise of God looked grim; God gave him the promised son after waiting twenty-five years. And now this? Now, after all he has gone through, God wants him to kill his one and only son through whom the covenant of God will be fulfilled?

Sounds messed up does it not? If I heard news about this for something in my life for example, if I went to school for years to be a teacher and was just starting to get in the rhythm of teaching and God told me to give it all up and leave it completely and go become a lumberjack in the Canadian Rockies, I would not believe it. Something that I have worked so hard for and I know was my calling from God and He wants me to give it up? But I must because He asked me to and I must obey my King, no matter the instructions. We cannot forget in the darkness what we know to be true in the light.

As we know from the text, Abraham did not even question God! That is utter faith and trust in the Lord, and good reason because of all God has done for him so far. I want that faith, faith where I cannot even see because "We live by faith, not by sight" (2 Corinthians 5:7) as Abraham did. He was able to do so because he remembered the Lord's promise to him and knew that God cannot lie. We know in this passage that it was a test from God so that Abraham could fear God (22:12), but in the moment I doubt he knew it was a test.

God tests us constantly. I pray that we can see when we are being tested, knowing that good will result. We know how this chapter ended. Not in the death of Isaac, but in his life. Much like Jesus, whom God had sentenced to death for our sakes, but it did not end in death, but in resurrection and life that is given to all who believe. God may call us to sacrifice the thing we love most, like how He sacrificed His one and only Son, but we must obey because He is Sovereign and we know that He knows what is best. Our love for God must be so much greater than our love for anything else because only out of our love for Him are we be able to love others. May we worship the Promiser and not the promise itself.

February 17

"Apart from me you can do nothing" - John 15:5

Human babies are the most vulnerable of all the babies in the mammal kingdom, and possibly the whole animal kingdom. They literally cannot do anything by themselves. They are utterly defenseless and would die if they were on their own without their parents. This is but an analogy of how we are in Christ, even though the passage uses the vine and the branches as a great analogy as well. "I am the vine; you are the branches. If a man remains in me and I in him, he will bear much fruit; apart from me you can do nothing" (15:5).

In horticulture, as Jesus is describing, the branches have to remain in the vine if they are to bear fruit, otherwise they would be away from the vine, wither and die. It is in the vine that the branches are able to exist because the vine is what digs down into the earth to gather nutrients in the soil and water and transport them to the branches and the fruit. So it is with us, that it is only in Christ that we are capable of living and moving and breathing. "Apart from me you can do nothing."

"Remain in me and I will remain in you" (15:4). By this we can take that it requires effort to remain in Him. This is a command that is followed by a promise. If we remain in Christ, He will remain in us. This is such a close and necessary fellowship and union that needs to take place. *We need to abide in the vine that is Christ.* As with babies that rely on their parents for everything, so we need to live in utter dependence upon the Living God who is the center of life and who is Life. "Because I live, you also will live" (14:19) if we abide in Christ. There is not a care in the world when we trust in Him completely and rely on Him as our Father and Shepherd.

My brothers, if we can comprehend and live out this truth day after day, oh how sweet that will be! To truly live in such reliance and dependence upon Christ, walking in step and unison with Him as He guides us, for "Your word is a lamp onto my feet and a light for my path" (Psalm 119:105). Without Christ, we are dead and nothing. We cannot pretend to be a part of Him because our fruit will be shown for what it is, "By their fruit you will recognize them" (Matthew 7:16). Father, I pray that we can be dependent on you in everything because from you and to you and through you are all things. Help us to live in absolute reliance on You in the things where we think we know it all or can do it by our own strength or knowledge. Apart from you we can do nothing. Help us to live as such, as is the truth. We love you Father, thank you for providing for your children. Amen.

"They could find no corruption in him, because he was trustworthy and neither corrupt nor negligent" – Daniel 6:4

Daniel was a man extremely high in the Babylonian government at this point. In fact, King Darius made Daniel one of the three administrators that are in charge of 120 satraps that rule throughout the kingdom. "Now Daniel so distinguished himself among the administrators and the satraps by his exceptional qualities that the king planned to set him over the whole kingdom" (6:3). That is indeed a prominent position for someone who is a foreigner taken out of captivity many years before.

So what makes Daniel so special? Yes, he was "handsome, showing aptitude for every kind of learning, well informed, quick to understand, and qualified to serve in the king's palace" (1:4). But what sticks out to me in 6:3 is that he was distinguished amongst his colleagues "by his exceptional qualities"; his character is what made him stand out. I believe this is something that is lost in today's world and especially in our culture and has even crept into the church.

Image has taken the place of character. We care so much more about our image or the image of someone else than we do about their character. For example, in the Kennedy and Nixon debate in 1960, the first one ever televised, Kennedy appeared confident and looked good while Nixon, recently hospitalized, looked pale and unhealthy. Most people watched the debate whereas only 11% listened on the radio. Those who listened to the debate on the radio thought Nixon had won and those who watched it on TV thought Kennedy had won. Needless to say, Kennedy won the election most likely because of how he looked that night, not because of what he said. (But what do I know, I was not around then).

But God places a great deal more emphasis on our character than how we appear. We can make ourselves look like anything we want, especially in this day and age of social media and plastic surgery, but who we are inside is what really matters. What we are on the inside, our character, eventually will be what we will look like on the outside. Jesus called out the Pharisees here saying "You are like whitewashed tombs, which look beautiful on the outside but on the inside are full of dead men's bones and everything unclean" (Matthew 23:27). If you have ever read the Sermon on the Mount, you know that it is about the heart of things, your character development and your nature. Do not work so much on how you appear before men, for the Lord knows what you really are. Work on your character my brothers so that no corruption may be found against you and so that you may be a pleasing sacrifice to your Father in heaven.

"Whom have I in heaven but you? And earth has nothing I desire besides you. My flesh and my heart may fail, but God is the strength of my heart and my portion forever" – Psalm 73:25-26

Over the past year I have learned more and more what it means to know and live that God is truly all that I need; not women nor money nor work acceptance nor comfort. Nothing but Himself alone. It is a hard thing to learn because we love to rely on other things for, well, everything and we tend to convince ourselves that we *need* this and that when truly we only just *want* it.

The first verse here, "Whom have I in heaven but you? And earth has nothing I desire besides you" is such a truth that, I do not know about you, but it cuts deep within me. "Earth has nothing I desire besides you." Nothing. That seems like quite the feat right there. How many of us can say that we desire nothing on this earth besides the Lord? I wish I could. I desire a woman who could be my wife, a job I love which provides for my family, good food, and many other things I am sure. I also greatly desire the presence of God, but it is not my sole desire as it should be.

Our one and only yearning should be rooted and established in the Lord God, who alone gives us everything we have, for "Every good and perfect gift is from above" (James 1:17). But we should not seek the Lord for what He can give us, even though He "rewards those who earnestly seek him" (Hebrews 11:6), but we should seek Him for who He is and what He has done and what He is doing right now.

"God is the strength of my heart and my portion forever." He is the Sustainer and Preserver of all things, especially when we try and try and in our own power and doing continually fail because we think we can do it on our own. His portion is enough for us because "God gives the Spirit without limit" (John 3:34). What is your biggest desire right now? A good job? A happy home? Adventure and travel? Peace and quiet? Whatever they may be, I implore you brothers that we can pray to the Lord to centralize our desires in Him, that earth may truly have nothing we desire besides Him because "The Lord is my shepherd, I shall not want" (23:1). God provides. May we trust Him this day with all of our being, knowing that we are in His good and gracious hands and that He knows what He is doing with our lives because He formed us with His hands.

"Then Peter remembered the word Jesus had spoken: 'Before the rooster crows, you will disown me three times.' And he went outside and wept bitterly" – Matthew 26:75

I have been there, to Caiaphas' house in Jerusalem, where one of Jesus' trials took place. I walked up those steps to his house leading to the courtyard where Peter was during this time. I saw the statue of Peter that inscribed this verse as he realized what he did to his rabbi and teacher of the last few years, weeping and distraught as he remembered Jesus' words of his predicted denial of Him. Earlier in the chapter, "Peter declared, 'Even if I have to die with you, I will never disown you'" (26:35).

Those words hurt. They hurt especially because we know the passion that Peter had for Jesus, but in the heat of the moment his words meant nothing and he ended up disowning his Savior three times. What is even worse is that in Luke's account of this, right after the rooster crowed his last, "The Lord turned and looked straight at Peter. Then Peter remembered" (Luke 22:61). Talk about eyes that would have pierced his very soul, hearing those words come out of his mouth as His Lord and King looked at him. No wonder he wept bitterly; I would be crushed.

What would devastate me the most is declaring earlier that "Even if all fall away on account of you, I never will" (26:33). What does it mean to disown Jesus? It means to deny him as Peter did saying "'I don't know what you're talking about'…He denied it again, with an oath: 'I don't know the man'…Then he began to call down curses on himself and he swore to them, 'I don't know the man!'" (26:70,72,74). Well that escalated quickly. The pressure of the people around him got to him and caused him to fall lower than ever before.

"Whoever acknowledges me before men, I will also acknowledge him before my Father in heaven. But whoever disowns me before men, I will disown him before my Father in heaven" (10:32-33). How have we denied Christ in our lives? Are we afraid to mention his name in a conversation? Do we shy from declaring that we are Christ-followers? Do we cower to society's pressure and not stand up for what the Bible says is true and right? I am quite guilty of these and I need continual repentance for my cowardice. As you can see from 10:32, we should be acknowledging our Father in heaven by not shrinking away from admitting the power and grace of Christ's work in our lives and being ever-mindful of His presence in our days. Father forgive us for disowning you before men and for being ashamed of who you are out of fear of rejection. Produce in us a spirit of courage that stands up for you at all times. You are worthy of it all. Thank you for your grace.

"Do not conform any longer to the pattern of this world, but be transformed by the renewing of your mind. Then you will be able to test and approve what God's will is—his good, pleasing and perfect will" - Romans 12:2

As a child, I conformed and mimicked what people were doing around me because I did not have the proper concept of right and wrong and thought that because they were doing it, I also should be doing it. But as I grew older, I have discerned that the way of the people around me, especially non-believers, is not how I should be acting because they do not know the Lord Jesus Christ and thus follow the people around them who believe that this life is all there is.

We are told here to "not conform any longer to the pattern of this world" because the world's way of thinking does not align with God's. The way of the world is me, me, me; a dog eat dog world where it is every man for himself and you must do whatever is necessary to make it to the top, no matter how many people you hurt. It is rooted in selfishness and greed and pride. But we are to "be transformed by the renewing of your mind." So if the world is dominated by selfishness and pride, we should be guided by selflessness and humility, particularly because that is the way of Christ whom we are to imitate.

"Finally, brothers, whatever is true, whatever is noble, whatever is right, whatever is pure, whatever is lovely, whatever is admirable—if anything is excellent or praiseworthy—think about such things" (Philippians 4:8). These are things that we can be thinking so that our minds may be renewed by the Lord. Reading the Word is also a wonderful way to be renewing your mind because you are digesting and meditating on the Living Word of God that is "Sharper than any double-edged sword, it penetrates even to dividing soul and spirit, joints and marrow; it judges the thoughts and attitudes of the heart" (Hebrews 4:12).

One of the most widely asked questions in the Christian life is "What is God's will for me?" I cannot answer that for you explicitly, but this verse gives you a clear path to how you can determine that, by not conforming but renewing your mind and aligning it with Christ. "Then you will be able to test and approve what God's will is." So what are you waiting for? Do not live as the world lives any longer my friends! Be transformed by the Spirit within you, sanctifying you day by day, conforming you to be like Christ to do His bidding. Take time right now to renew your mind, to lean on Christ and to think godly thoughts, full of love and joy and peace. Get after it.

"When the angel of the Lord appeared to Gideon, he said, 'The Lord is with you, mighty warrior'" – Judges 6:12

Last night I saw *The Lego Movie* with a group of friends and it was unbelievably hilarious. Every part of it was funny and extremely creative where anything could happen. The main character Emmet was only a normal construction worker that happened to stumble upon the piece of revolution and because of that, he was seen as The Special, the one who would overthrow Lord Business who was trying to destroy the world as they know it. But he wasn't anyone special; he only was because other people believed he was special, giving him the courage that he needed to try and be The Special.

Gideon was just the same way. He was not anyone special at all, in fact, when the Lord appeared to him, "Gideon was threshing wheat in a winepress" (6:11) while hiding because he was afraid of the Midianites. And later he said, "How can I save Israel? My clan is the weakest in Manasseh, and I am the least in my family" (6:15). He did not see himself as someone of importance or capable of doing anything that could really make a difference. He was hesitant again and again to believe that it was the Lord speaking to him: "Give me a sign that it is really you talking to me…If there is dew only on the fleece and all the ground is dry, then I will know that you will save Israel by my hand as you said…Let me make one more request. Allow me one more test with the fleece" (6:17,37,39).

He was continually reluctant to believe that God could work through him, a normal person, because no one has ever believed in him to do great things, just like Emmet. No one ever spoke into his life and told him that he was special and has great talents and can do so much in the world. But "The Lord does not look at the things man looks at. Man looks at the outward appearance, but the Lord looks at the heart" (1 Samuel 16:7). God knows who we really are and what we are capable of through His work in us; that is why He told Gideon, "The Lord is with you, mighty warrior." He saw who he could become if someone nudged him in the right direction.

Every one of you is special. Do not let anyone tell you otherwise and do not listen to the voice of the enemy. God has called you "a chosen people, a royal priesthood, a holy nation, a people belonging to God" (1 Peter 2:9). You are someone because you are made in His image, created "to do good works, which God prepared in advance for us to do" (Ephesians 2:10). So go. Do something because the Lord is with you and has called you to great and marvelous things through His Spirit. See yourself through the Lord's eyes.

"Yet when I surveyed all that my hands had done and what I had toiled to achieve, everything was meaningless, a chasing after the wind; nothing was gained under the sun" – Ecclesiastes 2:11

The book of Ecclesiastes was written by Solomon who has been deemed one of the wisest and richest men of all time. He wrote the majority of the book of Proverbs as well. He has had it all: money, palaces, women, and a kingdom. He has done many things and pursued many paths in order to find fulfillment and satisfaction in something, but he starts off his book saying, "'Meaningless! Meaningless!' says the Teacher. 'Utterly meaningless! Everything is meaningless!'" (1:2).

All of his pursuits came up empty. He worked and worked and still discovered that "everything was meaningless, a chasing after the wind; nothing was gained under the sun." He could not find life's meaning and joy in his work and toil; it was "a chasing after the wind." Have you ever tried chasing the wind to catch it? It is useless and you come up empty. Even in all that you have accomplished, no matter how great it was, the happiness and such that you feel is only temporary and truly nothing in the grand scheme of things because what does it produce? Something that is here today and gone tomorrow.

This is why Jesus has called you and "appointed you to go and bear fruit—fruit that will last" (John 15:16); to "store up for yourselves treasures in heaven, where moth and rust do not destroy and where thieves do not break in and steal" (Matthew 6:20). All the chasings of the world: fame, wealth, pleasure, materials, prestige, security, it all amounts to absolutely nothing without Christ in the picture. He and eternity are what makes everything else worthwhile.

"A man can do nothing better than to eat and drink and find satisfaction in his work. This too, I see, is from the hand of God, for without him, who can eat or find enjoyment?" (2:24-25). Solomon shows us in this book that we should enjoy life, but do not make enjoying life your main pursuit. We should make knowing and obeying God our main purpose. Many of us in today's world love to enjoy life, but then some of us forget to obey God's commandments in the midst of enjoying the great gifts He has given. Obeying God should be above having fun with friends and living merrily. Our purpose in life is found in God and God alone, not in "chasing after the wind" and everything that makes us happy. He ends the book like so, "For God will bring every deed into judgment, including every hidden thing, whether it is good or evil" (12:14). May these final words give you a perspective on the things you are doing in this life, knowing that you will be held accountable for them.

"He was made king, however, and returned home. Then he sent for the servants to whom he had given the money, in order to find out what they had gained with it" – Luke 19:15

This is from the Parable of the Ten Minas, which is one of Jesus' last parables recorded in Luke. The "man of noble birth [who] went away to a distant country to have himself appointed king and then to return" (19:12) is Jesus of course, in regards to His second coming. "So he called ten of his servants and gave them ten minas. 'Put this money to work,' he said, 'until I come back'" (19:13). We are his servants who have been entrusted with the future King's possessions.

From this we can gather that everything belongs to God in the first place, it is never ours, but he has bestowed it upon us and entrusted us to take care of it as He would have desired. If you make money from your job and you think it is yours to do whatever you wish, think again, "But remember the Lord your God, for it is he who gives you the ability to produce wealth" (Deuteronomy 8:18). It is all God's to begin with, so throw away the mentality that you can do what you want with it, but remember from yesterday that you will be held accountable for everything you did in this life. Do not squander what God has given you, but "Put this money to work."

We have all been entrusted with something, whether it is finances or intellect or strength or artistic ability or whatever it is, we have been given gifts. "We have different gifts, according to the grace given us...if it is serving, let him serve; if it is teaching, let him teach; if it is encouraging let him encourage..." (Romans 12:6-8). What talents have you been given by God for the sake of His kingdom, for His glory? If you do not know, take time to think and pray about that today so that you do not squander the gifts you have been given and thus "for the one who has nothing, even what he has will be taken away" (19:26).

We are all held responsible for what we do with the things God has entrusted us with in this life. We spend a lot of our time striving to get and gain what we do not have instead of embracing and stewarding what we do have. We should be multiplying what the Lord has given us as in the parable, "The first one came and said, 'Sir, your mina has earned ten more.' 'Well done, my good servant!' his master replied. 'Because you have been trustworthy in a very small matter, take charge of ten cities'" (19:16-17). Have you been faithful with what God has given you? Can He say to you "Well done, my good servant!"? I pray brothers that we can be great stewards of the Lord's possessions He has given us, showing us to be worthy servants responsible of bigger and better things for His kingdom.

"Do everything without complaining or arguing" - Philippians 2:14

Children love to complain about everything that does not go their way. They do not get what they want so they throw a temper tantrum, hopefully manipulating their parents. When they grow into adults, their antics and tactics however do not always fade away as they should. I see it all the time and it is quite sad to see a middle-aged man sit and complain about everything that a coworker does, only because he does not like it and did not do something his way.

In the context of the passage, Paul is speaking to the church in Philippi right after describing Jesus' humble and giving character while on earth. Complaining and arguing are both devices of creating dissension among people, and dissension is not of God because God is all about unity. If a non-believer walked into your church and saw everyone complaining about everything, would they get a true representation of who Jesus Christ is? By no means! When we complain about something, we are believing that we know the right way to do things and everyone else is wrong; also that the world revolves around us and what we want instead of around Christ and what He desires.

"Do everything without complaining or arguing, *so that* you may become blameless and pure, children of God without fault in a crooked and depraved generation, in which you shine like starts in the universe as you hold out the word of life" (2:15-16, emphasis added). We do not argue or complain *so that* we may represent Christ in His fullness, showing that we are God's children and that children of God do not argue and complain because the world does those things and creates divisions among themselves, not unity. This is but another way to "not conform any longer to the pattern of this world" (Romans 12:2).

Do you see yourself as someone who complains and argues on just about everything? Do you do it for the sake of arguing (to tick people off), or because you want your opinion to be heard and obeyed? Be careful if you are around those who are this way because their behavior is contagious like any bad behavior is. "Bad company corrupts good character" (1 Corinthians 15:33). Do not let them corrupt who you are by changing how you act, as I have noticed in myself some when I am at work too much, where I see lots of complaining at play. It just puts a negative attitude on everything and nobody wants to be around that and it definitely does not show others the love and mercy of our Lord Jesus Christ. May we put aside the depressing acts of complaining and arguing and take hold of the humble and peaceful acts of our Savior and King, for the praise of His glory. Take a look at yourself today to see what camp you are in.

"Jesus turned and said to Peter, 'Get behind me, Satan! You are a stumbling block to me; you do not have in mind the things of God, but the things of men'" – Matthew 16:23

I do not know why, but we as people like to control things; whether they are situations in our lives or other people or nature, we like to control it. Maybe because we then think that we are in charge of it and can manage the outcome and manipulate it to do what we want it to. This is how most if not all of our scientific and manufacturing developments came to be, by taking something and dictating it to do what we wanted. Not so the way with God.

Jesus said these words to Peter after he "took him aside and began to rebuke him. 'Never, Lord!' he said. 'This shall never happen to you!' (16:22). All of this was said following Jesus describing how "he must go up to Jerusalem and suffer many things at the hands of the elders, chief priests and teachers of the law, and then he must be killed and on the third day be raised to life" (16:21). I do not know about you, but if I heard Jesus, the man I left everything to follow, whom I have been following for the past three years, tell me that that is what was going to happen to him, without knowing what I know today, I probably would have said near the same thing to him and I would feel like crap being called Satan from the Son of God!

Jesus called him that because it was Satan who also tried to dissuade Jesus from taking the necessary way of the cross (4:10), as Peter was then doing. He was trying to tell Jesus, the Son of the Living God, what He should do, in other words, he was trying to control Him. He did not believe that the Savior of the Jews should have to suffer and die, but that He should reign supreme in Israel and overthrow the Romans' rule. Thankfully, Jesus was not that king, but He was the one for whom "it was the Lord's will to crush him and cause him to suffer, and though the Lord makes his life a guilt offering" (Isaiah 53:10).

God is not a genie that we can get out of the lamp whenever we want Him to and have Him do our bidding. He is the God of the universe! The Almighty One who is in control of the whole world from the beginning of time and who is outside of time. He is not a God of convenience for us; He is not a vending machine. He is the Eternal God whom cannot be manipulated to fit Himself into our will. We are the ones who should be fitting ourselves into His will! We need to "have in mind the things of God." Know who the God you worship and adore is, praise and thank Him for who He is. Ask Him to mold yourself into His perfection for His purpose. Do not try and manipulate God; be shaped by Him.

"Because judgment without mercy will be shown to anyone who has not been merciful. Mercy triumphs over judgment!" – James 2:13

In *The Lord of the Rings: The Fellowship of the Ring* while the fellowship was passing through the Mines of Moria, they were lost and Frodo saw Gollum following them and told Gandalf, "It's a pity Bilbo didn't kill him when he had the chance." Gandalf then wisely told him, "Many that live deserve death. And some that die deserve life. Can you give it to them Frodo? Then do not be too eager to deal out death in judgment. Even the very wise cannot see all ends."

Beautiful. It is scenes like this where I see Gandalf as the Jesus character in the films. He takes pleasure in showing mercy, even to someone as Gollum who told the enemy in Mordor that the One Ring was in the Shire with Baggins. "You do not stay angry forever but delight to show mercy" (Micah 7:18). God delights in giving us mercy for our iniquities, especially when we have screwed up big time, as in the case of Gollum. And think, if Bilbo or Frodo had killed Gollum earlier, then the One Ring would never have been destroyed in Mount Doom. That is why Gandalf said, "My heart tells me that Gollum has some part to play yet, for good or evil, before this is over."

"Mercy triumphs over judgment!" Boy am I glad that this is the truth! If judgment ruled, I would be scared because of all the wrongdoings I have done in my life and because of them, that is how I would spend eternity. But thanks be to God that He sent His Son and "bore the sin of many, and made intercession for the transgressors" (Isaiah 53:12), because "without the shedding of blood there is no forgiveness" (Hebrews 9:22). Since mercy rules, the blood of Christ will "cleanse our consciences from acts that lead to death, so that we may serve the living God!" (Hebrews 9:14).

We are not God; therefore we not shall assume the role of God in choosing who should live and who should die. God alone is God. We are but His servants and friends; His creation. The wooden cabinet that I made cannot try and take my position and make decisions about my life. That is not how it works. Why are we so eager to deal judgment on people because of what they have done? Is it because we see that same sin in our lives and have not come to terms with it? I do not know, but I do know that "Blessed are the merciful, for they will be shown mercy" (Matthew 5:7). Bestow mercy on those in your life whom you want to impart judgment. Be like Christ in this way brothers. He will smile down upon you and be glad.

"Those who cling to worthless idols forfeit the grace that could be theirs" – Jonah 2:8

There is a story of a man who was a kingpin drug dealer in Detroit. Cops always knew where he was but did nothing because they were on his payroll. People feared him. Until one day he changed and found Jesus Christ as his Lord and Savior. He ended his drug dealing ways, found a nice Christian wife, and luckily the cops did not do anything to him. Everyone would say that he was a born-again Christian who saw the error of his ways, but one thing he could not do; he could not stop using drugs as he was completely addicted. His wife tried to have him stop, but he just loved his drugs too much and relied on them for everything.

This is what Jonah meant in his prayer to God, "Those who cling to worthless idols forfeit the grace that could be theirs." The man could not loosen the grip of his idol of drugs, thus giving up his grace from the Lord and chose to follow a different master. "Do not turn away after useless idols. They can do you no good, nor can they rescue you, because they are useless" (1 Samuel 12:21). Only God can truly rescue you and do you good. Paul urges us to "not receive God's grace in vain" (2 Corinthians 6:1). The drugs here are what is useless, while God is the most useful being that has ever been or will be.

What are you serving that is not God? "No one can serve two masters. Either he will hate the one and love the other, or he will be devoted to the one and despise the other" (Matthew 6:24). "Don't you know that when you offer yourselves to someone to obey him as slaves, you are slaves to the one whom you obey...? (Romans 6:16). Are you serving yourself and your desires? "Those who live according to the sinful nature have their minds set on what that nature desires; but those who live in accordance with the Spirit have their minds set on what the Spirit desires" (Romans 8:5).

What worthless idols are you clinging to? Success in life? Money? A past relationship, or even a new relationship? Your job? Comfort and security? Whatever your worthless idol may be, cast it aside at once and run to the Master that has and can fulfill what you truly need! In Jesus Christ, there is no shortage of any kind; "he will have an abundance" (Matthew 25:29). In Christ alone will you find satisfaction and purpose. Do not rely any longer on anything but God! They are useless and will fade to dust, for "The world and its desires pass away, but the man who does the will of God lives forever" (1 John 2:17). May it be Christ to whom you are clinging to; there are plenty of nice footholds to stand on.

"Each one should use whatever gift he has received to serve others, faithfully administering God's grace in its various forms" – 1 Peter 4:10

Last night I watched *Good Will Hunting* for the first time in a long while, so long in fact I forgot what it was about. In it there is a man who is extremely gifted and a genius, but he is a janitor and construction worker. He does not want to go anywhere in life or do anything and he squanders his amazing gift until a professor and a counselor come into his life and try to have himself find a purpose for his abilities. He had all this knowledge and facts in his head, but he did not know the feelings and the experiential parts of it because he distances himself from anything or anyone that may potentially hurt him.

If you have not seen it, I would recommend it, even though there is a fair amount of language throughout. We all have been given wondrous gifts from the greatest gift giver of them all. We have been given different talents and abilities from the One whose image we are formed from. Like Will in the movie, our talents are unique to us. "Just as each of us has one body with many members, and these members do not all have the same function, so in Christ we who are many form one body, and each member belongs to all the others. We have different gifts, according to the grace given us" (Romans 12:4-6).

Our gifts we have been given are not only for our own benefit, but mainly for the benefit of those around us. "Each one should use whatever gift he has received to serve others." I know these passages are mostly referring to spiritual gifts, but I want to focus on actual gifts like the ability to look at a piano and play it like Mozart, or to see a canvas and paint like Picasso, or the ability to excel greatly in sports or can fix anything you see that is broken.

What gift(s) have you been blessed with? Take this question and seriously pray and think about it if you do not know already. I honestly do not know what mine are, even though yes, I am good at sports and have a passion for helping people, but I still do not really know what I excel in. Whatever it is that you are talented it, do not throw it away and just settle with not using it like Will originally did, but train yourself in it and make it grow, using it for God's glory and the benefit of others in your life and the world. "Do not neglect your gift" (1 Timothy 4:14). You have the potential for greatness in God's kingdom; do not waste what He has given you. Be thankful for it and use it for His purposes.

"You adulterous people, don't you know that friendship with the world is hatred toward God? Anyone who chooses to be a friend of the world becomes an enemy of God" – James 4:4

If this verse is not pushing you towards self-reflection of your life and your actions, it should. James just called you an adulterous people, meaning that you have forsaken your love for God for the love of the world and its ways. This verse is to each and every one of us who professes Jesus Christ as Lord of our lives. Of course I am guilty of this and that is why repentance needs to become a part of your life with God. Repentance precedes forgiveness and blessing.

What does it look like to be friends of the world? It means to love the world and the pattern of thinking and principles that govern it. It means to seek and desire things that are not of God and to pursue them with the same fervor that should be directed towards Him. It means to copy what the world does in spite of what God says we should do and it means choosing to be one with the world and to blend in so much that they do not even know that we are "followers" of Christ. It means that our thoughts never rise to God when are doing activities or witnessing His creation, although He is the One that makes everything that you see possible.

God is our portion, not the world. When you do the things listed above and more, you are no longer friends of God but you are His enemies and have become friends of the world. We love to quote that Jesus has called us friends. Yes, He has, but He said "You are my friends *if* you do what I command" (John 15:14, emphasis added). You must do what God commands if you are to be His friend and I guarantee you brothers that friendship with the world is not one of them.

Everything that you do matters. Are you seeking to be friends with the world and its customs, to fit in and be one with them? Or are you seeking to be friends with God and direct your passions for Him and His Kingdom? What do you spend your time doing? Does everything you do relate back to God? It should! We need to stop separating the secular from the spiritual. We need to stop keeping Jesus out of our conversations within our Christian circle because they are sick of hearing it and just want to "relax". Why is that? Why is God's name sickening you? You should be in love with Him! He should be involved in everything you do and He wants to be! "For from him and through him and to him are all things" (Romans 11:36). Are you friends with the world, or are you friends with God?

"The man said, 'The woman you put here with me—she gave me some fruit from the tree, and I ate it.' Then the Lord God said to the woman, 'What is this you have done?' The woman said, 'The serpent deceived me, and I ate'" - Genesis 3:12-13

One day a man went for a walk on the beach. He saw that a ship full of passengers struck a rock and capsized in the sea. The ship went under water and all the people on board fell into the sea. As they did not know how to swim, they drowned one by one. The man watched all this from the shore but could not do anything to help the people. In the evening, he narrated the sad event of the ship's drowning to his friends. Everyone felt sorry for the dead people. The man said, "God has not been just. To kill one sinner aboard the ship he killed so many other innocent people."
As he was saying this, he felt a pinch on his feet. He looked down. A red ant was biting his toe. Many other red ants were near his feet. In anger, he started stamping his feet to crush the red ants.
God appeared at the spot and said, "See, how you are killing other innocent ants to kill the one which bit you. You were blaming me for my unjust act. Look at your own actions before blaming me for anything."
The man felt ashamed as he realized his mistake.

A simple fable with no author on how stupid blame shifting is. Adam was the first to do it in the third chapter of the Bible and Eve was quickly the second. Why did they shift the blame? They believe it will take the responsibility off their shoulders and rid them of the guilt of having the blame. Doing this however does not work and only further deceives yourself, blinding you to the truth.

It is just like making an excuse; you are deceiving yourself over and over and you begin to believe the lie and excuse you have told. You can never deceive God however. He sees what is invisible and what is in our hearts. He is light and "everything exposed by the light becomes visible, for it is light that makes everything visible" (Ephesians 5:13). So why continue in blaming others and making excuses if you will still be found out in the end?

Temporarily it may work out for you, but in the long run the result is the same; you will be exposed for who you really are. Why hide the truth? Do not be ruled by fear brothers, but be ruled by faith in the Son of God and by truth which sets you free. It is convenient to blame someone else for your failures, but that is not what we are called to do; convenience does not characterize a believer's way of life, but hardship does. "In fact, everyone who wants to live a godly life in Christ Jesus will be persecuted" (2 Timothy 3:12). Do not blame those around you for your wrongs or make excuses. Be honest with people and be honest with yourself and be honest with God. Own your faults.

"For God did not give us a spirit of timidity, but a spirit of power, of love and of self-discipline" – 2 Timothy 1:7

The other night I joined some members of 35 churches from around the area to worship our God and King as one body, one church. It was part of Jesus Loves Kalamazoo, which is the body of Christ in Kalamazoo coming together as one to show Christ's love to those in the area who desperately need it and need to see the unity that God intends. It was a wonderful night full of God's presence that, sadly to say, I have not experienced to that extent in a few years. It was filled with God's power and His Holy Spirit stirring among all of us as one, as we praise the King of kings for all that He is.

For too long, we as a church have stood idly by to the evils in this world, but no more my brothers! We need to unite together as one church, the bride of Christ, and then we can walk in the power of the Holy Spirit. We could then say that when the Spirit came down at Pentecost, that it was not a one-time event but that it can happen again and the church can be as it was in the first century and more! Jesus himself prayed "that all of them [the church] may be one, Father, just as you are in me and I am in you...May they be brought to complete unity to let that world know that you sent me and have loved them even as you have loved me" (John 17:21,23).

The world needs to see the unity of the church so that they can see how much God loves them and cares for them where they are at. The unity of the Christ's bride is what gives them power because Jesus and the Father are one and desire that unity for His church, with each other and with Him. That is why Paul wrote that "God did not give us a spirit of timidity, but a spirit of power, of love and of self-discipline." And right after that he says, "So do not be ashamed to testify about our Lord" (1:8). That is what a lot of this is all about, so others can see God through you as you testify about Him with your words and with your actions, so this can be true that "I no longer live, but Christ lives in me" (Galatians 2:20).

Are you a slave to the spirit of fear and hesitation? Do not be any longer because that is not the spirit that is within you! Inside of you there lives a "spirit of power, of love and of self-discipline." Walk in that authority that is within you which Christ Himself bestowed upon you. Walk in the power that the Spirit is so that everywhere your feet touch, God's glory and presence may be made known and that His kingdom may come. Have faith like a child in this and walk in communion with your Father in heaven and His children.

"The Lord Almighty has sworn, 'Surely, as I have planned, so it will be, and as I have purposed, so it will stand'" – Isaiah 14:24

Have you ever planned to do something and then did not do it? Or have you willed to complete something or even start something but could not come to terms to finish it because something else came up or you decided it was not worth it? I know I have and I like felt crap because I told myself I was going to do this or that and then I did not. I felt as if I was cheating myself, like when I wanted to become a police offer and found out that I was too optimistic to be a cop, so I decided not to pursue it further. Or when I wanted to be a teacher or a college ministry worker or an adventure guide and then I stopped.

But when God plans to do something, He means to follow it through to the end because He knows everything and "Nothing in all creation is hidden from God's sight. Everything is uncovered and laid bare before the eyes of him to whom we must give account" (Hebrews 4:13). He is "the Beginning and the End" (Revelation 22:13), meaning that He is outside of time, seeing the whole of creation as if it is all happening at once, so yes, God can see all of your life right now, knowing how the decision that you make later today will affect your tomorrow and so forth.

That is comforting to me because I know that the choices I make really do matter and that what God says He will do, He will actually do. When He says that "if I go and prepare a place for you, I will come back and take you to be with me that you also may be where I am" (John 14:3), then I know without a doubt that that is in fact what will happen because He said it would. "As the rain and the snow come down from heaven, and do not return to it without watering the earth and making it bud and flourish, so that it yields seed for the sower and bread for the eater, so is my word that goes out from my mouth: It will not return to me empty, but will accomplish what I desire and achieve the purpose for which I sent it" (55:10-11).

The Lord's will *will* be done my brothers. If He wills it, it shall be so. May this be an encouragement to you as you walk about your day, knowing that God's word is His word and His word is trustworthy because "the Word was with God, and the Word was God" (John 1:1). If God has said something over your life, believe that "the one who calls you is faithful and he will do it" (1 Thessalonians 5:24). The Bible was for people back then and it is His revelation for us still today, His very life breathed throughout its pages. Where in your life do you need to walk in this confidence?

"Whatever you do, work at it with all your heart, as working for the Lord, not for men"
– Colossians 3:23

This past week I have working on setting up for the Kalamazoo Home Expo with my landscaping company. We are the headline sponsor and have the largest display right in the front and another smaller one to the side. It was a lot of hard and tedious work, but it looks beautiful in the end. A lady that I do not know came up to me and complemented me on the work I was doing, telling me that she was proud of my attitude towards the work and my work ethic to make it look nice, even though it is all going to be torn down in a couple of days.

That felt really nice to hear that from her, knowing that she owns a landscaping company of her own and appreciates the work I put in for all of this. My mindset for those couple of days is what got me through it, knowing that in all the work that I do, I do it unto the Lord for His glory because He has given me the ability to work. It was quite pleasant to be able to have artistic liberty with a certain section and to beautify that area with flowers and rock and mulch.

"Whatever you do, whether in word or deed, do it all in the name of the Lord Jesus, giving thanks to God the Father through him" (3:17). That may have been one of the few select times in my work life where I enjoyed what I was doing and felt peace about it, even though I still desire another job. But this should not be a rare occurrence my friends, but a lifestyle. "Whatever your hand finds to do, do it with all your might" (Ecclesiastes 9:10).

I know that we may not always like and enjoy the work that we do, but we should do it nonetheless as to the Lord. Yes, we have bosses over us for whom we work in order to take home a paycheck, but our ultimate boss is God above who allows all of this to happen. If working as to men, then our only purpose for the job would be to make money, but when we realize that we are working to the Lord, we can know that God has given this to us to be able to work for Him and not to skimp out on our work, but that we can give our all to it because it is to God! Once this comes to realization, I believe that none of us would ever desire to be lazy in our work again, but work at it diligently. I say to you, "Rejoice in the Lord always. I will say it again: Rejoice!" (Philippians 4:4). May you find joy in your boring workload, knowing that God is your boss who blesses you with gifts much more than a paycheck and that last longer too. He has the best retirement package money cannot buy, but you must only have faith in what He says He will do because He is trustworthy and worthy of it all.

"Whoever claims to live in him must walk as Jesus did" – 1 John 2:6

I have many Christian friends from my time at college and I love all of them dearly. They have a great passion for the Lord and for others to come to the knowledge of Him in their lives. I see their fervor as they study the Word and learn how it applies to them today and how it can affect the lives of those in their sphere of influence. But I also notice how in different settings they tend to separate themselves from what they have learned and lean more towards what the world has taught them.

Do not get me wrong brothers, I also struggle with this, but over the years the Lord has enlightened me in the error of me ways. Today goes along well with March 2 in how we must act and think differently than the world because the Holy Spirit dwells within us. "But the Counselor, the Holy Spirit, whom the Father will send in my name, will teach you all things and will remind you of everything I have said to you" (John 14:26). The Spirit will teach us and remind us of how Jesus lived and we have the Bible so we can read how He lived and how we must live.

Why do we have a tendency to separate our spiritual lives from our "secular" lives? First, we should not have a spiritual life and a secular life; it should all be spiritual because we are spiritual beings. Second, Jesus never compartmentalized his life, for "the Son can do nothing by himself; he can do only what he sees his Father doing" (John 5:19). He did not get out of the synagogue and then get with his friends and get drunk, but everything that Jesus did was in obedience to His Father, not the world and its pressures. He has said to us, "As it is, you do not belong to the world, but I have chosen you out of the world. That is why the world hates you" (John 15:19).

Does it look like the world hates us or loves us? Are we dividing the areas of our lives so that we are godlier in one area over another? This should not be my friends! "Whoever claims to live in him must walk as Jesus did." Jesus was godly in every area of His life without compromising to the whims of those around him. "If we claim to have fellowship with him yet walk in the darkness, we lie and do not live by the truth" (1:6). I pray that we do not compromise with the ways of the world and so dishonor our Father in heaven, but that we can stand firm, knowing that God is always with us and that through Him we can make the right decision in every situation. May we be people of wholeness and integrity in the Lord Jesus Christ, representing His light to a world shrouded in darkness and falsehood.

"The men of Israel sampled their provisions but did not inquire of the Lord" – Joshua 9:14

As people, we learn how to do things as we experience life. We learn from a young age not to touch fire because it will burn us, so we do not touch it when we are older. We learn that something works in a situation, so we believe that doing it the same way will make it work in a similar scenario. We assume that because we made it a ways in life, that we know what we are doing and do not need advice or counsel in things because we believe we know what is best or that the decision is simple enough for us to make on our own.

The Israelites had just destroyed the cities of Jericho and Ai and heard Joshua read all the words of the Law of Moses (chapter 8). Then the Gibeonites fooled them into making a treaty of peace with them so they could live and not be destroyed as they have heard what the God of Israel was doing to the people in the land (9:3-15). But God told the people of Israel earlier that they should "Be careful not to make a treaty with those who live in the land where you are going" (Exodus 34:12). But yet they did with the Gibeonites.

What strikes me here is that this happened right after they heard the Book of the Law, so they reheard that they should not make a treaty with the people in the land they are conquering. This reminds me of when the Israelites, in full view of the glory of the Lord on Mount Sinai, built the golden calf for themselves to worship, all because Moses took awhile to come down the mountain (Exodus 32).

Do we do that? Do we, in full view of the Lord (although everything is always in His view), or after just hearing and reading His Word, forget what we have seen and heard and learned, so quickly go back to doing things our own way? Do we forget to inquire of the Lord, even in things that seem so straightforward that we should be able to do them on our own? How easily we forget that "apart from me you can do nothing" (John 15:5)?

"David inquired of the Lord. 'Shall I go up to one of the towns of Judah?' he asked. The Lord said, 'Go up.' David asked, 'Where shall I go?' 'To Hebron,' the Lord answered" (2 Samuel 2:1). There are countless more accounts of David inquiring of God for what to do, even in menial matters. So I urge you today brothers, do not leave God out of your life in how you should go about your day. Talk to Him and listen to Him and be willing to go where He is taking you. God delights in your obedience to Him and loves it when you ask Him what to do and lean on His understanding and not your own.

"Blessed is the man whom God corrects; so do not despise the discipline of the Almighty" - Job 5:17

There once was a man who was well-loved by everybody, everywhere he went. He had a great job, a loving family, and he loved to live life. Then one day, a crippling disease hit him, forcing him to lose his job and have a different outlook on his life. He was now depressed and cynical, but then God came to him and told him everything was ok, that all of this is for his betterment, just wait and see. So he waited, and waited, and waited twenty years until he was finally healed and during this waiting, he learned to love life again and became an even better man than he once was.

I am someone who has been corrected on many occasions by the Lord God. He has been and always will be a wonderful Father to me. He has shown me that "God disciplines us for our good, that we may share in his holiness. No discipline seems pleasant at the time, but painful. Later on however, it produces a harvest of righteousness and peace for those who have been trained by it" (Hebrews 12:10-11). I could not have said it better myself. Discipline does stink; it hurts and I do not know anyone that likes it, whether it be self-discipline for getting in shape or a child being disciplined by their parents, it is not fun.

We tend to get so caught up in the moment, in the pain of the present, which we then forget that God is outside of time and sees the fruit of what He is causing us to endure. "My son, do not despise the Lord's discipline and do not resent his rebuke, because the Lord disciplines those he loves, as a father the son he delights in" (Proverbs 3:11-12). Is God disciplining you now? Great! He delights in you as His child! Praise Him for loving you so much. We need to get out of our current mindsets of the pain that is caused, and see the greatness that comes in the end.

When we are being disciplined, we are being corrected and moving forward towards holiness. It is not fun being corrected either because it shows that we are not doing something right. But Job says that "Blessed is the man whom God corrects." He is blessed because the Lord loves him enough to not have him stay as he is, but to bring him to righteousness and wholeness. Where has God been correcting you lately? In how you treat your family? In your reading of the Bible? In the workplace? Take a step back for a moment and see where He is correcting you and guiding you towards a more Christ-like life in Him. If He is not correcting you or disciplining you, I would check to see where you are with Him, to see if you are really with Him at all. I pray that is not the case. See beyond the moment with God's eyes and see how much He cares for you, His children.

"For he wounds, but he also binds up; he injures, but his hands also heal" – Job 5:18

Continuing from yesterday, God may not be the cause of your pain, because in the New Jerusalem, heaven, "There will be no more death or mourning or crying or pain" (Revelation 21:4), but He will use your pain for your benefit. You most likely will not see it in the moment of the hurt and pain, but in hindsight with the Lord's eyes, you will see how marvelous He was in those times and how you would not be the same person today if you had not gone through that ordeal.

C.S. Lewis said that "We can ignore even pleasure. But pain insists upon being attended to. God whispers to us in our pleasures, speaks in our conscience, but shouts in our pains: it is his megaphone to rouse a deaf world." It is in the pain where some of the greatest revelations and the best breakthroughs we receive from God come from. I know for me in some of my lowest and most painful moments of my life, I could think the clearest and see life more from God's perspective because He was all that I was relying on as everything else around me crumbled.

In a distressing moment for Paul and Silas, after being severely beaten and thrown into prison, "About midnight Paul and Silas were praying and singing hymns to God...Suddenly there was such a violent earthquake that the foundations of the prison were shaken. At once all the prison doors flew open, and everybody's chains came loose" (Acts 16:25-26). In one of their dark moments, they prayed and sang and they were delivered. I see our verse played out in this, for God allowed them to go to jail and be flogged, but he also had them be released. All these great things happened so that His name may be known and glorified on earth and through their testimony.

He puts people in impossible situations and circumstances so that everyone can see that only by the divine intervention of God in heaven is it made possible to get out of there. This is made evident throughout the story of Job, where even though nearly every single thing was taken from him, "he fell to the ground in worship...[and] The Lord blessed the latter part of Job's life more than the first" (1:20, 42:12). I would say His healing hands were manifested in his life! And they are manifested in your life too. Pain is a tool that the enemy uses, but God uses that same pain for something so much greater that the enemy never sees coming! It shall bring us into a more Christ-like life, relying on every movement of the Father, and "sharing in his sufferings" (Philippians 3:10). Do not shy away from the pain in your life, but look towards your loving Father and what He is trying to teach you that He cannot do any other way.

"For we brought nothing into the world, and we can take nothing out of it" - 1 Timothy 6:7

I am sure that many of you, like myself, like to gather more and more things in this life, whether that is more clothes, more money, more movies, just more. But why do we think this way? Why do we think that more is better? Is it because we have more options or choices? Or is it because of fear, that if one or more of them gets taken away, we will still have the others? Or is it just our culture once again rubbing off on us, telling us that we *need* certain things in order to be cool and seen as up to date?

I believe all of those are valid reasons why we like to collect more of things than we truly need, if at all. Only a verse before this Paul told Timothy that "godliness with contentment is great gain" (6:6). Not buying into the concept of materialism and the greed of acquiring so many useless objects that we "need" to survive, but being *content* with what we have, this is what we need if we want to be godly. He then says that "if we have food and clothing, we will be content with that" (6:8). The basics of life, food and clothing, and most others would include a shelter, is all that you really need. Everything else is but a gift (those others are gifts as well) from your loving and graceful Father in heaven, whom is worthy of praise and thanksgiving.

"A man's life does not consist in the abundance of his possessions" (Luke 12:15). Producing and obtaining wealth does not prolong your life at all because once you have passed on, your wealth is given to someone else who you do not know what they will do with it. A man's life consists of what he stores up in heaven and what he does for others, not himself. "Naked a man comes from his mother's womb, and as he comes, so he departs. He takes nothing from his labor that he can carry in his hand" (Ecclesiastes 5:15).

Jesus was a man who did not really have any possessions because He did not need them. He did not live to acquire wealth and riches, but to do the will of His Father, to love those around Him and to show them the most excellent way of living, simply for God who takes care of our needs. Why do you think Jesus, after telling the people not to worry about food and clothing and life, says "But seek first his kingdom and his righteousness, and all these things will be given to you" (Matthew 6:33)? He wants us to know that life is not about the things we get, but about God. He is what life is all about. Brothers, learn what it is to be content in this life by living simply and not clouding your mind and spirit and life with trivial things. Life a life of giving, not getting. Jesus, be the center of it all.

"But he was pierced for our transgressions, he was crushed for our iniquities; the punishment that brought us peace was upon him, and by his wounds we are healed" – Isaiah 55:5

Last night with my Bible study group, we watched the *Passion of the Christ*. It was some of my friend's first time seeing it, while I have seen it a few times before, but it does not mean the movie does not affect me; in fact, I believe it affects me more each time that I see it because of how my walk with the Lord has grown. I know His Word more each time and I get a glimpse of the pain and agony and the sheer weight that the sin of the world put upon our Savior, my sin on His shoulders.

It is but a glimpse, a faint shadow, of what Jesus actually had to bear and the suffering He went through so that you and I may live with Him now and eternally, so we may come to Him. After Jesus' death, "The curtain of the temple was torn in two from top to bottom" (Mark 15:38) by God, symbolizing that we were no longer separated from Him because Jesus made a way by his death. I am still and always will be baffled by how much Jesus loves each and every one of us, to willingly choose to go through all of that torment and affliction so that we "may have life, and have it to the full" (John 10:10). He did so out of obedience to the Father.

Jesus' wounds and inflictions, they have healed us and brought us salvation and life and without them, we would still be walking in death and destruction. "Death has been swallowed up in victory...But thanks be to God! He gave us the victory through our Lord Jesus Christ" (1 Corinthian 15:54,57). Only when I see Jesus face to face do I think that I will ever even begin to grasp how wonderful His love is for us and why He had to suffer and die, but we are told that He, "who for the joy set before him endured the cross, scorning its shame" (Hebrews 12:2). For joy Jesus did those tremendous things, for the joy of obeying His Father and to see His chosen people come back to Him and for Him to "[sit] down at the right hand of the throne of God" (Hebrews 12:2).

If we asked Jesus about these things, I believe He would tell us that His joy for us and His Father far outweighed any of the pain that He had to endure. He knew where He was going, and I hope we know where we are going too brothers. If you count yourself as one of His disciples and have the Holy Spirit within you, you are going to the New Jerusalem, the heavenly city where all things are made new! Oh the joy! May this encourage us and compel us to Christ-likeness, granting us joy against any suffering we might have to undergo, keeping our eyes on our Savior King Jesus.

"When I am afraid, I will trust in you. In God, whose word I praise, in God I trust; I will not be afraid. What can mortal man do to me?" – Psalm 56:3-4

Fear is a strong motivator that grips you. It paralyzes you, flooding you with anxiety and worry, keeping you in bondage to something that is most likely irrational. This is the fear of man, while fear of God is healthy because it is exercised in its proper context. "The fear of the Lord is the beginning of wisdom" (Proverbs 9:10). I heard once that fear is a gift of God, as we must have reverence and respect for the Creator of the universe, but like most gifts, sin perverts it.

We should have a good fear of God as commanded to us, but sin perverts that and instead of fearing God, we fear people and what they think of us or can do to us; we fear the future and whatever it may hold; we fear getting caught instead of living a righteous and God-honoring life of freedom. Fear and anxiety are debilitating to the body and mind. Why do we fear what people think of us? Why do we care so much what they think? Should we not be caring more what God thinks? Pastor Michael Youssef said that sin switched the questions that we ask ourselves: Instead of thinking "What would God think or say or view what I am about to do", we switch to "What would people think or say or view what I am about to do?"

"Fear of man will prove to be a snare, but whoever trusts in the Lord is kept safe" (Proverbs 29:25). Fear of man entraps you, while trusting God frees you. "In God I trust; I will not be afraid. What can mortal man do to me?" When you fear God, you will not fear man. Jesus said, "Do not be afraid of those who kill the body but cannot kill the soul. Rather, be afraid of the One who can destroy both soul and body in hell" (Matthew 10:28). Simply put, fear God because He is the one who is in control of your life and we need to constantly remember that and His promises which should shake away any and all fear of anything that is not of Him.

Instead of fearing, we should trust God. "When I am afraid, I will trust in you." When Jesus told us that "So if the Son sets you free, you will be free indeed" (John 8:36), He was talking about freedom from all sin, including fear of man. So do not live in fear any longer my brothers, but live in the freedom and trust of God who knows us inside and out, despite all of our failures and faults. He is the Pilot that flies the plane of our lives; do you trust your Pilot to fly the plane where He said it would go?

"If my people, who are called by my name, will humble themselves and pray and seek my face and turn from their wicked ways, then I will hear from heaven and will forgive their sin and heal their land" – 2 Chronicles 7:14

Do you consider yourself as belonging to the people of God, as those who are called Christ-followers? Then that verse is for you. Everything written there is then applied to you and are instructions for us to this day. My land of America needs the Lord's healing; it is a land that is filled with sickness and death, both within and outside the church. We cannot have this! As a nation that is supposed to have been founded on Christian principles, we have sunk so low and moved so far away from our roots, as the church has as well.

Firstly, we are told to humble ourselves. What does that mean? It means to confess to God that you are not a perfect person and that you have sinned and that you need Him all day every day. Ask for forgiveness and mean it, and throw pride by the wayside as well because pride and humility are polar opposites and cannot reside together. God does not want to hear how great you are, He wants to hear someone who knows his place before the Mighty God in the scheme of things.

Secondly, pray and seek His face. "Pray continually" (1 Thessalonians 5:17), and "seek his face always" (Psalm 105:4). This does not say to do it only when you feel like it or when it seems right, but all the time! It should be our way of life; living and moving and breathing while seeking the face of God and praying constantly to Him, always in communion as the Father and Son are.

Thirdly, you *must* turn from your wicked ways, from sin, from the areas in your life where you are not walking with God but are bringing shame to His name. "I take no pleasure in the death of the wicked, but rather that they turn from their ways and live. Turn! Turn from your evil ways! Why will you die, O house of Israel" (Ezekiel 33:11)? If we do all those things without turning from our sin, what good is it? It all should result in changed behavior, a changed life, a new life.

Finally brothers, after all these are accomplished, God will hear us and forgive our sin and heal our land. He is a God of His Word, who always keeps His promises and never changes. We can trust Him because He is faithful. Do you want revival to flood across your land and healing to arise? You know what you have to do as part of Christ's body: humble yourselves, pray and seek, turn from sin. Pray for arrival and revival in your land and in the lands of the world, that all may come to the knowledge of the truth and be healed.

"I urge, then, first of all, that requests, prayers, intercession and thanksgiving be made for everyone—for kings and all those in authority, that we may live peaceful and quiet lives in all godliness and holiness" - 1 Timothy 2:1-2

I know these may not be everyone's favorite verses to read and abide by, but they are important ones if we are to live godly lives. Those in government and who make decisions for our country have a huge responsibility on their shoulders and should know that the choices they make while in office affect everyone in the nation, not just themselves or a select few. This is becoming more evident to me in these recent months as I am noticing how our president is struggling to lead this country.

This is why it is extremely important to pray for those in authority as Paul told Timothy. They need divine guidance in how to lead millions of people because if they are only out there to get their own agenda across, countless people will suffer because of their selfishness and desire to make a name for themselves, even if it is in a negative context. Paul then tells us that praying for those governing us "is good, and pleases God our Savior, who wants all men to be saved and to come to a knowledge of the truth" (2:3-4). If we are appointing people in leadership with loose morals and no desire to work for the common good, then the country will soon follow suit, leading to its downfall.

This is seen all throughout the age of judges and kings in the Old Testament. When a selfish and childish person was leader of Israel, they were given over to idolatry and were oppressed, but when a selfless and God-centered person became the leader, the nation prospered and had peace. Pray that your leaders can come to the knowledge of the truth that is in Christ Jesus our Lord. "The authorities that exist have been established by God" (Romans 13:1), whether we think so because of their actions or not, but God has ordained them.

I urge you then to pray for your leaders; for state representatives, senators, governors, presidents, bosses, principals, parents, whoever is in authority over you, so "that we may live peaceful and quiet lives in all godliness and holiness." Pray for their families and their spiritual lives and that they may be blessed, as hard as that may be. By doing so, you will become more like Christ and less like the culture around you. Know in your heart and mind that God is the supreme authority that has given them authority and that His will *will* be done. It is hard to do brothers, but it is required of us and it leads to good.

"Remember how the Lord your God led you all the way in the desert these forty years, to humble you and to test you in order to know what was in your heart, whether or not you would keep his commands" – Deuteronomy 8:2

Remembering something is easy. We remember things all the time, like that 2+2=4 and that the earth revolves around the sun and that if we do not let the dog out, they will relieve themselves in the house. But along with remembering comes bringing it to mind and applying it; this is where it benefits the person even more because I could remember that drinking and driving is a dangerous mix, but if I do not actually live in such a way, then I could kill myself and possibly someone else too.

Why is it so hard for us to remember what we read in the Bible and what we are told by those who have gone before us? I believe one reason could be that we live in an information-loaded environment where we are taking in so much that we only tend to remember the latest stuff that gets uploaded into our brains and do not really filter how much goes in. So along with that comes the second reason that we are easily distracted by things, especially new things.

We forget because we do not think and try to remember and constantly meditate on it so it is ingrained within us. About these things in the Word we are told to "Impress them on your children. Talk about them when you sit at home and when you walk along the road, when you lie down and when you get up. Tie them as symbols on your hands and bind them on your foreheads. Write them on the doorframes of your houses and on your gates" (6:7-9). All throughout the Old Testament there are constant reminders of how God delivered the Israelites out of Egypt and led them through the desert to the land He has given them.

How can we remember? Get in the Word! Every single day, get in the Word of God and have those living and active words be ingrained into your very soul so that when situations arise, you can think of how God will think in a situation because "[you] have the mind of Christ" (1 Corinthians 2:16). The people of Israel who continually fell into idolatry did so because they forgot what God has done in their lives and how He rescued them from their enemies and gave them into their hands. What has God done and what is He doing in your life that you need to remember Him for? Remember that He never leaves you nor forsakes you and remember to keep the Lord's commands and to walk in His way of obedience. Do not take the grace of the Lord in vain friends; remember His work in your life and that He is not finished with you.

"Elijah was a man just like us" - James 5:17

It is St. Patrick's Day, a day where we celebrate the Irish heritage, but more importantly, the life of St. Patrick and his work. He was Scottish and at the age of 16 was taken captive to Ireland, where he was a shepherd for six years. There God spoke to him in a dream telling him to leave Ireland, so he did and when he got home to Britain, God gave him another revelation, this time to go back to Ireland as a missionary. He then became a priest and fifteen years later returned to the land that enslaved him, on a mission to minister to the Christians that were already there and to the pagans that roamed the land, using what they already knew in their religions and applied it to Christ.

"Elijah was a man just like us." St. Patrick was also a man just like us. Yes he had some things happen to him like being enslaved, but he worked a job (nonetheless the job of a shepherd, quite biblical) and many of us work jobs, both boring and exciting alike I am sure. Elijah was not special either; he was a prophet of God who spoke for him, but James tells us that "[He] was a man just like us." This was right after he said that "the prayer of a righteous man is powerful and effective. Elijah was a man just like us. He prayed earnestly that it would not rain, and it did not rain on the land for three and a half years. Again he prayed, and the heavens gave rain" (5:16-18).

Do you think that you will never accomplish great things for the Kingdom of God like the prophets and saints of old did? I do not think that they thought so either because they were all men and women just like us. And we, like them, can hear the Lord as they did and do the things that they did and more! But are we hearing the voice of the Lord? Listen carefully my brothers this day for His voice, He is speaking. He has called you somewhere to bring His Kingdom. Like St. Patrick, we need to hear His voice, trust it, and follow it wholeheartedly, knowing that God always moves with power and that He is sovereign. St. Patrick himself said that "If I be worthy, I live for my God to teach the heathen, even though they may despise me." We are worthy because God has called us worthy enough to die for. The heathen are all around us and should be taught and shown the great and never ending love of God for each and every one of them. Are you willing to hear God's voice and change the course of a nation as St. Patrick did, like Elijah did? Are you willing to walk with Jesus, the greatest world-changer of them all? Go forth in faith and obedience, knowing that God is working with you and through you for the betterment of the world around you.

"Set your heart to honor my name" – Malachi 2:2

This was said by the Lord to the priests through the prophet Malachi. In full it reads, "'If you do not listen, and if you do not set your heart to honor my name,' says the Lord Almighty, 'I will send a curse upon you, and I will curse your blessings. Yes, I have already cursed them, because you have not set your heart to honor me'" (2:2). You have to know a little about priests to get what God is saying completely.

One of the priests' functions were to announce blessings to the people of God as instructed, saying "The Lord bless you and keep you; the Lord make his face shine upon you and be gracious to you; the Lord turn his face toward you and give you peace" (Numbers 6:24-26). God is then saying that if the priesthood, whose job was to give glory to God through their lives, that if you do not set your hearts to honor my name, the blessings that you are supposed to give to the people will be cursed. That hurts. That was their job and from the text we know that they did not fulfill it, thus dishonoring the Lord their God.

As we move forward in the Bible, we find that Peter tells us that "You are a chosen people, a royal priesthood, a holy nation, a people belonging to God, that you may declare the praises of him who called you out of darkness into his wonderful light" (1 Peter 2:9). We are now called priests, so when God said "set your heart to honor my name", that now applies to us. Our hearts must be set to honor His name, as it is our duty and our delight to do so. We are to also then bless the people around us and represent God to a people who desperately need to see and hear Him.

First off, how do we set our hearts to honor God's name? Unlike the priests Malachi described in his first chapter, we are to bring our best to Him, not our second-best or our leftovers. "Bring the whole tithe into the storehouse" (3:10) and also tell the truth at all times, which gives glory to God (see Joshua 7:19, John 9:24). Secondly, we must be representing Christ fully to those in the darkness around us, not just to those on Sunday morning or Wednesday night (if that is even like Christ at all). People need to know of the love of Jesus and how else would they see and experience it if it is not shown to them? Finally, people need to be blessed through our lives and if they are not, we are not living as we ought. There is the common phrase, you are blessed to be a blessing, and it is true. What good can you offer the people in your lives? Much good! People need you. We are God's vessels to a broken world. Do not hinder or downplay the role you may play in someone else's life. Do not wait until tomorrow what you can do today.

"At this they covered their ears and, yelling at the top of their voices, they all rushed at him, dragged him out of the city and began to stone him" – Acts 7:57-58

What do you picture when you read this? I picture a mob of children after hearing something they did not like hearing and throwing a temper tantrum because they did not get their way. Imagine it: "They covered their ears and, yelling at the top of their voices." It is like a bunch of children! But these were not children however, they were adults and members of the Sanhedrin, the Jewish ruling council in the city on religious matters. The religious rulers that the people should be looking up to are the ones acting like children who did not get their way.

But why were they acting this way? Stephen, the first Christian martyr, after giving them a speech about the failures of Judaism and them as leaders, along with their rejection of Jesus, said "Look... I see heaven open and the Son of Man standing at the right hand of God" (7:56). That was the last thing they wanted to hear from that man, so that is why they did what they did and began stoning him. He had just spoken against everything that they have been representing and believing for centuries, even though what he said was all true.

That might have been the hardest thing for Stephen to do, to speak the truth amidst his circumstances, knowing that it was not going to be accepted or understood and that it would most likely lead to his death, but he said it nonetheless. He said it anyways because those listening were living in darkness and they did what followed because they are afraid of the light because the light exposes their wicked deeds and their true selves. They could not handle the light that Stephen was, just like he said earlier, "You always resist the Holy Spirit! Was there ever a prophet your fathers did not persecute? They even killed those who predicted the coming of the Righteous One. And now you have betrayed and murdered him" (7:51-52).

Do you consider yourself a follower of Christ? Then "You are the light of the world. A city on a hill cannot be hidden" (Matthew 5:14). A light, as Stephen was a light to a corrupt generation, so are we to a lost and wandering people who are living in shadow because "Everyone who does evil hates the light and will not come into the light for fear that his deeds will be exposed" (John 3:20). May the light that we are, reflecting the supreme "Light of the world" (John 8:12) that is Jesus, expose other's sinfulness, leading to their repentance and freedom.

"Father, forgive them, for they do not know what they are doing" – Luke 23:34

These were some of Jesus' last words as He hung on the cross. Not "Father, burn them, for they made me do this for their sake" or "Father, strike them down, for then they will know that they have crucified your Son", but they were "Father, forgive them, for they do not know what they are doing." Some of the most profound and weighty words ever spoken and nothing can capture God's heart for His people better than those words do.

At the climax of Jesus' suffering, after He had been troubled in Gethsemane, after He had been betrayed and beaten severely, and now after being hung on a cursed cross, He uttered these wonderful words of love and mercy to all who had put him up there, both past, present and future because of their sins, "Father, forgive them, for they do not know what they are doing." Stephen also spoke in that same spirit in yesterday's passage right before he died; "Lord, do not hold this sin against them" (Acts 7:60).

How can someone forgive another person after they had done something absolutely terrible to them like the Jews did to Jesus? With love, that is how. Jesus' love is the only thing that allows us to be able to forgive someone else for the wrong they have committed against us, no matter how awful it may have been. And that love is given us through the indwelling of the Holy Spirit. I think it is quite necessary to keep Jesus' words to these people in mind when we begin to have an unforgiving and hardened heart towards someone because if Jesus can forgive them of the horrific wrongs they (also us because He is on the tree because of our sins) committed, then how much more can we forgive one another for the incredible lesser wrongs done to us? They are petty in comparison my friends.

We hold so many unnecessary and insignificant grudges, like something a family member did to us twenty years ago or a friend that forgot your birthday. Just let it go. It is not worth it. Just think if Jesus held grudges against us? Oh the pain and misery and death! But thanks be to God that He forgave us for disowning His name and lying to our parents and stealing from our neighbor and being selfish in our relationship! Follow Jesus' example and forgive the people in your life. They do not always know what they are doing just like you do not always know what you are doing. Do not hold a grudge; forgive and begin to live.

March 21

"Come, follow me" - Mark 1:17

If a random stranger came up to you and said "Come, follow me", would you? Most likely not, which means there must be something about the person of Jesus that just shone around him to have these fishermen drop all that they had known and lived for and follow him. Maybe it was the desire to be wanted or chosen. Or even the desire for change. I do not know, but I do know that "At once they left their nets and followed him" (1:18).

When Jesus said those three words to them, they had a choice to make: to either keep doing what they were doing and go about their lives or to leave it all and follow Him. They did not know what following Jesus would entail, but they had enough faith to try it out and go for it, but those words should not be taken lightly. Those words are a call to discipleship and to a life that requires total commitment, not a half-hearted spirit, but one that is ready to learn from and imitate the life of the one who has called him.

In Luke's gospel, Jesus asked another person to follow him and he replied "Lord, first let me go and bury my father" (Luke 9:59) and yet another said "I will follow you, Lord; but first let me go back and say good-by to my family" (Luke 9:61). Jesus called these people, but they only wanted to follow Him on their terms and in their time frame, not His. That is not what following Jesus is about; it is about answering His call to you now. You are to follow Him; He is not to follow you. And when you do follow Him, there is no going back. You are either all in or all out. "No one who puts his hand to the plow and looks back is fit for service in the kingdom of God" (Luke 9:62).

Following Jesus requires that you imitate Him in all things, not just the areas that are comfortable or convenient for you, but all of them. And when He asks you to follow Him and you have decided to follow Him, then actually do it! Do not only do it in word, but in deed also! It is a transformational life for those who do follow Jesus, a life that is way better than the life they are leaving behind and that is how we have to view it. "Come, follow me" Jesus says. The invitation is given to you; the invitation to a lifetime of worth and adventure and mystery. Just like the first disciples that chose to follow Him, we do not know where this road of discipleship will lead us, but we know we are following the only One who is worth following.

"What do you have that you did not receive? And if you did receive it, why do you boast as though you did not?" – 1 Corinthians 4:7

I remember in high school when I played football and baseball and being really fast and having a good arm. We trained and trained to improve and hone our skills and to make all of us better and more efficient athletes, but being fast and throwing the ball well were not two skills that I learned or acquired because of training. I was born with those traits, whether I exercised them or not, I had them. They were gifts given me from God because I received them by mercy, not by merit.

Paul was speaking these words to the Corinthian church after talking to them about the divisions they were creating amongst themselves because they were following certain apostles teachings and not realizing that all of them were speaking Christ crucified; that it was God who has bestowed them with the words, not themselves. That is why he told them "'Do not go beyond what is written.' Then you will not take pride in one man over against another" (4:6).

It is easy to get attached to a spiritual leader who has made an impact in your life. Like right now, I am attached to my pastor at my church because he speaks the truth in love and is not afraid to offend those who are a part of the church. But in the past year or so I have learned that I should not show favoritism towards him or get mad when he is gone and another pastor fills in for a week or two; that I should treat all pastors, no matter what church I go to, as God's representatives, knowing that they have nothing to offer that God has not given them. Our loyalty should be to Christ, not to leaders. This should not cause division among the body of Christ, otherwise we would still be infants and worldly (see 3:1-4).

We need to keep in mind what John the Baptist said, "A man can receive only what is given him from heaven" (John 3:27). Everything that I have, I have received from God because He has been gracious enough to give them to me. And the same with you brothers. "Every good and perfect gift is from above" (James 1:17). Everything is given from our loving Father in heaven, especially His son Jesus Christ, the best gift of all. "What do you have that you did not receive?" Nothing, we have nothing that we did not receive. Even the things that we think we earned and achieved and merited on our own, they were still given to us and so we received them. Remember these things, and thank your Father that He has blessed you in abundance and may these things humble us and remove any sense of pride.

"They will be called oaks of righteousness, a planting of the Lord for the display of his splendor" – Isaiah 61:3

I have always liked trees, ever since I was little. I liked climbing them and looking at them and watching them sway during storms and turn orange and red in the fall and green in the spring, giving color to the world after the brown and barrenness of winter. Both conifers and deciduous trees, I like them all: conifers in how they stay green all throughout the year and deciduous in their massive size and distinct leaves.

So when we are named "oaks of righteousness", I just love it. Trees are a great analogy of what the Christian life is about. First off, they have roots that dig deep for nutrients and water, allowing it to sustain life, as Christ is our Sustainer and Provider of life. Plus, trees are not self-sustaining, in that they need groundwater and rain water in order to survive and thrive.

Secondly, if they are rooted well in the ground with their nutrients and water, they can grow. It is only when their roots are strong that they can truly grow, and so it is with us. If we are not rooted and established in Christ, we will never grow because "apart from me you can do nothing" (John 15:5). We need to be strong in Christ, relying on Him to keep us in order to grow.

Thirdly, as trees face the winds and storms that nature throws at them, the tops tend to sway back and forth until it stops, then it returns back to its normal position. As in our walk with Christ, when we face the storms of this life, the tip of us may be moved by it, but if we are standing firmly in Christ and remaining rooted in Him and what He stands for, then our being will withstand the storms and not be moved, but will return back to where we were in alignment with Him.

There is still much more about trees and how they relate to our walk with God, like how they go through seasons of change as we do and how they sort of have a "resurrection" after winter with the trees having an appearance of being dead, but are very much alive. If you think about it, trees are mentioned from the beginning to the end in the Word. There is so much more yet to be said, but for now I leave you with this, "Blessed is the man... [who] is like a tree planted by streams of water, which yields its fruit in season and whose leaf does not wither" (Psalm 1:3). May we remain planted by the river of life who is Christ and display His splendor for all to see.

"Whoever acknowledges me before men, I will also acknowledge before my Father in heaven. But whoever disowns me before men, I will disown him before my Father in heaven" – Matthew 10:32-33

Last night I saw *God's Not Dead* with a few of my friends in theaters. It is about a freshman in college in a philosophy class whose teacher's first thing was to have everyone write and sign that God is dead. This kid was the only one who did not and had three chances to speak to the class and try to prove why God is not dead. There were side stories that eventually all came together at the end from people of all walks of life coming to the same conclusion that God is not dead but is surely alive!

Yes it is a Christian movie where the acting is not as great as in big films and may be corny in some spots but who cares, it got its point across, which was to tell the story that God is still very much alive and active in our lives here and now. This is the verse that prompted the kid to stand up for what he believed in with his teacher, even though his parents and girlfriend said otherwise. He discovered (thanks to a pastor in the film) that this may be the peers in his class' only chance to hear about God and Christ and to make the decision for themselves to believe or not. He also learned both parts of this verse, that if he denied Christ in front of these people, He would deny him before the Father, but if he acknowledged Him, so would He be before the Father, giving him the clear choice of what he had to do, which was defend his faith and stand up for his Lord and Savior.

A good motivation for us to remember when situations like these come up in our lives is what Jesus said to the church in Sardis, "He who overcomes...I will never blot out his name from the book of life, but will acknowledge him before my Father and his angels" (Revelation 3:5). "He who overcomes" indicates that we have to overcome those conditions that we face in order for Jesus to recognize and approve of us before His Father.

If you have not seen this movie, I would recommend it to give you a kick in the pants to stand up for your faith wherever you are in life and to proclaim that God is good all the time, even amidst the muck and mire of the trenches. Do not be afraid of saying the wrong thing or that you do not know the answer, for "at that time you will be given what to say, for it will not be you speaking, but the Spirit of your Father speaking through you" (10:19-20). That is no excuse to not prepare yourself, but should be a waking call to know the Word that God has given you and to meditate on it and ingrain it in your heart. Are you standing up for your faith, or are you following whatever the popular vote is in order to avoid confrontation?

"Do not follow the crowd in doing wrong" – Exodus 23:2

Lately I have been thinking of the "mob mentality" that I see of the people around me. Many of my friends have a strong individual personality, but when they get in a large group together, that tends to dissipate into whatever the group wants to do. When one starts, the other chip in, whether that is picking on something someone said and blowing it up continuously, or something as neutral as deciding to go to the store to get candy before the movie starts. This is a two way street; one that leads to good and the other that leads to evil.

I hope the good of this can clearly be seen, for instance if the notion comes up to do an outreach event on campus to reach the students there and they all follow along and do it. That is great and a good example of the mob mentality in the advancement of God's kingdom and getting people out there to do things they would not do otherwise. But on the other end, I have seen a few of my friends lose their principles and values I know they usually stand up for because the group consensus said otherwise and they want to please the group and be a part of them.

This is when mob mentality is not right and that is why Moses told the Israelites to "not follow the crowd in doing wrong." He knows the temptation of following the crowd and the wrong that can become of it, as we see in the case of the golden calf (see Exodus 32). When this way of thinking becomes your main mode of life, then you persistently do things that you would not do otherwise.

I do not care if your Christian friends are doing it. If you have that gut feeling inside of you, your conscience (aka the Holy Spirit), telling you not to do something, then do not do it! Simple as that. Go against the grain and stand up for the things of God that He has convicted you of. If the people are doing something godly and good, great! Follow along and worship and praise the Lord together with them, if the Lord wills you. The Old and New Testaments are filled with crowds, both good and bad, but Jesus, the Son of God, followed His Father in heaven and did only what He saw Him do and say (see John 5:19). So I say to you, beware of the mob mentality in your life. Know who you are in Christ and that you do not need to compromise your convictions in Him for the sake of pleasing your friends and doing what is cool. "And whatever you do, whether in word or deed, do it all in the name [character, nature] of the Lord Jesus, giving thanks to God the Father through him" (Colossians 3:17).

"There he built an altar, and he called the place El Bethel, because it was there that
God revealed himself to him when he was fleeing from his brother" - Genesis 35:7

This was Jacob who named this place El Bethel. It was years earlier, twenty-six years I believe, when Jacob had a dream from God after running away from his brother. This dream made him exclaim "'Surely the Lord was in this place...How awesome is this place! This is none other than the house of God; this is the gate of heaven'...He called that place Bethel" (28:16-18). It was God who called him back to Bethel to "settle there, and build an altar there to God" (35:1), even though he also built an altar there twenty-six years ago (28:18). Bethel's name was changed to El Bethel; from the "house of God" to the "God of the house of God".

Why was there this change in name? Maybe it was because Jacob had matured and gained new revelations of God during that time. He was gone twenty-six years. But what is also interesting to note is that it was here where God changed Jacob's name to Israel; from "he deceives" to "he struggles with God" and also renewed Abraham's covenant with him. A.W. Tozer writes in *Of God and Men* that "Many years later, after he had suffered and sinned and repented and discovered the worthlessness of all earthly things, had been conquered and blessed by God at Peniel and had seen the face of God in an hour of spiritual agony, he renamed the place...The change is significant. Jacob had shifted his emphasis from the house to the One whom he met there." It was God who was now at the center of Jacob's eye, not the place where he met God, but God Himself. This is huge. This is a slap in the face to many of us professing American Christians today who are so stuck up with worshiping the King of kings in a certain place (in church or youth events) when we need to realize that it is not about the place, but about God who should be the sole focus of everything we think and say and do.

God must be first, as He is in El Bethel and not in Bethel, in the meaning of the names. Is our focus and attention on the things of God or God Himself? Tozer says "Where is the primary interest? Is it Beth-el or El-Beth-el? Is it my church or my Lord? Is it my ministry or my God? My creed or my Christ?" May things never come before God in our lives and our walk with Him. We are missing so much when we center our lives around the religious things and forget to align them with the One for whom we have those things. I have been guilty of this lately. Father, forgive me of my wrongful attitude towards you and my walk with you. Bring me on track with your ways. Be my center where you have every right to belong. Thank you for hearing me. You are good all the time. Amen.

"For this world in its present form is passing away" – 1 Corinthians 7:31

That is kind of hard to believe at times, is it not? That everything that we see on a day to day basis, everything (well a lot of the things) that we work and strive for and put effort and time into, is all passing away and will be no more. If we had this mindset all the time, I guarantee we would not be doing a majority of the things that we do now.

"For this world in its present form is passing away." From this we can know that since this world will soon be no more, a better and new world will arise that will last for eternity. "Then I saw a new heaven and a new earth, for the first heaven and the first earth had passed away" (Revelation 21:1). There is so much evil and death in this current world that it is destroying itself, making the way for God's new and perfect world that is to come where "He will wipe every tear from their eyes. There will be no more death or mourning or crying or pain, for the old order of things has passed away" (Revelation 21:4).

With these things in mind, hopefully we can see the triviality of lots of the things that we do. Trivial in the sense that not everything that we struggle to gain and keep will last, but also that this should awaken us to see that this world is passing away and that we are passing away. "You have made my days a mere handbreadth; the span of my years is as nothing before you. Each man's life is but a breath" (Psalm 39:5). How we relate and treat everything really does matter. "So then, each of us will give an account of himself to God" (Romans 14:12) for the things we do in this life.

What are you striving for? What are you putting your hope in? Know and apply that if you are striving for and hoping in anything other than Jesus Christ, it will be gone and will not be stored as treasures in heaven. "His work will be shown for what it is, because the Day will bring it to light. It will be revealed with fire, and the fire will test the quality of each man's work. If what he has built survives, he will receive his reward. If it is burned up, he will suffer loss" (3:13-15). This is how your work will be treated when the time of Christ's coming arrives. Are you building up and accumulating things in this life or are you building up and accumulating things for the life to come? I pray that our hearts and our living may be in the right place with Christ and our Father, seeing the meaninglessness of so many things while seeing the necessity of many other things.

"Be very careful, then, how you live—not as unwise but as wise, making the most of every opportunity, because the days are evil" – Ephesians 5:15-16

This verse goes along with yesterday in that it deals with how we spend our time and energy in our lives. The teaching should have given us some wisdom on how we should live our lives and what we spend our days doing. An old friend once told me that "The way we live our days is the way we live our lives." It is simple yet so true. The things we spend our days doing, what we are doing right now, is reflective of how we live our lives in the grand scheme of things.

In relation to yesterday, we need to remember that our time is fleeting and that we may not have tomorrow to love on our neighbor, that is why the Psalmist writes "Teach us to number our days aright, that we may gain a heart of wisdom" (Psalm 90:12). And in relation to today, to apply that wisdom so we may be "making the most of every opportunity." And do not forget that the days are evil because that is why we must not be missing countless chances to show the world around us some good and light and not the evil and darkness they are used to. The foolish person is the one that misses these opportunities to live for God amidst an evil atmosphere, but we are called to be wise and not miss them.

We are to keep our eyes open for these situations that God puts in our path everyday; situations where we can spread His goodness and love and live for Him and not ourselves or the world. I believe that many of us try and plan our days to a T, rarely allowing anything unexpected to find its way in, and this gives us a sense of control over our lives and what happens to us. But what a lot of us are inclined to do is be so rigid in how we let our days happen that if something comes into it that we do not want, we shy away from it without trying to see how it can be beneficial.

For instance, last Friday I had the day off work and I was looking forward to having a peaceful morning and afternoon of reading and writing and just me and God, but my friend wanted to meet for lunch in town and I did not want to go because I had this awesome and quiet day of rest planned for me. I went anyways because I wanted to know him better since I did not know him that well, and it was great just eating and talking about life, relationships, work, the whole shebang. I am really glad I went, even though it changed the rest of my "planned" day. Brothers, we must be flexible in our lives to allow God to give us opportunities for growth and His kingdom to advance. Keep your eyes open, there are God-given opportunities everyday to make His name known. Make the most of it.

"Then Peter got down out of the boat, walked on the water and came toward Jesus. But when he saw the wind, he was afraid and, beginning to sink, cried out, 'Lord, save me!'" - Matthew 14:29-30

This has always been one of my favorite stories ever since I was a kid. I do not know if it was because I loved storms and water and wind, or because Peter actually walked on the water, but I loved it. I still love it because it is epic and I have actually been to the Sea of Galilee and I would be absolutely terrified being caught in the middle of that lake, surrounded by mountains, and have an intense squall come up, so I understand why Peter looked at the wind.

Just imagine it though: Jesus walking on the water towards you in the middle of the night during a storm and He tells you to come and join Him. Merely thinking about myself in Peter's situation is daunting because my whole view of things would be turned upside down. People cannot physically walk on water for starters, but then again, Jesus is no ordinary person but the Son of God. Also, during a storm, a boat seems like a much safer place than being on the water, so why would I want to willingly put myself in more harm?

But Peter did it anyways. He said "Lord, if it's you...tell me to come to you on the water" (14:28) and Jesus' reply was simply "Come" (14:29). It is an act of obedience on Peter's part because Jesus told him to come. Simple obedience that requires a singular focus on the one who called him to do it, that is all this is. What Peter realized when he first stepped out of the boat and onto the water was that where Jesus was is the safest place for him, even though logic and reason would tell him the boat is the safest, but Jesus was not in the boat, but on the water.

Peter did walk on water my friends, but he began sinking because "he saw the wind" and took his eyes off Jesus. He got distracted by the storm around him although he started off right, looking at his Lord who called him to join Him on the water. What is distracting you from doing the impossible in your life? In what areas are you taking your eyes off of Jesus and looking at the situations and anxieties that surround you? Jesus is the one who allows you to do the impossible and He is the one that allows you to do anything really, so why take your eyes off of him? You do not know better than Jesus, I can guarantee you that. Lord I pray that we keep our focus solely on you and the commands you give us and throw away any doubts and anxieties. Help us to get out of the boat by looking at you and trusting you wholeheartedly. You are greater than anything we can know or imagine. Thank you Father. We love you.

"When Jesus saw her, he called her forward and said to her, 'Woman, you are set free from your infirmity.' Then he put his hands on her, and immediately she straightened up and praised God" – Luke 13:12-13

I must first apologize for not writing about the healings of Jesus beforehand in this book, it must have slipped my mind for some reason. Anyways, this was one of many of Jesus' healings throughout His ministry and this one in particular was performed on the Sabbath in the synagogue, which was a no-no to the religious rulers of the day. This was so because of their take on the fourth commandment, "Remember the Sabbath day by keeping it holy. Six days you shall labor and do all your work, but the seventh day is a Sabbath to the Lord your God. On it you shall not do any work" (Exodus 20:8-10).

They saw healing someone on the Sabbath as doing work (13:14), even though Jesus only laid His hands on her and told her that she is set free from her brokenness. She "had been crippled by a spirit for eighteen years. She was bent over and could not straighten up at all" (13:11). But what the rulers failed to understand is that they themselves disobeyed the same commandment by untying their donkey so it can get a drink (13:15). They were so set in their interpretations and traditions of the Old Testament that they made it nearly impossible to do anything at all on the Sabbath, although that is not what is meant in the spirit of the law.

Jesus however saw the woman who had been in bondage and, being who Jesus was, could not have it because He came to set people free from evil and bondage and bring them into the glorious freedom and life that He offers. He did not care how the rulers would view it; He saw someone in need and came to her in that need and offered what He could, even if it was against their laws. Isaiah wrote about Jesus in this way, "He has sent me to bind the brokenhearted, to proclaim freedom for the captives and release from darkness for the prisoners" (Isaiah 61:1).

He healed her because He loved her and wanted her to be free to stand up straight. The woman's response could not have been any better, "[she] praised God." What has been keeping you bound up for many years, not allowing you to be as you know you ought to be? Jesus loves you so stinking much and He desires for you to be free from what binds you, so what is it? A past sin that you cannot let go? A generational woe? Anxiety about things that have yet to happen? An actual physical infirmity? Whatever it may be, give it to Jesus, allow Him to put His hands on you and heal you from it. He wants you to stand up straight and praise His holy name.

"Because of the Lord's great love we are not consumed, for his compassions never fail. They are new every morning; great is your faithfulness" – Lamentations 3:22-23

This day was the warmest day since last fall, being sixty-eight and sunny with the wind blowing, keeping you cool. It was also my longest day of work in awhile, something I did not expect this Monday. I was planning on getting let out early like I have been lately because there has been nothing to do at the shop, go to Bible study and then bring my car in to get fixed. Instead, I worked over ten hours and my body aches from head to toe, making it miserable waking up from my nap just twenty minutes ago.

It was not the day I have planned, but it was still a beautifully warm and amazing day that I did get to work and make money. He could have given me a job where I would be in a windowless room and I would not even know that the sun was shining or the birds chirping, but He blessed me this day with being able to be outside and enjoy it. It is only "because of the Lord's great love" that I was able to enjoy this day, even though I injured myself at work and it hurts to just sit here and type. "His compassions never fail" me, for He allows me to enjoy His wonderful world and to see the good in it, despite the scenarios.

The Lord's compassion is filled with blessings, blessings that "are new every morning." Today's was the warm sun and wind after a harsh and cold winter; tomorrow may be a spring rain that always brings me peace, who knows. Or it may be a good conversation with a coworker about Jesus. I do not know what tomorrow may bring, but I know that God's compassion will be there and it will be new as He opens up our eyes and hearts to see the wondrous things He puts before us every day that will turn us to praise Him.

The sunrise this morning was so bright and beautiful, full of color and life. "As surely as the sun rises, he will appear" (Hosea 6:3). That is only part of the faithfulness of God. As the sun is faithful to rise each and every morning, so is the Lord faithful in every waking moment of our lives, whether you think so or not, He is always faithful to us. Have you had a bad day lately? Why is that? Have you been focusing on the negative things that happened? It is so easy to do so brothers, but we must remember the Lord's great love for us and His faithfulness towards us, otherwise we would get sucked in and only see the bad that has happened and totally miss out on the good and the praise of His name! Do so now, praise Him for the day He has blessed you with and the day He will bless you with tomorrow, for He is faithful and it shall be so. Thank you Father.

"You come against me with sword and spear and javelin, but I come against you in the name of the Lord Almighty, the God of the armies of Israel, whom you have defiled. This day the Lord will hand you over to me" – 1 Samuel 17:45-46

This is the account of David and Goliath, one of the most well-known in the entire Bible. Here we have David, the youngest of his father, a shepherd of sheep, coming against the champion of the Philistines, Goliath. He stood over nine feet tall and was fully decked out in armor and weaponry, while David only had a sling with five stones from the river. And as the story goes, David killed Goliath with only one stone and thus triumphed over the Philistines.

Why do we love this story? I think it is because David, who has never seen war, is viewed as the underdog against the battle-worn veteran, Goliath. The skirmish between the man that nobody knows versus the man that many know. It is the way of March Madness which is coming to a close, and it is the way of God as revealed through His Word. By the looks of it, the battle may not be in David's hands, but when you remember that he is coming "in the name of the Lord Almighty, the God of the armies of Israel", he no longer seems like the underdog, but Goliath does.

We tend to forget that key part in all the stories and even in our own, that God is with us. Yes, it does not say that explicitly, but it is greatly implied when David was talking about his fights with the lion and the bear and how God had delivered him from them and defeated them (17:34-37). When we know that God is with us, nothing is impossible and the odds are in our favor, even if it may not seem like it. But even though it appeared as if Goliath had the upper hand, David went forth boldly and with much courage.

Brothers, we need to go forth with that same boldness and courage because we know that God is with us no matter where we are. Whether we are in a den of lions (Daniel 6), facing tremendous odds (Judges 7), or speaking in front of thousands (Acts 2), know that the God who was with these people and more, who was with Jesus Christ, who gave us the Holy Spirit to dwell within us, is with you also as you face your foes and battle through your day in a world of evil and darkness. "Be on your guard; stand firm in the faith; be men of courage; be strong. Do everything in love" (1 Corinthians 16:13-14). Go forth in Christ's love and do something courageous.

"About midnight Paul and Silas were praying and singing hymns to God" - Acts 16:25

This single verse reminds me once again of *The Lord of the Rings: Return of the King,* when Sam believes that Frodo has been killed by the great spider Shelob and that their quest to destroy the ring had failed. He follows the orcs as they carried Frodo's body up the tower and then lost him. It was here that Tolkien writes, "And then softly, to his own surprise, there at the vain end of his long journey and his grief, moved by what thought in his heart he could not tell, Sam began to sing."

In what may be seen as Sam's darkest moment on his journey thus far, he begins to sing. We are not told why he did so, but we can take a guess that it is because he needed the words of that song then and that it is something to fall back on. In the same way I believe, after a long and arduous day of casting out a demon and being beaten and thrown in jail, Paul and Silas began to sing and pray because they found in those words, hope. Hope that the work they have done for Jesus Christ was not in vain and that no matter what happens next, they have obeyed their calling.

In *Return of the King,* after Sam sang, he found out then where Frodo was being held, and in Paul and Silas' case, after they sang and prayed, "there was such a violent earthquake that the foundations of the prison were shaken. At once all the prison doors flew open, and everybody's chains came loose" (16:26). Great things happen when you sing to God, especially in your darkest hours. In their situation it was dark because it was midnight and dark because of all they had just gone through, yet right in the midst of the darkness, they sang and prayed to their God in heaven, knowing that there is no darkness in Him, only light, and no matter the circumstances they are in, He is still worthy of praise!

What are your darkest moments? What do you do in them? Do you wallow away from everyone and sink into depression, or do you go about publicly and complain about the awfulness you are going through, not caring if people show you sympathy or not, but you just want them to know your life sucks? Whatever your situation may be, I urge you brothers to pray and sing glory to God amidst them all. He is beyond your circumstances and He is there with you in them. Nothing is too great for Him to handle and He wants you to come to Him and remember the truth He has told you, that "In this world you will have trouble. But take heart! I have overcome the world" (John 16:33). Do not forget in the darkness what you know to be true in the light.

"Build houses and settle down; plant gardens and eat what they produce. Marry and have sons and daughters; find wives for your sons and give your daughters in marriage, so that they too may have sons and daughters" - Jeremiah 29:5-6

This sounds like a pretty cool mandate to me, to start a family and settle down, building my own house and gardening and I am sure having cattle and such too. It kind of does make me wish I was born in an earlier time or just had a time machine so I can go back to those simpler days where life was not so distracting, but where I got up and worked my land and built things for my family and potentially others.

This is what God told the Israelites who were exiled to Babylon by Nebuchadnezzar. He told them to settle down and have a life. How could God tell them that? They just got taken away from their homeland and carried off into captivity and God wants them to accept it and settle down? The nerve! He then goes on to tell them, "seek the peace and prosperity of the city to which I have carried you into exile. Pray to the Lord for it, because if it prospers, you too will prosper" (29:7). Ok, settling down is one thing, but to pray for the city and for its peace and prosperity? Come on God! Why would I want to do that?

I am sure they probably thought somewhere along those lines, I mean, at least I would have. Maybe they wanted to band together all the Israelites and increase and then take over the Babylonians, or just all escape somehow. But God had other plans. He encouraged them to get settled in because "I have carried you into exile." It was His purpose to do so. He desires for His people to adjust to what happens to them and to keep on moving with their lives.

God continues with "For I know the plans I have for you" (29:11). Whether it looks like it or not, God knows what He is doing in your life and in the world. He has you where you are for a reason, even if you do not know what it is or how that could be so. Like right now in my life it is hard to see that, but I know it is true and that He wants me to trust Him with it all. Do you know why you are where you are right now? If so, great! Thank God for it and do what you have to do diligently. If not, continue to walk with Him and trust Him with your life because "we live by faith, not by sight" (2 Corinthians 5:7). Life does not stop during hard times, it keeps going. May we also not stop during hard times, but to pray for the people and places around us, for their peace and prosperity.

"Go and lie down, and if he calls you, say, 'Speak, Lord, for your servant is listening.' So Samuel went and lay down in his place. The Lord came and stood there, calling as at the other times" – 1 Samuel 3:9-10

Hearing the voice of the Lord is tough sometimes. Maybe it is tough because we make it tough by putting distractions in our way. Such distractions could include: work, friends, money, movies, busyness, ourselves, and many more. But why do we put distractions in our way? Do we really not want to hear God speak to us? Or do we think that we know how to act in a situation, so we do not need to hear His voice?

We need to hear God's voice to us. Some of you may say that God is not speaking to you, but I assure brothers that He indeed is! "For God does speak—now one way, now another--though man may not perceive it" (Job 33:14). He is speaking to us, but we merely need to settle down, throw aside distractions and anxieties that may get in the way of us hearing His voice, and actually attempt to listen to the God of our lives. He eagerly desires to speak to you and to have you hear Him because He loves you dearly and wants communion with you and communion is a dialogue, not a monologue.

To hopefully make this clearer, I will use an illustration I heard last night on the subject. God is our Father and we are His children right? And so when children speak to their fathers, the fathers do not just sit there and listen to everything their kids say without saying something back to them that may be beneficial to them, right? In the same way, as God is our Father, He does not stand idly by, keeping silent in matters that are important, but He speaks to us constantly because He loves talking with us as I pray that we love talking to Him.

As in this story of Samuel, God calls to us "as at the other times", meaning that He is always desiring to speak to us, but are we willing to quiet ourselves, get away from the world, humble ourselves and listen to the Lord of the universe speak to us? We are told that "My sheep listen to my voice" (John 10:27), and you are His sheep if He is your Lord and Savior. So do we as His sheep listen to His voice? I am sure He has something important to say to you because it is God and every word that comes out of His mouth is truth and full of love. Right now, He is telling me to say, "I love you dearly, do not forget that. I have shown you the way that is good and have told you what you must do, to obey Me and trust Me with your life. I need all of you, not just the parts that are convenient. Step out in My faith My son, and you will learn that I am your Guide and Father. I love you." The Lord is good my friends. He loves you so much. Try and hear from your Father.

April 5

"Rejoice with those who rejoice" – Romans 12:15

Last night there were many of us out having a goodbye party for one of our dear friends who is heading to Africa for two years in the Peace Corps. We had dinner, went and saw the new Captain America movie, and then to a piano bar for a couple hours for drinks and music. This was probably one of the best nights of fellowship with both new and old friends that I have had in quite some time. The conversations were great and simply enjoying time with each other, celebrating the times we have had with our friend and the times that have yet to be had. It was wonderful and I am thankful for last night.

He is a great friend who I have gotten to know these past four years in college and got to work with last summer. I know he will do great things in Africa, teaching there and sharing God's light and love to those he encounters. There was so much love in that place, love I know that stems from God's love for us and our love for Him that allows us to love others in the same way. There was no judgment or condemnation amongst us, only rejoicing and laughter and merriment. He is happy to leave and go do what God is calling Him to, which allows us to rejoice with him as Paul encourages us to.

That is a part of what love is, for love "Rejoice[s] with those who rejoice; mourn[s] with those who mourn." Love goes to where the people are, as Jesus is the greatest example of that by coming down from His throne in heaven to be with us. He loves us so much that He was willing to give up Himself so that we may have life and in abundance. Not only that, but so we can love each other because "Dear friends, since God so loved us, we also ought to love one another. No one has ever seen God; but if we love one another, God lives in us and his love is made complete in us" (1 John 4:11-12).

What we did last night was love one another with the Lord's love, verifying that God lives in us and that we should "Rejoice with those who rejoice." Celebrating life with friends is what Jesus showed us as He constantly ate and drank with His disciples and created food and drink for others to enjoy. There is always a reason to rejoice. What do you need to rejoice in that you know you should? "Rejoice that your names are written in heaven" (Luke 10:20).

To my friend and brother in Christ, Jason: Never forget that God is always with you. I know you will do amazing things in Tanzania for their people and God's kingdom. Never stop loving them as you never stop loving your Father in heaven. You will say, "I have fought the good fight, I have finished the race, I have kept the faith." I love you man.

"Have mercy on me, O God, according to your unfailing love; according to your great compassion blot out my transgressions" - Psalm 51:1

Recently I watched the movie *Prisoners*, where two young girls get abducted on Thanksgiving and it shows how one of the fathers takes into his own hands trying to find them by whatever means necessary, even if that means torturing a man relentlessly almost to death. The thing is too, that this was a man of faith and he struggled with what he was doing all through the film, but he kept on coming back to the point that he wanted to find his daughter.

It is movies like this that I love and hate. I hate them because of the pure evil that is so prevalent throughout it and I love them because they get me to think. They have me think of what would I do if my daughter was kidnapped and I think I had the perpetrator in my mitts but he was not telling me anything. Would I do what he did, or would I have the police do their jobs and I show the man mercy? That is really what it all boils down to in the end; would we condemn and judge the man, or would we show him mercy?

We should not have to think too hard about this, but we do anyways because our human nature tends to take over and we leave our spirituality on the back burner like the father did. "Father, forgive them, for they do not know what they are doing" (Luke 23:34) uttered Jesus on the cross after what His accusers had done to Him. How can He say such a thing to such evil that He just endured? Because even though they did wrong to Him by hanging Him on that tree, He still loved them and said, "O Jerusalem, Jerusalem...how often I have longed to gather your children together, as a hen gathers her chicks under her wings, but you were not willing" (Matthew 23:37). He has no need to condemn them because He is love and it is not He who condemns anyways, the people condemn themselves.

We are called to "Be imitators of God... and live a life of love" (Ephesians 5:1-2) right? What better way to do that than follow the example that Jesus set before us by not condemning us but showing us mercy as we cry out to Him as David did? So right now I can firmly say that if I was in the situation as in that movie, I would do my best to show the person who took my kid mercy as I have been shown mercy, for I know without a doubt that that is what Jesus would want me to do and I want to please Him because He is my King. Do you want to please your King, no matter how hard it may be? I sure do, though it may go against every emotion I am feeling in the heat of the moment, but God is stronger than our emotions. Lord, may we show mercy to those to who do not deserve it, as you have shown us mercy when we did not deserve it.

"For our struggle is not against flesh and blood, but against the rulers, against the authorities, against the powers of this dark world and against the spiritual forces of evil in the heavenly realms" - Ephesians 6:12

We are in a world at war. This war however, is not of man against man, or of man against the government or another country, but it is against "the ruler of the kingdom of the air" (2:2), the devil. So often we think that the enemy that we are fighting really is the devil and we even call them that at times because of their actions and our hatred for them, but I assure you that they are not. The devil and his forces are not flesh and blood, but they are spirit and that is why we are called to engage in spiritual warfare because it is happening.

Brothers, we cannot be ignorant of the fact that the devil actually is real and there is a battle going on that is unseen in the spiritual realm as we speak that obviously influences all the evil and destruction that is so prevalent in our world today. Paul tells us directly before this, "Finally, be strong in the Lord and in his mighty power. Put on the full armor of God so that you can take your stand against the devil's schemes" (6:10-11). Now why would we need to be strong in the Lord and put on His armor if there was no devil and war to be fought? There indeed is and we need to be ready to stand and fight, but it is not in our strength and power, but in the Lord.

This armor that we are to arm ourselves with (which will be discussed further over the next few days) is the Lord's and we cannot forget that. It is not a physical armor like that of a knight, but it is a spiritual armor to protect and fight against a spiritual foe. The devil has a hold of this world because people are ignorant of him and of sin because he is "the spirit who is now at work in those who are disobedient" (2:2). The Kingdom of light must take a stand against the kingdom of darkness and destroy it.

Know that the ultimate war was already won by Jesus' death on the cross and resurrection from the grave! "But thanks be to God! He gives us the victory through our Lord Jesus Christ" (1 Corinthians 15:57). As you can tell, Jesus' battle was not against the men of this world, but against the devil and his forces, whose main weapon is sin which leads to death. I will leave you with this: Know your enemy and his tactics that he uses to destroy the church and you individually and know your God and King even more, who gives you the ability to stand and who gives you His armor.

"Therefore put on the full armor of God, so that when the day of evil comes, you may be able to stand your ground, and after you have done everything, to stand" –Ephesians 6:13

I have always loved the concept of armor. I love it in epic medieval or fantasy movies and in video games, where I try and get stronger and stronger armor so I can take more blows from the enemy and tire him out. Armor protects your body, whether you have lighter, leather armor or heavier, steel armor, it protects you and each piece is there for a reason. Without armor, one is more prone to attack because it is just their clothes versus the weapon and the weapon always wins.

We are called to "put on the full armor of God", not half the armor or only the pieces we want, but all of it. And if we are called to put it on, it implies that we were without it before; we were susceptible to assault. God's armor is not the same as the world's armor because it protects our spiritual body and health and this armor is something that we should never take off, even though we do at times.

We should always have it on because we do not know when "the day of evil" will come upon us, whether tomorrow or next week or now. We know that our "enemy the devil prowls around like a roaring lion looking for someone to devour" (1 Peter 5:8). He is constantly waiting to pounce on his pray when they least expect it, so we must keep God's wonderful armor on so "[we] may be able to stand [our] ground." God willingly gives us His armor so that we do not falter; another awesome example of His great love for us. David once said that "I was young and now I am old, yet I have never seen the righteous forsaken" (Psalm 37:25), showing how God does not want us to fall but to rise, so He gives us His armor.

"You may be able to stand your ground, and after you have done everything, to stand." God's armor allows us to take on the enemy and to stand because he cannot take us down. I once had a dream where I was in a standoff with the devil and he tried all he could. He pressed his finger against my chest, but it did nothing, so I walked forward with his finger still there and I was moving him back and finally he was flung through closed doors. My brothers, that is what God desires of His children wearing His armor; the enemy cannot touch us. May we put on your whole armor O Lord and walk as you do with it on, being able to stand the ground you have given us. Your Son showed us the ultimate way to defeat the enemy, through love. Help us to walk in your selfless, giving love and your victory. Thank you Father. We love you.

"Stand firm then, with the belt of truth buckled around your waist" – Ephesians 6:14

The first piece of God's armor listed is the belt of truth. To start off, I did not even know that a belt was considered armor, but it is. It is a part of the soldier's uniform as it held the scabbard for the sword, so without it they would have no weapon. It also holds up the loose garments covering the legs, keeps the breastplate in place and tight, making itself once again invaluable and essential.

Now let us talk about the belt as holding the scabbard in view of God's armor: the belt of truth holds up "the sword of the Spirit, which is the word of God" (6:17). Without truth, the word of God would be void because "In the beginning was the Word, and the Word was with God, and the Word was God" (John 1:1) and Jesus said "I am...the truth" (John 14:6). Without this belt of truth wrapped around us, in which Jesus is truth, the whole purpose of the soldier crumbles because His only offensive weapon, Jesus, is faulty. But thanks be to God that He is not and that He is the truth that is wrapped around our waist that holds up the Scriptures of thousands of years!

We need to make sure first and foremost that we have the truth of God holding us up so that we do not have lies and falsehoods anywhere near us. We know that when the devil speaks, "he speaks his native language, for he is a liar and the father of lies" (John 8:44). What better way to stand against the devil's attacks than by being girded with the belt of truth which holds up the sword of the Spirit? Truth should be at the foundation of everything we do and without this proper foundation, everything else after it with fall because it is not set on Christ.

The truth that we wear must be absolute in Christ, not relative and changing like how the world perceives it, but firm as Paul tells us. We as soldiers of Christ (2 Timothy 2:3) are to never depart from the truth that Christ has revealed to us. To put on truth, we must know what truth is and what better way to know truth than to dig in the Word of God! Even more so, to deepen your relationship with Christ who is truth and the Word. Know who it is who is giving you their armor and for whom you are standing. We are standing for God and for the truth that He is and represents to a world that does not accept absolute truth. Stand firm in Him. Are you girded in God's truth? How is it affecting your day to day life?

"With the breastplate of righteousness in place" - Ephesians 6:14

The breastplate is usually the first piece of armor that I think about when I hear armor, probably because it is visible and right in front of you. I most likely would have a breastplate of leather because it is lighter and more flexible, so I can move quicker and not grow weary as easily. But once again, this is spiritual armor that we are to put on, God's armor, and I bet that it is the lightest and most flexible armor there is, along with being the strongest and the best.

God himself is described as putting on this breastplate; "He put on righteousness as his breastplate" (Isaiah 59:17), just in case we did not believe that it was a part of His armor. The belt, as we learned yesterday, helps keep the breastplate in place, and so truth helps keep righteousness in place. Without truth, how would we know what is righteous and what is unrighteous?

The breastplate is probably your most important piece of armor covering the largest portion of your body (besides the legs). It protects your vital organs like the heart, lungs and liver. A strike to the chest without this piece of armor would most likely be deadly but with the armor, you will be fine the majority of the time. We need to put on righteousness as our breastplate so that our hearts will be protected from the enemy. Righteousness is following God's way in uprightness and holiness, which is done by Jesus' death and resurrection. We cannot attain righteousness ourselves, but it is given us. "God made him who had no sin to be sin for us, so that in him we might become the righteousness of God" (2 Corinthians 5:21).

In essence, "clothe yourselves with the Lord Jesus Christ" (Romans 13:14) who made you righteous. When we are on the path of righteousness, we are on the path of life and sanctification and not the path of destruction and desolation. And when you are on God's path, you will desire and do the things that are godly and of love and you will not have a desire to sin and do evil. This may be why the breastplate of righteousness is at our center, our core, because that is where holiness and obedience to God shall be, in the center of it all. God is pleased with you right now because Christ became your righteousness so it is not because of good works you do, but all because of Him. Put on the breastplate, protect yourself from the devil's attacks and walk in the Light of Life set before you.

"And with your feet fitted with the readiness that comes from the gospel of peace" –
Ephesians 6:15

When I think of armor, I usually do not think about protecting the feet, but the chest, the back and the head. When you stub your toe, it hurts even though you barely hit it and that is because the feet are fragile and need protecting. That is why people wear shoes, to protect their feet from rocks and dirt and the elements and anything else that may harm their feet. Though I usually prefer to be barefoot or at least wear flip flops, there are times when I have to wear shoes to protect myself.

My first reading of this verse and I have no idea what it is trying to say. I know it is a part of God's armor to protect ourselves from the devil's attacks so we can stand firm through the onslaught, but why is readiness something that we must put on? When I initially thought of readiness, I thought of quickness and being impatient to get things done, but as I think about it more, I began to realize that I was way off, but that it in fact refers to our willingness and eagerness.

This "gospel of peace" refers to the gospel itself, that is, the good news and revelation of Jesus Christ who is the "Prince of Peace" (Isaiah 9:6). This beautiful gospel brings peace to our lives because Jesus has brought peace between us and God, making a way for us to enter the Holy Place and have communion with God. The prophet Isaiah also said that "How beautiful on the mountains are the feet of those who bring good news, who proclaim peace, who bring good tidings, who proclaim salvation" (Isaiah 52:7).

To make proper use of this piece of armor, we must have an eagerness to advance God's kingdom, His gospel of peace to the world. The joy that His message brings to us should impart in us a readiness that moves us to people who need to hear that goodness and love that His peace alone brings. Are you ready and willing to share the message of the cross and the resurrection? I know I am scared sometimes to do so, even though I have no reason to be because I know the truth about Jesus, but...I have no excuse. God does not want my excuses, He wants my willingness to obey and love Him enough to yearn to tell others about Him so that they may have peace in life and spend eternity with Him. Are you willing?

"In addition to all this, take up the shield of faith, with which you can extinguish all the flaming arrows of the evil one" - Ephesians 6:16

The Roman war machine was probably the most organized and most efficient in all of the world's history, continuously slaughtering their enemy with their unity and their advanced weaponry and armor. They were quite known for their large shields that could deflect literally everything that came at them and they made such a formation that nothing could penetrate if all their shields were up. They sometimes would also be covered in leather which would then be soaked in water so it could extinguish flame-tipped arrows.

Paul calls this piece of armor the shield of faith. The shield was used to protect attacks so they would not even hit the body, but the shield instead. It could protect the head, the heart, the back, anywhere the shield was. The shield made the soldier feel secure. So it is with our faith. Without faith, how can we feel safe about where we are going? Without faith, the other lifestyles of God's armor become more vulnerable. Without faith, it is almost impossible to believe in truth and righteousness and to be willing to share the good news of Jesus Christ. "Without faith it is impossible to please God" (Hebrews 11:6). Faith guards these other features of our walk.

The flaming arrows of the devil could be anything that is meant to spread destruction in your life. A.B. Simpson said that this assault from the enemy could be to drive the believer into self-accusation and condemnation. "This is Satan's objective point in all his attacks upon you, to destroy your trust. If he can get you to lose your simple confidence in God, he knows that he will soon have you at his feet." Put simply, faith is required to deflect the devil's accusations against us, trying to bring us down.

But God, my brothers, He longs for you to trust Him when He tells you "I am your Father, and you are My child whom I dearly love." This trust in your Father will quench anything the devil hurls at you because you know who you are and you know that the Lord is there for you, to strengthen you and help you and uphold you (Isaiah 41:10). We must be trusting of Him in every single area because He is Sovereign and in control and He is good. The antithesis of faith is doubt and doubt has no place in the life of a child of God, for "You are all sons of God through faith in Christ Jesus" (Galatians 3:26). Are you taking up the shield of faith and walking by it in confidence and victory? "For everyone born of God overcomes the world. This is the victory that has overcome the world, even our faith" (1 John 5:4).

April 13

"Take the helmet of salvation" - Ephesians 6:17

Now we come to the helmet which protects the head, also quite prone to attack and fatal when struck. The second part to the verse from the other day also speaks of God with "the helmet of salvation on his head" (Isaiah 59:17). The head is undeniably worth protecting and that is why we wear helmets when riding bicycles, playing football and baseball, and in the military. We want to protect our head and what is inside it.

Why is salvation a helmet according to Paul and Isaiah? The helmet was sometimes seen as a symbol of victory, so with wearing this helmet of salvation, we know in our heads that we have the victory through Christ that we will spend eternity with Him. In another letter Paul tells us to put on "the hope of salvation as a helmet" (1 Thessalonians 5:8). You have already been saved "if you confess with your mouth, 'Jesus is Lord,' and believe in your heart that God raised him from the dead" (Romans 10:9). So why would Paul tell already believers to put on the hope of salvation?

Salvation is not just a one and done thing, but it is a continual process that requires a whole life of devotion. "Therefore, my dear friends, as you have always obeyed—not only in my presence, but now much more in my absence—continue to work out your salvation with fear and trembling" (Philippians 2:12). It is the progression of maturation and sanctification, leading to Christ-likeness, as everything in a Christian's life should be. So when Paul tells us to put on the helmet of salvation, he is calling us to take up holiness while moving forward in the hope that we believe we will see our Lord face to face.

We are saved from death because of the salvation we received from Jesus. It is key to remember that it was Christ's suffering, death, and resurrection that saved us, not our own merit and power. This is precisely why we put on this helmet, to never forget what Christ did for our sake and for the sake of humanity. So with the helmet of salvation on our head, we are being "transformed by the renewing of your mind" (Romans 12:2), not to the ways of the world, but to God's way, the only way. May this helmet give us hope of Christ's return and of His final victory being manifested and may it protect our thoughts from the devil's attacks and schemes to lead us astray from God.

"And the sword of the Spirit, which is the word of God" - Ephesians 6:17

We come to the last piece of God's armor, even though it is more of a weapon than armor, but still. The sword of the Spirit is perhaps my favorite item in the passage because it is the only piece that is offensive while all the rest are defensive, suggesting that we are to use this weapon to combat the devil's attacks and not just defend them, but refute them. In battle, if you are constantly on the defensive, you never gain any ground. Think of Joshua and the Israelites: do you think they would have taken possession of the Promised Land if they did not go in there and try to take it? Not a chance.

I honestly do not know why this is listed last though. You would think that it being the Word of God that you would want that listed first, but maybe it is there last to remind us the conflict is spiritual as the next verse supports, "And pray in the Spirit on all occasions with all kinds of prayers and requests" (6:18). What I try to do is point a lot of the things we talk about to Jesus because we are to follow His example in becoming more like Him, so let us take a look at Him shall we.

While Jesus was tempted by the devil in the wilderness, three times He was tempted and to each temptation Jesus responded using Scripture (Matthew 4:4,7,10). If Jesus used the Word (as He is the Word) to combat the devil's schemes, how much more shall we do the same? This is why Scripture memorization is essential because how often do you have your Bible with you when faced with something or have to make a decision? The Psalmist wrote "I have hidden your word in my heart that I might not sin against you" (Psalm 119:11). I am sure Jesus had this in mind when the devil attacked Him.

I may have said this phrase more than any other so far in this book but repetition is great for ingraining things into your being. Know the Word. We must know the Word and be people of the Word. Then when you are tempted, you can use God's Word against the devil. Using the Bible, you are capable of invading the enemy's territory and putting a new flag in its fortress. Paul tells us to "Let the word of Christ dwell in your richly" (Colossians 3:16). The Word of Christ is Jesus Himself! We need to acknowledge His presence within us so that more of the flesh shall die and more of His life be manifested in our lives every day. Know the Word of God. I urge you to put on all of God's armor "so that when the day of evil comes, you may be able to stand your ground, and after you have done everything, to stand" (6:13).

"I am the Lord your God; consecrate yourselves and be holy, because I am holy" – Leviticus 11:44

The book of Leviticus is probably most peoples' least favorite book of the Bible because of all the rules and regulations, most of which are irrelevant to us today. I personally have not read through it all (I think) but I know I must because it is still God's Word to us, His people. The word holy appears more times in this book than any other in the Bible, so I would say that this is a worthy book to read because holiness is a topic that is not talked about as much as it should be.

So what does it mean to be holy? To be holy means to be set apart for consecrated/sacred use like the priests were. And that further implies that this consecration leads to purity in all areas of life. As God is holy and note that He says "I am holy" and does not say "I am holy when I do…" but "I am holy", meaning that all of Israel in every single aspect of its life is to be set apart for God's use and be fully dedicated to Him because "I have set you apart from the nations to be my own" (20:26).

We are God's representatives, "Christ's ambassadors" (2 Corinthians 5:20) to the world around us. So as a country's ambassador is supposed to be representative of their country's character, so we are to be representative of Christ's character at all times, not just on Sunday mornings or during Bible study or whenever you do things unto the Lord. All of our being at all times should be giving the world a glimpse of what Christ is like because "You are the light of the world. A city on a hill cannot be hidden" (Matthew 5:14). And we know that God is pure and perfect and He calls us also to "Be perfect, therefore, as your heavenly Father is perfect" (Matthew 5:48).

To be holy is to be set apart and pure. This is only possible by sanctification through the Holy Spirit within us. Sanctification of our lives, the purging of the old self as the new self emerges through us, to where "I no longer live, but Christ lives in me" (Galatians 2:20). That is the beauty of the sanctified and holy life that God calls us to, to become more like Christ in every situation that comes our way. Someone once said that every decision that you make either makes you more Christ-like or more like the world. I could not agree more. Are the decisions that you are making today leading you to a holier life for God's purposes or are they leading you to a disillusioned life for the world's purpose?

"I have set you an example that you should do as I have done for you" – John 13:15

In the movie *The Matrix*, after Neo received the message from the Oracle and where he, Morpheus, and Trinity almost died in a helicopter crash, Morpheus utters these words to Neo, "There is a difference between knowing the path and walking the path." It was in these moments that they began to realize even more so that Neo was the one who would end the war between the humans and the machines.

Jesus set the standard for us to follow. Granted, He set the bar extremely high, but He gave us His Spirit to help us of course. He said our verse following the washing of His disciples' feet, giving us the example that as He, our Lord and Master, humbled Himself and served us, so we must humble ourselves and serve others. But in a greater context, everything that He has done up to that point has been an illustration of how we must live our lives.

That phrase that Morpheus says is true for us Christ-followers as well. Many of us *know* the path because we have been versed in the Bible and its ways ever since we were in Sunday school, but to *live* the path is a completely different story. We know the stories of the patriarchs and prophets in the Old Testament and of Jesus and the early church in the New Testament. We, like the rich young ruler, know what commandments to obey and what must be done to inherit eternal life, but to go and do what Jesus asks us to do and follow Him, that is something else entirely (Matthew 19:16-24). Jesus set the example for the path of life; He asks us to trust Him and walk that course with Him.

"But set an example for the believers in speech, in life, in love, in faith and in purity" (1 Timothy 4:12). Jesus set that for us: His words were full of love and compassion (Mark 6:34), His life was doing what His Father told Him to do (14:31), He loved us so much that He willingly chose to suffer and die so that we may be with Him (3:16), He believed that nothing was impossible with God (Mark 10:27,11:22-24), and He was without sin in this life (Hebrews 4:15). My brothers, there is a difference between knowing the path and walking the path. May we begin to walk the path set before us and so "live by faith, not by sight (2 Corinthians 5:7). Notice that it says "live by faith" and not "Sit and wait by faith", implying that our faith must be active and moving, keeping in step with our Savior and King. Monkey see, monkey do. We see, now let us go and do. Father, help us to walk in faith and in your ways that you set before us, the way of life and love and peace. You have called us out into the deep things of you, not the shallows. Increase our faith. We love you.

"Freely you have received, freely give" – Matthew 10:8

Two brothers worked together on the family farm. One was married and had a large family. The other was single. At the day's end, the brothers shared everything equally, produce and profit.

Then one day the single brother said to himself, "It's not right that we should share equally the produce and the profit. I'm alone and my needs are simple." So each night he took a sack of grain from his bin and crept across the field between their houses, dumping it into his brother's bin.

Meanwhile, the married brother said to himself, "It's not right that we should share the produce and the profit equally. After all, I'm married and I have my wife and my children to look after me in years to come. My brother has no one, and no one to take care of his future." So each night, he took a sack of grain and dumped it into his single brother's bin.

Both men were puzzled for years because their supply of grain never dwindled. Then one dark night the two brothers bumped into each other.

Slowly it dawned on them what was happening. They dropped their sacks and embraced one another. – A Second Helping of Chicken Soup for the Soul

I thought this was a wonderful illustration of this verse played out. Jesus said our verse when He sent out His twelve disciples just after telling them to "Heal the sick, raise the dead, cleanse those who have leprosy, drive our demons" (10:8). He wants His disciples to realize that they have been shown and given wondrous things by God and that they need to extend that same mercy to those they come in contact with.

It is the same reason why John wrote that "If anyone has material possessions and sees his brother in need but has no pity on him, how can the love of God be in him?" (1 John 3:17). We as Americans have been blessed with so much, yet we are the most selfish and greedy nation that has ever existed. We are obsessed with ourselves and accumulating things that we believe we need in order to be cool and accepted in society. So yes, most of the wealth that we have is used on ourselves, but that should not be the case.

If your money is hindering you from loving God wholeheartedly, then I believe you need to rethink your lifestyle choices. Yes, you may have earned your money from your job by doing your work, "But remember the Lord your God, for it is he who gives you the ability to produce wealth" (Deuteronomy 8:18). He is the one who gave you that job that allows you to make money. Remember to thank Him for your job, whether you like it or not. I do even though I do not like my job and want a new one because it permits me to help my friends who are in need. God has entrusted you with so much, how are you using it? What do you do with your money and possessions? You say you do not have any, so then what do you do with what you do have? Trust God with what He has given you; He knows what He is doing. "One man gives freely, yet gains even more; another withholds unduly, but comes to poverty" (Proverbs 11:24).

"It was now about the sixth hour, and darkness came over the whole land until the ninth hour, for the sun stopped shining. And the curtain of the temple was torn in two. Jesus called out with a loud voice, 'Father, into your hands I commit my spirit.' When he said this, he breathed his last" – Luke 23:44-46

Today is Good Friday. The day where Jesus suffered unjustly and was put to death on the cross. How can this day, the day where our Savior who was supposed to save us, died, be called good? Should it not be a day of mourning and sorrow because Jesus, our Friend and King, was crucified and buried? Should it not be a time of reflection on the sins we have committed that hung Him on that tree on Calvary?

But it is a good Friday my friends. It is good because Jesus *did* take up our sins on that cross and died so that our countless wrongs may be atoned for! What can be better than that? It is good because it allows Him to resurrect from the dead and defeat death once and for all so that we may have eternal life with Him! It is good because it shows the extent of Jesus' great love for us that He was willing to be "pierced for our transgressions, he was crushed for our iniquities; the punishment that brought us peace was upon him, and by his wounds we are healed" (Isaiah 53:5). The punishment that was meant for us because of our sins was upon Him on that cross. He willingly took them because "for the joy set before him [He] endured the cross, scorning its shame" (Hebrews 12:2).

Talk about a beautiful love; a love that tore the curtain of the temple from top to bottom, signifying that it was God who tore it and not man. This curtain divided the Holy Place from the Most Holy Place, symbolizing for us that now we can come directly to God through Christ. "Since we have confidence to enter the Most Holy Place by the blood of Jesus, by a new and living way opened for us through the curtain, that is, his body" (Hebrews 10:19-20).

Today is a good day, a great day to praise and thank our Savior for bearing our burdens on the cross so we do not have to. It is a day to thank Him for making a way for us to enter the Most Holy Place so we can commune with Himself. It is especially good because we know what happens in a couple of days that makes His death even more beautiful. He is such a good God and loves us with a great intensity that "Many waters cannot quench [this] love; rivers cannot wash it away" (Song of Songs 8:7). How did Jesus make this a Good Friday for you personally?

"It is for freedom that Christ has set us free. Stand firm, then, and do not let yourselves be burdened again by a yoke of slavery" – Galatians 5:1

This morning I listened to a radio show of a friend of mine on human trafficking. The broadcast was mainly put on to show awareness of the subject and how vast it is and how it is even happening in our communities, but how not much is really done about it. And even the small bits we can do we definitely cannot do alone; we need God to help fight the injustice that is done all throughout the world.

They ended it with this verse, signifying that we were all in bondage at one point or still are and that there is a God who came to release us from that bondage. And that is wonderful news. "It is for freedom that Christ has set us free." Have you been freed from your sins by the blood of the Lamb? If not, I am praying that the eyes of your heart may be enlightened to the truth that Christ died to give you freedom to not obey the devil and his whims. If you have been freed, are you living in Christ's freedom?

Well, are you obeying God in what He commands of you? Or are you obeying yourself and following your desires above God's? If you are doing the latter, then you are not walking in the freedom Christ came to give you, the freedom to live unselfishly and to obey God and not the devil. "You are slaves to the one whom you obey—whether you are slaves to sin, which leads to death, or to obedience, which leads to righteousness" (Romans 6:16). So if you have been set free, you no longer *have* to sin, but you *choose* to. When you were enslaved, you had to obey the devil because he was your master, but now that you are free, you have the freedom to choose obedience to God over the ways of the enemy.

If you are free, what are some issues that tend to enslave you from time to time and take your eyes off of Jesus? For me, pride is something I get caught up in without much thought, so I have to consciously think about whether the thing I say or do will be prideful and draw people towards myself or humiliating and draw people towards Christ. I am being sanctified day by day towards the latter and all because of the beautiful and undeserving grace of God. As I have learned, falling back into sin is awful and yes, sin may bring happiness and comfort in the temporary, but in the long run it eats like a canker. "For what is seen is temporary, but what is unseen is eternal" (2 Corinthians 4:18). Learn to run and dance in the glorious freedom that Christ offers, the freedom to love and live for Him without guilt and shame, but to praise and thank Him for His presence and love.

"The angel said to the women, 'Do not be afraid, for I know that you are looking for Jesus, who was crucified. He is not here; he has risen, just as he said'" – Matthew 28:5-6

Today is Easter Sunday, or Resurrection Day as I like to refer to it, the day where Jesus rose from the dead after being in the grave for three Jewish days (A Jewish day refers to any part of a day as a whole day). This is where we celebrate Jesus having risen, "freeing him from the agony of death, because it was impossible for death to keep its hold on him" (Acts 2:24). That is fantastic news my friends, that death could not keep our Savior in the grave "for love is as strong as death" (Song of Songs 8:6).

That is why this day is one of the most important days in the Christian calendar because without Resurrection Day, our faith would be for nothing because we need the resurrection to happen for our faith to mean anything. "And if Christ has not been raised, our preaching is useless and so is your faith...And if Christ has not been raised, your faith is futile; you are still in your sins...But Christ has indeed been raised from the dead, the firstfruits of those who have fallen asleep" (1 Corinthians 15:14,17,20). What does it mean to be the firstfruit? The firstfruit was when the first bundle of the harvest was given to the Lord as an indication that all of the harvest would belong to the Lord and be dedicated to Him. In other words, it was a representation of the whole harvest, so just as Jesus Christ was raised from the dead and made alive, so shall we be.

Of course this shall be cause for such wondrous celebration! He is risen indeed! Our Lord is no longer dead, but He is fully alive and we also will have that life! The women who went to the tomb and found it empty were in shock when He was not there, and they "hurried away from the tomb, afraid yet filled with joy, and ran to tell his disciples" (28:8). They were "filled with joy" so they ran to tell Jesus' disciples the good news.

Are we filled with joy when we remember this magnificent news? Do we run and tell others of this because of the overflowing of our joy that our God is not dead but that He is very much alive? This should be the day where we are even more intent on inviting non-believers to church because I know the Holy Spirit will stir in them a thirst for the risen King of kings when they see the body of Christ rejoice in such a manner as we should. Oh, what a glorious day! "Rejoice in the Lord always. I will say it again: Rejoice!" (Philippians 4:4). And rejoice we must. Our hope is in Him. May you rediscover the joy of your salvation.

"For what I received I passed on to you as of first importance: that Christ died for our sins according to the Scriptures, that he was buried, that he was raised on the third day according to the Scriptures" – 1 Corinthians 15:3-4

There are many who do not believe that Jesus rose from the dead. There are some that say He did not completely die on the cross, but they thought He was dead and then His disciples nursed Him back to health and made the whole resurrection story up. Still others believe that there is not legitimacy to it because the first recorded documents of the resurrection did not come out until nearly half a century after it occurred. But we are among those who do believe that Jesus indeed rose from the dead.

Why do we believe it actually happened? First off, I believe it because the Word of God says it happened and that is my highest authority because "All Scripture is God-breathed" (2 Timothy 3:16), meaning that it is all inspired by God Himself. Paul continues above, "and that he appeared to Peter, and then to the Twelve...to more than five hundred of the brothers at the same time...then he appeared to James, then to all the apostles, and last of all he appeared to me" (15:5-8). There are over five hundred witnesses who saw Jesus after He rose from the dead. Also, if the disciples were to fabricate a story of His resurrection, they would not have had women be the first witnesses because in those days, women were not seen as a reliable witness because of their emotional instability and weakness.

But you said that some believe that Jesus was not entirely dead? Oh my friends, but He was! Pilate in the last chapter of Mark asked his centurion to go check to see if Jesus had died before Joseph of Arimathea takes down His body from the cross to put in the tomb he prepared for Him, and he confirmed He was indeed dead (Mark 16:43-45). He confirmed that Jesus was dead when the soldier "pierced Jesus' side with a spear, bringing a sudden flow of blood and water" (John 19:34). This happens after someone is in hypovolemic shock, which helps fluids gather around the heart and lungs and thus explains why that flowed out after he pierced Him, confirming His death because of massive blood loss.

That is some historical and medical evidence for you, and if you want to learn more history on it, I would suggest reading the writings of Flavius Josephus and Tacitus. The Bible is true brothers, the whole of it, and especially Jesus' death and resurrection which makes Christianity possible. Our Savior is all-powerful, conquering death, and bringing us into communion with Him through unconventional means of love. Jesus is alive!

"If anyone would come after me, he must deny himself and take up his cross daily and follow me" – Luke 9:23

Here in America, we love making ourselves known and heard. We love speaking our mind and opinions on both important and trivial matters. We take great pride in the things we have accomplished in school or sports or the workplace. We enjoy great pleasures because we can and it feels good. We fancy following our desires and being led by our emotions; "follow your heart" they say and it will not steer you wrong.

This is the message that is ingrained in so many of us most of the years of our lives in America. We do not even have to think about it, but this is what a lot of us habitually do because we grew up in it. However, this is not what Jesus has called us to. He calls us to deny ourselves, or in other words, to forget ourselves. When following Jesus, we must cast aside our own selfish desires that we naturally have day in and day out for the sake of Christ and His desires for us. In forgetting ourselves, we have a greater ability to see what God wants of us and how we can better serve others because our eyes are no longer on us, but on Christ where they should always be.

We are then called to take up our cross on a daily basis. Not once, or every other week, but daily. What does this mean? It means that dying to ourselves and the world should become our lifestyle. It means we do not always have to speak our mind because it would not be loving towards another. It means not to constantly follow our heart because "the heart is deceitful above all things" (Jeremiah 17:9). It means letting others get the credit or win an argument if it would bring unnecessary conflict otherwise. In this, by bearing others' burdens as Christ bore ours, we can "always carry around in our body the death of Jesus, so that the life of Jesus may also be revealed in our body" (2 Corinthians 4:10).

We are to follow Jesus. We must take up our cross daily and deny ourselves if we are to follow him. Anything less is not discipleship, but something we conjured up ourselves to make it easier for us. This is what Jesus asks of His disciples. The cost of discipleship is hefty, but it is so worth it. Are you willing to follow Him? In what ways do you need to deny yourself? And what is your cross that you need to bear? My cross that I constantly bear is my pride in past accomplishments and in my knowledge. I have to die to it continually and it is hard because it is a cross and that brings denial and suffering. But for the joy set before me, I will continue on as my King did, through His strength.

"I would rather be a doorkeeper in the house of my God than to dwell in the tents of the wicked" – Psalm 84:10

High positions of authority and rank are places we love, being able to go and tell others what to do and have power over them. We tend to throw away the mundane activities of our lives because they are too boring and we need excitement and adrenaline. We like to be noticed when we have done something right or even anything at all because we like receiving recognition for our actions when good. But we forget that what makes civilizations go round from the beginning of time are people who hardly ever get noticed or the recognition they deserve for the incredibly hard and dirty work they do.

The doorkeeper was one such person who probably never got appreciated or seen by those entering the doors at which he stood watch. In this case, the doorkeeper would stand outside the house of God, the temple, and keep watch at his post, not being able to stray from it. He could not even enter the temple while on duty, but could only look inside it. That is what the Psalmist, one of the sons of Korah, who were gatekeepers, would rather do than to dwell with the wicked.

They would rather be able to gaze into the glorious house of God without being allowed to enter than to roam about freely in the tents of the wicked, doing as they wish. They never cared about getting noticed; they only cared about doing their duty and serving their King. They would rather work this humble and ordinary position than to be entertained as a guest where wickedness makes its residence. The sight of just looking into the temple during worship was enough for them. They did not need acknowledgement or thanks or freedom, they had all they needed right there. Just before this in the same verse it says that "Better is one day in your courts than a thousand elsewhere" (84:10).

Can we say the same? Can we be satisfied with the ordinary and mundane if it involves Christ? But then again, being with God should never be mundane but joyful, as I am sure that it was for the Korahites. Can we not tolerate dwelling with evil? But we do all the time with what we permit our eyes to see and ears to hear and tongues to say and feet to do. May we find fulfillment in witnessing God where He is and where He has put us. May we not meander about the tents of the wicked, but stay with our God and King who alone can gratify us and brings true joy.

"Naked I came from my mother's womb, and naked I will depart. The Lord gave and the Lord has taken away; may the name of the Lord be praised" – Job 1:21

These are the words of Job after the Lord allowed the devil to do whatever he wanted to him other than laying a finger on him. So the devil then killed his oxen, donkeys, sheep, camels, all his servants with those animals, and his children (1:14-19). And that is saying a lot because Job "had seven sons and three daughters, and he owned seven thousand sheep, three thousand camels, five hundred yoke of oxen and five hundred donkeys, and had a large number of servants" (1:2-3).

But the devil came and took it entirely away with the Lord's permission, and Job sees that it was God indeed who did take it away. He recognizes God's sovereignty in everything despite it looking bleak with all the calamity surrounding him. God is and always will be in control and we must realize that as Job did. We must comprehend that God has the right to do what He wishes with what He created, which is everything and we cannot tell Him how He should live His life. He is life (John 11:25) and "Shall what is formed say to him who formed it, 'He did not make me'? Can the pot say of the potter, 'He knows nothing'?" (Isaiah 29:16).

Following this scene, the Lord allows the devil again to do harm to Job. This time "he afflicted Job with painful sores from the soles of his feet to the top of his head" (2:7). Yet, Job does not curse God for all this as his wife encourages him to, but he replies to her, "You are talking like a foolish woman. Shall we accept good from God and not trouble?" (2:10). Is that not the truth brothers! God has the right to do as He pleases with His creation and everything He does serves a purpose. In Job's case, it was to test him to see if he would maintain his integrity and devotion to God regardless of his wealth and health.

Other times the Lord may discipline us in such matters that would culminate in our spiritual gain to make us more like Him. Like we learned from the other day, suffering and denial of self is a part of the Christian life. But if we can teach ourselves to be able to say "The Lord gave and the Lord has taken away; may the name of the Lord be praised", then we will go far my friends. We will walk in such a way that will shock those around us and make them question why we live that way. They will want to know the hope that is "an anchor for the soul, firm and secure" (Hebrews 6:19). Christ is that hope that we hold onto at all times. Keep your eyes and hearts on Him and you will stand firm and not turn your back on the Lord.

"My heart is set on keeping your decrees to the very end" – Psalm 119:112

For those of you who have not read Psalm 119, the largest chapter by far in the entire Bible, you should. It is filled with repetitive themes, which then embeds them into your mind and soul. The constant topic that I see the most in it is the Psalmist's absolute love for obeying the commands and statutes of God. That is a foreign thought though; when have I ever said that I delighted in the Lord's commands that He has set for me?

I cannot say that I have until I read this psalm, but why should we find gladness in obeying God's laws for us? Do we not usually see rules and decrees as binding and hindering to our freedom, or just another thing that we *have* to do in order to make God happy? It does not have to be that way at all! We can enjoy obeying the commandments God has for us because He must have put them there for a reason because He is God and His purposes are divine and for His glory, so obeying Him must also be for His glory and help bring to fruition His plans.

The Psalmist says, "I have run in the path of your commands, for you have set my heart free" (119:32). Running in obedience? That is unheard of in my upbringing. I have been raised thinking that we obey because we have to and God asks of us, which is certainly true, but what the Psalmist brings to light and what Jesus shows is that there should be joy and happiness in obedience: "For I delight in your commands because I love them" (119:47), "Your decrees are the theme of my song wherever I lodge" (119:54), "I will hasten and not delay to obey your commands" (119:60), "Oh, how I love your law! I meditate on it all day long" (119:97), "Because I love your commands more than gold, more than pure gold" (119:127).

I do long to delight in God's law because His law is "Love the Lord your God with all your heart and with all your soul and with all your mind... [and] Love your neighbor as yourself" (Matthew 22:37,39). This is what we should revel in, loving others as Christ loves us. That is what we should run into and love doing more that accumulating wealth and living for worthless things. The Lord and His commands are one and the same because His Word is His commands to us and Jesus is the Word. "Delight yourself in the Lord" (37:4). Father, may you help guide us to obey your law and your Word to the very end so that we may be more like your Son who did whatever you asked of Him. Make us like Christ and let us not stray from your commands. We love you Father.

"Blessed are the poor in spirit, for theirs is the kingdom of heaven" – Matthew 5:3

This begins the series on the Beatitudes that Jesus spoke to the crowds and His disciples on a mountain side. I have actually been to this mountain that scholars believe Jesus gave the Beatitudes and the Sermon on the Mount on in Israel on the northwestern coast of the Sea of Galilee. It is a beautiful mountain surrounded by other mountains overlooking the sea, so I can see why Jesus would want to teach on it. The sayings that Jesus speaks of here go against whatever we think is the norm and what the world preaches.

It is daring of Jesus to say "Blessed are the poor in spirit" because we typically look down on those who are poor in spirit because it is their fault they are that way. But what does it mean for Jesus to say "Blessed are the poor in spirit"? To be blessed is to be made happy by God; more than that, it is not dependent on our emotions and outward circumstances, but on the joy of the salvation of the kingdom of God. To be poor in spirit could either refer to physical poverty or that someone's confidence and reliance are only on God and not on their own ability or strength. This phrase speaks against those who were spiritually proud in Jesus' day and in our day.

"For theirs is the kingdom of heaven." Matthew uses the terms kingdom of heaven and kingdom of God interchangeably, thus implying that they were one and the same. Jewish people would understand this as referring to the future tense of God's reign to come, but we must also see this in the present aspect that the kingdom of God has indeed come and has the authority. We want it to be manifested in our world and lives today as Jesus later teaches us to pray that "Your kingdom come, your will be done on earth as it is in heaven" (6:10). Why are the poor in spirit made happy though? Is it because the kingdom of heaven is theirs and that gives them hope for this life and the one to come?

Jesus for surely tells them that the poor in spirit are blessed because they have the kingdom of God in their possession. It *is* theirs. Their spirits should no longer be poor for they now have everything! Newness and change is upon them and they now have a hope that they never had before. Do you feel like you are poor in spirit, as if everything is against you and life just sucks? There is no need brothers, for yours is the kingdom of heaven. Take a hold of it. Grasp the hope that Jesus Christ sets before you for your freedom and His glory. You are blessed. Never forget that.

"Blessed are those who mourn, for they will be comforted" – Matthew 5:4

As I said before, the qualities that Jesus lists in the Beatitudes are not what the world would use to describe those who are blessed in the slightest. Jesus is counter-cultural and that is why many hated Him. But the characteristics that Jesus uses are to be envied and emulated because they make up the good and blessed life of His people. The spoken reasons of why these people are blessed are always positive and promising, despite what the current circumstances may seem like.

This time Jesus tells us that "Blessed are those who mourn." People that mourn, that cry out in the dark, who are grieving the loss of a loved one, who are in perpetual pain, who feel hopeless, who mourn over both personal and corporate sins, it is they whom Jesus calls blessed. It is these people whom Jesus recognizes as being made happy by Him. He is telling them that they have a hope and that they are loved and that He hears them and that they will indeed be comforted by God. They only need to look outside their present situations into the unseen reality which in actuality is more real than what they see (2 Corinthians 4:18).

How great it is of our Savior to say that these people will be comforted! This is the attitude of those in the kingdom of God. This is who Jesus is saying He loves, those who are cast aside because of their mourning. The prophet Isaiah wrote about the man who would "bind up the brokenhearted, to proclaim freedom for the captives and release from darkness for the prisoners, to proclaim the year of the Lord's favor and the day of vengeance of our God, to comfort all who mourn, and provide for those who grieve in Zion" (Isaiah 61:1-3).

Jesus is that man. Jesus is the one who comforts us in our troubles and despair and allows us to confidently say "I waited patiently for the Lord; he turned to me and heard my cry. He lifted me out of the slimy pit, out of the mud and mire; he set my feet on a rock and gave me a firm place to stand" (Psalm 40:1-2). He is the one whom will "wipe away every tear from their eyes" (Revelation 7:17) because their robes have been washed clean by the blood of the lamb. How has God comforted you lately in your mourning? Accept His comfort.

"Blessed are the meek, for they will inherit the earth" – Matthew 5:5

This is one of the most baffling of the Beatitudes to me. The word translated meek is the Greek word *praeis*, or *praus*, which typically means mild or gentle. I wish I could see the crowd's response to this one, especially because the Jews believed that the Messiah that was to come would overthrow the Romans and bring about a restoration of Israel and a new golden age for the Jews. How bizarre it would then be to hear that the gentle and meek people that Jesus calls blessed will inherit the earth, when it is usually the strong and harsh people that inherit lands.

This declaration of Jesus is an echo of what David wrote about hundreds of years before saying "But the meek will inherit the land and enjoy great peace" (Psalm 37:11). Another word that people use instead of meek is humble. We know that Jesus paved the way for us to follow in His footsteps, the way of humility that He chose as described by Paul; "[He] made himself nothing, taking the very nature of a servant, being made in human likeness. And being found in appearance as a man, he humbled himself and became obedient to death—even death on a cross!" (Philippians 2:7-8). The way of the world is pride and assertiveness and force but the way of the kingdom is meekness, gentleness, and humility as set forth by Jesus Christ.

How will the meek inherit the earth? Is it by their own doing, or, like the other beatitudes so far, is it something that is given them because of their attitude and heart towards God and others? I believe it is the latter because it is like that with most of the things that Jesus talks about, that they are a gift given by grace. Also because Jesus uses the word inherit, which implies something that was left for us. Like an inheritance from our parents, we did not earn it by merit or works, but only because we are their children.

I just noticed that in Psalm 37, it mentions a lot about inheriting the land: "those who hope in the Lord will inherit the land" (v9), "those the Lord blesses will inherit the land" (v22), "you will dwell in the land forever" (v27), "the righteous will inherit the land and dwell in it forever" (v29), "He will exalt you to inherit the land" (v34). The bulk of these have righteousness and the effects of it being the determining factor of inheriting the land, and we are made righteous through Christ (2 Corinthians 5:21). Humility and mildness, like our Savior represented, is what we are supposed to emulate and live like. These are the things Jesus desires in us, that only He Himself is, "for I am gentle and humble in heart" (11:29).

"Blessed are those who hunger and thirst for righteousness, for they will be filled" –
Matthew 5:6

For one reason or another, I like this beatitude. That may be because hunger and thirst are physical occurrences that we may face because our bodies need food and water to survive. It is instinctive for us to eat and drink. But since the fall of man, we began to hunger and thirst for other things to fill us up. We hunger and thirst for success, for recognition, for pleasure, for whatever fixation gives us a rush, for anything that keeps us busy and makes us look good in the eyes of others, for power, for the world, for self.

These objects have become natural for us to crave, but as you know, that is not how it should be. Jesus tells us that those who hunger and thirst for righteousness are blessed. What does righteousness look like? I would say that it would lead to a person's actions being justified, as in, being made right with God. So then Jesus is saying that blessed are those people who hunger and thirst for becoming right with God and pleasing Him. This is only done through faith, as Paul says, "For in the gospel a righteousness from God is revealed, a righteousness this is by faith from first to last, just as it is written: 'The righteous will live by faith'" (Romans 1:17).

As stated earlier, we know that we unfortunately hunger and thirst for worldly things that only "satisfy" us temporarily, but how many of us can honestly say that we yearn and ache for righteousness and holiness? Can we truthfully say "Yes, I desire righteousness as much and even greater than I desire to have a well-paying job and to be happy and live in luxury and ease"? This is utterly convicting for me right now. I know that I do crave for holiness and sanctification, but lately I believe my heart and mind has been so preoccupied with finding a new job that pays well and where I can work with people and not do manual labor.

Nevertheless, we cannot forget the ending of this verse, "for they will be filled." There is no denying it, if you long for righteousness, you will be filled. Jesus tells us that "He who comes to me will never go hungry, and he who believes in me will never be thirsty" (John 6:35). They shall *never* hunger and thirst again. That brings peace to my soul and hopefully yours as well. But we cannot overlook the first part, in which we have got to hunger and thirst for righteousness, for God's justice, for holiness, for wholeheartedness. Are you desiring to become more and more like Christ each and every day as righteousness entails? What do you need to stop desiring so that you can be more wholly God's?

"Blessed are the merciful, for they will be shown mercy" – Matthew 5:7

We all know the story of the Good Samaritan found in Luke 10, but in case you do not, here is a quick synopsis: There was a man going from Jerusalem to Jericho who got robbed and beaten almost to death. A priest and a Levite walked by and did nothing, but the Samaritan who saw him did and took care of him above and beyond what was required of him (even though Samaritans did not associate with Jews). Then Jesus asks the law expert who was a neighbor to the man and he said the one who had mercy on him. So Jesus told him to go and do likewise.

That is what this beatitude is all about. To be merciful, strangely enough, means to show mercy and Jesus tells us that those who bestow mercy to others are blessed. But what does it mean to show mercy? In the case of the Good Samaritan, it meant helping out someone who was in need. Another example could be in the story of Jonah where God spared the lives of over 120,000 people in Nineveh because they turned from their wicked ways. I guess we can subsequently say that to be merciful is to display compassion for those who desperately need it, and if we know anything about sin and brokenness in the world, we all need it.

God has certainly shown us mercy already as Paul states, "But because of his great love for us, God, who is rich in mercy, made us alive with Christ even when we were dead in transgressions" (Ephesians 2:4-5). However, that does not at all mean that we should not be merciful because clearly Jesus commands us to after the parable of the Good Samaritan and also earlier saying "Be merciful, as your heavenly Father is merciful" (Luke 6:36). We need to be continually showing mercy to our neighbor, who is everyone, because God is continually showing us mercy for the stupid and selfish decisions that we keep on making.

James gives us another reason to be merciful; "because judgment without mercy will be shown to anyone who has not been merciful. Mercy triumphs over judgment!" (James 2:13). God delights in showing us mercy for our wrongdoings because He knows how we forget and mess up, like how a father knows their children simply forget and make mistakes. But like the good Father that He is, He shows us the way of life as portrayed through His Son. Are we delighting to show mercy to those we come in contact with, quick to forgive them and help them out as we have been helped? That is what love is and that is what we need to do to become more like Christ which is what this is all about, my friends.

"Blessed are the pure in heart, for they will see God" – Matthew 5:8

Just this past week I was volunteering at Cedar Campus, which was the camp I worked at all last summer, and it was lovely up there. I got to run into a lot of the staff and other workers I had gotten to know that summer and it really made me want to work there again. I would if it paid as well as my job here, haha. They have a slogan for that camp, *A place to meet God*. What the camp director will tell you however is that you can meet God anywhere, but at Cedar there are less distractions and you can be more intently focused on Him and His doings.

"Blessed are the pure in heart, for they will see God." This is an amazing beatitude. I know they are all grand, but the promise here is that they will see God! How many people can say that? Moses never even got to do that, but only could see His backside and then had to be veiled because his face was so radiant from the Lord's glory and the people could not stand it. God told him, "you cannot see my face, for no one can see me and live" (Exodus 33:20). But yet we are told by the Son of God that the pure in heart will see God. I am sure there are some of you out there who will say, "Yeah, we will be able to see God in the lives of others and in creation and see manifestations of His kingdom on earth."

But I believe that it plainly means we shall see God because all the promises so far are both presently and eternally minded in a literal sense. Like yesterday's for instance, "for they will be shown mercy." I am pretty sure that is literal, along with "for they will be filled" and so forth. We shall indeed see God my friends, although we have to be pure in heart. What does that look like? It can look like having right attitudes and motives in your heart and mind, not only in external and public settings like the Pharisees, but maintaining real integrity at all times for the right reasons. It includes being single-minded towards things of the kingdom and not of the self. It consists of being purified from the world and evil by the blood of the Lamb and having Christ live within you.

David foreshadows this beatitude hundreds of years earlier saying, "Who may ascend the hill of the Lord? Who may stand in his holy place? He who has clean hands and a pure heart, who does not lift up his soul to an idol or swear by what is false" (Psalm 24:3-4). This purity of heart is holiness; "without holiness no one will see the Lord" (Hebrews 12:14). Do you want to see the Lord? Are you willing to become holy by the indwelling of the Spirit? This sanctification is a process, a painful procedure that will stretch you and change you so you can be molded into the image of Christ and look upon His face in full glory. Do you want that?

May 2

"Blessed are the peacemakers, for they will be called sons of God" – Matthew 5:9

Peacemakers. Those who make peace. It is a bit different from peacekeepers, which is something we hear of often, like "keeping the peace." But it raises a question, at least in the grand scheme of things, "How can one keep the peace if there is no peace to begin with?" When you look out into the world, there is so much violence and prejudice and wars and hatred and chaos and injustice. There is not much peace and even where there is, it is merely superficial for the sake of saving face or support, not because they actually want peace.

But Jesus tells us that peacemakers are blessed. Why? Because where there is peace, there is disorder and dissension and not love and unity. As peacemakers, we should be trying to reconcile opposing parties and promoting peace within our own little worlds. Paul tells us that "If it is possible, as far as it depends on you, live at peace with everyone" (Romans 12:18), and James says that "Peacemakers who sow in peace raise a harvest of righteousness" (James 3:18). We are called to bring about peace wherever we are. Jesus himself was called the "Prince of Peace" (Isaiah 9:6), and so we, who are called to be like Christ, should be about making peace where there is none.

Jesus says that we shall be called sons of God if we are peacemakers. "May God himself, the God of peace, sanctify you through and through" (1 Thessalonians 5:23). Our Father in heaven is a God of peace, and "the Son can do nothing by himself; he can do only what he sees his Father doing because whatever the Father does the Son also does" (John 5:19). Jesus is the Son of God and we are children of God, so furthermore we should do what we see our Father doing and our Father is the God of peace. That is why we will be called sons of God because we will be reflecting the character of our heavenly Father.

As a child of God, "we are heirs—heirs of God and co-heirs with Christ" (Romans 8:17). And as an heir and child of God, we get to share in what are His possessions, which is everything! All that has ever been or will be created is Christ's. None of this can be obtained by merit or effort, but by the free grace and love of God in our lives. In what ways can you be promoting peace with those around you? Are you creating discord instead of peace in your walk? *Lord, make me an instrument of Thy peace; where there is hatred, let me sow love; where there is injury, pardon; where there is doubt, faith; where there is despair, hope; where there is darkness, light; where there is sadness, joy. – St. Francis of Assisi*

"Blessed are those who are persecuted because of righteousness, for theirs is the kingdom of heaven" – Matthew 5:10

And so we come to the last of the Beatitudes. These sayings of Jesus have come full circle, with the first promise being "for theirs is the kingdom of heaven" and the last promise declaring the same. The whole of them are a proclamation of character traits that Jesus defines for being godly and righteous people, those His kingdom needs for kingdom living.

"Blessed are those who are persecuted because of righteousness." I really do love this, even though living in America does not really allow me to live this one fully out. I think of believers in the Middle East, Africa, and Asia who are treated with hostility and being ostracized and face death day in and day out because the culture and people they are around cannot stand Christians and the love they preach and live. They know what being persecuted is about because their families have kicked them out or turned them over to the authorities because it is illegal to be a follower of Christ.

Many believers in those parts of the world are killed because of their faith in Christ, but does that hinder their advancement? Not at all! Just last week I heard about the country with the largest amount of IFES (International Fellowship of Evangelical Students) students in it. Can you guess? It is not America, even though we are second, but it is Nigeria! They have more students involved in IFES than anyone and there is a tremendous amount of Christian persecution in that country because of the terrorist group Boko Haram. The only type of "persecution" that we may face in America is having people call us names or no longer be friends with us and say that we are narrow-minded and archaic.

Brothers, those who are persecuted for their faith are blessed. For those of us, Matthew goes on to say "Blessed are you when people insult you, persecute you and falsely say all kinds of evil against you because of me. Rejoice and be glad, because great is your reward in heaven" (5:11-12). That gives us hope that we may live that way as well. We are summoned to live for Christ and what He stands for, so may no persecution or suffering hinder us from living out this kingdom lifestyle. If you have not noticed throughout history, wherever there is persecution of God's people, there is an expansion of His kingdom. Persecution gives us an opportunity to prove out fitness for the kingdom of God. Are you fit for it? Are you willing to suffer hatred and discrimination for the sake of Christ? Are you even willing to die for Christ's name? May you be blessed my friends.

"But the prince of the Persian kingdom resisted me twenty-one days. Then Michael, one of the chief princes, came to help me, because I was detained there with the king of Persia" – Daniel 10:13

The person speaking here is an angel. He came to the prophet Daniel in a vision after he mourned for three weeks following a revelation he received concerning a great war. During that time of mourning however, we know from the previous verse that Daniel had "set [his] mind to gain understanding and to humble [himself] before [his] God" (10:12). The angel then spoke these comforting words to him, "your words were heard, and I have come in response to them" (10:12).

This is where our verse comes in. The angel said that he had heard Daniel's cry for understanding and humility, but he met some resistance along the way. This is one of the greatest examples in Scripture of the reality of spiritual warfare in our lives. Daniel mourned and prayed for these three weeks and heard nothing from the Lord. Have you ever been in a similar situation, where you are setting apart time and energy to intently hear and get a response to your fervent prayers, but it comes up empty? Maybe the reason for this could be that angels and demons are fighting over it in the heavenly realms like they were here.

We are at war brothers. Whether you think so or not, we are. Demons are having influence over political leaders (prince of Persia, king of Persia), aiding in their evil advances and fighting against the goodness and light that God's angels represent, as you can depict from the text. The angel said that he heard Daniel "Since the first day" (10:12). And David tells us that "The righteous cry out, and the Lord hears them" (Psalm 34:17). We know this to be true, God *does* hear us when we cry out to Him and He *does* answer us.

That may be why there is a delay in God's answers to us because of the war being fought in the heavens. But as I am writing these things, I think about the absolute sovereignty of our God and how His timing for everything works out beautifully, even of the delays that happen because of spiritual battles! He truly is a great and wonderful God who loves His children so much and hears them. I recently discovered this passage and the truth of it when I got a phone call from the TSA after months of prayer for a new job and I finally got it. It was great that there was this delay because me and my girlfriend, whom I have mentioned before, were no longer together and I was able to transfer the TSA job here in Michigan. God *always* hears us and answers us, maybe not in our timing, but always in His wondrous timing. What are you waiting for?

"So Elisha left him and went back. He took his yoke of oxen and slaughtered them. He burned his plowing equipment to cook the meat and gave it to the people, and they ate. Then he set out to follow Elijah and became his attendant" – 1 Kings 19:21

At church this morning, we were going over part of our vision as a church: Belong, Believe, Become. We desire our church to be inviting and welcoming so that anyone regardless of social class, ethnicity, what they are wearing, etc can come and belong. But we do not want to be like other "clubs" where people just belong so they can go and do good things, but so that they may then believe in the name of the Lord Jesus Christ and become more like Him.

God had Elijah choose Elisha as his successor as prophet of Israel (19:16), but Elisha had to break apart from his previous way of life before he could truly follow Elijah and be his aide, much like how the disciples had to leave their nets and follow Jesus. Even though his former life of plowing in the fields was not sinful and wrong, but it was unnecessary in the new calling upon his life from God, which was to be His prophet, His voice for His people. In order for someone to believe in Christ so that they become Christ-like in all they do, something has to change about them; they have to do a 180 and follow Christ and His ways and no longer their own ways.

Billy Graham said that you should "Come just as you are. But when you come, you must leave your defiance and rebellion behind and come in submission, for in that moment of repentance the Savior of your soul will become the Master of your life." Jesus loves everyone and wants them to come as they are to Him. Some think that they have to have everything together before they can come to Christ, but if that was the case, no one would come to Him because they will never have it all together. God wants the world to belong so "that at the name of Jesus every knee should bow, in heaven and on earth and under the earth, and every tongue confess that Jesus Christ is Lord, to the glory of God the Father" (Philippians 2:10-11).

Elisha burned away his previous life so that he may be completely devoted to his new life and have no chance of ever turning back. Jesus says that "No one who puts his hand to the plow and looks back is fit for service in the kingdom of God" (Luke 9:62). You must leave behind that rebellious nature as Billy Graham said and submit your life to Christ who will become the Master of your life. Are you looking back at your former life, missing some aspects from it, and thus being a hindrance to God's kingdom? Do not look back.

"Are you so foolish? After beginning with the Spirit, are you now trying to attain your goal by human effort?" - Galatians 3:3

"Are you so foolish?" Apparently the Galatians were foolish (3:1), foolish for forgetting the simple truth that Paul taught them, which was Jesus Christ crucified, the Gospel. Have we forgotten the Gospel and traded the eternal truth for a cheap grace that diminishes the work of Christ on the cross?

The context of our verse is Paul preaching against the Galatians because they had begun to believe the Judaizers, who were Jewish Christians who believed that a number of the Old Testament's ceremonial laws were still to be practiced by the church. What made it worse is that the Galatians were Gentiles, so everything would be brand new to them, and thus to find out that they had to carry out all these Jewish practices was daunting. That is why Paul is frustrated with the Galatians for forgetting the Gospel he had preached to them, the Gospel that is by faith and not by works, as the Judaizers tried to push forth.

This is the same gospel spoken to us; that "it is by grace you have been saved, through faith—and this is not from yourselves, it is the gift of God—not by works, so that no one can boast" (Ephesians 2:8-9). Yes, we may go out and do good deeds or practice spiritual disciplines, but that does not save us or make us righteous before God. We are made righteous because He is righteous, not because we did something right or observed the law. It begins with the Spirit which is by faith, and it ends by the Spirit, which brings sanctification and justification.

"Since we live by the Spirit, let us keep in step with the Spirit" (5:25), for if we live by the Spirit, "you will not gratify the desires of the sinful nature" (5:16). Brothers, trying to make yourself right before God does not work, only He can make you right before Him. "All who rely on observing the law are under a curse...the law is not based on faith...now that faith has come, we are no longer under the supervision of the law" (3:10,12,25). We must be trusting God and His Spirit within us that we are right with Him if we believe in Him. Christ is worth believing in and when we submit to Him and stop doing things in our own strength and effort, we will find rest for our bodies and souls.

"May the words of my mouth and the meditation of my heart be pleasing in your sight, O Lord, my Rock and my Redeemer" – Psalm 19:14

This week at work, I have been learning how to mow with one of those zero-turn lawnmowers and it is much harder than it looks. I am one who learns how to use things quickly and with this, I just cannot mow a straight line for the life of me. Granted, the mower they gave me is not the greatest because the two handles do not line up and are ultra-sensitive, so that is why my lines look like I have been drinking on the job. I am getting better at it though, compared to the first section I mowed.

The same is true with this verse and our living it out; it may not be easy to do, but with practice and time, we will get better at it with the help of the Spirit. We may not be going directly down the path we have desired, but we are heading that direction. David knew the importance of our words and how they affected us and those around us and, whether we meant all the words or not, "out of the overflow of the heart the mouth speaks" (Matthew 12:34). He understood that words held power and influence and that "The tongue has the power of life and death, and those who love it will eat its fruit" (Proverbs 18:21).

David, better than most, also understood how imperative the condition of the heart was for our own well-being and for a follower of God. He knew that "Above all else, guard your heart, for it is the wellspring of life" (Proverbs 4:23). David recognized the pertinence of having a pure heart and mind before God who saw all of who he was. How important these need to be for us as well brothers! Not only for our conscience's sake, but so that our lives may be pleasing to the Lord of lords.

How can the words of our mouth and the meditations of our heart be pleasing in the sight of our Father in heaven? Practice. Asking God to purify your mind and heart daily. Watching what you take in via television and music. Being wary of your bad thinking habits and the first thoughts that come to mind in situations and whether or not they are positive or negative and glorifying to God. You must be on the alert friends. You cannot just let things happen to your heart and mind, they are precious to God. They matter and it really does affect your walk with Him. I know it may be a struggle at first, but keep at it, Christ's Spirit is with you. Are the words of your mouth and the meditation of your heart pleasing to the Lord our God, or are they pleasing to you and those around you?

"Consider it pure joy, my brothers, whenever you face trials of many kinds, because you know that the testing of your faith develops perseverance" – James 1:2-3

James knows the greatest way to start a letter: telling the recipients to be joyful in their trials. Really? That is how he begins his epistle, "To the twelve tribes scattered among the nations" (1:1). The one thing I have always loved about the Book of James is that he is not afraid to boldly speak against the norm, which he does quite often. James was the brother of Jesus who originally doubted his brother's mission, but later become a prominent leader in Jerusalem.

Ever since the dawn of creation, God has tested man. He longs to know that he will be obedient to Him and trust Him when He tells him something. God's first test to Adam was, "You are free to eat from any tree in the garden; but you must not eat from the tree of the knowledge of good and evil, for when you eat of it you will surely die" (Genesis 2:16-17). Unfortunately, we know that Adam failed this test and that is why it did not produce fruit, but when you do pass the tests that God throws at you, fruit is produced. Maybe not right away and you most likely will not see it in the moment, but God will bless you.

Why should we be joyful during times of trial and testing? Because they are opportunities to make us more like Christ. They give us the chance to choose Christ over ourselves and the world. These tests occur every day and range from small to great. For instance, today I believe I failed the test at work and let the rainy and cold weather make me negative and pessimistic instead of finding a way to experience joy and thank God for it, although it is not what I would have wanted for work. It is the small things like that that make up our days and where we have the chance to live and act like Christ.

When we pass the tests of our God, our faith develops perseverance as we learn to wholly trust Him as our Rock and Sovereign Lord. Every day we have the opportunity to either say yes to Christ or yes to ourselves. On the one hand, we can react to our circumstances with cheerfulness and a thankful heart, or on the other hand, a grudging and complaining attitude. Which do you think pleases Christ? As we talked about yesterday, even if we do not outwardly show frustration and resentment, God sees our inmost being and knows our mind on the issue and desires that the meditation of our heart be pleasing to Him. How are you responding to what life throws at you?

"Swarms of living creatures will live wherever the river flows" – Ezekiel 47:9

This is where my church, The River, got its name. They desired to be a place that wherever they went, life would flow forth from it because of the Spirit's moving and life-giving nature. I believe that decision was God-led because it puts a new spin on what the church should actually be doing because for years, the church in America has been dying, and the church was meant to bring life.

For those who do not know the context of this passage (even though I hope you always read these in context), I will bring you up to speed. The prophet Ezekiel is experiencing a vision and is being led by a man in it. The man brings him to the temple in Jerusalem and they see water flowing out of the east and south sides of it. The water then gets deeper and turns into a river that then flows into the Dead Sea, which is the saltiest body of water in the world, so salty that nothing can live in it. But yet, there is this fresh water river that pours into it. This river has trees on both sides of the bank (remember, this is in the middle of the desert), and "There will be large numbers of fish, because this water flows there and makes the salt water fresh; so where the river flows *everything* will live" (47:9, emphasis added).

The Dead Sea is well, dead, hence its name. However, this river that flows from God's temple is bringing life to the sea that has not bore life in a long time. Not only that, wherever the river goes, life follows it. From Jerusalem to the Dead Sea, it is extremely barren and dry and it takes no effort for the river to flow there because it is over a three thousand foot drop in only fifteen miles. But what I am trying to say is this: we need this river. We need to be bringing life wherever we go, both individually and as a church. The world is the Dead Sea; dry, lifeless, and it needs the river of life to flow into you and have everything come alive.

Brothers, can this happen? I truly believe it can. No matter how dead the world or even our own personal world may be, we know that the Spirit of the Lord our God is life and there is not death in Him. He brings life everywhere He is, it is in His nature. That same Spirit dwells within us, which means we too can and should be bringing life everywhere our feet touch. Is this so? Are we enhancing the regions that we come into contact with or are we making no difference at all, or even a negative impact? May we bring the life of Christ to the comatose and deceased sea of people so they may flourish with life!

"The Lord is my shepherd, I shall not be in want" – Psalm 23:1

I am beginning a new series on what may be my favorite psalm because it contains many truths about our Shepherd and God that we tend to forget. Except for the first two writings, I am going to be sectioning these off not in verses, but in couplets, which is one line of Hebrew poetry because they are paired nicely.

"The Lord is my shepherd." We have talked about this before awhile back, but it is really good to be reminded of what it means that God is our Shepherd. A shepherd first and foremost takes care of his sheep, and sheep are very dependent on a leader. We are the sheep; the dumb, near-sighted, and gullible sheep and Christ, the Lord, is our Shepherd. It says that "The Lord is *my* shepherd." The focus here is on my, indicating that we are not our own, but we are Christ's. Christ owns us. Paul says that "You are not your own; you were bought at a price" (1 Corinthians 6:19-20). And so if we are not our own, why do we think that we can go out and do whatever we want and think it will be ok? What if your car that you own, starting doing whatever it wanted and did not do what you were telling it to do? It was made for you to drive it, so should it not do what you tell it? I know, maybe not the best analogy but the question still remains provoking.

"I shall not be in want." Going with what I mentioned earlier, the shepherd takes care of his sheep. He provides for his sheep in such a way that they shall not be in want. He gives them *everything* that they need. Do you know that this is true in your life if you call yourself a child of God? Because if so, you are His sheep and He is your Shepherd, your God, Jehovah-Jireh, The Lord who provides. And we know that God does not give sparingly, but in abundance. He created and owns everything that ever was, is, or will be and He does not waste anything.

Do you know God is the one who takes care of you? Do you know that He gives without wanting? This verse is making a statement, not asking your opinion, so it is true and trustworthy. But we may not always realize that these things are true because we do not see their fruit. Maybe you are in need of something right now. Are you trusting in the Lord as your Shepherd, that He will do what He says He will do? Have faith my friends in our Good Shepherd who owns us and takes care of us, so much in fact that we are not in want. Father, show yourself to us as our Shepherd. We need it; we need you in order to live. We are dependent on you. Help us to realize this. We love you.

"He makes me lie down in green pastures, he leads me besides quiet waters, he restores my soul" – Psalm 23:2-3

This morning at church was just what I needed. Worship was good where I could just praise my King as always and declare His Holy Name. The message was more of an info session on infant baptism and dedication and how there has been bloodshed in church history because people did not agree on this, so our church does both because of Romans 14:1, knowing that they both point the children to Christ. It was relaxing and beautiful as we dedicated and baptized six babies to the Lord and I even cried some when we were praying for them.

Green pastures are the places where sheep go and eat. Once again, we see God as our provider as He takes us to these pastures, but they are also places where sheep rest and lie down for some peace and tranquility. And they do that knowing that they are safe because their shepherd is watching over them. They are also content because they are not in want, but are satisfied as their shepherd has fed them and brought them to this place of rest.

The sheep also are being led to still and quiet waters where they too can satisfy their thirst and not have to worry about a mighty river sweeping them away. These quiet waters are just that, quiet, and the sheep love it as it lulls them to sleep. I am sure that you also love the sound of a slow and calming river as a place of peace and serenity. This whole time we have to remember that we are being led to these places; we are not finding them on our own, but our great Shepherd is leading us to them because He loves us and cares for us because we are His. Rebelling against His leading is rebelling against our own best interests.

Both of these scenes of a life-flourishing meadow and a bubbling brook are places that our Shepherd knows will bring restoration to our souls. They do provide nourishment and refreshment for our bodies, but they may more importantly bring a restoration to our spirits, which I am sure that if any of you are in school or the working world, you know how pertinent that really is. Our Shepherd, Christ, knows these things full well and that is why He brings us there. That is why I believe He went on a mountainside to get away and pray (Matthew 14:23). Jesus Christ knows what we need as He created us and we are His. He loves us dearly and delights to bring us rest. What do you need rest and restoration from?

"He guides me in paths of righteousness for his name's sake" – Psalm 23:3

We see our Shepherd as our guide. Previously we have talked about how sheep need to follow someone, they need a leader. They also tend to follow each other, whether that is somewhere good or somewhere bad, that is why they need a good leader who knows where he is going and leads them to safe areas. I am so glad that Jesus Christ is that leader, the only true leader worth following because He does know the way as He is the Way. He guides His sheep and they follow Him because they trust Him because He has never steered them wrong. He has never misguided them.

But here, our Shepherd guides us in the paths of righteousness. These paths of righteousness are all throughout the wilderness. These ways are right because Christ is leading us through them. They are good and just paths. "I walk in the way of righteousness, along the paths of justice" (Proverbs 8:20). That is where Jesus leads us; He leads us to right and proper understanding of the world and of Himself. As we have talked about before, righteousness and holiness go hand in hand, so as our Shepherd leads us in the paths of righteousness, He leads us into holiness and sanctification through His Spirit that makes us holy.

These paths lead us to Himself however. Because He is holy and pure and He guides us to that holiness, He guides us to Himself. He knows that if we went down a different path, it would lead to ruin, as the whole Book of Proverbs can attest. These paths bring a justification to us, as we know that "we have now been justified by his blood" (Romans 5:9) and they bring a sanctification as we go along them because we are coming closer and closer to Himself.

We cannot forget that this is all for His name's sake. Yes, it makes us righteous and more like Christ and that is good for us, but it is still all for Him. Oh how we need to always realize that everything is for His name's sake! My brothers, this truth has to be ingrained in our hearts and minds, that it is "Not to us, O Lord, not to us but to your name be the glory, because of your love and faithfulness" (115:1). Are you being led by Christ down the path that leads to Him and to life, or are you being led by another down the path that leads to death and destruction?

"Even though I walk through the valley of the shadow of death, I will fear no evil, for you are with me; your rod and your staff they comfort me" – Psalm 23:4

This section starts off oddly. David is telling us that we sometimes walk through the rocky ravine that is dark and full of gloom, and he would know because he has gone through some rough patches in his life. And so shall we if we have not already. Life is full of darkness and shadows, dreariness and trouble that just happen upon us because there is evil in the world and they follow the devil, "the ruler of the kingdom of the air" (Ephesians 2:2). This path is also dangerous since it is the valley of the shadow of death. If you have been around death, you know there is a stench in the air, a dampness that is unsettling. There is evil lurking around the corner waiting to pounce on you and wound you when you least expect it, tempting you to turn your back on Christ. But what will you do? Will you give in?

Say "I will fear no evil, for you are with me." We know that the world is full of evil, but we are to boldly declare that we will not fear the darkness that surrounds us, albeit we do not see what lies there because it is veiled in shadow. That may be what brings fear upon us the most: not knowing what is there, the uncertainty. But we are told that God is with us and that is all that we need to know in that moment because why should we fear what we do not know when our Shepherd is with us? We should be certain of Him. All else in this earth could be a mystery and unknown to us, but if we are assured and confident in Christ, why be afraid?

His rod and His staff bring us comfort. The rod was an instrument of authority that was used for counting, guiding, rescuing and protecting the sheep and the staff was used as a support. We have reassurance in our walking through the darkness because our Shepherd holds his rod and staff high and knows how to use it. It brings us great comfort and soothes us, knowing He is right there with us amidst the shadows. So why fear? Charles Spurgeon said that "It is beautiful to see a child at perfect peace amid dangers which alarm all those who are with him. I have read of a little boy who was on board a vessel that was being buffeted by the tempest and everybody was distressed, knowing that the ship was in great peril. There was not a sailor on board, certainly not a passenger, who was not full of fear. This boy, however, was perfectly happy and was rather amused than alarmed by the tossing of the ship. They asked him why he was so happy at such a time. 'Well,' he said, 'my father is the captain. He knows how to manage.'" And so it is with our Father in heaven, our Captain, our Shepherd. Do you have faith in your Shepherd?

"You prepare a table before me in the presence of my enemies" – Psalm 23:5

I just woke up from a lovely nap. I am sure you all know exactly how great a nap is after a hard day's work. I laid down my head and two minutes later I was out like a trout for an hour and a half, and the only reason I woke up was because I heard noises outside my window. You know when you had dreams during your nap but you forget them because you got up too fast? Yeah, that happened to me, but I still knew they were good dreams.

This verse speaks of something that is even better than naps (hard to believe, I know). David tells us that our Shepherd-King Jesus sets up a table before us right in front of our enemies. It means what you initially think it means; Christ prepares for us a feast of choice foods and wine in the presence of those who hate us and want us dead. This is coming out of the valley of the shadow of death, so that is now behind us and we are back to the tranquility that our God offers us. All our adversaries can do is look on with disgust and annoyance at us as we are being treated with royalty because of our good God; our God and Shepherd who brings us to a place of prosperity and blessedness after traversing through shadowed valleys.

God is the God of plenty and His people and His sheep are never left scarce. As we know from yesterday and from our walk in Christ, life is not always comfortable and rich, but has its ups and downs, its mountains and valleys; from the valley of death to the mountain of our God. "The mountain of the Lord's temple will be established as chief among the mountains; it will be raised above the hills, and peoples will stream to it" (Micah 4:1), but not until "they pass through the Valley of Baca" (84:6). Baca means weeping, which could be another example of the valley of death.

Our enemies cannot prevent our God from blessing us. Even though they look on with envy, there is nothing they can do about it but look. The people of God triumph in the very presence of their foes. This shall be the same on the last day when the people are separated from one another, "He will put the sheep on his right and the goats on his left" (Matthew 25:33). The sheep on their way to heaven and glory; the goats on their way to hell and anguish. Christ provides sufficiency for you in your time of need. Are you making it through the rough patches of life to the place of prosperity and blessing through Christ?

"You anoint my head with oil; my cup overflows" – Psalm 23:5

It has been really nice weather this week for working outdoors. It is my last week working for the landscaping company I have been with for the past two and a half years. It is kind of nice to leave on a good weather note, knowing that God has allowed me to finish my time there strong and in good standing with the company and with the outdoors. Plus, I got to get some sun this week, maybe a little too much, but it feels good.

As I have been blessed in my work, so we have been blessed by our Lord. In the Ancient Near Eastern culture, it was customary for an honored guest's head to be anointed with fragrant oils or lotions at a banquet or feast. Jesus was a special guest once at a Pharisee's house, but He told him "You did not put oil on my head, but she has poured perfume on my feet" (Luke 7:46). The Pharisee did not honor Jesus with anointing His head, showing what was really in his heart towards Him, but the woman knew who Jesus was and poured her perfume on Him.

Jesus anoints us with oil because He welcomes us to eat at His table with Him. He wants as many people as possible to come to His banquet. "Go out to the roads and country lanes and make them come is, so that my house will be full" (Luke 14:23) says Jesus. "Blessed are those who are invited to the wedding supper of the Lamb!" (Revelation 19:9). A great feast awaits those in God's family; a feast where our cups overflow because the Master fills it and He has an abundance that never runs dry. There is no want or need at the Lord's table, only satisfaction and fullness of life.

After trudging through the wilderness where shadows lurk on every side and we come out of it wearied and exhausted, still being surrounded by our enemies, our great and wondrous God and King makes up a table before us and makes us feel right at home and content because He is with us. He invigorates us with His food and drink and presence, so much so that we forget where we are and our sole focus is on Him. Some think that this is in the returning of Christ in His future kingdom, but I tell you brothers, that this is how it can be right now! God longs to bless you. St. Augustine once said that "God wants to give us something but cannot because our hands are full— there's nowhere for Him to put it." Are your hands full? Are you willing to empty what you rely on to embrace and take a hold of what God has in store for you which is exponentially better?

"Surely goodness and love will follow me all the days of my life" - Psalm 23:6

Just when I thought the weather at work could not get any better, it did! Today was perfect: 68 and partly cloudy with a good breeze. I could not ask for a more beautiful day for working outside. I did not get really hot even once because of the breeze. And now I have softball in an hour and it is going to be good. God continues to amaze me day in a day out. In addition, I saw a lovely fox with a big bushy tale at work, with horses galloping in the distance. That is right, be jealous.

David goes on to say even more wonderful things that God is doing in our lives besides giving us a feast and anointing our heads. He tells us that goodness and love will follow us all the days of our lives. The Hebrew word for love here can also mean mercy and favor, so David is proclaiming that the Lord's goodness and mercy and favor and love will follow us. It will pursue us all of our days; HE will pursue us all of our days because He is love. "The fruit of the Spirit is *love*, joy, peace, patience, kindness, *goodness*, faithfulness, gentleness and self-control" (Galatians 5:22-23, emphasis added).

Instead of our enemies following us, we now know that our God, our Shepherd and His attributes will follow us. Do you not know that Christ's Spirit dwells within you, making you holy because that is what He does? He sanctifies you and draws you into nearness to the God of the entire universe, making you more like Him. That God, my God, my Shepherd, my King, He cares about us enough to do us good. That is why He is personified as our Father because He truly loves us like one. "Do not be afraid, little flock, for your Father has been pleased to give you the kingdom" (Luke 12:32). We are the sheep of His flock, and *He is pleased* to give us the kingdom of God and so much more.

My friends, do you want goodness and love to follow you as long as you live? Who does not? And that means even more to us because our life does not end, but only begins with death, and even more goodness and favor will be bestowed upon us only for the reason that God loves us. Our Father knows how to give good gifts to His children, as an earthy father gives gifts to his kids, not necessarily because they did something right, but because he loves them because they are his. We are God's, not our own. Thank God for that! He shall never leave us nor forsake us. This is good news. How could it be any better?

"And I will dwell in the house of the Lord forever" – Psalm 23:6

Just the other night I went to the premiere of *X-Men: Days of Future Past*. It was quite good and makes you think about some things. It was a saddening movie throughout, but the ending, like most good movies, makes you happy that you went through all those troubling and depressing moments because it allows you to cherish the goodness that does come at the end. It concluded with joy that I even did not expect.

And so it is with this psalm as we have come to its end. There were some bumps and gloom along the way, but no more. We have made it to the finale. David said that we will get to dwell in the house of our Lord forever! Could you even think of a better ending? He is confident of this truth coming to pass, and so shall we be. We may have had comfort and plenty at first in our walk with Christ, and then He puts trials in our path where He longs to see us trust Him as our Shepherd. What is more, we make it out of those valleys of shadow and death and into a place of blessedness and fruit, and finally into the dwelling place of our King.

In the movie, the future version of Xavier told his younger self, "Just because someone stumbles and loses their way doesn't mean that they are lost forever." During those darker days of our lives, and even some of the brighter ones, we may stumble and fall by the wayside, but that does not mean that we are not going to make it on the path of life again. Thank God that is not the case! We know that He is right there with us, pushing for us to be more like Him. That is why He put His Holy Spirit within us, to make us holy as He is holy.

We keep trudging along the path set before us by Christ to make it to His dwelling place, to His home that He has prepared for us. Jesus comforted His disciples saying "In my Father's house are many rooms...and if I go and prepare a place for you, I will come back and take you to be with me that you also may be where I am" (John 14:2-3). Christ's heart yearns for us to be with Him where He is, and right now He is in heaven, preparing a room for us in His house where we will spend eternity with Him. This gives us hope brothers and "hope does not disappoint us" (Romans 5:5). Does knowing this bring you joy of a future hope with Christ? It does me, making me smile and even shedding a tear because I ache to be there with Him.

"They claim to know God, but by their actions they deny him" – Titus 1:16

The past couple days have been really fun. I went skeet shooting and had a bonfire, went to the lake and swam and relaxed on the boat, and also went to the pub with friends to have a good time with a buddy who is going away for a couple months. Some of his friends did not show up and we really do not know why, they never responded. That was saddening to me because I thought they were good friends of his and would at least try and make an effort to spend some time with him.

Only later did I find out why they did not come, but they at least could have responded to it because I know they all saw the invite. Nevertheless, we come to Titus. Paul was writing this about the Judaizers again like I talked about on May 6; they were ruining households with their deception and leading others away from the truth that they were taught. That is why Paul told them this verse.

Oh how this is true for so many believers today! Countless claim to know God and Christ, but after seeing what they do, it makes you question the authenticity of their faith. I know people can stumble every now and then, but to continuously live a lifestyle that is not representative of Christ, that is living in denial of Him. John wrote that "The man who says, 'I know him,' but does not do what he commands is a liar, and the truth is not in him" (1 John 2:4). The prophet Jeremiah also had something to say on this, "You are always on their lips but far from their hearts" (Jeremiah 12:2). I hope this is not the case for the majority of believers out there, even though it pains me to say that I have seen many a follower of Christ unfortunately fall into this line of deceit because it is easier to live that way than in the commands of God.

This is why honesty truly is the best policy, because the only reason this happens is because of falsehood and lies that people are preaching and believing. My brothers, do not only claim to know the truth, which I know many of you do if you are rooted and established in the Scriptures, but may your actions follow suit. I do not care if it is hard or something you do not want to do, do it anyways. Heed the guidance of the Holy Spirit within you so that you may be "eager to do what is good" (2:14). Are your actions denying or affirming your walk with Christ? Truthfully think about this today and analyze why you do the things you do.

"It teaches us to say 'No' to ungodliness and worldly passions, and to live self-controlled, upright and godly lives in this present age" - Titus 2:12

The previous verse is perhaps necessary to understanding what the "it" this refers to; "For the grace of God that brings salvation has appeared to all men" (2:11). Paul is telling us that it is the grace of God, the undeserving love that He gave us through Christ while we were still sinners, that instructs and pilots us towards godly and upright lives in Him. It is imperative that we grasp that we are unworthy in and of ourselves to do anything good for the kingdom of God, but that only by His grace and mercy *given* to us are we even able to begin to live for Him.

The Greek for "no" here implies that we are to firmly deny and repudiate the wickedness and unholy passions that the world throws at us and wants us to live by. I admit, this is hard at times because we are constantly surrounded by it and it is thrust upon us in school and the workplace and the media. It seems as if the odds are against us because the entire world really is against us because it is against Christ, but we have God on our side and He is greater than the whole earth. He tells us to "take heart! I have overcome the world" (John 16:33). Indeed He has and that should give us hope and the ability to say no to the world and yes to God and His ways.

Paul calls us instead to live lives in which we are sober minded and controlled, not giving way to our fleshly passions or to the wind, but being in mastery over them and not the other way around. Some commentators put self-controlled, uprightness and godly living under three aspects: to ourselves, to others and to God. Maybe that's why the NIV uses the word self-controlled and not moderately or soberly as some others have, to indicate more to self. We are to be controlled in our actions and emotions, to be honorable and righteous in regards to our neighbors, and to always live as if we are in the Lord's presence, which we are.

It is only because of God's grace to us, this gift that we did not earn or deserve, that teaches us that the world and its ways are not the ways of God, but polar opposites. It is this grace that instructs and trains us to be holy and godly in a godless world, to show love and mercy to all we come in contact with, not just a select few. What say you? Is God's grace that prevalent in your life that you are indeed saying no to the world and yes to Christ? I pray that is so in all our lives brothers. Grace and peace be upon you.

"You need to persevere so that when you have done the will of God, you will receive what he has promised" - Hebrews 10:36

In *The Fellowship of the Ring,* when the company is lost in the Mines of Moria after Frodo had decided to take up the burden to destroy the Ring in Mordor, he said to his wise and dear friend Gandalf, "I wish the ring had never come to me. I wish none of this had happened." Keep in mind that he said this shortly after choosing to bear the ring and all its weight, and that is why I believe Gandalf told him this, "So do all who live to see such times, but that is not for them to decide. All we have to decide is what to do with the time that is given to us."

If you have ever seen the movies, you know that Frodo suffered much because of the Ring, but he endured and completed the task to which he chose. He took the advice of Gandalf and that made all the difference. As followers of Christ, we too may have to suffer, in fact, Jesus tells us that "If they persecuted me, they will persecute you also" (John 15:20). And if we know anything about Christ, He was indeed persecuted, so shall we be. The writer of Hebrews, who many believe to be Apollos, explains to us that we need to persevere through the suffering inflicted upon us.

What I see when reading this is that this suffering that is thrust upon us is because we are doing the will of God. So I say that if you are suffering because of your own selfish ambitions instead of the will of God, then that is your own doing and the responsibility is on your head. Many things may come upon us through our walk in this life, things that we ourselves may have brought up or that were forced upon us by outside circumstances. But how we react to the latter is when we truly can reflect the work of Christ in our lives.

If you think about it (you probably do not have to try hard), the majority of life is pushed upon us and out of our control, much like with Frodo. What Gandalf says is true, "All we have to decide is what to do with the time that is given to us." We all go through crappy times, but what do you make of it? There are many occurrences that we wished had never come to light, but they did anyways. A close friend unexpectedly dies. You lose your job. But what do you make of it? What are you going to do now that that has happened? The ball is in your court. The responsibility is yours.

"From the time he put him in charge of his household and of all that he owned, the Lord blessed the household of the Egyptian because of Joseph" – Genesis 39:5

Have you ever thought that what you are doing is insignificant and does not make a difference? I urge you to think again, that you look at the story of Joseph and find some encouragement and wisdom to know that you can bring significance wherever you are and produce change for the better.

Joseph was sold into slavery by his own flesh and blood, his brothers, because they were jealous of him and how much their father loved him. He was bought by one of Pharaoh's officials in Egypt, Potiphar, who then put him in charge of all that he had because he "saw that the Lord was with him and that the Lord gave him success in everything he did" (39:3). But look at Joseph here. Never once in this passage did it say anything about him complaining or thinking of ways to get back at his brothers. It only says time and time again that the Lord was with him.

It gets even better. Potiphar's wife tries to seduce Joseph and he flees, but she tells her husband something different and he has him thrown into prison. He does not even try to hear his side and we never even know if Joseph tried to tell him the truth. But what we do know is that "The Lord was with him; he showed him kindness and granted him favor in the eyes of the prison warden. So the warden put him in charge of all those held in the prison" (39:21-22). How cool is that? It seems that everywhere Joseph goes, he makes an impact and is placed in a position of leadership and authority, all because the Lord was with him. Read the second half of chapter 41 to see Joseph then become second in command in all of Egypt.

What I want to get at is this: you were made to make a difference wherever your feet would take you because the Lord is with you. The latter part is key, especially if you want the difference you make to be good and benefiting to all. You may not get to the influence or status of Joseph, but you still come in contact with people all the time, unless you are a hermit. He may not have asked for his circumstances of being sold into slavery and then later into prison, but he did not grumble or complain. Instead, he made the most of where he was at regardless of where he was at. Can you say the same? Are you making the most of where you are in spite of where it is and whether you chose it or not? Look to those who have gone before you and take courage.

"Someone told him, 'Your mother and brothers are standing outside, wanting to see you.'
He replied, 'My mother and brothers are those who hear God's word and put it into
practice'" – Luke 8:20-21

Yesterday for the first time, I finally met my brother's fiancés' family. They
are getting married in two months and I just met them, although they are only an hour
away. I wish I had met them sooner though because they are pretty cool and they even
allowed me to stay the night. In addition, they have a fun dog who kind of reminds me
of my cat. They will become my family soon, though not directly.

This is what most think of when they think of family, yet Jesus once again
turns what we grew up believing on its head. He states it a little differently in
Matthew, but still says the same thing, "For whoever does the will of my Father in
heaven is my brother and sister and mother" (Matthew 12:50). So now our family is no
longer only those with whom we came from and share the same blood, but those who
obey our Father in heaven and put God's word into practice. Mr. Feeny from my favorite
childhood show *Boy Meets World* said that "You don't have to be blood to be family",
and he was saying that to boy who never had a good family life and always felt like he
did not belong.

But God wants us to belong to His family, to share in His inheritance and to
dwell in His house. However, He has a few house rules that we must abide by: We have
to be men and women of the Word, those who hear the Word and do what it says. Like
the "wise man who built his house on the rock" (Matthew 7:24), so when the storms of
this life come (and they do come), you will not fall because your foundation is on the
rock of Christ that nothing can shake. Do you willingly welcome those from different
denominations than you as part of your family, even though you may not agree with all
their church doctrine and theology? I am sure that they also are doing the will of the
Father because they love Him and love to obey Him. Brothers, they are your family as
well, along with your own bloodline because they were purchased by the blood of Jesus
Christ as you were. "But now in Christ Jesus you who once were far away have been
brought near through the blood of Christ" (Ephesians 2:13). So I say to you, are you
deliberately obeying the will of God and putting His Word into practice every day and
are you realizing that your family is much bigger than you expected?

May 23

"They went backward and not forward" - Jeremiah 7:24

I am recalling a message I heard from my first year in Intervarsity, which might be the only thing I truly remember from any speaker at Western. He later became an IV staff worker there and he was talking about our walk with Christ. He brought up the analogy of a down-escalator and how you have to keep on walking up it in order to make it to the top because if you just stand still and do nothing, you will go back down to the bottom and that is not where you intended to go.

This is what God was saying to the prophet Jeremiah about His chosen people Israel after He brought them out of Egypt, after He made His covenant with them, which was "Obey me, and I will be your God and you will be my people. Walk in all the ways I command you, that it may go well with you" (7:23). But as we know from biblical history, "they did not listen or pay attention; instead, they followed the stubborn inclinations of their evil hearts. They went backward and not forward" (7:24).

How often have we done the same thing in our walk with Christ? How frequently have we given way to the selfish methods of our malicious nature? Like Paul who said "For what I want to do I do not do, but what I hate to do" (Romans 7:15). We know the good that we ought to do, the thoughts we ought to think, and the words we ought to say because God has told us what He requires of us. Nonetheless, we do not obey Him or walk in His commands although if we did, we would be the most free and liberated people on the face of the earth and they would all know it, but instead, they see us as the most captive because we are not living as we should as children of God.

Do you want to be the person that people look at and say "I do not know why this is, but that person, something is different about them. I can see it on their faces. Joy and peace and rest, I wonder why that is?" Because that person has believed and said of God, "I run in the path of your commands, for you have set my heart free" (Psalm 119:32). They are constantly moving up the down-escalator and are not stagnant and still in their faith, but continually striving to become more like Christ, not by works or strength, but by trust and faith. Are people looking at you and wondering why you are going backward and not forward, or the other way around? I pray it is the latter because the power of the Holy Spirit in our lives permits us to move in the right direction, towards Christ.

"He has showed you, O man, what is good. And what does the Lord require of you? To act justly and to love mercy and to walk humbly with your God" – Micah 6:8

This has become one of my favorite Old Testament verses, mainly because it outlines what the Lord requires and asks of us, the children of God. In addition, these requirements are not bad or impossible, but they are good according to Micah and God has shown us them so that we are without excuse.

He desires for us to act justly, but what does that mean? In the Bible, justice and righteousness are closely linked, and Amos explains it quite well, "But let justice roll on like a river, righteousness like a never-failing stream!" (Amos 5:24). What this is getting at is that as plant and animal life flourishes where there is water, so human life flourishes where there is justice and righteousness. Are you acting justly and fair to those around you, or are you showing favoritism which is forbidden (Deuteronomy 1:17)?

Secondly, God longs for us to love mercy as He is merciful. But to love mercy does not merely mean to love the mercy that God is showing to us, but to love extending mercy to people in your lives, as God has graciously extended His mercy, Himself, to you. The prophet Hosea told us that "I desire mercy, not sacrifice" (Hosea 6:6); He delights in granting us forgiveness and giving us a second and third and fourth chance, and so we, who are supposed to be in growing likeness of Him, shall delight in giving others the same chances. Are you showing mercy to those who have wronged you?

Lastly, the Lord requires that we walk humbly with Him. To humbly walk with God, with Christ, means to be low before Him, knowing who we are and *whose* we are and more importantly knowing who He is and where He is seated on high. And this is not just a one-time act that we are supposed to be do, but a lifestyle as we are told to *walk* humbly with our God, not be humble for a moment and then go back to our selfish and prideful ways. These are the aspirations of our God in heaven for us, to act, to love, and to walk in justice, mercy, and humility, the parts of His character that Israel often forgot as we often get swept up in the motions of doing church and other disciplines because we think they please God. But God wants us to love what He loves and do what He does and think as He thinks and burn for what burns Him. These are ways to do that, to be more Christ-like. Are you walking in these? Father, help us to live as you require of us because we are your people and you are our God. We are not our own. Thank you for your grace. We love you.

"Heaven and earth will pass away, but my words will never pass away" – Mark 13:31

One day ends and another day begins. You leave one job and you start a different one. You depart from your parents and you go establish a new family. The world is constantly in motion and ever changing. Some believe that we will live forever in this world, so they do everything in their power to create such a place, but Job tells us that a man "springs up like a flower and withers away; like a fleeting shadow, he does not endure" (Job 14:2).

This world seems so unstable with all of its acts of terrorism and changing climate, and that is why Jesus uttered these words to us. He knew this and He knew that we needed something solid to hold on to and stand on, His Word, Himself. He says that even "heaven and earth will pass away, but my words will never pass away" and in Matthew He says "I tell you the truth, until heaven and earth disappear, not the smallest letter, not the least stroke of a pen, will by any means disappear from the Law until everything is accomplished" (Matthew 5:18).

Jesus is talking about stability for us in an unstable world. We see daily how things seem to come and go, whether it be fashion, politics, sports, work, food, etc, but we know for certain that Jesus and His words will never go away. Instead, He will be the ruling foundation for our lives in this life and the coming one. This should give us hope brothers! Hope along with responsibility because we know these truths and that we must abide by them if we are to live full lives for our King.

Is this world causing you to doubt and lose hope? Well, it should because this world is not all there is and it is in fact hopeless. It will be here today and gone tomorrow, as we shall be. If this world of evil and chaos will be no more, that means something better, something more beautiful will be fashioned in its place. "But in keeping with his promise we are looking forward to a new heaven and a new earth, the home of righteousness" (2 Peter 3:13). Christ's words come with authority from above. His statement, His promise, proves His immutability, which means He cannot be altered. Malachi wrote hundreds of years before that "I the Lord do not change" (Malachi 3:6). So in this world of change, Christ does not, and that gives us hope and strength to stand upon Him as our Rock that does not wear or move.

"This day you have seen with your own eyes how the Lord delivered you into my hands in the cave. Some urged me to kill you, but I spared you" – 1 Samuel 24:10

In the film *The Hobbit: An Unexpected Journey* (prequel to *The Lord of the Rings*), we meet Bilbo Baggins and how he comes about obtaining (more like stealing) the Ring of Power from Gollum in a game of riddles. Now Gollum knows that his name is Baggins and that he is from the Shire and this ring that Bilbo stole was his precious that has been his life source for the past five hundred years. So Bilbo planned on killing him so he would not have to worry about him ever again, but in that moment, pity overtook him and he could not do it. Gandalf then told him, "True courage is not about knowing when to take a life, but when to spare one."

Those are wise words that maybe were running through David's mind when he had this chance here in a cave to kill Saul who has been relentlessly pursuing him throughout Israel. David's men were encouraging him to kill Saul, not only because then all their running and hiding could come to an end, but also so that David could take his place on the throne of Israel as he was anointed to. Nevertheless, David did not kill him because he said that "I will not lift my hand against my master, because he is the Lord's anointed" (24:10). I do not know about you, but that is loyalty to a T, even though Saul is bent on killing him.

The same type of scenario happened again merely two chapters later where David once more spared Saul's life. Now as I am reading this however, our verse says that the Lord delivered Saul into David's hands, so did God allow that just so David could spare him and show how he was the better man or did David not do what the Lord wanted him to, which was to kill Saul? Then I read on and David said "'From evildoers come evil deeds,' so my hand will not touch you" (24:13). I think that may have the answer in it, like the old principle, "eye for eye, tooth for tooth" (Exodus 21:24), but Jesus turned that upside down (Matthew 5:38-42).

People talk of having courage when they are going out and fighting battles and wars, and that tends to always be in relation to destroying the enemy. And Gandalf changed that, "True courage is not about knowing when to take a life, but when to spare one." But Christ changed it first, who is all about mercy and who said "Love your enemies and pray for those who persecute you, that you may be sons of your Father in heaven" (Matthew 5:44-45). Because Christ did that, so shall we. What do you think about that?

"God is light; in him there is no darkness at all. If we claim to have fellowship with him yet walk in the darkness, we lie and do not live by the truth" – 1 John 1:5-6

The writer, who is the disciple and apostle John, has always been my favorite writer in the New Testament. All of his books I love, including Revelation even though it is a tough read. Maybe what I love most about the way he writes and what he writes is that he tends to often use the metaphor of light and darkness to contrast God and the world.

John starts off by saying that God is light, which he then explains that because God is light, there is no darkness in him. If you think about the concept of light, it casts off darkness wherever it touches, revealing what was hidden in shadow. And that is what God is! Because God is light, wherever He is, darkness flees and He exposes what was concealed in the dark, showing the true reality of the world because darkness can mess with our minds and give us a false perspective.

So John continues by declaring that if we state that we have fellowship with God who is light and yet we walk in darkness and secrecy, we are liars because the truth is not in us. Paul exclaims, "For what do righteousness and wickedness have in common? Or what fellowship can light have with darkness?" (2 Corinthians 6:14). This goes back to us being a people of a singular focus and mindset, of being a true follower of Christ, one "who has left houses or brothers or sisters or father or mother or children or fields for my sake" (Matthew 19:29). For "No one who puts his hand to the plow and looks back is fit for service in the kingdom of God" (Luke 9:62).

We used to live in darkness, but since we came to believe in Christ, we crucified the old self and put on the new self, which is Christ and we walk in the light, free from guilt and have no need to hide anymore. In the dark, good and evil are seldom labeled, but in the light that Christ is, they can be clearly distinguished. Because we claim to be in the light, let us walk and live in the light and live by the truth that we now know because the light revealed it; the truth that our world is full of sin and that its ways bring death. Martin Luther King Jr. said that "Every man must decide whether he will walk in the light of creative altruism or in the darkness of destructive selfishness." What will you decide? Will you follow through with your claim to walk in Christ's light, or will you lie to yourself and God and continue to flirt with the darkness?

"Live such good lives among the pagans that, though they accuse you of doing wrong, they may see your good deeds and glorify God on the day he visits us" – 1 Peter 2:12

Just this past week, I believe for the first time in my life, I have had someone say that I have influenced them more than I could imagine, not merely with my words but with my actions and how I treated them. And this did not only happen once, but twice this week. The other person, whom I have only known for a month, praised God because of the encouragement I gave him and looks forward to what the rest of our friendship may bring.

I did not see those things coming in the slightest and neither should you because "You are the light of the world. A city on a hill cannot be hidden" (Matthew 5:14). Jesus did not say "You must give all you have to the poor and then you will be the light", but He said "You *are* the light" right now because He said "I am the light of the world" (John 8:12). Because Jesus is the light, we are the light, and this is what it means to live good lives among the pagans, letting the light of Christ shine within us.

Peter is telling us that people will notice the way we live and that the only way that they will praise our Father in heaven is if the lives we are living are indeed good lives emanating from Christ Himself."I know that nothing good lives in me, that is, in my sinful nature" (Romans 7:18), but it is only because of the indwelling Spirit that makes us holy are we allowed to live such good lives that people will notice and glorify God. Just before this however, Peter urges us to "abstain from sinful desires, which wage war against your soul" (2:11) because how can we live good lives while still living in sin and walking in darkness like we talked about yesterday? It cannot be done; they cannot have fellowship together.

I am sure that you have all been accused of doing wrong at some point, whether by a friend or boss or parent, but did you actually do something wrong? You probably did deserve it. But if you "walk in the light, as he is in the light" (1 John 1:7), the lives you live will truly become attractive to those living in darkness around you and they will want what you have. They will see the joy and the freedom and the love that you are constantly basking in to overflowing and hopefully someday will praise God with you instead of accusing you of wrongdoing. I pray for that brothers, that we may live as the light, not because of our works, but because of who Christ is, who is in us and His influence in our lives.

"The Lord said to Abram, 'Leave your country, your people and your father's household and go to the land I will show you'" – Genesis 12:1

Yesterday I finally moved out of my parent's house for good, not going back. Granted, I only moved an hour north, but still, I am out and on my own. I know I did not just leave the country and head off to some distant land that I do not even know where it is like Abram, but I did leave my father's household and went to a new place, a different place, and hopefully a better place.

Abram was called by God to leave the only land he knew and the only people he knew and go to a place that God will reveal to him. We know from earlier in the passage that his brother Haran died and that was when his father decided to move them all to Canaan, but when they came to a place that was also called Haran, they stayed there and that is where his father died (11:28,31-32). I see this as Terah, the father, not being able to live beyond his son's death; the pain was too much for him and that is why he moved in the first place. What I then learned is that we cannot permit the wounds of our past to nullify what God has for us in our future. Moving on is a part of life.

And that is what Abram decided to do, and God called him to it, so an even better reason to leave. We are told that "Abram left, as the Lord had told him….and they set out for the land of Canaan, and they arrived there" (12:4-5). Abram obeyed the call that the Lord gave him, even though I am sure it was scary to uproot himself and go to an unknown land. Think about it: If God right now told you, "Get in your car and drive to where I will show you", that would be kind of hard to do I feel. The first thing that rushes to mind is "What if I go the wrong way" or "I kind of like it here though." But that is not what Abram did. He got up, obeyed, and left. "By faith Abraham, when called to go to a place he would later receive as his inheritance, obeyed and went, even though he did not know where he was going...he was looking forward to the city with foundations, whose architect and builder is God" (Hebrews 11:8,10).

It is by faith that he left. It was by faith that I left all I knew back home for this new life with new people. It is because Abraham and countless others "were longing for a better country—a heavenly one" (Hebrews 11:16). Their eyes were on the prize that is Christ. Are our eyes that focused on Him, or are we stuck where we are out of fear, even though He is calling us elsewhere? Do not be led by fear my brothers, but by the Lord.

"For we are God's workmanship, created in Christ Jesus to do good works, which God prepared in advance for us to do" – Ephesians 2:10

Have you ever thought that you were not special or had any value? I am here to tell you that you do indeed have tremendous value and are exceptional in God's eyes. Paul says that "we are God's workmanship", meaning that God made us and we know that to be true because of David's writings over a thousand years prior, "For you created my inmost being; you knit me together in my mother's womb" (Psalm 139:13). But workmanship may also carry the connotation of being a work of art, and that is what you are!

You are not an accident. You were made for a purpose. One of those purposes is to "Love the Lord your God with all your heart and with all your soul and with all your strength" (Deuteronomy 6:5) and another is to "love your neighbor as yourself" (Leviticus 19:18). Another purpose that God fashioned us for was to do good works, as today's passage points out. Notice how Paul orders these phrases, with earlier stating "it is by grace you have been saved...not by works, so that no one can boast" (2:8-9), and then brings up the notion of doing good works.

Many a person believes that doing more good deeds will earn them a higher and more beloved status with God but that simply is not the case. It is "because of his great love for us, God, who is rich in mercy, made us alive in Christ even when we were dead in transgressions" (2:4-5). Because it says "when we were dead in transgressions", then it cannot be because of the works we have done since what we have done produced death. But God made us alive with Christ because of His wondrous grace; the life-giving grace that says "You are loved and you are created for a purpose."

You are a work of art. You are loved. If anyone says otherwise, merely tell them the truth that you are and do not further listen to any lies they may spit at you. You cannot keep on living the redeemed life without accepting God's grace at work in you to allow you to do good deeds for Him. We need to accept it from His giving hands every day. D.L. Moody once said that "A man can no more take in a supply of grace for the future than he can eat enough today to last him for the next six months, nor can he inhale sufficient air into his lungs with one breath to sustain life for a week to come. We are permitted to draw upon God's store of grace from day to day as we need it." We always need it my friends, to move closer to Him and to others for His glory and their benefit.

"Do not say, 'Why were the old days better than these?' For it is not wise to ask such questions" – Ecclesiastes 7:10

Last night I was watching *Back to the Future* for the first time in forever and that is odd because I grew up watching that movie because of my brother. In the first installment, they go back to 1955 and every time it makes me want to travel back to that time period when life seemed simpler, with better music and dancing and styles. I get that feeling whenever I watch any movie that takes place in the 40's or 50's. Sometimes, I believe I was born in the wrong age, and others have said that about me too, haha.

The wisest man who has ever lived who wrote the book of Ecclesiastes convicts me of this. I never thought it was an issue to wish I was in another time, a simpler and better time, but Solomon tells us that it is not wise to do so. Because I honestly do think that that stretch of time was better than the age I am living in now, with less cares and worries and a higher sense of priorities. But they indeed did have their cares: WWII, Korean War, segregation and the Civil Rights Movement, threat of a nuclear holocaust, and more.

I only learned of this sin in my life recently. It was not beneficial to me because it made it tend to not live in the moment where God has put me. God created me exactly when He desired to, and the same with you. I am *where* I am and *when* I am for a reason determined by God alone. I do not precisely know why I am here and now, but I strive to walk every day in faith believing that I am here in this time for His purpose and glory.

We are where we need to be to best praise the Lord and do His bidding. The old days were not necessarily better than these, just different. We need wisdom to see this and it does not come from ourselves, but by revelation through the Holy Spirit. "As the heavens are higher than the earth, so are my ways higher than your ways and my thoughts than your thoughts" (Isaiah 55:9). We think this heavenly-minded way when we are walking in a thankful attitude for all the Lord has done, is doing, and will be doing for us. As the saying goes, "Gratitude is the best attitude", and that is truth. Be thankful today for all God has done for you and maybe you will walk in the higher wisdom that you have been looking for from Christ.

"If you fully obey the Lord your God and carefully follow all his commands I give you today, the Lord will set you high above all the nations on earth" – Deuteronomy 28:1

I have been in TSA training for the last few days and a question came up that our instructor brought to the table: What good are we if we pick and choose which rules to follow on the job? If we did that in the line of duty, we could end up costing the lives of many people because we were unwilling to follow through with a certain procedure that we did not necessarily agree with. In the work of counterterrorism, you do not take shortcuts, but you fully obey the rules that are set before you for the public's safety.

I am glad I made a note of that during class because it relates to our walk with Christ so much more. Moses told us thousands of years ago that we must fully obey God's commands if we wish to fulfill His goal for us. Notice how he had to use the word *fully,* as if just telling God's people to obey was not good enough because I am sure there were some smart aleck people who would say "Moses, you only told us to obey God, you never said we had to obey everything He told us." So that may be why he added *fully* just to shut them up.

We cannot simply pick and choose which commands of God we want to obey and not obey, but we must obey all of them because God said them and He is the highest authority. "This is how we know that we love the children of God: by loving God and carrying out his commands. This is love for God: to obey his commands" (1 John 5:2-3). If we lived with this picking and choosing mentality, we are saying that God is not supreme and that we have a higher authority than God, which obviously, we do not. If we pick and choose what to obey, then we are not truly obeying Christ but merely doing what we want to do and then we would be no different than our former selves before we knew Christ.

We must follow all that God commands of us, then and only then can we be true children of God that represent Him in a way that is true. It would be as if Christ told the Father that He will do all the miracles and fun stuff, but then not decide to go through with the suffering and dying on the cross because He did not feel like it. Thank goodness that is not the case! As Christ obeyed all that the Father sent Him to do, so we must follow suit if we are to be like Christ. There is no other way brothers; we either follow Christ 100% or we follow ourselves and the way of the world. There is no middle ground. There is no 50/50. You are either all in or all out. What do you choose to do this day?

"Greater love has no one than this, that he lay down his life for his friends" – John 15:13

I was reading through some journal writings of mine from last summer and I came across an excerpt that affected me then and still does today: *The notion of letting go of my dreams and aspirations for the sake of others came up again as reading Tolkien's Ordinary Virtues on friendship, like when I saw The Hobbit and The Ultimate Gift. It was mentioned on January 1 too. Help others achieve their dream, even if we do not know our own.* That last line is what hit me the most and I believe it is unbelievably true in the life of a Christian today.

As far as we know, Jesus spoke our verse to His disciples during The Last Supper. He then went on to call them friends, thus fulfilling the statement of greater love, which Jesus accomplished on the cross when He willingly gave up His life for us, His friends. In *The Hobbit: An Unexpected Journey,* Bilbo was just an ordinary hobbit that had no great ambition or goal in life but to live a quiet and peaceful life in his hole in the ground. But when he got caught up in the adventure with the dwarves who had a set goal to take back Erebor, their homeland, he wanted to help them achieve it, even though he did not have a dream of his own.

I can relate to that immensely because I also do not really have a dream for my life other than to please my God in heaven. But I have helped others take steps closer to theirs by helping them out along the way, encouraging and pushing them and not dampening their spirits. I do believe that is what love does. Love does not have all the answers and nor does it need it, but what love needs is a willingness to put itself out there for the sake of someone else and for their betterment.

Jesus is the prime example of such love and that is why we should be willing to do the same because He cared so much for us to suffer and die, not for His own benefit, but for ours, so we must desire doing the same for our friends and Christ. I still do not know what God has for me in this life but to bring Him glory and praise, and so I will continue in faith to do so and to help others achieve the mission God has put them on. We are blessed to be a blessing to others, not for our own gain. And always remember, "Do to others what you would have them do to you" (Matthew 7:12). Grace and peace brothers.

June 3

"Out of the same mouth come praise and cursing. My brothers, this should not be" –
James 3:10

Today I learned about how to effectively communicate to those I come in contact with at work through actively listening and putting ourselves in their shoes when communicating. This involved treating them with respect and being all about them, while still being able to do our job the best we can. I think this was the best day of classroom training so far.

As followers of Christ, communication with our fellow brothers and sisters is essential and that is mainly why I really liked learning that stuff in class. We have to be treating one another with love and respect, whether they are in the family of Christ or not. So often I see believers talking down to others and talking to them as if they did not matter and they were better than them. This should not be the case.

James tells us that from the same mouth comes both praise and cursing, but as sons and daughters of the Living God, that should not be! He goes on to say "Can both fresh and salt water flow from the same spring? My brothers, can a fig tree bear olives, or a grapevine bear figs? Neither can a salt spring produce fresh water" (3:11-12). It is just like what we talked about on May 28 on our walk with Christ and how we should be living in the light and not the dark which is full of deception. "For what do righteousness and wickedness have in common? Or what fellowship can light have with darkness?" (2 Corinthians 6:14).

Blessing and cursing shall not come out of the same mouth. How can anyone trust you if one day you bless them and then the next you curse them? What would that person think? Would Jesus Christ do that to you? By no means! He will only speak blessings onto you. The one who speaks both of these things not only deceives others, but he deceives himself because he has become double-minded and a false disciple of Christ. What fellowship can light have with darkness? It cannot have any. There is either light or there is darkness. There is either blessing or there is cursing. The tongue is powerful my friends and it must be controlled and that can only be accomplished through the power of the Holy Spirit in your life. Are you speaking life onto your brothers or are you speaking death and judgment? I pray that we all can be speaking life and love upon each other for the praise and the glory of our Father in heaven.

"Who is wise and understanding among you? Let him show it by his good life, by deeds done in humility that comes from wisdom" - James 3:13

Many claim to have wisdom but have none. They assert that God has indeed blessed them with knowledge and understanding, but when you see how they live their lives and interact with others, you wonder how that can be so. They may even be along in years and so assume that they are wise because of their long life, but when noticing their deeds you discover that they are simply a grown up child and have not an ounce of wisdom about them.

One aspect I have always loved about the book of James is that he does not beat around the bush or speak in parables, but straightforward truths that cut to the core of the matter. He says it plainly that those who claim to be wise and understanding must show it by the good life that they live and by the good deeds they do for the sake of others and not themselves. This comes to show that wisdom is not merely saying the right words at the right times, but it involves actions and a lifetime of goodness and righteousness that people see (but not for the sake of being seen). They will say of this man that "He lives a great life in which I can find nothing false to pounce on or leverage against him."

"The wisdom of the prudent is to give thought to their ways" (Proverbs 14:8). That is an excellent way to live a good life, by giving thought to what you are doing and not being led by feelings and emotions which come and go. The wise man often times will be criticized for not reacting by how he feels because they would say that he is not being true to himself, but he is indeed being true to himself because emotions are deceiving. "A man's wisdom gives him patience; it is to his glory to overlook an offense" (Proverbs 19:11).

Wisdom and good deeds go hand in hand, much like faith which is discussed in James 2 which I would urge you to read. The wise man is inspired by the Holy Spirit who has blessed him with discernment and revelation so he may act in a godly manner at all times, knowing what to do and when. In himself he cannot know, but only through the Spirit can he accomplish good deeds done in humility because it is the right thing to do and because Christ asks it of him. Are you one who claims to be wise and understanding? If so, is your life proof of it? If not, what are you going to do about it?

June 5

"Where were you when I laid the earth's foundation? Tell me, if you understand" - Job 38:4

This morning was my first time at my new church and I think I am going to like it. They talked about the first chapter of Job and how he was a blameless man who was wealthy and successful and then how God allowed Satan to do as he wished to him without taking his own life. So Satan takes away all his possessions and even the lives of his children and even then he did not falter, but worshiped God. Later in the book however, Job begins to question God and asks the age-old question, "How can a good God allow such evil and suffering in the world?"

This question has baffled many, both believer and nonbeliever alike, causing a migration for numerous people away from God. But I believe that our verse and the surrounding better help explain why and I am sure that many of you are not going to be ok with the answer: I do not know why God allows such things. I know that Sin (from the fall) and our own personal sin help play a role in it and that God certainly does use evil and suffering for His glory and purposes, but I cannot honestly answer why because I am not God and I cannot speak for Him on such a matter.

Chapter's 38-41 of Job is the Lord's response to everything that has happened and He asks countless rhetorical questions that all return back to Him, showing that He is indeed the all-knowing, all-powerful, and all-good God that we claim Him to be. Here are just a few of the things He says: "Have you ever given orders to the morning, or shown the dawn its place...Can you bring forth the constellations in their seasons...Do you give the horse his strength or clothe his neck with a flowing mane?" (38:12,32, 39:19). God does all these things and we will never understand how or why He does them and in the same way, we may never understand fully why He allows so much pain and suffering in the world.

Job replies "I know that you can do all things...Sure I spoke of things I did not understand, things too wonderful for me to know" (42:2-3). And that is the truth brothers. It may just be too wonderful for us to know in this life with our finite minds since His is infinite. Something we have to keep in mind is this, "As the heavens are higher than the earth, so are my ways higher than your ways and my thoughts than your thoughts" (Isaiah 55:9). I hope you can see how beautiful and comforting this is, and though there is no definite answer, there is definitely a God who has always been there and always will be.

"Do not be afraid. I am the First and the Last. I am the Living One; I was dead, and behold I am alive for ever and ever! And I hold the keys of death and Hades" - Revelation 1:17-18

This was near the beginning of John's first vision in Revelation, which he describes as "The revelation of Jesus Christ" (1:1). That is what the book of Revelation is all about, Jesus Christ. It is a reminder of who Jesus really is. It does not reveal to us many new things, but it rekindles our love for the gospel and the man Jesus Christ who is our life.

These are Jesus' words. By starting off saying that He is the First and the Last, we know He is the one who has all authority because He was there before everything else and He will be there at the end of all things. "For from him and through him and to him are all things" (Romans 11:36). He is also the Living One, not merely one who was once alive or is now alive, but one who has life in Him and gives life to others (John 1:4, 14:6). As the Living One, in relation to being the First and the Last, death has no mastery over Him, but He does death as seen in the second half of the verse.

It is Jesus who holds the keys of death and Hades and it is He who has power over it. "I have authority to lay it down and authority to take it up again" (John 10:18). How sweet of news is that? Our Savior Jesus Christ is sovereign over life and death, and life wins because He is alive forever and ever, so also we shall be alive. Jesus told us that "Because I live, you also will live" (John 14:19). We know for certain that He lives because there were numerous witnesses who saw Him after His death and watched Him ascend into the heavens, where He is now seated at the right hand of God the Father until the time of His return.

My friends, do these truths comfort you? Do they give you a future hope that the good things you are doing in this life will not be for naught, but that you will see the Living One who formed the earth and separated the seas and called us by name? Oh, how they reassure me and bring me peace amidst the chaos of life, generating a smile on my face with tears that I get to see the one who bore my sins and made me alive in Him because of His great love! This is good news. Father, may these revelations of you come to fruition. "Come O Lord", or an early Aramaic expression, *Marana tha*!

"I know your deeds, your hard work and perseverance. I know that you cannot tolerate wicked men" – Revelation 2:2

I am going to attempt to write a series on the seven churches that John writes to at the beginning of Revelation. I believe that this is good and relevant for us because throughout these churches, there are many issues that are still being struggled with in today's churches and I think this could help shed light on it.

The first church that John addresses is the church in Ephesus. Keep in mind that the words to these churches are the words of Jesus Himself. He starts off saying that He knows their deeds, which He says to five of the seven churches. Jesus Christ knows our deeds; He knows the things we have done for Him and for ourselves. He knows. That is both terrifying and refreshing, that He knows what we have done, that our work is not all in vain. He sees the hard work that we have done for Him (and I pray we have done work for Him) and He does not forget it. He notices how we persevere through trials and keep our eyes attentive on Him throughout it.

He also knows that we cannot tolerate wicked men, that there can be no false teachers among the body of Christ so that the truth of Christ may be manifest. He recognizes the Ephesians' desire for purity and holiness in the church and that sin should be dealt with and not ignored. Christ then tells them "You have persevered and have endured hardships in my name, and you have not grown weary" (2:3). They did not let the adversity they faced deter them from their walk with God, but saw the end goal which is Christ and kept strong in His name.

We know that the church in Ephesus did not grow weary in their work for Christ. Even though it was the capital of the province of Asia and home to the Temple of Artemis, the church grew amidst the pagan influences all around them. These are the things that Christ commends them for: hard work, perseverance, purity and truth in the church. How would Christ characterize your church? Would He say that you have worked diligently and endured through trials in being part of a church that represents Him? My brothers, the church exists to draw men to Jesus Christ to make them like Christ. Is your church aligned with that same mission?

"Yet I hold this against you: You have forsaken your first love" - Revelation 2:4

In the first half of Jesus' message to the church in Ephesus, He commended them on what they were doing right, but now in the second half He is revealing where they still lack. This is the basis of any exceptional teaching because it is wise and good to praise people for what they are doing correctly without forgetting to inform them where they could yet improve.

We see here that Jesus told the church that they have forsaken their first love. They had forgotten about Christ and had lost their joy for Him like they had when they first began. The church of Ephesus' love towards Christ and others has cooled down over time. I am sure that you have been here at one point or another my brothers, where you started off with such zeal and passion for God and His workings and then over time, that passion and vision waned and your love grew cold. It is a terrible thing to happen to a church since we are supposed to be representative of Christ and how can we if our love for Him is not strong and at the heart of all we do?

They are told to "Repent and do the things you did at first. If you do not repent, I will come to you and remove your lampstand from its place" (2:5), and this is what we shall do in our day and age. We are in need of repentance of our complacency and forgetting the basics of our faith. It is on Christ which we stand, nothing else. And note that He says that if we do not repent, He will remove our lampstand, which is our church because "the seven lampstands are the seven churches" (1:20). I know that when I was first baptized with the Holy Spirit, I was living in such exuberance and joy that all the things from my life before that point had no effect on me. I indeed was a new creation! I preached and prayed and did things that I never would have dreamed I would ever do and now as I look back at that, I am proud of that man and wishing I could have that boldness and fervor again, which I know I can.

All that needs to be done is to trust God like I did and to love and live for Him and Him alone; not myself or my parents or the world, but solely Jesus Christ. He was and always shall be our first and true love. Without our hearts and minds focused on Him, we slide off the path designed for us and if all are doing it, then the whole of the church is missing its mark. Friends, may we not miss the mark. May we not forget our first love.

"To him who overcomes, I will give the right to eat from the tree of life, which is in the paradise of God" – Revelation 2:7

This is how Jesus ends all of His messages to the seven churches in Asia, "To him who overcomes." But before He gets to that He says, "He who has an ear, let him hear what the Spirit says to the churches" (2:7). In other words, "Everyone listen to what the Spirit of the Lord is saying" because we all have ears, so we all must be attentive to the Spirit's working in the church throughout the world.

"To him who overcomes" is a challenge to the church in Ephesus; a challenge to be victorious in the problem areas that Christ previously spoke to them about. John loves talking like this, for in a previous letter he wrote, "for everyone born of God overcomes the world" (1 John 5:4) and Jesus Himself said to His disciples that "In this world you will have trouble. But take heart! I have overcome the world" (John 16:33). Christ tells the church that if they overcome, He will give them the right to eat from the tree of life.

Now there were two trees in the Garden of Eden: the tree of life and the tree of the knowledge of good and evil. Adam and Eve were allowed to eat from the tree of life, but the tree of the knowledge of good and evil, they were told not to eat from, but they did anyways because we humans love to cross the forbidden line. When they ate of it, they were cast from the Garden and no longer could eat from the tree of life. But now, Christ is informing us that we can once again eat the fruit of the tree of life.

This tree is in paradise, which in fact is heaven itself. So what Christ is saying is that to him who conquers, he will surely be rewarded with not only an entrance into heaven, but will be able to enjoy all of its pleasures. In the Hebrew and Greek contexts of the word paradise, it implies a beautiful pleasure garden that is full of good and pleasing joys. What Jesus does here is restore man to where He was before the Fall and even to a higher place than that in a more blessed state where he will live and be with Christ and His people forever, free from sickness and death. My brothers, is this not beautiful? Is this not an encouragement for us to overcome worldly pleasures and say no to ungodliness? I urge you then, to live such victorious lives in Christ Jesus with Him as your strength, so that you may overcome and enjoy Him forever and He can say to you, "Well done, good and faithful servant…Come and share your master's happiness!" (Matthew 25:21).

"I know your afflictions and your poverty—yet you are rich! I know the slander of those who say they are Jews and are not, but are a synagogue of Satan" - Revelation 2:9

We now come to the church in Smyrna, which was a beautiful city just north of Ephesus, of which many believe that the famous martyr Polycarp, one of John's disciples, was the first bishop of the church there. It is in this opening that Jesus says, "These are the words of him who is the First and the Last, who died and came to life again" (2:8). We talked about this name of Christ a few days ago, so I think you are set on that.

This is one of the times where Jesus does not say that He knows the churches deeds, but instead He tells them that He knows their afflictions and poverty. What a great way to start a letter! The Son of God, the King of kings tells you that He knows of your sufferings and persecutions. He has been watching and is not absent, but He sees the pain you are enduring, and He is right there with you. He knows what you are going through. I know some would say that no one can understand what they are going through, but I assure that Christ does, not only because He suffered more than anyone has ever suffered, but because He has created each and every one of us.

He also says that He knows of their poverty, so the church must have been poor at the time, but He tells them otherwise. He knows their poverty, but He knows even more that they are rich in Christ! Jesus Himself was a poor man, yet He was the most blessed that has ever lived, and so all His disciples, the first apostles, were also poor yet were closer with the Lord than most. Those who are poor in worldly goods do not rely on them, but depend on Christ and His goodness because they have the kingdom of heaven as discussed on April 26 in accordance with the Beatitudes.

I pray that we can live in such a way that we are always aware that Christ knows everything about the situations we are in. And now a prayer from St. Augustine:

Look upon us, O Lord, and let all the darkness of our souls vanish before the beams of thy brightness. Fill us with holy love, and open to us the treasures of thy wisdom. All our desire is known unto thee, therefore perfect what thou hast begun, and what thy Spirit has awakened us to ask in prayer. We seek thy face, turn thy face unto us and show us thy glory. Then shall our longing be satisfied, and our peace shall be perfect.

"Do not be afraid of what you are about to suffer. I tell you, the devil will put some of you in prison to test you" - Revelation 2:10

One of the most common phrases throughout the entire Bible, "Do not be afraid", is what Christ tells the church in Smyrna. He encourages the church by telling them this. I just envisioned being told this and pictured myself wandering through a forsaken wilderness knowing that the road ahead was dangerous and dark, and coming upon hearing these words, strength came to me and I walked with hope and faith in my steps. I believe this is how it made the church in Smyrna feel, confident in Christ because He charged them to not be afraid of what they were about to suffer.

We know from Paul that "everyone who wants to live a godly life in Christ Jesus will be persecuted" (2 Timothy 3:12) and additionally Jesus told His disciples that "If they persecuted me, they will persecute you also" (John 15:20). So why should we be afraid? We should expect it to happen and to be counted worthy to share in the sufferings of our Savior. But what is cool about this verse is that Jesus says, "the devil will put some of you in prison to test you." They are not being punished. They are not suffering by mere happenchance, but they are being tested and we know that "suffering produces perseverance; perseverance, character; and character, hope" (Romans 5:3-4), and "the testing of your faith develops perseverance" (James 1:3).

Jesus goes on to tell the church to "Be faithful, even to the point of death, and I will give you the crown of life" (2:10). We know that persecutions *will* happen; we should not shy away from them, nor should we dive headfirst into them, but when they come, we should listen to our Captain and King who commands us to be faithful and to stand firm, and the reward will come.

Brethren, this is our call; to stand amidst the volatility and the tribulations that are coming for us or already upon us and to see Christ, who is the First and the Last. It is He who was faithful to the point of death because His Father asked Him and because He loved the world for whom He was giving up His life. Our call is to Christ. Are we in love with Jesus Christ to the point that we are willing and ready to suffer for His sake, even onto death? Are we as faithful to the Father as Christ was?

June 12

"He who overcomes will not be hurt at all by the second death" – Revelation 2:11

This morning I made a quick run to one of my friend's garage sales which was also a fundraiser for her and her friend's mission trip. I have not been to a garage sale in years and they did not have anything priced, but it was a donation-based sale so we paid what we thought was reasonable. I ended up buying a lot more than expected and they estimated that it would be around $15 but I ended up paying $80 and they were shocked. I like helping out people for trips because I know they need it and fruit will come of it.

I share this not to pride myself like a Pharisee, but to help illustrate that we overcome when we band together as the church of Christ, His body, His bride, rooted in Him. "God has arranged the parts in the body, every one of them, just as he wanted them to be" (1 Corinthians 12:18). When we have communion with fellow believers, we are stronger because "If one falls down, his friend can help him up" (Ecclesiastes 4:10). The same is true when we are undergoing persecution and affliction, when done together, there is a greater chance that it will be conquered and the experience would be more joyful and rewarding.

Jesus here tells the church that he who does overcome will not be hurt by the second death. What is the second death? "The lake of fire is the second death" (20:14) as John later describes as the place where death and Hades are thrown into, along with "If anyone's name was not found written in the book of life, he was thrown into the lake of fire" (20:15). That does not sound like a pleasant place. In essence, if your name is written in the book of life, you have without a doubt overcome and will be spared from the second death.

And to be spared from the lake of fire means that you will dwell in the paradise of our Father. Unity with one another and unity with Christ as Jesus talks so much about in John 17 is essential to overcoming the obstacles we face. Otherwise we might more easily get discouraged, give up and lose hope and thus miss the prize we set out for. May we be like the victors who "overcame [the accuser] by the blood of the lamb and by the word of their testimony; they did not love their lives so much as to shrink from death" (12:11). May we love the Lamb of God who takes away the sins of the world and our brothers so that we do not shrink back, but strive forward to Christ Jesus our Lord, the Victor of our lives.

"I know where you live—where Satan has his throne. Yet you remain true to my name. You did not renounce your faith in me" – Revelation 2:13

Jesus moves on to the church in Pergamum, a city known for its cone-shaped hill it is set upon, making it a natural fortress. It is located north of Smyrna and it is believed to be the place where Antipas, the bishop of Pergamum, was martyred for persuading the people to stop sacrificing to idols and to follow Christ.

This is why Jesus notifies the church that He knows the place where they live, the citadel on the hill, where Satan has his throne, where pagan worship dominates and persecution of Christ-followers is prevalent. Christ knows that the church in Pergamum lives among such idolatry and wickedness, and yet He knows that they have remained true to His name throughout it. How strengthening is that to hear? Does it not hearten and inspire you?

If this church nearly two thousand years ago could stand firm amidst persecution in its own city, even witnessing the torturous murder of its own bishop and yet not renounce their faith, why cannot you? Are you staying true to Jesus' name? I am quite certain that the majority of you have not even been ostracized because of your faith, let alone suffering for it. Who am I to talk? I have only been rejected because of my faith in Christ by strangers, not by my own family or friends. I honestly have no right to be judging anyone in this matter, but I want all of us to think about these things.

Why are we not suffering as the founders of our faith have? Why are we afraid to speak up in the name of Christ? Do we so easily forget the price He paid to set us free from sin and death? We compromise our stance on things so often for the sake of avoiding confrontation and not being seen differently. But we are different! We have the Holy Spirit actually living within our very beings! We have been born again because of the blood of Christ! We are a new creation and we do not live by the standards of the world, but we live by a higher standard, God's standard, so yes, we are different. Yet we are afraid brothers. May we heed the wise words spoken for centuries, "Do not be afraid." Follow the example of this church and remain true to Jesus' name. I guarantee you, you will not be disappointed and you will for surely be rewarded, whether in this life or the next. I love you all so much and I pray for you daily. Pray for me also.

"Nevertheless, I have a few things against you: You have people there who hold to the teaching of Baalam, who taught Balak to entice the Israelites to sin by eating food sacrificed to idols and by committing sexual immorality" – Revelation 2:14

He really does have a few things against them. The main thing here is that the teaching of Baalam is being upheld. The story of Baalam takes place in Numbers 22-24 and that is where he advised the Moabite women to lead the Israelites astray. "The men began to indulge in sexual immorality with Moabite women, who invited them to the sacrifices of their gods. The people ate and bowed down before these gods. So Israel joined in worshiping the Baal of Peor. And the Lord's anger burned against them" (Numbers 25:1-3).

The church in Pergamum must have been teaching and permitting the people to indulge themselves in sexual immorality and idolatry. But why? How could a church, who Christ just said remained faithful to His name and did not renounce their faith in Him, having something this negative said about them? It could be the result of poor leadership of which Baalam was also a bad leader because he wanted to do harm to his own people. He had a strong desire to do what he knew was wrong and forbidden by God, and he did it anyways; he led them into idolatry.

Christ's body should not have leaders who try to deceive believers into compromise with worldliness. We should *never* compromise with worldliness because its ways are not God's ways, but are for the most part opposite. Idolatry is putting anything else in the place of the one true God. It begins within us and is manifested in outward adoration when we nudge God off the rightful throne as the King of our lives. We must trust in nothing or rely on anything more than God Himself. If we do, we too are idolaters and that is why this sin is rampant in this church and in many churches today.

One may say God is their King, but when they make decisions solely for financial reasons, then money is king. Or when all we think about is women or comfort or success instead of thinking about how to please God in this situation, that is idolatry. Martin Luther said that "If you have a heart that can expect of Him nothing but what is good, especially in want and distress, and that, moreover, renounces and forsakes everything that is not God, then you have the only true God. If, on the contrary, it cleaves to anything else, of which it expects more good and help than of God, and does not take refuge in Him, but in adversity flees from Him, then you have an idol, another god." My friends, keep Christ on His throne, from whom all things flow and return. He is good and He does not lead us astray.

"To him who overcomes, I will give some of the hidden manna. I will also give him a white stone with a new name written on it, known only to him who receives it" - Revelation 2:17

Jesus is now telling those who overcome that He will give them some of the hidden manna. This is in contrast to the unclean food that they were eating from those who held to the teachings of Baalam. From what we know of manna is that it was bread given to the Israelites from God during their time in the wilderness on their way to the Promised Land. Jesus mentions it once more saying "I am the bread of life. Your forefathers ate the manna in the desert, yet they died. But here is the bread that comes down from heaven, which a man may eat and not die" (John 6:49-50).

Manna in the Psalms is dubbed as "the grain of heaven...the bread of angels" (Psalm 78:24-25), but what is it? I think the latter half of that verse draws it out for us, that it is the food of heaven; that which will sustain us as it sustains the heavenly hosts. It is food that will never perish or rot and is incorruptible by the world and held safe by God, much like the jar of manna that was put into the Ark of the Covenant (Hebrews 9:4). We shall eat that food brothers, if we overcome.

Now unto the white stone: white symbolizes purity and so the white stone given to the overcomer would be a sign that he was considered pure by Christ. There is much debate on what the stone itself resembles, but some say that certain stones may have been used as tokens of favor and reward, or used to signify good and lucky days, and even acquittal or condemnation. So this stone is given to the one who is victorious in their walk with Christ, and it is given with a name on it.

We do not know if the name will be ours or another name of the Lord. The prophet Isaiah said a few things about new names: "To them I will give within my temple and its walls a memorial and a name...I will give them an everlasting name that will not be cut off" (Isaiah 56:5), "you will be called by a new name that the mouth of the Lord will bestow" (Isaiah 62:2). New names were common in Scripture to represent the change done in a person by God and what He has in store for them. They symbolize a new status, a better status, a heavenly status (Isaiah 1:26, 62:4,12). Help us overcome by the blood of the Lamb Father, so that we may receive the hidden manna and the white stone; that we may embrace the newness you have prepared for us in your heavenly realm.

"I know your deeds, your love and faith, your service and perseverance, and that you are now doing more that you did at first" (Revelation 2:19).

These words were spoken to the church in Thyatira, located southeast of Pergamum. This was the home of Lydia, who was a dealer of purple cloth who was converted by Paul and his company (Acts 16:14). As with every opening to these messages, Jesus is described in a new way; this time as "the Son of God, whose eyes are like blazing fire and whose feet are like burnished bronze" (2:18). Christ's eyes penetrate those in Thyatira as fire penetrates and purifies all. His whole being burns with fire for them as "The eye is the lamp of the body" (Matthew 6:22).

He tells the people once again that He knows what they have done; He has been keeping His burning eyes of fire on them, noticing their love and faith for their brothers and the lost in their city. He sees their good works and enduring spirit in spite of the persecution they are undergoing. One thing I have taken note of was that they were doing more than what they did at first, and that is one of the purposes of our faith, growth.

This aspect is vitally important in our walk with Christ and as a church. Countless Christians in America today stay at the stage of where they began in the faith and they never move on into maturity. They are stagnant; sitting still in the swampy waters producing a stench where few things can live. Paul said they are "mere infants in Christ. I gave you milk, not solid food, for you were not yet ready for it. Indeed, you are still not ready. You are still worldly" (1 Corinthians 3:1-3) and he urges that we should "no longer be like infants, tossed back and forth by the waves, and blown here and there by every wind of teaching" (Ephesians 4:14).

We *need* to be doing more than we did in the beginning. That is what growing in faith is, which we are called to do. In our old self, we were allowed to be worldly because we were a part of it, but no more! We are created anew and should no longer be worldly and tossed to and fro by every teaching that tells what our "itching ears want to hear" (2 Timothy 4:3), but we should train ourselves to be able to distinguish good from evil (Hebrews 5:14). The church in Thyatira matured and moved on to become a stream of water that moved throughout its city, serving and loving on them. Is that what we are like today? Are we mere infants, only able to process milk, or are we becoming adults and digesting solid food?

"Nevertheless, I have this against you: You tolerate that woman Jezebel, who calls herself a prophetess. By her teaching she misleads my servants into sexual immorality and the eating of food sacrificed to idols" - Revelation 2:20

Yet in spite of the line of praise that Christ told the church, He has an even longer list against them. This just comes to show that the church is not perfect and if you go to any church today, it is still not perfect. It shall not come to perfection until the day of His return, so until then, we will always fall short in some way.

Jezebel was a ruthless woman who was the wife of King Ahab in the second half of 1 Kings. She became an epithet for manipulating and evil women, as I am sure you have heard the saying, "You Jezebel!" It is not good to be called that name. Apparently in the Thyatiran church there was such a woman who claimed to be proclaiming the words of God, but she was leading others in the congregation to live sexually immoral lives. Jesus goes on and says "I have given her time to repent of her immorality, but she is unwilling. So I will cast her on a bed of suffering, and I will make those who commit adultery with her suffer intensely, unless they repent of her ways" (2:21-22).

God cannot and will not tolerate such wickedness and impurity in His body that He died for. How can He? He died so that we may be set free from the bondage of sin and death, not to serve it and make it our master. God and God alone is the Master and Head of the church; if there tries to be another, that is idolatry and He will spit us out of His mouth. Christ's body burns immensely for us my friends. So much that He wants us for Himself, to be wholly His, "For the Lord your God is a consuming fire, a jealous God" (Deuteronomy 4:24).

This jealousy causes Him to hate the evil that is in our lives, and so should we! We should not tolerate the Jezebel's and Ahab's in our churches or the world for that matter. Evil ought to be detestable to us because we are told to "Hate evil, love good" (Amos 5:15), and because God is only good and we should strive to be like Him through the working of the Spirit in our lives. The light that we are should cast off the darkness within us and around us. May there be no compromises with the enemy and their teachings brothers, but may there be a yearning for God that echoes His intense yearning for us; a longing that craves for purification within the body of Christ so that we may be more like Him in every way as we were created to be.

"I will strike her children dead. Then all the churches will know that I am he who searches hearts and minds, and I will repay each of you according to your deeds" – Revelation 2:23

The first sentence does not sound like the words of Jesus, but they are. He is starting to sound more like the God we know from the Old Testament, or at least the God that a lot of people see Him as; the God of judgment and condemnation. This is true. He is the God of judgment and He is the God of mercy. For how can an omnipotent, omniscient, omnipresent, and good God allow such evil to remain unpunished? He cannot by His very nature because He is a God of justice. "God is just" (2 Thessalonians 1:6).

Many forget that the Christ of the Gospels is the incarnation of the whole character of God. We forget that because that is true, He loves justice and justice is not always pretty, as in the case here. "I will strike her children dead." He is doing this because He cannot tolerate such wickedness in His church, for it would spread like gangrene and "A little yeast works through the whole batch of dough" (Galatians 5:9).

Christ said He had to do this so that the other churches will know that He is the one who searches their hearts and minds. He echoes the prophet Jeremiah saying that "I the Lord search the heart and examine the mind, to reward a man according to his conduct, according to what his deeds deserve" (Jeremiah 17:10). Christ desires His church, His body, to be "a radiant church, without stain or wrinkle or any other blemish, but holy and blameless" (Ephesians 5:27). And Paul feels the same way, "I am jealous for you with a godly jealousy. I promised you to one husband, to Christ, so that I might present you as a pure virgin to him" (2 Corinthians 11:2).

Do we aspire and hope for a holy church, where sin is being eradicated because of Christ's work and His peoples' desire to be pure and blameless? Do we utter the words of David saying "Search me, O God, and know my heart; test me and know my anxious thoughts. See if there is any offensive way in me and lead me in the way everlasting" (Psalm 139:23-24)? Do we, like Jesus, who wept over Jerusalem, weep over the condition of the church today and yearn and pray for its purity? May we be counted among the ones "who have come out of the great tribulation; they have washed their robes and made them white in the blood of the Lamb" (7:14).

"To him who overcomes and does my will to the end, I will give authority over the nations...just as I have received authority from my Father. I will also give him the morning star" – Revelation 2:26-28

In order for the church to overcome the troubles with their church and the world, they must also do Christ's will to the end. And we know what His will is: to not be persuaded by that Jezebel and to "be transformed by the renewing of your mind. Then you will be able to test and approve what God's will is" (Romans 12:2). His will is that we obey His commands, which are to love Him and to love others.

Why does Jesus say that He will give authority over the nations for the overcomer? I thought He Himself was the one who would rule? Oh, He is brothers, but as the Ruler, He bestows authority to those He trusts. As in the parable of the Ten Minas, the master tells the good servant, "Because you have been trustworthy in a very small matter, take charge of ten cities" (Luke 19:17). Christ has made us stewards on this earth, setting us here to help take care of it as best we can so when He returns, He will say "Well done, my good servant" (Luke 19:17). We need to remember that this world is God's and not ours, but He has entrusted us to take care of it, and that is a mighty responsibility that should not be taken lightly.

The reason we will have that authority (if we overcome and do His will) is because Christ gave it and it will be just like how the Father gave authority to His Son, for a purpose. And that purpose for us is to take care of something that is not ours so that someday it shall be given to us as our own in the heavenly realms. "I will also give him the morning star." Jesus later calls Himself "the Bright Morning Star" (22:16) and it is also mentioned by Peter, "until the day dawns and the morning star rises in your hearts" (2 Peter 1:19). So what Christ is saying is that He will give the overcomers of the church Himself.

What could ever be a better gift than that? But some may say, "Do we not already have Christ?" And we do to an extent, but John is referring to the day when we shall have the fullness of Christ Himself, sitting on His throne, right in our midst and we can physically touch Him. That is a beautiful promise brothers and it may well be my favorite from these letters. But what do these things mean for us? They mean absolutely nothing unless we overcome and do Christ's will to the end, and that requires faith and trust in Him who is trustworthy. "You, dear children, are from God and have overcome them" (1 John 4:4).

"I know your deeds; you have a reputation of being alive, but you are dead. Wake up! Strengthen what remains and is about to die, for I have not found your deeds complete in the sight of my God" – Revelation 3:1-2

The church in Sardis, the fifth letter of John's journey in modern-day Turkey, and once again Christ begins by saying that He knows the church's deeds, but unlike the previous churches, He starts off telling them what they need to work on instead of encouraging them in the good they are already doing. I am not sure why the change here. I do love how Jesus continues to tell the churches and us that He knows our deeds and what we have done. It is a necessary reminder that ought not to be overlooked, for repetition is there for a reason.

Christ says the church is dead, even though they were known for being alive. Does this ring any bells? It makes me think of churches nowadays where people flock to because they feel accepted and welcomed there, which of course every church should be that way; they are known for their loud and modern worship and for being liberal and radical in their teachings, but they indeed are dead. It is all a front to give the appearance that they are alive and well, when in fact they are rotting from the inside out and Christ knows that.

He sees their decomposition and declares for them to "Wake up! Strengthen what remains and is about to die." Death should have no place in a church because Christ came to give to them life. The church may be doing all those great things and not even know that they are dead, so Jesus Christ who is Life tells them to become vigilant and aware of what is going on about them! We must be attentive of where we are and what is happening and to know without a doubt that we are heading in the right direction, towards Christ and His likeness. Jesus urges them further to, "Remember, therefore, what you have received and heard; obey it, and repent" (3:3).

And He urges us to do the same. Remembrance is one of the biggest hindrances to going deeper with Christ. We are human and we simply forget. We forget the basics of our faith and who we are living for. We forget that our lives should be motivated by our love for God and love for people because of God's great love for us. We forget that life is not about us, but about Christ. This makes it pivotal to stay rooted in the Word and in prayer so that we do not forget why we are here, to live as light in the dark, reflecting the true Light of Christ to a world stumbling in darkness. Wake up.

"Yet you have a few people in Sardis who have not soiled their clothes. They will walk with me, dressed in white, for they are worthy" - Revelation 3:4

Sometimes we may think to ourselves that there are no righteous people out there, no one who longs to do the will of the Lord and we feel alone in our journey to do it. But we must bear in mind the story of Elijah where he honestly believes that He is the only one left who has not deserted God. However, the Lord said to him, "I have reserved seven thousand in Israel—all whose knees have not bowed down to Baal and all whose mouths have not kissed him" (1 Kings 19:18).

In the same way, there are a few believers in Sardis who do not look as though they are dead and thus wearing soiled clothes, but they are indeed alive! To have your clothes unsoiled signifies that you have remained above reproach in a society where people-pleasing and the mob mentality run rampant and are the norm. But what looks better not only in God's eyes, but in ours? To be wearing clothes that are stained and smelly, or clothes that are of the purest white? I do not even need to answer that question.

Christ notes that those who have not given in to the cultural woes around them, who have not defiled or polluted themselves in their way of thinking or in action, who have stood firm among shaky ground, they will walk with Him, clad in white. White is a sign of purity, spotlessness, and innocence. No wonder those who walk with Christ will be wearing such a garment. We must not overlook that Christ mentions that those with unsoiled clothes shall walk with Him! Does our heart not long for such intimacy with the Lord? Do we not pray for the days of Eden renewed where we can walk with Christ in the cool of the day in paradise?

My brothers, these wondrous days shall be restored and will be even greater than before; the days where those whose trust is in the Lord, who walk by faith and not by sight, shall walk with Him in all peace because He has considered them worthy. But why are they worthy? There have been many non-believers who have not given in to the world's ways, but refrained through self-discipline and avoidance, but that was done for their own sake and not for Christ's and selfishness has no place in His heavenly kingdom. "Rather, clothe yourselves with the Lord Jesus Christ" (Romans 13:14). That is why we are worthy, because we are wearing Christ who alone is worthy. Are your clothes being soiled by the world, or are you wearing the Lord Himself as your garment, following in His footsteps?

"He who overcomes will, like them, be dressed in white. I will never blot our his name from the book of life, but will acknowledge his name before my Father and his angels" – Revelation 3:5

God's will for the church has never changed since its creation: to be sanctified (1 Thessalonians 4:3) through the Holy Spirit so that it can become more like the Head, that is Christ. His will is for the church to be unified with Christ as the body should be unified with its head, for the benefit of itself and all around. And as Christ overcame the world to set this in motion, so we must overcome the obstacles put against us so that after going through these tribulations, we may take one step closer towards unity with Christ.

The promise that Christ gives the church in Sardis is that if they overcome the woes affecting their church and become what God intended for them, then He will never blot out their name from the book of life. We have talked about the book of life a few times before. It is the ledger that stores all the names of the citizens of heaven and if there was a name that has been erased or blotted out of it, that would indicate a loss of citizenship for that person. How awful that would be to have one's name removed from God's book, signifying that one is no longer a resident of His kingdom?

But thanks be to God that to him who overcomes, He *will not* blot out his name from that book and thus will be called a citizen of the kingdom of God! Not only that, but Christ shall also acknowledge our name before His Father in heaven, saying "Father, this is (Name), the man I was telling you about. See the good He has done for your kingdom and glory." Would that not be absolutely wonderful? Just think of it, the God of all things, the limitless and endless God of the universe, will know of you through His most trusted servant, His Son!

This past week I have been training at the airport and on my second day I had a fellow coworker acknowledge me and the good work I have been doing to my supervisor. My supervisor then told me that he was proud to have me on his team and to be learning the ropes quickly. My friends, that is no comparison whatsoever to Christ's acknowledgement of us to our Father in heaven. That is a hope worth looking forward to, as all these promises to those who overcome are, all guaranteeing that we will be citizens of God's kingdom in future glory. Are we as a church overcoming, or are we being succumbed to our attacks and sacrificing our upcoming reward?

"I know your deeds. See, I have placed before you an open door that no one can shut. I know that you have little strength, yet you have kept my word and have not denied my name" – Revelation 3:8

The church in Philadelphia is next on the trip through Asia and it is a beautiful city which means brotherly love. This church is near and dear to Christ I believe because throughout His message to it, He does not say anything negative about it like He does the other six churches. He merely encourages them in a multitude of ways so that they may become what He intended without raining down on them.

This door that Christ speaks of is referenced to through the prophet Isaiah saying "I will place on his shoulder the key to the house of David; what he opens no one can shut, and what he shuts no one can open" (Isaiah 22:22). What is this door? None other than the door to the kingdom of heaven! The church in Philadelphia has accepted and received Christ, and that will never be taken away from them. That door shall remain open before them because no one can tear them away from their love for Christ. Their salvation is sealed and they are the temples of the Holy Spirit, "who is a deposit guaranteeing our inheritance until the redemption of those who are God's possession" (Ephesians 1:14).

The Philadelphians have kept Jesus' word even though they do not have any strength because they know their strength comes from Christ. They utter Paul's words, "For when I am weak, then I am strong" (2 Corinthians 12:10) because for them, human weakness provides the opportunity for the display of divine power. Through their weakness and in Christ's strength, they kept His word and have not denied His name. Did you catch that brothers? They *kept* His word and did not deny His name. How can you keep the word if you do not know the Word?

Jesus Christ is the Living Word given for us. The Holy Scriptures are there for us so that we may know Christ more. If you have ever wanted to know more about who He is, you have to read and know the word of God if you are to keep it. This is not a new command, but an old one. "It is to be with him, and he is to read it all the days of his life" (Deuteronomy 17:19). Do you know His word inside and out? Do you know the Living Word on a personal level? Do you talk to Him all throughout the day, every day of the week because He is your God, your Guide, and your Friend? Just because the door to the kingdom is open before you, do not take it or the Word for granted, but make sure to step through the doorway.

"Since you have kept my command to endure patiently, I will also keep you from the hour of trial that is going to come upon the whole world to test those who live on the earth" - Revelation 3:10

Endurance is one of the most valuable traits in the life of those who are born again. It signifies a complete and utter trust in God that He will get you through one way or another. It produces great fruit in a variety of arenas that will be enjoyed in this life and the life to come. Not only did this church endure, but they endured patiently. Oh how that is immensely harder than mere endurance because you are going through some ordeal and not constantly complaining with the thoughts of "When is this ever going to end? I do not deserve this and just want it all to stop."

This patient perseverance is understanding that God has put you there for a reason and that allows our heads not to sulk around, but to praise God the Father for desiring us to be more like Him. And because the church in Philadelphia has done this, Christ says that He will keep them from the trial that is coming upon the whole world to test them; the test that will examine and reveal each other's true character, as most times of suffering do.

Christ continues to encourage His people because of His love for them. Because they have already endured patiently through what was affecting their church and city, Christ now urges them to continue on and He will keep them through it all. Since Christ, our Savior who bore our sins and rose from the grave, will be keeping us through the upcoming trials, why should we be afraid? We should not brothers because He is keeping us safe throughout and His arms are the safest place we could ever be.

He heartens them further saying "I am coming soon. Hold on to what you have, so that no one will take your crown" (3:11). I would love to hear such words when going through hardship, "I am coming soon." And He certainly is coming soon friends! He is coming to take us up with Him to be with Him where He is. But we must continue to endure what the world throws at us for the sake of Christ and His kingdom so that they may know His great and unending love. That love is what makes everything else possible. Father, may we love as you love. Help us to love one another with your sacrificial and selfless love that always puts the other first. May you strengthen us through times of trying so that we may be molded and shaped into your glorious image. Thank you Father for your everlasting grace. We love you.

"Him who overcomes I will make a pillar in the temple of my God. Never again will he leave it. I will write on him the name of my God and the name of the city of my God, the new Jerusalem, which is coming down out of heaven from my God; and I will also write on him my new name" – Revelation 3:12

The temple has always been considered the place where the presence of God dwells here on earth. But the apostle Paul states that "The God who made the world and everything in it is the Lord of heaven and earth and does not live in temples built by hands" (Acts 17:24), and Solomon basically said the same thing two thousand years earlier, "But will God really dwell on earth? The heavens, even the highest heaven, cannot contain you. How much less this temple I have built?" (1 Kings 8:27). So how can one me made a pillar in God's temple?

Easily. "I do not see a temple in the city, because the Lord God Almighty and the Lamb are its temple" (21:22). Even better. Him who overcomes will be built right into Christ Himself and He will never leave that place, thus fulfilling David's longing: "that I may dwell in the house of the Lord all the days of my life" (Psalm 27:4). As the overcomer gets to dwell with Christ forever, as all of these promises continue to point to and more, He will also be fashioned into Christ's image as the Lamb will also have the Father's name on Him (14:1).

But to bear the name of the New Jerusalem, that shows citizenship for he who overcomes. It reveals that his residence is now in heaven where the Lamb and the Father are. If you think about it, we are already citizens of heaven (Philippians 3:20) and members of God's household (Ephesians 2:19). But this refers to the manifestation of this citizenship, where earth will be no more and we will be in the new heaven, the place of rest and peace and joy.

Notice how Jesus says He will write on us *His* new name! The culmination of who we were meant to be, bearing the nature of Christ, will be ours. Do you want to be one who is victorious in this life because Christ is? Do you want to truly say, "we are not of those who shrink back and are destroyed, but of those who believe and are saved" (Hebrews 10:39)? I pray that you do want that, that you crave to stand firm for Christ in the slippery slopes of this life. Remember the old hymn, *On Christ the solid Rock I stand, all other ground is sinking sand.* Be the wise man whose house is built on the rock, so when the storms come, and they do come, you will not fall.

"I know your deeds, that you are neither cold nor hot. I wish you were either one or the other! So, because you are lukewarm—I am about to spit you out of my mouth" – Revelation 3:15-16

We finally made it to the last church that John writes to, the church in Laodicea. This church was well-known for their wealth in the banking industry, the textile industry, and their medical school that is believed to have specialized in optometry. However, their weakness was their lack of a sufficient water supply, so it is then no mistake that Christ mentions the notions of hot and cold and lukewarm which can easily be related with water.

He warns them that they are neither hot nor cold. Cold water is refreshing to drink. Hot water is soothing to drink with teas and coffees, and also is seen as healing waters, which could be like a hot tub of sorts. But lukewarm water, what is it good for? Absolutely nothing. It is useless. Christ says that this church is in fact lukewarm and wants to spit them out of His mouth. The church supplied neither healing for the spiritually sick nor refreshment for the spiritually weary. They became useless all around and were not living as the church of Christ.

Oh, but Christ is not done attacking them yet. "You say, 'I am rich, I have acquired wealth and do not need a thing.' But you do not realize that you are wretched, pitiful, poor, blind and naked" (3:17). He is bashing the very things that the church in Laodicea relied on (wealth, textiles and optometry) instead of relying on Christ. Not only does He want to spit them out of His mouth because they are of no use, He is attacking their society and way of life because they have become idols to them.

What would Christ say of you and the church you are a part of? Would He call you hot, cold, or lukewarm? He would without a doubt rather have you be on fire for Him or completely against Him; He hates mediocre Christianity where they only go to church on Sunday morning and live for themselves and the world the other six and a half days of the week because they believe God's grace will cover them and their foolishness. My brothers, He will spit you out of His mouth! That is detestable and you are taking the grace of God in vain! Be either hot or cold, do not be a compromiser in the middle. So what are you? What are things you are relying on besides Christ? They may even be good things, but if it is not Christ, it will not last and you will fall. Rely wholly and fully on Him my friends; His gold is refined, His clothes do not wear out, and He will help you see more than ever (3:18).

"Those whom I love I rebuke and discipline. So be earnest, and repent. Here I am! I stand at the door and knock. If anyone hears my voice and opens the door, I will come in and eat with him, and he with me" – Revelation 3:19-20

"My son, do not despise the Lord's discipline and do not resent his rebuke, because the Lord disciplines those he loves, as a father the son he delights in" (Proverbs 3:11-12). It is good that Christ says these things to the church because it shows His perfecting love for them and His desire for them to be holy. He loves them and He loves us too much for us to stay as we are in our sin and brokenness; He wants us to have life to the fullest.

It is then that we know we have strayed a little from the path that leads to life and that is why He asks us to repent. Repentance is oft overlooked in today's church and that is chiefly because of the peoples' belief of cheap grace, which Dietrich Bonhoeffer said that "Cheap grace is the grace we bestow on ourselves" and that is when people say things like "It is ok, God will forgive me." Yes brothers, God will forgive you because of His mercy, but if you are living with that mentality, then you truly have no desire to become more like Christ, but to keep on living your own selfish life in a state of cheap grace and not one that produces fruit and life.

I pray that you heed the call to repentance. We are human; we mess up often because we get caught up in the moment and forget whose we are, but we should never forget to repent of our wickedness when it comes. John the Baptist, Jesus, and even Peter's first messages in their ministry were about repentance. But even though we have continually failed Christ, He still says "Here I am! I stand at the door and knock. If anyone hears my voice and opens the door, I will come in and eat with him, and he with me."

Despite ourselves letting down Christ time and time again, even now He longs to be with us broken and self-centered children because He is our caring and loving Father who wants to see His kids succeed and live a life of worth onto Him. Do you want to eat with Christ? Do you want that level of intimacy with the one who suffered and died in your place? Eating together is a sacred thing and should not be taken lightly. Welcome Him in; open the door in your heart and in your church and allow the Head to be with you and lead you to greener pastures where you will indeed become more like Him.

"To him who overcomes, I will give the right to sit with me on my throne, just as I overcame and sat down with my Father on his throne" - Revelation 3:21

We come to the last on the series of letters to the churches in Asia. This is the final promise given to those believers who overcome the woes facing them in the world. Christ has that authority to allow us to sit with Him on His throne. The other time that Christ mentions His followers sitting on a throne is in the Gospel of Matthew saying, "I tell you the truth, at the renewal of all things, when the Son of Man sits on his glorious throne, you who have followed me will also sit on twelve thrones, judging the twelve tribes of Israel" (Matthew 19:28). This was spoken to His disciples after they had asked what there will be for them because they left everything to follow Him.

A throne; that is what will be for them and that is what there will be for us if we stay true and follow Christ to the very end, throughout all sorts of trials and tests. There are times when we are in the midst of such a test and we come to believe it is the end and there is no way out and that we will fall, but I tell you the truth, you will not falter brothers because there is One who went before you who had said "I have overcome the world" (John 16:33)! There is much hope and encouragement in those few words; enough for us to keep our heads up and fastened on Christ to make it through as He did.

To be able to sit down on a throne signifies that we have been given some authority, as is evident in the verse from Matthew and in the Parable of the Ten Minas when the master said, "Because you have been trustworthy in a very small matter, take charge of ten cities" (Luke 19:17). Furthermore, we will be given the right to share in Christ's glory and kingdom, as kings and priests of our heavenly Father. This is as close as you can get to Christ, to sit *with* Him *on* His throne. It is even better than to have our own throne because we get to partake in the glories of the kingdom with Christ on His throne.

We are the church. To be the church is to be united with its Head, Jesus Christ. There is no church, no body, apart from Christ. "Apart from me you can do nothing" (John 15:5). We need Christ more than anything this world has to offer. He chose us, the church, to be His hands and feet in this world that desperately cries out to Him without even knowing it. They search and search for things to bring them joy and contentment and always come up empty because they are looking in the wrong places. There is only one who can bring true joy and rest for the soul, and that is Christ, and as His body we must be the light that fully represents Him to the world that needs Him. Are you willing to live a life of faith so that others may know the joy you have and want to partake in it? Be an overcomer.

"There is no one holy like the Lord; there is no one besides you; there is no Rock like our God" – 1 Samuel 2:2

Yesterday I spent the vast part of my day hiking throughout the sand dunes along Lake Michigan's shoreline in Grand Haven. I have not had an adventure like that is quite some time and it was breathtaking. It was unbelievable how something could just be created like that over thousands of years. There was also a section of the woods that was full of brighter and more slender trees with limbed branches that brought a new life to the area because it was rather dreary outside. I could not have asked for a more wonderful day.

Such beauty should always point you back to the Creator of all things and bring upon a time of praise and thanksgiving for the work He has done. That is what Hannah has done here after God had answered her prayers for a son because she was barren. How could she not praise the Lord after He heard and responded to her prayers of misery and desperation? It was the only thing that seemed fit to do and that is the truth; the best thing we can do in such situations is thank and praise the Lord because He has done a wondrous thing!

There is no one like our God. There is none besides Him and none that compare to His insurmountable deeds and wonders. Just think about it: "Who can straighten what he has made crooked?" (Ecclesiastes 7:13). Who can bring life through death? Who has laid the earth's foundations and set the world in motion? Who created the heavens and the earth; told the sun to rise and set and come back again in the morning? Only God can do these things. "The Lord brings death and makes alive; he brings down to the grave and raises up" (2:6). My friends, this is a foreshadowing of Christ's resurrection and ultimately our resurrection when He returns. Hannah's womb was barren and dead, but through God was made fruitful and alive!

She can then say, "My heart rejoices in the Lord" (2:1) because the Lord has delivered her from the grave. He can do the impossible and He does it every day. But notice how she rejoices in the Lord and not in the son that the Lord gave her; that is key in how we should be praising the Lord because He does indeed bless us in abundance day in and day out, but we *must* rejoice in Him and not the gift He gives. I am at fault in this as of recent. Father, forgive us for putting the gift above the Giver. Remove all idolatry far from us and may we thank and praise you and you alone because there is none like you in all the earth. Thank you for hearing your servant's prayer. We love you Father.

June 30

"Didn't you know I had to be in my Father's house?" – Luke 2:49

This is what twelve year-old Jesus told His parents after they accidentally left Him at the temple in Jerusalem one Passover. His mother asked Him, "Son, why have you treated us like this? Your father and I have been anxiously searching for you" (2:48) and boy Jesus' response was "Why were you searching for me?" (2:49) and that is when we come to our verse.

At such a young age, Jesus already knew where He had come from, realizing that He had both an earthy father and a Father in heaven. Not only that, He understood that He had a personal duty to his Father in the temple, the dwelling place of God. Do we ever say things like that? Do we ever say to people, "Didn't you know I had to be in my Father's house?" Why do we not say that? As believers of Christ, should not we be people who love being in the presence of the Almighty Father in heaven? I know some of you are saying, "The Holy Spirit dwells within me, so I am always in the presence of my Father", but are we truly?

Do we live in such a way as if that is the reality of things? More often than not, I see us living as if we ourselves are the "god" of our own lives, even though we claim to have the Spirit of God dwelling within us. Should not we be living the opposite? Of course we should! Our Father's presence should be the safest place for us to be and the source of all our joy. It is where we come to rest and abide in Him, growing in intimacy with the One who made us and knows the purpose we are here for. Are we as bold as the twelve year-old Jesus to purposefully take time and make it evident that we need to be spending time with the Lord of hosts?

I urge you brothers, to be able to say those words with confidence and actually abide by them for your sake and for God's glory. "Didn't you know that I had to be in my Father's house?" As the first question and answer of the Westminster Shorter Catechism states, "What is the chief end of man? Man's chief end is to glorify God and to enjoy Him forever." Simple as that folks. That is our chief objective, to glorify God and enjoy Him forever, so we might as well start now.

July 1

"You will keep in perfect peace him whose mind is steadfast, because he trusts in you. Trust in the Lord God forever, for the Lord, the Lord, is the Rock eternal" – Isaiah 26:3-4

This past week, it has been hard to fall asleep at night because as soon as my head hit the pillow, my mind started racing. Night after night this occurred and it greatly affected my sleep; it did not help that I had to be up at 2:30 the following morning for work. I guess there were more things my mind was worried about than I thought, causing the restless maneuvering of my brain.

However, it does not have to be this way. I was unusually stressed about a few things and I never really get stressed so I was not used to it. But with these anxieties and cares, we must, I repeat *must,* give them to the Lord. He is ever the only one who can keep our mind in perfect peace and contentment. What is this perfect peace? Nothing less than having our trust be in the Lord God for every facet of our lives. From relationships to work to family matters to things outside of our control (which is more than what is actually in our control), we must bear them upon the Lord who alone can do what is best and make us light again.

The prophet also mentions that with this perfect peace, this contentment of the soul because One who is greater is in control, our mind has to be steadfast, unwavering and resolute in the statutes of God and who He is. This can be accomplished through the renewing of the mind (Romans 12:2) and the continual labor of the Holy Spirit within. It can also be done by reading the Scriptures and meditating on them. I have always found the Psalms to be great at setting my mind straight and thrusting peace upon it.

When we begin to trust in God as our Rock, we too shall be a rock, a living stone (1 Peter 2:5) that is strong so when the tempest of life comes, we shall be firm and steadfast in the winds and rain and we will not falter (Matthew 7:24-25). No matter what this world throws at you or what the devil tempts you with, you shall stand strong in the Lord God, the Rock eternal, if you remain in Him and trust Him like you have never trusted anyone or anything else. Everyday most of us trust our cars to take us to and from work without even thinking about it, yet our cars break down every now and then, so we fix them, and continue to trust them. God never breaks down; so why do we not trust Him like we do our cars? We need to endlessly put our trust in Him because He has never failed us. He is much greater than all we can ask or imagine!

"Now faith is being sure of what we hope for and certain of what we do not see. This is what the ancients were commended for" – Hebrews 11:1-2

The eleventh chapter of the Book of Hebrews is commonly referred to as the Hall of Faith because it is all about the heroes of the faith in the Old Testament. From God's creation, to the patriarchs and on to the Age of Kings, this chapter moves forth the notion that the ancients did wonderful things with God in their lives because they lived by faith in the unseen God.

But what is this faith? Is it a strong belief in God and the things He is and stands for? Is it a conviction that the Holy Scriptures are true and reliable and relevant today? Or is it an unwavering trust in God that will compel us to do great things that we would not otherwise do? I would say all of the above. It takes faith to believe in a God we cannot see and to rely on a book that was written by multiple authors over many centuries. And it also takes faith to do things that are out of our control, to trust in Someone who is in control and has the most caring and grace-filled hands that always has the end goal in sight as He sees the end from the beginning because He is outside of time.

The author of Hebrews, whom scholars believe to be Apollos, wrote that "faith is being sure of what we hope for and certain of what we do not see." In other words, faith is the lifestyle of banking on God that everything that was written about Him and Christ is true, that He really did die on the cross and rose from the dead to release us from the bondage of sin so we may be justified before the Father and sanctified by the Spirit and glorified through Christ. It is all unseen my friends, this truth, we cannot prove it, but we accept it as truth because of the Holy Spirit's nudging on our souls.

We can be sure of this hope that is unseen because of what Paul wrote to the Romans; "But hope that is seen is no hope at all. Who hopes for what he already has? But if we hope for what we do not yet have, we wait for it patiently" (Romans 8:24-25). We have this blessed assurance, this promise that allows us to live Christ-like lives, believing that the One we have faith in, Christ, is true and will do what He says He will do for those who believe. This is faith. This is hope. This is love. Brothers, we must not be afraid to believe wholeheartedly in the Christ of the Scriptures, to fall head over heels over the Savior who is Lord of our lives and gave Himself for us that we might be with Him. Are our lives characterized as living by faith? Or are they exemplified as only believing what can be confirmed by our senses and experiences? Believing is seeing.

"By faith we understand that the universe was formed at God's command, so that what is seen was not made from what was visible" - Hebrews 11:3

This goes right along with what was being said yesterday, that an aspect of faith is having hope in what is said in the Scriptures, that it is indeed absolute truth and not just an intriguing mythical story that some come to believe, even those who claim to be followers of Christ. They believe that the creation account in Genesis is similar to other Ancient Near Eastern creation stories, so it cannot be taken literally, but more like a parable of the Gospels.

But I am here to tell you friends that "In the beginning God created the heavens and the earth" (Genesis 1:1). This is not a myth, nor a legend, but it is historical and it is truth. Adam and Eve really were the first people created and those in the New Testament treat them as such because they are the reason why Christ came because of the Fall in the garden. And it is only by faith that we can recognize it as truth. If you profess to be a believer, a child of God, and you cannot believe that God said "Let there be light…Let there be an expanse between the waters…Let the land produce vegetation…Let the water teem with living creatures…Let the land produce living creatures…Let us make man in our image, in our likeness" (Genesis 1:3,6,11,20,24,26), what other parts of the Bible do you not believe as truth?

We are told not to "devote [ourselves] to myths…have nothing to do with godless myths and old wives' tales" (1 Timothy 1:4, 4:7), but to devote ourselves to Christ and His Word. And this can only be done through faith in Him. This verse alone in Hebrews goes against what some more modern scholars believe, that God made the world from primordial chaos, one of the reasons being that they simply cannot conceive of something being formed out of nothing. But I believe in the concept of *creation ex nihilo,* or creation out of nothing, that by God's words in the formless void, the world and everything in it came to be.

Faith is being sure of what we hope for and certain of what we do not see. We were not there at the creation of the world, so we cannot know for certain that what Genesis and the rest of the Scriptures say on the matter of the formation of the universe is in fact truth, but we can believe and have faith that what God said happened did indeed happen, exuding His limitless power and sovereignty. What say you on the matter? Is the Word of God indeed the very word of God in how you are living your life?

"By faith Abel offered God a better sacrifice than Cain did. By faith he was commended as a righteous man, when God spoke well of his offerings. And by faith he still speaks, even though he is dead" – Hebrews 11:4

This story of Cain and Abel occurs in Genesis 4 and if you do not recall it, here is a brief summary: Cain is Abel's older brother and he worked the ground while Abel kept the flocks. Cain offered a sacrifice to the Lord of some of his fruits whereas Abel offered some of the fat from the firstborn of his flock, and God favored Abel's offering, so Cain became angry and killed his brother.

Why did Abel offer a better sacrifice than Cain? Does God like fatty steaks more than He likes luscious fruits or hearty grains? Unlikely. However, we are told that it was by faith that Abel offered his sacrifice to the Lord, and so in contrast Cain did not. But how was Abel's sacrifice offered in faith? Maybe it was because he actually chose something of value to give to the Lord like the fat portions, which were considered the best pieces of meat and most valuable. It may have also been that he presented the fat portions of the firstborn of the flock, indicating that the entire flock belonged to the Lord and he trusted Him with it.

After reading the story of Cain and Abel however, it is quite easy to recognize why Abel's offering was accepted and Cain's rejected because following Cain's rejection, he became extremely angry to the point of him killing his own brother. If he had offered his sacrifice in faith to the Lord and was still rejected, I do not believe he would have killed Abel since he would have hopefully trusted God with the sacrifice and that would have been enough for him. The writer of Hebrews merely tells us that it is by faith that Abel's sacrifice was better than Cain's and that he was commended as a righteous man, and so we must believe that the writer was inspired by the Holy Spirit to make such a truthful claim. And so by faith, trusting in our Creator, we must offer Him our best. Here is an excerpt from a hymn by Frank von Christierson:

In gratitude and humble trust
we bring our best today,
to serve your cause and share your love
with all humanity.
O God, who gave yourself to us
in Jesus Christ your Son,
teach us to give ourselves each day
until life's work is done.

"By faith Enoch was taken from this life, so that he did not experience death; he could not be found, because God had taken him away. For before he was taken, he was commended as one who pleased God" – Hebrews 11:5

Enoch is only mentioned in a few verses but he was still considered a man of faith, yet he was only one of two men who never had to experience death, the other being Elijah (2 Kings 2:11). Enoch came from the line of Seth, Adam's third son, and he was "the seventh from Adam" (Jude 14), the number of completeness. We do not know much more about Enoch other than he "walked with God 300 years...then he was no more, because God took him away" (Genesis 5:22,24).

He is contrasted with all the others in Adam's line in Genesis 5 however, as the rest are said to have lived and died, while Enoch was said to have walked with God and was taken away. None of the others are even said to have known God, yet alone walked with Him. Why was Enoch chosen to be taken from earth and not have to experience death like everyone else? We know that he was one who pleased God, but so have countless others mentioned in this chapter, yet they all were given over to death. Once again, the only tangible answer was that he lived by faith and God chose for him not to undergo death. We cannot fully understand the Lord's ways nor do we need to.

But I believe that he possibly was spared from physical death so that he could give us a glimpse of the followers of Christ not having to experience the second death that will come upon the world as mentioned on June 12. This occurrence confirms that there is in fact another world that they went off to, heaven. "And without faith, it is impossible to please God, because anyone who comes to him must believe that he exists and that he rewards those who earnestly seek him" (11:6).

Because Enoch pleased God and walked with Him, that was proof of his faith. For there to be faith, there must be a confidence that God is certainly there and if there is any distrust or jealousy on our part, there will be discord and misery and faith will be no more. We believe that God does exist and that is why we are able to come to Him. How can God be pleased in a man who has no confidence or trust in Him? If we do not trust that the promises of God are true and that He is who He says He is, how can we have faith in Him? We must put our confidence in the only One who is worthy of such confidence and dependence. Are we walking with God like Enoch where God is pleased with us, or are we like his forefathers who merely lived and died without believing that God rewards those who seek His face?

"By faith Noah, when warned about things not yet seen, in holy fear built an ark to save his family. By faith he condemned the world and became heir of the righteousness that comes by faith" – Hebrews 11:7

"Noah found favor in the eyes of the Lord" (Genesis 6:8). Noah was a man like us; a child of God who stood out in the world because He did not live as they did. The world and its evil inclinations were growing and the shadows were taking over the light up to the point where "The Lord was grieved that he had made man on the earth, and his heart was filled with pain" (Genesis 6:6). He wanted to destroy the men and creatures He had made, but Noah indeed found favor in His eyes.

The Lord could have just destroyed everyone, but He gave instructions to Noah to build an ark with which he could save his family and creatures of every kind. Why save them? Why not simply start over afresh? Because even though God is a God of justice, He is also a God of mercy and He trusted Noah because "Noah was a righteous man, blameless among the people of his time, and he walked with God" (Genesis 6:9).

Noah must have appeared as a lunatic before his peers, since it took him probably around seventy years to build the ark, all for a flood that was supposedly going to happen over the whole earth. But faith in God looks like that sometimes and not only to unbelievers, but other followers of Christ as well. Faith may seem foolish, especially if you are saying the world is going to flood and you have been saying it for nearly a century and not even a drop of rain had yet fallen. Think of the movie *Evan Almighty,* which is the modern-day version of Noah's story and how everyone around him doubted what he had been told by God, even his own wife and kids.

Faith in God *will* do that to you. When you are told something by God, if it lines up with Scriptures and you are convinced in your heart by the Spirit, *do not* let anyone persuade you otherwise what you have been told. They may say that whatever He had told you is wrong and unwise, but do not waver or give in; play it out and prove them wrong by having your faith come to fruition. My brothers, "the righteous will live by his faith" (Habakkuk 2:4). Noah continued to build the ark God told him to build, despite what was happening around him, which was no flood or any sign of it. He, by faith, believed in what was to come because the Lord he has been walking with told him so. They were close. Are you close to Christ so that you are walking and believing in the promises He has told you, although you see nothing of it at the moment?

"By faith Abraham, when called to go to a place he would later receive as his inheritance, obeyed and went, even though he did not know where he was going" - Hebrews 11:8

Abraham is seen as the patriarch of faith, considering he has eight verses mentioned of him and his faith in Hebrews 11. Paul said that Abraham "is the father of all who believe" (Romans 4:11) because "Abraham believed God, and it was credited to him as righteousness" (Romans 4:3).

God had told Abraham to "leave your country, your people and your father's household and go to the land I will show you" (Genesis 12:1). That sounds like he might need some faith for that. If God told you right now to quit your job, sell your house, get in your car and drive to where He tells you, leaving behind everything you have ever known, all the people you consider friends, everything familiar and comfortable, and go to a place unbeknownst to you and do something that you know not of, would you do it? Would you, like Abraham, just get up and leave as the Lord told him? Would you at any moment doubt that this was what you should do, or think that perhaps you have misheard what God asked of you?

We do not know what went on through Abraham's mind or heart in the matter, but we do know that He obeyed what the Lord had told him. He went even though he did not know where he was going. Obedience is the prerequisite to walking by faith in Christ. If we cannot obey, we cannot have faith in the invisible God because we do not obey for the reason that we see something, but because we are told something. And we are to do what we are told by God because He is our Maker and our Father if we have been redeemed by His blood.

Abraham made it to the Promised Land after journeying through lands he knew nothing about because He saw Him who was invisible. He made it his home because of the promise the Lord had spoken to him. Hebrews says that "he lived in tents...for he was looking forward to the city with foundations whose architect and builder is God" (11:9-10). He held the Lord's promise in his heart as he voyaged across the land, keeping the end goal in sight, pushing him further, believing he will be in a better place one day, and he made it there. He made it to the even better place, the heavenly Jerusalem whose builder and maker is God Himself, whose walls will never fall down and whose food supply never suffers. This is living by faith. Are you being obedient to what the Lord has called you to do, despite whether you think it impossible or not?

"By faith Abraham, even though he was past age—Sarah herself was barren—was enabled to become a father because he considered him faithful who had made the promise" - Hebrews 11:11

Why is it that God loves making the impossible possible? Is it that He enjoys blowing people's expectations or proving them wrong? Or possibly that He does not want them to have a limiting view of Him? I think all of the above are good reasons, especially the last one because God cannot be limited since He is limitless, omnipotent. Abraham, the father of faith, did not always believe God wholeheartedly.

After God told Abraham that his wife Sarah would have a son, he "fell facedown; he laughed and said to himself, 'Will a son be born to a man a hundred years old?'" (Genesis 17:17). Sarah was no exception, she also laughed after hearing the words of the Lord that she would bear a child at ninety years of age and while being barren. God's response to her laughter is priceless, and it is His response to us as well: "Is anything too hard for the Lord?" (Genesis 18:14). A rhetorical question of course with the answer of no, "For nothing is impossible with God" (Luke 1:37) and "This is an easy thing in the eyes of the Lord" (2 Kings 3:18).

And yet, despite Abraham and Sarah's unbelief, God still allowed the miraculous to flow into their lives, and we learn from our verse that it was by faith that he was chosen as the father of whom the Lord's covenant would come forth. Out of Sarah's barrenness, out of the death within her womb, the Lord brought life, and not just any life, but life that would bring the Lord's promise to realization, which is to have descendants like the sand on the seashore and life and blessing for all who believe.

From this one act of God came countless who would believe in His name. And do not think that these are rare occurrences of barren women having children, for the Lord continues to do these deeds every day. He thrives in the impossible because our minds are so limiting, so doubting and He wants to change how we think so that we can come to trust Him for anything and everything. That is living by faith, believing God when the odds are against you, and if you think about it, the odds usually are against you. But remember you have the King of kings on your side, and the Spirit of God within us to make us holy and pure. Never doubt the Word of the Lord for it is never false and it *will always* come to fulfillment.

"All these people were still living by faith when they died. They did not receive the things promised; they only saw them and welcomed them from a distance" - Hebrews 11:13

Did these patriarchs of faith know that they would not receive what they had hoped for? Of course not. That is what kept pushing them further in their walks with the Lord and doing what needed to be done because they saw the promise given them at a distance and strived for it because He who gave it is right and true.

And that is the essence of faith my friends; confidence in the Lord that what He says will in fact come to pass. Think of *The Lord of the Rings* for instance: the people of the West were hoping that the One Ring of power would be destroyed in Mount Doom and that Sauron and the dominance of evil would be abolished forever. Some of them believed in a young hobbit from the Shire to help make this happen, but there were many who had lived their entire lives in expectation of its destruction and never saw it come. They dreamed and foresaw a better world free from darkness, and several times even came close to its fruition, yet still fell short, but that did not impede them from believing that it will happen someday.

So it was with Abel, Enoch, Noah, Abraham, and the ones to come; they anticipated the dimly lit promises of the Lord and even when their lives were coming to a close and they still did not have the promise in their hands, they nonetheless walked by faith and not by sight. What is more is that they believed in the resurrection, ultimately, the resurrection of Christ and even their own because they were still clinging on to the promise when they died, believing that they would see the promise fulfilled although they are dead.

There is much hope in that promise and much faith as well. And even more love as their trust and dependence is shown through their lifelong dedication to the Lord despite not seeing the fruit of the covenant. Is there something in your life that Christ has promised you that you cannot yet grasp? You can see it far away, but you cannot grab a hold of it so far. I am here to tell you that Christ Jesus Himself is that promise, who dwells within you and whom you will surely see face to face in the life to come, if you are His child. Do not quit, do not stop living by faith, but rather keep Him in your sights, knowing that He is worthy of it all and will reward you fully. Stay strong brothers. Be men of faith.

"If they had been thinking of the country they had left, they would have had opportunity to return. Instead, they were longing for a better country—a heavenly one. Therefore God is not ashamed to be called their God, for he has prepared a city for them" - Hebrews 11:15-16

They dreamed of more than what was presently with them. They saw beyond their predicament and with help of the Spirit were able to envision a city in which they would no longer be aliens or strangers, but citizens and even part of the King's family. What made these men great was that they had not constantly been thinking of where they had been, but were intently focused on where they were going to be because they inspirationally knew that this life was not all there was, that there was indeed a heavenly country awaiting them.

This heavenly country is the fulfillment that these men were waiting for and they are now there, as we also shall be if Christ Jesus is the Lord and Savior of our lives. When you hear of this heavenly city, what comes to mind? For me, I picture a giant castle on a hill, with rolling hills surrounding it, with forests beyond that which include rivers and lakes, and then soaring mountains in the distance; a place where the sun never sets because "The city does not need the sun or moon to shine on it, for the glory of God gives it light, and the Lamb is its lamp" (Revelation 21:23). It is a land full of song and dancing, joy and merriment because the Lamb of God is presently with us and absolutely nothing could be better. I long for that city. I long for that country. It is the culmination of everything we had ever hoped for on earth, yet we scarcely knew that was our hope.

So often we put our hope in things and ideas in this life and we strive for that which seems good and enduring, but is in fact trivial and then when our lives come to its end, we realize that everything we had hoped was misguided. Brothers, this is why our hope *must* be in Christ alone and not in things of this world, for they fade and do not bring life. Like the song *In Christ alone, my hope is found.* Not in the things Christ gives me, or in my friends or work, but in Christ alone. He can fulfill that longing within you because He truly is the One you are longing for whether you know it or not. He put that craving inside of you to so that other things will never truly bring you satisfaction, but disappointment. Christ said that He is preparing a place for you (John 14:2) in the city of our God if you believe in Him, that He died, rose again and ascended to the right hand of God the Father. Believe brothers, have faith in the only One who is faithful and can satiate your deepest longings.

"By faith Abraham, when God tested him, offered Isaac as a sacrifice. He who had received the promises was about to sacrifice his one and only son" - Hebrews 11:17

The devil tempts us to bring out the worst in us, while God tests us to bring out the best in us. "Remember how the Lord your God led you all the way in the desert these forty years, to humble you and to test you in order to know what was in your heart, whether or not you would keep his commands" (Deuteronomy 8:2). When God tests us, it is an opportunity for us to show our trust and faithfulness to Him, which in turn will make us more like Him if we pass the test. These tests happen every day in both big and small ways, and that is why we must be "making the most of every opportunity" (Ephesians 5:16).

Abraham had waited twenty-five years until part of the promise given him even came in view, and that through his son Isaac. However, God told Abraham to sacrifice the promise he had waited for, through which the covenant God gave him would be fulfilled. But notice how there is not a single verse or word that mentions Abraham questioning God through this. Abraham had waited for this son for a long time and now God was asking him to give it all up? That does not make sense, but Abraham followed through with it until the Lord had him stop just before he tried to kill him.

He passed the test. Abraham understood that obeying God, who gave him Isaac in the first place, was more important to him than the promised heir. I have come to believe that if Abraham did follow through with sacrificing his one and only son, he knew that God could resurrect him from the dead because he was one who lived by faith in the God who had never led him astray. And I know this because "Abraham reasoned that God could raise the dead, and figuratively speaking, he did receive Isaac back from death" (11:19).

I honestly do not know what I would have done in that situation. I believe that I would have reasoned myself out of thinking that God wanted me to sacrifice my son because He is God and He does not like murder so I would have thrown away the whole notion of it. But Abraham reasoned better than I because his faith was vibrant and strong. He was one who worshiped the Promiser and not the promise. Like I have said before, the things given us can fade away, but the Lord never will. He alone shall be the object of our desires, not things of this life. God may call you to sacrifice the thing we love most, the thing promised, even though He is the one who promised it. Our love for God must supersede every other love, as Abraham's did and Christ's did. If God asked you to give up something you love deeply, would you?

"By faith Isaac blessed Jacob and Esau in regard to their future" – Hebrews 11:20

If you do not know the story of Jacob and Esau, read Genesis 25 and 27. The name of Jacob means "to grasp the heel" or "he deceives" and that is rightly so for that is what he did. He had first deceived Esau into giving him his birthright as firstborn and later he deceived Isaac into giving him the blessing also intended for the firstborn Esau. So how can it say that it was by faith that Isaac blessed them when it clearly seems to be by the deception of Jacob that they were blessed?

Let us look deeper into the story shall we. When Esau sold his birthright to Jacob for a bowl of soup, Esau was not in the right state of mind because we are told that he was famished (Genesis 25:29) and if you have ever gone without food for awhile and tried to make an important decision, you know that food is really the only thing on your mind. This is why we should not let our appetites control us, whether that is for food, success, pleasure, relaxation, but we must be in control of them. Do not, like Esau, give up something of great importance for something temporary.

But what is oft overlooked in this is that the Lord did tell Isaac's wife Rebekah that "Two nations are in your womb, and two peoples from within you will be separated; one people will be stronger than the other, and the older will serve the younger" (Genesis 25:23). It may have not been recognized, but God did tell her that Jacob would indeed rule over Esau, so the only way for that to happen would be to get the birthright and blessing from Isaac. Why did God not just have Jacob be the firstborn so that he would not have to deceive his father and brother? I do not know, but it is something to think about.

However, Isaac by faith blessed Jacob and Esau each according to what was revealed to him by the Lord. And they were prophetically spoken since they both came to be true and they were binding. The future things that were spoken of Jacob, or Israel, were taken literally as blessings were and were taken by faith because their fulfillment was not in sight, thus satisfying the definition that "faith is being sure of what we hope for and certain of what we do not see." Isaac was sure of it when he gave each their blessing, even though it was not as he thought, but the words spoken were legally binding and would happen. He did what he thought was right because he was living by faith, believing his blessings to his children would come true and the covenant made to his father concerning his heirs would be realized. Know that God works through you in ways that you know not of in the moment, but see its true power and truth down the road as you continually walk with Him. All truth is revealed in hindsight.

"By faith Jacob, when he was dying, blessed each of Joseph's sons, and worshiped as he leaned on the top of his staff" - Hebrews 11:21

The faith of an old man is priceless. To see someone who has lived a long life, gone through trials and tribulations, and can still wake up in the morning and praise the Lord, living a life of faith, that is wonderful. After seeing life at its best and its worst, they continue on in faith in the Lord. Jacob was no exception, since he knows what it means to endure, bearing in mind that he worked fourteen years for two wives and his favorite son was taken from him by his own brothers.

Not many know of the part of the story where Jacob blesses Joseph's two sons, Manasseh and Ephraim, which occurs in Genesis 48. He blesses Ephraim, the younger son, with the greater blessing as he himself being the younger was blessed, along with his favorite wife being the younger of two sisters. What is interesting here is that Jacob gives Joseph's sons the status of his own sons, and even greater than his two eldest. This is huge because now Manasseh and Ephraim are included among the tribes of Israel and have some of the largest portions of land.

But before he blessed Joseph's sons, he had Joseph swear to him that he would be buried with his fathers, and that is when he leaned and worshiped on his staff in reverence of the great and glorious God who has remained faithful to him through the end, allowing him to be buried in the land promised to his forefathers. One commentary mentioned that even though the order in this verse is not chronologically accurate, it may have been that way to show how Isaac performed the former and the latter will be done by Joseph. Faith was before and after Jacob, and it shall continue on for many generations to come.

By believing in his son to bury him in the land of the promise, he had faith the promise would indeed come to fulfillment. His sons would later become the twelve tribes of Israel, the Promised Land indeed. Jacob trusted the Lord with his life, as is evident by his encounters with Him, with his dream at Bethel and his wrestling match. I do not know why the writer of Hebrews chose this story of Jacob's to emphasize his faith in God, possibly because it had to deal with the covenant promise and its accomplishment. Just because you do not see something happening, that does not mean it is not happening. Always keep in mind the first verse of this chapter.

"By faith Joseph, when his end was near, spoke about the exodus of the Israelites from Egypt and gave instructions about his bones" – Hebrews 11:22

I love how these ancients stood by the Lord for all the years of their long lives. For Isaac, Jacob, and now Joseph, their mentions of faith in Hebrews 11 are regarded as occurring as they were on their deathbeds. And with Isaac and Jacob, it was about them blessing their children, but with Joseph, it was concerning the whole of the people of God and the promise given his forefathers and their trek to the Promised Land.

I believe that when one's end is near, they have such clarity of life that we cannot comprehend. They know their time is coming to a close and so their priorities are in proper view, unlike ours which are clouded by everyday trivialities and nonsense, ever-changing depending on our mood and circumstances. But Joseph, when his end was in sight, was reminded of his father's words, "but God will be with you and take you back to the land of your fathers" (Genesis 48:21) because he said on his deathbed that "God will surely come to your aid and take you up out of this land to the land he promised on oath to Abraham, Isaac and Jacob" (Genesis 50:24).

This could have only been spoken in faith on Joseph's part since there was no end in sight of his people leaving Egypt because at this point in time, the Israelites were welcomed there. It was only after Joseph died and the Hebrew people began multiplying greatly in Egypt that Pharaoh had made the people slaves to try and diminish their numbers. Even though nothing was visible and there was no sign of their slavery, Joseph foresaw that his people would not always be welcomed in the land of Egypt. Only God could have spoken these words to him. They might have even sounded crazy since he was second in command of all of the land and God told him all that would change.

How do you react when you hear something from God that makes absolutely no sense? Do you inquire further, doubt, or do you trust it in spite of the facts surrounding you? You must remember however the fact that God is outside of time and is all-knowing and He says that "my word that goes out from my mouth; It will not return to me empty, but will accomplish what I desire and achieve the purpose for which I sent it" (Isaiah 55:11). Do not be afraid to listen to the voice of the Lord and follow through with it. They are words of truth and they are hope to those who need it. Put your hope in God.

"By faith Moses' parents hid him for three months after he was born, because they saw he was no ordinary child, and they were not afraid of the king's edict" - Hebrews 11:23

Parents have the knack of noticing things about their children that no one else can see, for they are closer to them than anyone else because they sprang from their loins. For instance, we came from God and we are His. He is our Father and He sees the deep things in us that He put there and He notices our potential and what we may become.

And so it was with Moses' parents, who saw that their son was no ordinary child even though he was just a baby. The Spirit of the Lord told them that he was someone special and more than just their own son. By putting him in the basket, which was like an ark for him in the waters of the Nile, his parents believed he would be alright and no harm would befall him. They could not know for sure what would happen to Moses once they placed him in the river, but their faith and trust was in the Lord that he would be protected and their faith rewarded.

Their confidence in the Lord allowed them to not fear the edict of the king, which was to murder all newborn Hebrew boys by throwing them into the Nile because the Hebrew population was becoming too vast for the Egyptians to handle and Pharaoh feared an uprising. How courageous of them to stand against the king's proclamation and not fear his thousand chariots, countless other horsemen and foot soldiers, and the might of his wrath.

Two ordinary parents stood up to the king of one of the most powerful nations in history because they had faith in the Word of the Lord that was spoken to them concerning their son. They trusted what they heard because who it was from. They knew they were rebelling against the king's orders, but they knew even more that they had to obey the King of kings' orders, who alone was the master of their lives. Heed Joshua's words saying, "choose for yourselves this day whom you will serve...but as for me and my household, we will serve the Lord" (Joshua 24:15) and Peter's declaration that "We must obey God rather than men!" (Acts 5:29). Whom will you serve? A worldly king who does not have your best interests in mind, or the King of the universe who never forsakes those who seek Him (Psalm 9:10)?

"By faith Moses, when he had grown up, refused to be known as the son of Pharaoh's daughter. He chose to be mistreated along with the people of God rather than to enjoy the pleasures of sin for a short time. He regarded disgrace for the sake of Christ as of greater value than the treasures of Egypt, because he was looking ahead to his reward" – Hebrews 11:24-26

Moses was forty years old at this point (Acts 7:23), so he had lived a long time in Pharaoh's palace. He grew in the wisdom and education of the Egyptians, becoming strong and leading armies as Pharaoh's grandson. He *was* in fact an Egyptian in all ways except by blood. His lifestyle was most likely full of sin and pleasure, having everything in the kingdom at his disposal with his mother being the daughter of the king. But when he got older, something within him clicked; he had grown up watching the Egyptians beat the Hebrews, but this time, after seeing that happen, he chose to kill the Egyptian and help his fellow people.

But they did not see it as such. They rejected him and he fled the land. I do not know if he knew why he did what he did, but we know that it was by faith that God stirred within him something deep, a yearning for justice and the deliverance of his people from slavery. He lived the high life, why would he just throw it all away for the sake of his people? He could have merely ignored the oppression like many do today and go on their merry ways, but he did not. He chose to leave. He chose to be counted among and mistreated with his people because of the presence and words of the Lord given him in the account of the burning bush. God spoke life into him then and told him to go to Pharaoh to release His chosen people.

He was never the same after that encounter. How can he be, after being in the very presence of the Living God, the God of his ancestors? No one has ever said words like that, words with such weight and authority that gave him a purpose in life, not just shepherding the flocks in Midian. Moses saw that his pleasurable life in Egypt was a fleeting vapor, absolutely nothing compared to the notion of liberating his people, the people of God, from the oppression of those whom he grew up with. He decided to become nothing in the eyes of his former peers for the sake of Christ and His chosen people because he was told that they would dwell in the Promised Land, "a land flowing with milk and honey" (Exodus 3:17). Are you willing to throw it all away, all the things you worked for your entire life, all your ideologies and desires, for the sake of Christ and following His desires, looking ahead to your reward that He offers?

"By faith he left Egypt, not fearing the king's anger; he persevered because he saw him who is invisible. By faith he kept the Passover and the sprinkling of blood, so that the destroyer of the firstborn would not touch the firstborn of Israel" – Hebrews 11:27-28

When someone wants you dead, you do not normally stay around in their vicinity because well, they could kill you. But that did not scare Moses. He stayed around for a bit while God brought forth ten plagues upon the Egyptians because Pharaoh would not let the Lord's people go. What gave this man such courage, while forty years earlier he found himself fleeing the king? He saw the burning bush and heard the voice of the Lord speak! He realized then why his parents did not fear the king because they saw something in him and believed that their people would be freed and the covenant of the Lord would be accomplished. He saw Him who was invisible and simply seeing Him and witnessing His power in the plagues gave him the faith to believe that his people will go the Promised Land.

The Passover in Exodus 12 is the first Passover for the Hebrew people. It was when the Lord would "pass over" all the land and would not kill the firstborn in the houses with the blood of the lamb they slaughtered on the doorframe. From Hebrews we identify that it was only by faith that the people believed when the Lord saw the blood, he would not kill them. As you know, this is a foreshadowing to Christ in our lives, where because He shed His blood for us on the cross, God's judgment passed from us to Him because God sees the blood of His Son, thus extending His mercy to us. "Mercy triumphs over judgment!" (James 2:13).

Moses was a man inspired by the Spirit of the Lord. He walked in His ways and conversed with Him constantly, being led by His instructions. He had confidence that God would spare the children of Israel if they did what He commanded, and it was so. He saw Him who was invisible; he saw what would become of his people if he did not do what he knew he had to, which was to stand up to Pharaoh with command presence and the Lord's authority. He was certain of things unseen, which was his people's deliverance, acquirement of the land promised to their forefathers, and ultimately of the Messiah's coming. Even though we physically cannot see the day of His return, do we live our lives as if He is indeed returning and rewarding men according to the things they have done?

"By faith the people passed through the Red Sea as on dry land; but when the Egyptians tried to do so, they were drowned" – Hebrews 11:29

The people of Israel were freed from the oppression of the Egyptians, but then Pharaoh changed his mind because of all the labor he had now lost with the Israelites gone. So he chased them across the desert and the Israelites panicked, but Moses reassured them, "Do not be afraid. Stand firm and you will see the deliverance the Lord will bring you today" (Exodus 14:13). He then raised his staff over the sea and it divided, allowing the people of God to crossover on dry land, and then did the same after they crossed and it collapsed on the whole army pursuing them.

That is daring to think about. You start walking towards the Red Sea, then there are pillars of water on both sides of you because the Lord is holding it up, so you walk through the sea. What if it fell back down while you were still crossing over? What if the Lord was not strong enough to keep it up for such a long time? But my friends, He is strong enough and the people of Israel believed the water would stay divided until they had finished crossing. We are told that "the people feared the Lord and put their trust in him and in Moses his servant" (Exodus 14:31). They would not have been able to cross and live if they had not had faith in the Lord because no amount of their insignificant human strength would have allowed them to cross the sea without the Lord's mighty hand.

The Israelites' faith must have constantly been growing ever since Moses showed up on the scene after Midian because the Ten Plagues cast upon Egypt had to show the people of Israel that there is but one God who alone is able to do the impossible; one God who alone can bring deliverance to His oppressed people, and one God who alone is worthy of their confidence and trust. But as their time in the wilderness goes on over the next forty years, the faith of many falter, regretting their choice of leaving Egypt because it was there they never had to worry about food or water or anything of that sort. In the desert they grew impatient of the Lord, wanting to just be in the Promised Land already, but His work with them was incomplete. He needed them to continually have faith in Him, to trust Him for absolutely everything and be totally dependent on Him. That is why the people of Israel were not mentioned again of having faith in God in this chapter because after the emotions of this event occurred, they lost it. But they had it for a brief time, indicating that even if you have faith in the Lord at one point in your life, that does not guarantee you will have it in another. Brothers, continue to put your faith in Him who never leaves you nor forsakes you. He has never steered you wrong, nor will He.

July 19

"By faith the walls of Jericho fell, after the people had marched around them for seven days" – Hebrews 11:30

Joshua was a man of God who always heeded His guidance. He was Moses' right hand man when wandering through the wilderness those forty years. He was one of the twelve spies that scoped out the land of Canaan to determine whether or not they could take it. He, along with Caleb, were the only spies to bring back a positive report on the land, knowing God has given it into their hands. They were also the only two people of the generation that left Egypt to make it to the Promised Land, all the others had died.

Jericho was a city where the people were stronger and taller, an oasis of a city with walls up to the sky (Deuteronomy 1:28). It seemed impossible to win a battle against them because of the pessimistic reports by the other ten spies, but the Israelites had God on their side and nothing is too hard for Him. Joshua and Caleb knew that. They were the leaders appointed by Moses to lead the Lord's people into the Promised Land. God loves to be put in situations where it seems as if the odds are against His people, and then has them do bizarre things so that the world will know that it was God and not man who won the battle.

God's battle strategy: to walk around Jericho for seven days and then blow their trumpets on the last day and the walls would come down. And it was so. The Israelites did not question this command from the Lord because just previously, He had all the people cross the Jordan River on dry land during flood stage. They trusted Him because He had never let them down, even in the desert, and that He would not let them down against the people of Jericho whose walls were impenetrable. They may have thought the Lord's command was peculiar and unorthodox, but they obeyed Him anyways, believing that when He said the town would be theirs, it in fact would be.

Has God recently told you anything that you second guessed yourself on? Has He told you to go and talk to someone about something completely random or go to a certain event that you would never have otherwise thought of attending? If so, try out what He said in faith, believing He did speak those words of truth to you. Obedience is one of the essential keys to faith in Christ. How can you trust someone you do not obey? Like the Israelites with Jericho, do not be afraid to do something silly for the Lord's sake. Take a chance at it and watch the Lord's provision burst forth.

"By faith the prostitute Rahab, because she welcomed the spies, was not killed with those who were disobedient" – Hebrews 11:31

Throughout the history of the world, people's enemies could not be trusted because they wish ill favor upon them and have different beliefs about life. They want to see them fail and be destroyed so they can live in peace and have their ideology reign supreme. Why would someone want to protect their enemies from harm? Maybe because they have come to realize that they are people with hearts and families just like us, who usually want peace for their loved ones as well.

Or like Rahab who did not live in fear of her enemies but heard of the might and presence of the Lord with the Israelites and risked her life by committing treason because she lied to the king and hid the spies of Israel. What right did she have to harbor the spies of her enemies? How could she trust them to not torture her for information or to keep their word on saving her and her family from the battle to come? It is only by faith brothers, faith in the One in whose name they came, the Name above all other names.

She put her faith in the God she had never met, who went against the gods of her people, and because of what He had done in Egypt and east of the Jordan to kings Og and Sihon (see Numbers 21), the people feared Him. They believed that "the Lord your God is God in heaven above and on the earth below" (Joshua 2:11) and that if He wanted to accomplish something, He would and there is nothing they could do about it.

So what about you? Rahab the prostitute, who later gets mentioned in the genealogy of Jesus in Matthew 1, a pagan, had faith in a God that was not her own and believed that His servants would keep their word to spare her family. She had faith in the goodness of the God who promised goodness to His people and has proved faithful in it. What does this look like? It may be as simple as trusting the word God has spoken to you as truth. It may seem odd what God wants you to do and go against your instincts and previous notions, but obedience is the key here. Are you willing to risk your life for the chance of a better one, although there is no tangible guarantee that will happen? Rahab did, the disciples did, and countless others have since then. Will you?

"And what more shall I say? I do not have time to tell about Gideon, Barak, Sampson, Jephthah, David, Samuel and the prophets" - Hebrews 11:32

Do you think that only those mentioned earlier were the ones who lived a life of faith? Not at all! There were countless more men and women who had dedicated their lives to the service of the King and walked by faith and not by sight.

" *Who through faith conquered kingdoms, administered justice, and gained what was promised; who shut the mouths of lions, quenched the fury of the flames, and escaped the edge of the sword; whose weakness was turned to strength; and who became powerful in battle and routed foreign armies. Women received back their dead, raised to life again. Others were tortured and refused to be released, so that they might gain a better resurrection. Some faced jeers and flogging, while still others were chained and put in prison. They were stoned; they were sawed in two; they were put to death by the sword. They went about in sheepskins and goatskins, destitute, persecuted and mistreated—the world was not worthy of them. They wandered in deserts and mountains, and in caves and holes in the ground" (11:33-38).*

What can we really say? The things that these heroes of faith had done were incredible. They had endured the most treacherous and repelling of situations, stood in the presence of kings, proclaiming their allegiance to the King with confidence, not fearing what was to come because they knew that their lives were in the hands of the Living God. I like what Shadrach, Meshach, and Abednego said to king Nebuchadnezzar, "If we are thrown into the blazing furnace, the God we serve is able to save us from it, and he will rescue us from your hand, O king. *But even if he does not*, we want you to know, O king, that we will not serve your gods or worship the image of gold you have set up" (Daniel 3:17-18, emphasis added).

God never promised any of us that bad things would never happen to us, that we would not undergo persecution and that He would save us from all forms of injustice and suffering. In fact, He said the opposite! "In this world you will have trouble" (John 16:33). "Blessed are you when people insult you, persecute you" (Matthew 5:11). "Do not be surprised at the painful trial you are suffering, as though something strange were happening to you" (1 Peter 4:12). "In fact, everyone who wants to live a godly life in Christ Jesus will be persecuted" (2 Timothy 3:12). My brothers, we are indeed overcomers through faith in the Lord Jesus Christ (1 John 4:4). I say to you, do not fear what this world will throw at you, for they will throw all sorts of things in your direction, but you must remember Whose you are and Who you are living for. Keep your eyes on Christ on His throne in heaven, for He is our prime example of overcoming the world. Do not compare your faith to these men, but put your faith in Christ as they did, seeing beyond their present and onto the future.

"These were all commended for their faith, yet none of them received what had been promised. God had planned something better for us so that only together with us would they be made perfect" – Hebrews 11:39-40

At last we come to the end of this series on the heroes of faith from the Old Testament. Throughout all of their stories we have seen how by faith, they have accomplished remarkable tasks and things that are not normally occurring were happening in their lives and affecting those around them. They were commended for their acts and lives of faith, yet none of them had received what they were promised, which kept them going in the first place.

So what had been promised? The Promised Land was a promise to the early fathers, but those down the line dwelled in it, so they received that. Is it coincidental how the author stopped with the "By faith" verses after the Israelites had made it to the Promised Land, the land of milk and honey and rest? I do not think so. These heroes of the faith "saw [the promises] and welcomed them from a distance" (11:13) without having them come to pass. They embraced the idea that they would be fulfilled in future times, as Jesus told the Jews saying, "Your father Abraham rejoiced at the thought of seeing my day; he saw it and was glad" (John 8:56).

The others must have believed that that day would indeed be fulfilled as well. They all saw glimpses and aspects of the coming of the Christ because that is ultimately where their eyes and desires have been set, allowing them to persevere through the adversity of life. The fulfillment is Christ himself brothers, of seeing Him and dwelling with Him forever. They never had the whole picture, but only a "poor reflection as in a mirror" (1 Corinthians 13:12). They had faith that One was coming someday who would say "I am the resurrection and the life. He who believes in me will live, even though he dies; and whoever lives and believes in me will never die" (John 11:25-26).

But why did the writer of Hebrews give us this chapter? So that we can live a life of faith as they had and give us cool stories about them? We could just read the Old Testament to read these stories and see they had faith, so why bring them back up? He did this to show us how the ancients, who only had a limited and obscure view of these future blessings, were able to persevere through their trials, so how much more reason is there for us to persevere as we have the whole picture? Brothers, we can endure whatever the world throws at us if we continually "fix our eyes on Jesus, the author and perfecter of our faith" (12:2), being certain of what we do not see. He has the victory.

"The rest of mankind that were not killed by these plagues still did not repent of the works of their hands" – Revelation 9:20

These were the worst plagues to ever hit mankind. It was so devastating that it wiped out a third of the world's population. People were choking on and spitting out fire, smoke and sulfur. Those who were not killed I am sure were still severely injured and affected because this destruction was worldwide; those three plagues are penetrating and they linger. But we are told that regardless of all the death around them, the other two-thirds of mankind that were not killed still did not repent of the works of their hands.

This refers to the end times in Revelation and the sounding of the Seven Trumpets. The time is near for Christ's return and the culmination of His kingdom coming, which in turn means that the time is short and our time for repentance of sins is coming to a close. The worst possible pain and torture had just been inflicted upon the world, elements that continually eat at you, and in the midst of it all, they would not ask for forgiveness of their sins, although they knew that the reason this was happening was because of their wickedness. "An evil man is snared by his own sin" (Proverbs 29:6).

He is in bondage to it and on the surface he loves it more than anything else, but deep down, he knows his ways are wrong but since he knows no other way to live, he continues on in his wicked ways as they completely devour him, much like what the Ring of Power did to Gollum in *The Lord of the Rings*. The time of repentance is now brothers because you do not know the day or the hour of Christ's return and then it will be too late. "Repent, then, and turn to God, so that your sins may be wiped out, that times of refreshing may come from the Lord" (Acts 3:19). We are told that these men still "did not stop worshiping demons, and idols of gold, silver, bronze, stone and wood— idols that cannot see or hear or walk. Nor did they repent of their murders, their magic arts, their sexual immorality or their thefts" (9:20-21).

Later, more plagues came on the earth, "but they refused to repent and glorify him" (16:9) once again. Brothers, do not be like these people who see the wrath of God in their lives, understanding wholeheartedly that if they simply repented of their evil ways and turned to the Lord, they would be saved and would be able to spend eternity in heaven and not in tortuous hell. There have been too many people who have gone through life without humbling themselves and asking forgiveness for their sins. Talk to those around you. Pray for them to be saved, that the Holy Spirit will work in their hearts.

"I have posted watchmen on your walls, O Jerusalem; they will never be silent day or night. You who call on the Lord, give yourselves no rest, and give him no rest till he establishes Jerusalem and makes her the praise of the earth" – Isaiah 62:6-7

I confess that I have not been praying as I ought as a child of God and as His ambassador; that I have not been interceding for those in my life and in the world for the sake of Christ, but have in fact prayed more selfishly for the things in my everyday life. Father, forgive me of my selfishness in prayer to you, for continually asking you of things for my benefit while ignoring the needs of my friends and family. Humble me Father, that I may ask selflessly of you, knowing that you already take care of my needs. Help me in this, I need it. Amen.

Brothers, intercession is what the prophet Isaiah is getting at here, the watchmen on the walls who are never silent because they are calling on the Lord day and night for their city. Intercession is mediating or intervening on another person's behalf for their benefit. Christ "is at the right hand of God and is also interceding for us" (Romans 8:34), mediating between us and the Father in our defense. He knows that we are sinners, so He stood in the gap and "bore the sins of many, and made intercession for the transgressors" (53:12). And that is what we are called to do, to stand in the gap for the lost and the broken, to pray for their salvation that they may come to the knowledge and faith of Christ and share in His glory.

But there is more to that; we must also "keep on praying for all the saints" (Ephesians 6:18), that they may be sanctified everyday by the Spirit that makes us holy. We ought to not forget about our brothers and sisters throughout the world who are suffering and undergoing persecution, for those who are afraid to share their faith because of what others may think, and for the new believers in the faith that they may become mature in the knowledge and wisdom of Christ and follow sound doctrine. The majority of Paul's letters deal with this type of prayer in some regards, teaching us to pray continually (1 Thessalonians 5:17) for God's work and will to be done in this world. So you know how selfish my prayer life has been, how about yours? Is it full of requests and needs for yourself to make your life easier, or is it full of grace and truth that other's burdens may be lightened and that mercy may overflow into their lives? I pray for the latter.

"Not to us, O Lord, not to us but to your name be the glory, because of your love and faithfulness" - Psalm 115:1

One of my old football coaches had this as his motto for his players, reminding us that even though we want to win the football game and play to the best of our abilities, we had to make sure that everything we were doing was for the Lord's glory and not our own. It is especially easy in a sports environment to do things for our own pride and glory, which he understood full well, thus teaching us this verse to keep in mind at all times.

In our American society of meritocracy and success-focused ideology, the Psalmist's words are faint and distant, trying to pierce through the dense fog of selfishness and conceit that is blinding the nation, including those of the faith. We are letting our culture affect us instead of us affecting our culture. It is seeping through the cracks and into our lives in such subtlety that we do not notice it unless others point it out. C.S. wrote in *The Screwtape Letters* that "the safest road to Hell is the gradual one—the gentle slope, soft underfoot, without sudden turnings, without milestones, without signposts." The moment you see a sin in your life, repent and turn to the Lord. Do not let it gain a foothold and open the door for more heinous acts.

"Not to us, O Lord, not to us but to your name be the glory." That should be our frame of mind for every thought and word and action that we have and do. We should be thinking to ourselves, "Is what I am doing or about to do bringing glory to God or to myself?" This is how we ought to approach everything in our lives. We came from God. "It is he who made us, and we are his; we are his people, the sheep of his pasture" (100:3).

"Whatever you do, whether in word or deed, do it all in the name of the Lord Jesus Christ, giving thanks to God the Father through him" (Colossians 3:17). Once we fully realize that the earth is the Lord's and everything in it and all things are to bestow to Him the glory due His name, we can then live a life of true worth and importance because we would not be living for ourselves and our desires anymore, but for the Lord and His desires. Our wills and longings would be molded into His so that we will begin to think and act as He would in everyday life, bringing love and joy and life everywhere our feet take us. This will bring glory to His name and not our own because of His love and faithfulness that transforms us into His likeness. Is God getting the glory in your life?

"Even youths grow tired and weary, and young men stumble and fall; but those who hope in the Lord will renew their strength" – Isaiah 40:30-31

Young people have this tendency to believe that they are invincible and that nothing bad could ever happen to them. They see themselves as being on top of the world and no one can dethrone them. "The world is my footstool" they say, so they will treat it as such, with no respect for anyone or anything that hinders them from doing what their young and immature minds set out to. But what they fail to realize is that as soon as something bad actually does happen, their worldview shatters and then they are shown their true selves and their place in the world.

The prophet Isaiah is teaching us here that youth really do grow tired and weak, even though they are in the prime of their strength. All the strength they think they have will in fact fail them at one point or another because they are human and their hope is in their own abilities and might which have limits. However, God's abilities and might are inexhaustible and never fail. "He will not grow tired or weary, and his understanding no one can fathom" (40:28), but He does give "strength to the weary and increases the power of the weak" (40:29) because they know they are weak and not invincible. He tells those in the Babylonian captivity to put their hope in the Lord, to wait upon Him because He will renew what little strength they have. They have tirelessly waited for deliverance, for a glimmer of hope, but Isaiah is telling them to put their hope and trust in God who will "renew their strength. They will soar on wings like eagles; they will run and not grow weary, they will walk and not be faint" (40:31).

When he talks about renewing their strength, it invokes a change, an alteration that was better than it was before, a replacing. This earlier verse has the same Hebrew word in it that helps illustrates it further, "The bricks have fallen down, but we will rebuild them with dressed stone; the fig trees have been felled, but we will replace them with cedars" (9:10). Because our hope is in the Lord, because we are waiting on Him to deliver, He will give us strength to overcome our trials of life. As eagles fly higher than any other bird, so we can ascend higher than the world because of our hope in the Lord and His Holy Spirit within us, allowing us to be above the world and its ways, flying closer to the sun and being in deeper communion with our God. Have you been tired and weary lately, exhausted in your own strength to the point of stumbling and falling? Do not wait another day to put your trust in God because you may not have another day. May your hope be in Him today so that you may walk in His strength and vigor, able to do what He has called you to.

"But I tell you who hear me: Love your enemies, do good to those who hate you, bless those who curse you, pray for those who mistreat you" – Luke 6:27-28

These may as well be the hardest words that Jesus ever tells us. These go against every natural instinct within us to maintain the "eye for eye, tooth for tooth" (Exodus 21:24) mindset of getting even and reciprocating the others' actions. However, that is what Jesus loves to do, grind against the grain of our culture so that His Kingdom's principles may be the guiding principles of our lives and not the heathens'.

While at work today I thought about this verse and repeated every action that Jesus wanted us to do and paired it with every group of people He mentioned. So it would sound like this "Love your enemies, love those who hate you, love those who curse you, love those who mistreat you..." and so on and so forth. Doing that really opened up my eyes that all these actions apply to all the groups and all the groups are essentially the same. If one is your enemy, they tend to hate you and mistreat you and hope for the worst to come to you. You hopefully get the picture that Jesus desires for us to love, do good, bless, and pray for those who are our enemies, hate us, curse us and mistreat us.

These truths and commands are at the heart of Jesus' teaching and are one of the main factors for Him being different than any other good teacher out there. Others would have told us to give the person who curses us what they deserve, but Jesus makes it so much better by having His people do what you would not expect and extend them grace and hope for their betterment. Like Jesus, we *must* be different than the society around us and stand above what people do to us and see that they are people who are hurting and broken like we have been and still are. To love them means to act with their best interests in mind, even though they are not doing the same to us.

Paul tells us to "Bless those who persecute you; bless and do not curse" (Romans 12:14) because when you treat others in a much better and counter-way than how they treated you, you will have them wonder why you would treat them in such a loving fashion and they may feel bad for how they had treated you. Brothers, we need to do this, no matter how hard it may be and how badly we want to give someone a piece of their own medicine. Do good to those who mistreat you, pray for those who hate you, love those who curse you and bless your enemies. Follow the example that Christ set before you, who gave us what we do not deserve and loved us while we were His enemies.

"Let not the wise man boast of his wisdom or the strong man of his strength or the rich man boast of his riches, but let him who boasts boast about this, that he understands and knows me, that I am the Lord" - Jeremiah 9:23-24

There are people who are very wise, extremely strong, and incredibly wealthy, and they will make it far in this life in the eyes of the world. People will look to them for help, support, and guidance on how to better live their lives. They are the A-team, those who are in leadership positions because they believe they can use their gifts that they boast in for the greater gain of their own cause. They take their complete identity in their forte and if they ever lost it, they themselves would be lost.

The prophet Jeremiah penned these words of the Lord with this in mind. He saw in his own day that people loved to pride themselves on the things they have, whether materials or insight or aptitude. They failed to acknowledge that it was indeed the Lord Himself who gave them these gifts that were to be used for His glory and not their own personal profit. God is the giver of all things, "For from him and through him and to him are all things" (Romans 11:36). "Every good and perfect gift is from above, coming down from the Father" (James 1:17). It is not wrong to use the talents we have been given, but when we give ourselves the praise in them, when we boast of them as if we somehow earned them ourselves and we merited it, that is when it becomes wrong. "Let another praise you, and not your own mouth; someone else, and not your own lips" (Proverbs 27:2).

The key to keeping our heads straight about this is to remain in a thankful attitude for everything the Lord has given you, which is in fact everything. When you do this, it takes your eyes off yourself and gives you the mindset and spirit that it is God who blessed you with that wisdom or strength or riches so that you can bless others through them. Paul tells us twice that "Let him who boasts boast in the Lord" (1 Corinthians 1:31, 2 Corinthians 10:17), referencing to Jeremiah who goes on to say "that I am the Lord, who exercises kindness, justice and righteousness on the earth, for in these I delight" (9:24). We should take pride in knowing the Lord, that we know the Creator of the heavens and the earth, the Lord Jesus Christ who suffered and died and rose again so that we may have life through Him. This is not a selfish pride however, but a pride that we are proud of the fact that we have a God who does those wondrous things and who Himself is marvelous. So are you struggling with boasting about the things you have done or acquired through your own efforts? If so, what can you do to change that and shift your focus on the one who truly gave you those gifts?

"Do not imitate what is evil but what is good. Anyone who does what is good is from God. Anyone who does what is evil has not seen God" - 3 John 11

The apostle John, the disciple whom Jesus loved, likes to talk about opposing forces, i.e. light and darkness, good and evil, death and life. There is something about these concepts in the nature of their simplicity and are oft portrayed in literature and movies, quite possibly because they are prevalent in everyday life. They usually make the best stories, even though you hear of ones like them all the time, but I believe something is rooted deep within us to continue pursuing such stories because they help reveal the larger story of the world.

John writes for us to imitate goodness and not evil. I think as believers we understand this concept and yet forget it at the same time. We overlook the fact that this world is evil and a number of its practices are as well. But John goes further to help us comprehend this and even gives us a reason as to why we should choose to imitate good and not evil because in this world, evil seems to have the upper hand and is always succeeding, so we need a concrete grounds for choosing good. "Anyone who does what is good is from God." Some of you may be thinking, "Does this mean that when I choose good I am from God but when I choose evil I have not seen God?" And my answer to that is no. This is referencing to a lifestyle of doing good or doing evil. If the Holy Spirit dwells within you, you will be doing more and more good because the Spirit is sanctifying you everyday into the image of Christ Himself and His likeness.

John goes on to say that "Anyone who does what is evil is has not seen God." And how can they? If you are doing what is evil, there is no love within you because we are told to "Hate what is evil; cling to what is good" (Romans 12:9) and that "No one has ever seen God; but if we love one another, God lives in us and his love is made complete in us" (1 John 4:12). When we love someone and do good onto them, God is shown in us because God is love and God is good. Christ is the incarnation of God Himself to us to help show us what it looks like to be people of goodness and love in this world of evil and hate. God is good and in Him there is nothing false or evil. "No one who lives in him keeps on sinning. No one who continues to sin has either seen him or knows him" (1 John 3:6). We can live a lifestyle of doing good my brothers; we do not have to do anything evil because we have the Spirit of the Living God within us. Would you say you are moving forward in your walk with Christ, walking in a routine of goodness towards your neighbors, or are you settling with the occasional good with a mixture of evil every now and then?

"I have not stopped giving thanks for you" - Ephesians 1:16

The notion behind giving thanks for someone or something is a humbling experience. Let us say there is a man who is in need of some money and his friend, without his knowledge, slips some money on his person to help him out. The man finds it, is puzzled, but thankful at the same time. He eventually finds out that it was his friend who gave it to him and tries to give it back, but instead the Lord convicts the man to accept the gift offered him, and he then thanks his friend for his generosity. A humbling incident for the man.

Giving thanks for something given to us is what the Lord desires of us. He is the greatest gift giver of all time and He loves it when we acknowledge that fact and thank Him for His generosity to us. We obviously do not deserve any of the gifts given us by any merit of our own doing, because if that was the case, we would probably get very little. But we have in fact been given so much and we are in such a need of offering thanks to God for everything.

Right now, it is quite hot and humid outside, miserable by my standards. I like it cool and breezy, but I am thankful nonetheless because "This is the day the Lord has made; let us rejoice and be glad in it" (Psalm 118:24). God could choose to take away the next day from us so that today is our last day, so how would you feel if your last day on earth was one of complaining and bitterness because the weather was not as you would have hoped? This is part of the mindset I try and keep to be in a thankful attitude because God could at any moment take one of his precious gifts away from us because He said so. If we do not appreciate something, why should He continue to give it to us?

Are you appreciative of your life? Are you living in a thankful frame of mind for the things you may not even like but because the Lord gave them, you will thank Him? My friends, the Lord gives and He takes away (Job 1:21); He does as He pleases. We know that He grants us things because He loves us, His precious children, and parents love to bless their children. May we be a people who never stop giving thanks as Paul said, "Give thanks in all circumstances" (1 Thessalonians 5:18). We are indeed blessed my friends, blessed beyond what is necessary. Be thankful today for what God has done, is doing, and will do in your life and in His kingdom. To the praise and glory of the King of kings, Christ Jesus our Lord, forever and ever. Amen!

"A fool gives full vent to his anger, but a wise man keeps himself under control" –
Proverbs 29:11

This is a proverb I have always appreciated because it attacks something that we Americans hold dear and that is the right to be emotionally unstable. We say, "Tell me how you really feel" and "Do not lie to yourself, but speak from the heart and let your emotions guide you." This is a faulty philosophy my brothers, faulty because 1: feelings do not always accurately portray how a person is really feeling, 2: lots of feelings are temporary, so they come and go, and 3: we may hurt someone in the process because we are not thinking clearly when acting out of raw emotion.

Anger is often one of the most popular emotions that is expressed today. People get angry about everything, from not getting something their way to simply getting mad because they lost a game or forgot to do something, or even when someone cuts them off while driving. In our fast-paced, high-stressed society, anger comes up readily and people love to resort to it and use their American "I have the right to be angry" and "I do what I want" mentality. But this is not how we are supposed to be living as followers of Christ. We see that a fool gives full vent to his anger, and I have pointed out that many people today are those fools, and even those in the Christian community have succumbed to this way of living, letting their anger run rampant, tearing apart relationships and giving disciples of Christ a bad and wrongful reputation.

But we also see that a wise man keeps himself under control. Some may say, "How can you do that? How can you remain calm in that situation? Do not hide how you really feel about this." I have heard this from friends in the church, friends I have respect for, but I have learned to disagree with them on this because it is not right. It is not that we are lying about what we truly think about something, but that we have begun to master our emotions and know that Christ calls for us to have self-control, as it is a part of the fruit of the Spirit (Galatians 5:23). "A man's wisdom gives him patience; it is to his glory to overlook an offense" (19:11). Do you want to be the wise man who has self-control, able to be temperate in all he does, the man who people do not have to worry about exploding randomly because something small and insignificant happened, or even something momentous? Or do you want to be the fool, the man who people have to continually watch what they say and do around, not knowing whether you would take offense and blow up in their faces? Do not give full vent to your anger and let your emotions get the best of you brothers, but use wisdom and temperance, representative of a life changed by the death and resurrection of Christ Jesus.

"I do believe; help me overcome my unbelief!" – Mark 9:24

Some of us may have come to the point in our walks with Christ where we understand the concepts and truths of the Gospel and the Bible as a whole, but then we take a look at our lifestyles and begin to doubt whether or not we really believe what we say we believe, whether we are striving to live out the Kingdom's way of life.

I know I have been here before/am occasionally entertaining this mentality. The verse itself seems somewhat contradictory, "I do believe; help me overcome my unbelief!" Does this mean that we do believe or that we do not believe? I see it as signifying that we may believe in certain aspects of Christ Jesus at the moment, but there are surely other arenas where we are still uncertain with in our faith. Take for instance, I believe that Christ died and rose from the grave and ascended into heaven to sit at the right hand of God the Father Almighty, from thence He shall come to judge the living and the dead. But I have trouble believing in the fact that Christ dwells within me and that He is ever-present, all throughout time, knowing all things. I may have trouble believing that such a perfect and infinite Being could ever love an infant-like, finite being who is just learning to walk and continues to make the same mistakes day in and day out. I may have trouble believing that God can do all things and that nothing is impossible for Him, that He does indeed care about my everyday life, including the small details that seem insignificant and cares about my thoughts and hopes.

These are but a few of the truths I struggle with, which is why I still utter the words, "Help me overcome my unbelief!" I do believe in Jesus Christ and God the Father and the Holy Spirit, but I also tend to doubt the other truths that make them what they are. I need to continually ask for "wisdom and revelation so that [I] can know him better" (Ephesians 1:17). I long to know the fullness of Christ that Paul talks about (Colossians 2:10), to know Him in every capacity, to thank Him for absolutely everything that is thrown my way, to praise Him because I am fearfully and wonderfully made (Psalm 139:14), to confess to Him that I need to drink from His fountain of grace and mercy. I desire to fully believe, and not doubt "like a wave of the sea, blown and tossed by the wind. That man [is]...unstable in all he does" (James 1:6-7). I want to always stand on the firm foundation, that is, the Rock of Christ Himself! This can only be done brothers through the sanctifying and teaching nature of the Holy Spirit in our lives. No amount of worldly wisdom and discipline can make this happen, only by the revelation of the Spirit of God. Father, help us in our unbelief!

"Now we know that if the earthly tent we live in is destroyed, we have a building from God, an eternal house in heaven, not built by human hands" – 2 Corinthians 5:1

Lately at work when I have been monitoring the exit, I am noticing when someone member returns home to their family after being absent for some time, the joy that not only the family receiving their loved one has, but the joy of the one who had been gone is exuberant. All I could do was smile as they embraced one another, making me think of *The Lord of the Rings* when Aragorn at last is crowned king of Gondor and he gets to hold his wife Arwen whom he has not seen in a long time, the intense elation they were both feeling was contagious.

As followers of the Lord Jesus Christ, we will have a homecoming of even greater excitement and jubilation than that because we will finally be home with our Father and family, free from all the woes and ills of this earthly tent. It will be a place of celebration and happiness, of worship and rest. Paul is speaking these words to the people to encourage them to continue on in their trials and sufferings because they do indeed have a heavenly home awaiting them because of their faith in Christ. He says just before to "not lose heart...For our light and momentary troubles are achieving for us an eternal glory that far outweighs them all" (4:16-17). Their work is not in vain, but there will be rewards for the labor they have toiled and there will be for us as well if we continue in the work given us by Christ.

This fleshly body that we dwell in was never meant to be a permanent dwelling, and that is why it is referred to as a tent, which is set up for temporary purposes, much like the tabernacle of the Old Testament. It is a fragile body that gets sick and is weak and deteriorates, while the eternal body in heaven will be strong and live forever. This life here on earth is not all there is friends, so may we never live as if it is such. May we never live for this world and the things of it, to satisfy our appetites and desires, because only God is able to satisfy completely. May we continue on in the work assigned to us, not losing heart because the road looks bleak, but looking ahead to our dwelling place in heaven, our homecoming that will have us forget all these tribulations we have undergone because the joy of seeing our Father and risen Christ face to face will supersede everything. Are you filled with joy and hope because of this wonderful news, giving you strength to carry on?

"I tell you the truth, unless you change and become like little children, you will never enter the kingdom of heaven. Therefore, whoever humbles himself like this child is the greatest in the kingdom of heaven" – Matthew 18:3-4

Jesus spoke these words to His disciples after they were arguing amongst themselves on who would be the greatest in the kingdom of heaven, which in itself is a very selfish and earthly mentality for the disciples of Jesus to be bearing. But if you think about it, they were behaving like little children who believe that the world revolves around them and they are always looking for ways to make themselves look better than others. However, Jesus was referring to a different kind of childlike frame of mind. Let us take a look at some of the positive traits of children.

Children are trusting of their parents. This is vital in their upbringing because if a child cannot trust their parents whom they are closest to, then who can they trust? As followers of Christ, we need to be trusting of Christ, believing He has our best intentions in mind and will not lead us astray. Children are also dependent on their parents. If the parents do not give children, especially younger children, food and drink and take care of them and protect them, they could very well easily die. As God's children, we have to be dependent upon Him in every way because we came from Him and Christ said that "I am the vine; you are the branches...apart from me you can do nothing" (John 15:5). The branches need to remain in the vine in order to have life; they have to be dependent upon it for absolutely everything as we do Christ, from whom everything came.

Another quality of children that goes unnoticed is that they do not claim titles for themselves or rights of their own, but they tend to do as they are told because they recognize they are under authority and without that, they would be lost. Jesus may have been asserting this attribute to His disciples in this passage because they were being petty and immature, desiring to sit at His right hand in His kingdom, while a child would simply be content by just being in the throne room in His kingdom. I hope you are catching on brothers, how Jesus wants His followers to have a *childlike* faith of dependence, trust and selflessness in Him and not a *childish* faith of selfishness, trivial pursuits, and lack of vision. Lord, help us to bear the qualities of a childlike faith in you, so we do not debate whether we have a great position in heaven or not, but that we can be unpretentious and lowly before your sight as we really are, relying on you for everything as the Vine that nourishes us.

"And whoever welcomes a child like this in my name welcomes me. But if anyone causes one of these little ones who believe in me to sin, it would be better for him to have a large millstone hung around his neck and to be drowned in the depths of the sea" - Matthew 18:5-6

If anything discourages me from working with children, this verse would be it. The amount of responsibility that Jesus places on His followers in their dealings with children is monumental, so much to the point that He says it would be better for the person to kill themselves than to cause a little one to stumble. I began to understand this last summer when I worked as camp counselor and noticed how much the kids emulate the things we do, almost to a T, and it was eye-opening. I really had to watch everything I did and said because they were always watching. Monkey see, monkey do.

Kids have a great memory and are always willing to recall something they saw you do to justify their actions. And this is why we have to be super careful how we live our lives, and not merely in front of children, but in front of everyone because believe it or not, people are constantly watching you, especially if you claim to be a Christ-follower. We must be welcoming of children in the way that Christ is welcoming of us, with open arms and open hearts, ready to love on them with Christ's love and mercy. Even though the responsibility with children is great, I would still love to work with them because they are so creative and adaptive and willing to learn, and a lot of us as we grow up forget this ingenuity and try to blend in with society instead of standing out and living differently. I love children, and I cannot wait to become a father someday (Lord willing), even though it is daunting, but fantastic nonetheless.

May we not hinder the children, and ultimately the people, that God has put in and around our lives. People are impressionable in all stages of life, so we must "make the most of every opportunity" (Colossians 4:5) to show them the grace and love of Christ who gladly showed us His. We need the Lord's help to live a life of the utmost stature, living and breathing the very words and nature of Christ Himself so that when others see us, they catch a glimpse of Him and their very encounters with us will bring out the best in them and not the worst. Brothers, are our lives above reproach? Are we living as if the world is watching, and ultimately as if God is watching, and would He be pleased on how we are representing Him?

"But when you give to the needy, do not let your left hand know what your right hand is doing, so that your giving may be done in secret. Then your Father, who sees what is done in secret, will reward you" – Matthew 6:3-4

Giving is quite the touchy subject in the Christian realm and I have no idea why. Maybe it is because people do not feel compelled to give so they do not, or they love their money too much to give it away for the Lord's sake, or even that when they give, they become like the Pharisees who try and do their "'acts of righteousness' before men, to be seen by them... [who] announce it with trumpets...in the synagogues and on the streets, to be honored by men" (6:1-2).

As Spirit-filled men and women of Christ however, that is not how we are to give, but we are to give so that our left hand does not even know what our right hand is doing, or in other words, do not tell others about your vigorous giving so that they can commend you for your generosity. "We are not trying to please men but God, who tests our hearts" (1 Thessalonians 2:4). The only reasoning for letting others know that we gave or how much we gave is for selfish gain and cannot glorify God, but ourselves, which in the end, is all for naught.

Our heavenly Father sees what is done in secret, so why parade it around? Why inform others of our good works? If you keep on going around and doing good deeds for the sake of your reputation with man, you are in fact living for them because you begin to care more about how they view you and less about how God views you. You have become a Pharisee at this point, a people-pleaser, not a God-pleaser. Pleasing God has been put in the back of your mind and not on the forefront where it belongs. You love the admiration that men give you because of your kindness and willingness to give.

Friends, this is the way of the evil one, the devil, "the ruler of the kingdom of the air, the spirit who is now at work in those who are disobedient" (Ephesians 2:2), not the way of our holy Father in heaven. Keep in mind that our Father sees everything that you do, even what is done in secret, and He generously rewards those who do so because when done secretly, it is only you and Him who know what you did. Selflessness. May we be a people who do not do anything to be honored by men because we live for an audience of One, not many. Are your spiritual disciplines of those that are done in the privacy of your home so it is just between you and God, or are you flaunting your righteousness and thus losing your rewards?

"I tell you the truth, unless a kernel of wheat falls to the ground and dies, it remains only a single seed. But if it dies, it produces many seeds" – John 12:24

At the first look, this is about Jesus and His death. If He failed to follow through with the plan to die to save humanity from their sins, then it would only have been Christ in heaven with the Father because He would have remained a single seed. But since Christ fell to the ground, that is earth, and died, He was able to save many and produce many seeds, allowing His grace and love and Spirit to flow to all, permeating life throughout the earth.

When we begin to look at it a little differently, we look at the grain more in depth. If you have ever seen a grain, you know that there is a strong shell on the outside and if that shell does not break, you cannot get to the grain. In other words, unless the grain dies, the life and goodness that is within the shell cannot grow. The shell must break for the grain within to grow, without that death of the shell, it stays as it is, single and dormant. Author Watchman Nee saw this outer shell as the human nature, the flesh, the body of man that must be destroyed in order for the life of the Spirit to flow forth in abundance to all. He said that "In order for the inner life to be released, the outer life must suffer loss. If that which is outward is not broken, that which is inward cannot be released."

The Lord's life is locked up within us, within our outer shell and it wants to be released! The Spirit of the Lord wants to go throughout all the earth and bless its inhabitants. But the only way this can be so is if our outer man, our flesh, dies so that the life of Christ can pour forth freely from within us. This life within us wants to be released, much like how the germ within the kernel wants to break free so that it can live and grow, but the outer shell wants to keep it inside so it can stay as it is and remain alive. They are in conflict with one another, but one has to make way for the other to thrive, otherwise they both will die. Paul said it this way, "For in my inner being I delight in God's law; but I see another law at work in the members of my body, waging war against the law of my mind and making me a prisoner of the law of sin at work within my members" (Romans 7:22-23).

Lord, release us from the shell surrounding us, hindering us and your Spirit from being released and having your life gushing onward to the world that needs it. May we fall to the ground, die, and be free as you have intended saying "So if the Son sets you free, you will be free indeed" (8:36). May we be fruitful for you Father, as you have been fruitful by sending us your Holy Spirit. Thank you for everything. We love you.

"Wait for the Lord; be strong and take heart and wait for the Lord" – Psalm 27:14

Remember way back on January 23 when I talked about walking by faith and not by sight, and how I thought the Lord was telling me I would receive a job in Boston. I actually did get that job, however I declined it because I was no longer in that relationship and thus had no desire to live out in Boston anymore. I saw the Lord as wanting me to take that step in trusting Him, although it was not the step I had anticipated. And as soon as that happened, I transferred that same application to Grand Rapids and got the job which I work at today because of my interview and job efforts in Boston.

We may think that the Lord is taking us one direction and then He calls an audible on us and brings us a different direction. The life of a Christian is a life of waiting. As the Jews all throughout the Old Testament had waited to enter the Promised Land; as they had awaited deliverance from their captivities, and as they still await the first coming of the Messiah, so we disciples of Christ live waiting for His final return when we meet Him up in the sky. Right now in Iraq, Christians are being persecuted, forced to convert to Islam or die, so many are fleeing to the mountains. This verse for them is a lifeline, words of hope that strengthen them in their time of distress. They will wait for the Lord and His deliverance; wait for His will to be done in their lives, even though they are starving at the moment.

Perseverance is the mark of a believer of Christ. It exemplifies how our hope is in Christ and His work and not in the world and our own strengths. When David wrote this Psalm, he needed patience and endurance to get through his days of running around and hiding from Saul and his men. When he spoke these words, he was reminded of the faithfulness of the Lord and thus further strengthened his trust and dependency on Him so that the next time he was in despair or danger, he could recall these words and be of good courage once more.

We have trying times of waiting where we need to be patient and persist in what we are doing, awaiting the Lord to come through. What is it for you? What are you waiting for right now? Are you waiting for the Lord's answer to a prayer to come to fruition or even an answer in general? Are you waiting for the culmination of Christ's kingdom to come and abolish wickedness and evil forever? Or are you awaiting something else? I know I am patiently and prayerfully waiting for Christ's return, to bring us home with Him and the destruction of sin in the world. Whatever you are waiting on the Lord for, do not forget to keep on praying and seeking His face.

"In those days Israel had no king; everyone did as he saw fit" – Judges 21:25

Those days sound a lot like these days where everybody does what they please and are not held responsible for their actions. It sounds like children with poor parents who do not discipline them and they run rampant; you see those kids all over the place and it truly shows how bad their parents are at being parents. Where there is good leadership, there is order and peace.

This does not come because the people are afraid of their leader because of potential punishment, but because they respect that person's ability to lead them effectively and with their best interests in mind. "When a country is rebellious, it has many rulers" (Proverbs 28:2). The verse of the day is the last verse in the Book of Judges. Israel physically did not have a king, but in their hearts, the Lord was not their king either because they did not want Him to be and that is why they did as they saw fit. You can see all throughout the media what happens when there is no good leadership; rebellions occur, riots ensue and the people are afraid.

The nation of Israel was swallowed up in sin because the Lord was not on the throne in their hearts and minds. I am sure you have noticed that when you forget about the Lord, that He really is the King of kings, it is extremely easy to fall back into the sinful habits of your old self before Christ came into your life. It becomes effortless to slip into your old mindset and routine of life before Christ came and saved you and began sanctifying you into His likeness. The Israelites knew the way of the Lord; they lived in it and had the commands of God memorized, yet they dethroned Him from their lives and He became a second thought.

They put idols and themselves as the chief authority in their hearts and not the rightful King. Who have you put on the throne of your life besides the Living Christ? Your job? Your significant other? Your comfort and security? Your government? Your children? If there is anything or anyone ruling in your life above Christ Jesus, take them off and allow Christ to reign supreme. When you died to your old self, that is just it, you *died* to it, which means you no longer live for it. T.S. Eliot describes a martyr as one "who has become an instrument of God, who has lost his will in the will of God, not lost it but found it, for he has found freedom in submission to God. The martyr no longer desires anything for himself, not even the glory of martyrdom." We have a King, a glorious King, who loves His people. Keep Him on His rightful throne.

"The Spirit gives life; the flesh counts for nothing" – John 6:63

Jesus spoke these words to His many disciples after He talked about how "unless you eat the flesh of the Son of Man and drink his blood, you have no life in you" (6:53). They had not quite accepted this and a lot of them followed Him no more. They could not come to grip with what He said, even though He goes on to explain that it was not to be taken literally, and that is why He said, "The Spirit gives life; the flesh counts for nothing."

It is in fact the Spirit of God that gives us life; the Spirit that was placed within us who believe. No action of the mind or of our emotions can bring about life. We may be the most clever, happiest person the world has ever seen, but without the Spirit, there is no life. Our mind shifts like shadows and our feelings fall and rise like the waves, but our Spirit remains constant because Christ who gave the Spirit is constant. We can *always* rely on the Spirit to gives us peace and joy that will last and not change when our thoughts and emotions change with our circumstances.

The flesh deceives and lies to us. It tries to get us to think that we need this or that in order to be satisfied or yet survive, but we can survive and even thrive on much, much less. It is only through the revelation and wisdom of the Spirit that we are able to see and do this. The flesh counts for nothing. The flesh fails us. The flesh does not meet the real needs of man; only the outward needs and not the true needs of the inner man. Only the Spirit can meet such needs and bring forth life and make it grow and flourish and generate fruit. "Man does not live on bread alone but on every word that comes from the mouth of the Lord" (Deuteronomy 8:3).

Brothers, are you actually alive? Are you, like the fig tree that had the appearance of life and abundance, deceiving others and even yourself that you are bearing fruit, when in reality you are not? (see Mark 11:12-14). Is the Spirit of God free within you to do as He pleases, or is your outer man hindering itself from the breakthrough life of joy and power that Christ promises? "Let us throw off everything that hinders and the sin that so easily entangles, and let us run with perseverance the race marked out for us. Let us fix our eyes on Jesus, the author and perfecter of our faith" (Hebrews 12:1-2). Let us fix our gaze on the One who alone is Life; through no other means can life come to us or the world except through His Spirit. Remember and live out these truths as you go about your day.

"When Israel was a child, I loved him and out of Egypt I called my son. But the more I called Israel, the further they went from me" – Hosea 11:1-2

Part of this verse is referenced to Jesus when, after He was born, fled to Egypt to avoid being killed by Herod (Matthew 2:15). But that is not what this is about; this is about the nation of Israel, the Jews of the Old Testament, which now refers to the followers of Christ today. When Israel first became a nation, when they were merely an infant learning how to get up and walk, that was when God called them out of Egypt and out of slavery. He was a Father to them and called them "my son." God loves using familial terms when referring to His relationship with His people: Father, Son, children, mother, son, daughter, those who are loved. The Father does love His children very much and that is why He calls us His own.

The Hebrew in this text, instead of saying "the more I called Israel" more correctly translates "the more they called Israel", referring to the prophets through whom the Lord spoke through. The NIV translators took the liberty to put "I" there because ultimately it is the Lord who is speaking through the prophets and it makes it more personal and corresponds with the rest of the text.

The more that the Lord called His son, the more He pursued them and showed them His love, the more He walked with them, the further that they went away from Him. They had ignored their Father's call for them and "they sacrificed to the Baals and they burned incense to images" (11:2) instead of following the Lord their God who brought them out of Egypt and into the Promised Land. How could they ignore such providence that was bestowed upon them? Such grace and mercy and favor that had them stick out among the nations? Moses said that "How will anyone know that you are pleased with me and with your people unless you go with us?" (Exodus 33:16). It is because of the Lord's presence with Israel that made them special because He chose them.

"It was I who taught Ephraim how to walk, taking them by the arms; but they did not realize it was I who healed them. I led them with cords of human kindness, with ties of love; I lifted the yoke from their neck and bent down to feed them" (11:3-4). The Lord did these loving actions for Israel, teaching them His ways, yet they kept walking away to others who caught their fancy. The same is true with us brothers; we get drawn away from the One we truly love to others that offer more instant gratification and catch our eyes and hearts. The Lord calls us daily. Will you choose to run away like Israel, like a wayward son, or will you go to your Father like a child that desperately needs and loves Him?

"Then you will know which way to go, since you have never been this way before" –
Joshua 3:4

A guest speaker preached on this verse somewhat yesterday at my church. It was in reference to the Israelites following the Ark of the Covenant, which was the presence of the Lord, into the Jordan River and then the Promised Land, the land sworn to their forefathers was finally coming to fulfillment. The crossing of the Israelites through the Red Sea was spectacular in and of itself, but it was not to anywhere, it was just running away. Yet the crossing of the Jordan went somewhere, to the land flowing with milk and honey, the land of promise where the people of God will make their homes.

The Promised Land to which they were heading, they had obviously not been there before, so they did not know the way. They merely went where the Lord told Joshua to go, and then he had the Ark of the Covenant always go before the people, so the Lord went before Israel, showing them the way as a king leads his troops and a father leads his family.

We constantly try and find things to do and places to go, striving to discover our own way through life and go where our imagination and emotions take us. One decision leads to another, and then to another, which treks us down a path that we never intended to go on, but it is where we are and the only way back to where you wanted to go is to backtrack. It is only through Christ Jesus and knowing Him personally that we are able to know which way to go, the way of denying and dying to ourselves and following Him with everything we got (Matthew 16:24).

It is Jesus who reveals the way to us through His Holy Spirit. Everyone's path is not the same length, nor does it contain the same obstacles, but they all eventually lead to the Holy Mountain. When we are following the Lord our God with our hearts and minds and strengths, we will go the way He intended for us. As the Israelites were following the Ark, so we are to be following Christ. Then we will never be lost or in disarray because we are following One who is trustworthy. The Lord "is faithful in all he does" (Psalm 33:4). We have not traversed through this life before and cannot possibly know what may happen five years from now, tomorrow or even in one hour, but the Lord has been there and He knows the way. He *is* the way.

"May God himself, the God of peace" – 1 Thessalonians 5:23

As I am writing this, it is raining pretty heavily outside and I love it. I just love when it rains, the smell that is in the air, the sound it makes, the coolness that comes with it. But I really love the peaceful atmosphere it sheds upon me when I hear and see it. I do not know what it is, I could be sitting in my chair on my patio watching the rain continuously fall, or I could be walking in the downpour and getting drenched, but the serene and peaceful feeling it gives off is wonderful.

This always makes me think of the story of Horatio Spafford, who was a wealthy lawyer and businessman in the latter half of the nineteenth century. He had a few traumatic events happen to him: his only son died of scarlet fever in 1870, he lost a lot of investments and property in the Great Chicago Fire in 1871, ruining him financially, then in 1873, he sent his family ahead of him to Europe and their ship sank and it killed his four daughters and only his wife survived. In spite of all these awful events that no one should ever have to go through, especially with such severity, he penned the famous hymn *It Is Well With My Soul*. The first lines of the song go as such:

When peace like a river, attendeth my way,

When sorrows like sea billows roll;

Whatever my lot, Thou has taught me to say,

It is well, it is well, with my soul.

After these incidents, Horatio was still able to say that it was well with his soul. The whole world sank from beneath him and everything was taken from him except his wife. I see him as the modern-day Job, and yet he was able to walk in the peace of the Lord because he understood that it is indeed the Lord who gives and the Lord who takes away, and who are we to try and understand His ways! He had "learned to be content whatever the circumstances" (Philippians 4:11). It is this peace that I experience when I hear the rain and watch the waves crashing into the shore and gaze into a campfire. This peace can only come from the God of peace because it confirms within us that everything really is alright because God is still in control. He is in control my brothers, if only we would continually acknowledge this simple fact daily, imagine the peace that would flood our hearts and minds!

"Seek me and live; do not seek Bethel, do not go to Gilgal, do not journey to Beersheba. For Gilgal will surely go into exile, and Bethel will be reduced to nothing" – Amos 5:4-5

The other day I was thinking about going on a vacation to Scotland or Ireland or another beautiful place that I have not been to before but always wanted to travel to. The reason for going to those places would be because of their physical beauty, their jagged and rolling landscapes, the cliffs by the sea and the crispness of the air. I believe it would be a place of rest and relaxation, of meditation and contemplation, to gather again my bearings away from worldly distractions and cares. It would be a much needed vacation for the growth of relationship with Christ.

That is what the people of Amos' day were thinking when heading to Gilgal and Bethel; they were recognized places of worship where people could "feel" the Lord's presence because of past incidents that occurred there and how the Lord helped His people at those locations (Genesis 35:1, Joshua 4:20). But these places have also become known places of idolatry, so in these areas of Godly worship are also areas of pagan worship. "What agreement is there between the temple of God and idols?" (2 Corinthians 6:16). This is preposterous of the people of God to do such a thing! How could they defile the Lord's sites of worship with idols and carvings made by man?

But we are guilty of this every day. We poison the places of worship, our lives, with worldly pleasures and things, "For we are the temple of the living God" (2 Corinthians 6:16). There shall be no fellowship between light and darkness. We are to seek the Lord and the Lord alone. We also do not need to go to these places of worship, these holy sites, in order to catch a glimpse of God like people were when going to Bethel and Gilgal; we have only need to seek the Lord of the universe where we are at because that is where He is, right there with us always. Places are not always what they seem to be. Yes, you may want to go somewhere to get a certain experience or feeling, but I assure you that you can get that same familiarity wherever you are. God is not limited to a particular location; God cannot be limited at all and we tend to do that constantly! Forgive us Father for limiting you to what our puny human minds can barely comprehend. May you expand our thinking and leave tons of room for you to move around unhindered by us, and may you open our eyes and hearts to see you right where we are, to acknowledge your presence and glory. Help us to seek you and live the life we were meant to live; a life full of wonder and peace and delight. You are so good to us Father, thank you for your kindness and for hearing our cries. We love you. So be it.

"I am the Lord, and there is no other; apart from me there is no God. I will strengthen you, though you have not acknowledged me" – Isaiah 45:5

As we somewhat talked about yesterday, God does not like sharing His throne and our devotion to false gods, things and ideas that have no value or authority. He says here that He is the Lord and apart from Him there is no other God with a capital G. Sure, we humans make lower case g gods because we believe they are more tangible to us, but "They have mouths, but cannot speak, eyes, but they cannot see; they have ears, but they cannot hear, noses, but they cannot smell; they have hands, but cannot feel, feet, but they cannot walk; nor can they utter a sound with their throats" (Psalm 115:5-7).

The gods that we create for ourselves *will* fail us because they have no power whatsoever because they are mere things, not the God who created all the world. There is no true god apart from our God! "I form the light and create darkness, I bring prosperity and create disaster; I, the Lord, do all these things" (45:7). No other god can say that about themselves but our God. When we put a false god into our lives, we are no longer trusting in the Lord to meet our needs. And this is usually when bad things happen to us and we wonder why and it is because we are putting our faith into something that cannot deliver.

The Lord said that "I will strengthen you, though you have not acknowledged me", but why? What did we do to deserve such a gracious God? We have not acknowledged or recognized the works of the Lord or even His presence, and yet He decides to strengthen us in times of need and plenty? I do not know, but this one line hits me hard and has me think of Christ and how while we were still His enemies, He died for us so that we may have life through Him (Romans 5:8,10)! The prophet Isaiah goes on to write from where we leave off saying, "so that from the rising of the sun to the place of its setting men may know there is none besides me. I am the Lord, and there is no other" (45:6). Because our God strengthens us though we do not acknowledge Him, that shows that He is the one true God of the world because no other god would ever do something so merciful because all other gods are about give and take, not grace and mercy. Brothers, do not forget to acknowledge the Lord your God and live out the truth that He is the Lord and there is no God besides Him. Is your life evident of this reality, shaping the very things you think and say and do?

"If one falls down, his friend can help him up. But pity the man who falls and has no one to help him up!" – Ecclesiastes 4:10

I finally saw *Guardians of the Galaxy* yesterday and it was both hilarious and moving. It spoke to me as good movies tend to, on sacrificing oneself for the benefit of those they love so that they may live, much like when Jesus says that "Greater love has no one than this, that he lay down his life for his friends" (John 15:13). The main characters in the movie did not really have any friends before they met each other, but over the course of the story, they became reliant on one another and in the end, were able to humble themselves and become the closest of friends and defeating the enemy because of it.

I know I may not have explained it that well, I guess you will just have to see the movie yourselves, haha. But I hope that my point was illustrated somewhat, that it is not good for us to go through this life alone; we can accomplish so much more together than we ever could by ourselves, especially when this is done in Christian fellowship and community. When we are attacked by the devil or his minions, we are to "Resist him, standing firm in the faith, because you know that your brothers throughout the world are undergoing the same kind of sufferings" (1 Peter 5:9). By understanding that others just like ourselves, of whom we are all a part of Christ's body, are also undergoing the same situations we are in, this shows that we are not alone in this fight against evil and that if one of us does indeed fall, his friend is right there to pick him back. "For though a righteous man falls seven times, he rises again" (Proverbs 24:16) because a friend, a brother in the faith, is there to lift him up and keep trudging along.

"A friend loves at all times, and a brother is born for adversity" (Proverbs 17:17). In the movie, if they had not grown to care and love each other, the enemy would have destroyed them and the galaxy would have been obliterated. But since they grew to love and rely and depend on each other in the direst circumstances, they were able to accomplish so much more and life abounded because of their sacrifices. My friends, I am one who loves to do things alone, so this has been a struggle for me in the past years, but the Lord is working in me to obtain a greater fellowship with my family in Christ for His glory. Are you having fellowship with your brothers and sisters, living vulnerably and depending on one another to help get through when times get tough? It is toilsome, but it is worth it.

"Therefore each of you must put off falsehood and speak truthfully to his neighbor, for we are all members of one body" - Ephesians 4:25

Communication is essential to any functioning and thriving relationship. Whether you are dating or married to someone and have a feud, or you and your friend have a little miscommunication about something vital, or you simply misunderstood some directions that were given to you at work and you failed to ask questions about it, communication mistakes do cause problems. And that is why there is the famous idiom, "What we have here is a failure to communicate."

Like any other relationship, our relationship with God and the body of Christ needs good communication as well. What do we know about good communication? Well, we know that when communicating, being honest with who you are talking to is a great way to start and that is why Paul told the Ephesian church to "put off falsehood and speak truthfully to his neighbor." When you are lying in a conversation, you are withholding information from the other party because you are either afraid they will not like what you are saying or you are just trying to save your behind from some sort of punishment. Either way, you are hurting the relationship with who you are talking to by destroying any sense of trust there was before.

But Paul does not leave us by merely saying to put off falsehood, but he encourages us to then speak truthfully to our neighbors. When you speak the truth to others and to God, you become a trustworthy and honest person, one people will look towards because they see you as responsible to handle whatever they might say to you. Earlier, Paul tells the church to be "speaking the truth in love" (4:15) because one can speak the truth, but in sensitive situations, simply telling the truth could be done in a harsh manner and may end up hurting the person. I am sure you can easily think of situations in which this is the case. When we communicate in a truthful and straightforward manner, we are best representing Him who is Truth, who Himself never told a lie. It is one thing to quit doing bad things, but it is even better and more wonderful to quit the bad habit and start to do good things. Make that complete 180 degree transition in your life to being an excellent, truthful communicator as one who desires the best in their relationships by speaking the truth in love and not falsehood in selfishness and fear. When you are honest with others, you have their best interests in mind which is to hear the truth, even if it hurts a little. Do you like being lied to? I doubt it, so how would you define your communicative effectiveness in this area of honesty?

"Everyone should be quick to listen, slow to speak and slow to become angry" – James 1:19

Another part of successful communication is listening. I honestly believe that this is the most critical component for communicating effectively. We need to be able to understand that communication is a two-way street that involves both speaking and listening, with listening taking the majority of the road. This is true for all forms of relationships with friends and family, colleagues, strangers, and especially God.

My brothers, note how James tells us that we should be *quick* to listen and *slow* to speak, indicating that listening should always come first and we should be swift to begin listening to others before we hastily jump in with our own opinions. Solomon wrote that "A man of knowledge uses words with restraint...A fool finds no pleasure in understanding but delights in airing his own opinions" (Proverbs 17:27, 18:2). He is saying that a fool hastily will speak his mind because he does not care about comprehending what the other person is saying, but only wants others to know what he is thinking, and that is why he is the fool.

This is plainly seen in our walks with Christ and sad to say, we are that fool that is spoken of quite often. We love talking to God. We love telling Him our issues and cares and dreams and I will admit, He loves hearing it because He loves listening to the cries of His children. However, that is usually where we end the conversation, with us talking; we never make it to the part of the discussion where we then listen to God and hear what He is trying to tell us. We have become the fool. "Do you see a man who speaks in haste? There is more hope for a fool than for him" (Proverbs 29:20).

I remember back in my classroom training for my job, one of the best things they taught us when communicating is to pause before speaking. When we take a moment and pause, we not only can gather our thoughts but we can avoid speaking rashly and out of emotion and hurt and not out of truth and sincerity. Listening shows the other person that you care enough about them to take time and listen to what they have to say, thus deepening trust and the relationship grows because of it. Is your relationship with Christ waning or at a standstill? Have you thought that is the case because maybe you have not been taking the time to listen to what God has to say to you? He is whispering to you brothers, I know that is the truth. He does so because He is just one step away. Take time today and listen to your heavenly Father who loves you very much.

"Pray that the Lord your God will tell us where we should go and what we should do" –
Jeremiah 42:3

Throughout our lives, we frequently come to the Lord and ask Him, "What on earth am I here for and where do you want me to go?" At times, we may think we know the answer, but actually are being led by our unbroken outer man and not our inner man, so we venture down the wrong path. Other times we believe we have the answer, and indeed we do, but God then changes the direction of our course and we question Him asking "You told me I was supposed to go this way and do that, and now you are taking that away from me and pushing me towards another route, why?"

Life is full of winding paths that sometimes seem to be going nowhere, but for the believer who is being led by the Spirit of God, it is always going somewhere, to a place that is sanctifying us and making us more like Christ. Watchman Nee wrote that "Everything that comes our way is meaningful and under God's sovereign arrangement. Nothing accidental happens to a Christian. Nothing is outside God's ordering." Everything *does* happen for a reason, whether we know it or not, and we hardly ever know it in the present, only afterwards in hindsight do we begin to realize the meaning behind it.

The Lord our God *will* tell us where we should go and what we should do. Like I have said many times before, He constantly desires to talk to us, all we have to do is take the time to listen. It is vital to know what our purpose on this planet is for the Kingdom of God, which is why it is vital to ask the Lord what that purpose is. For me, the Lord had said countless times that I will help people. I do not know whether that is in a physical or spiritual capacity, or both, but I do know that I will in fact help people in this life.

Are you lost and without direction right now? Are you setting aside time in your day to quiet your thoughts so you can hear the voice of the Living God? He desires for you to know the way, as He is the Way that we are to follow. Tolkien coined the phrase, "All that is gold does not glitter, Not all those who wander are lost." Just because you may be wandering to and fro does not mean you are lost however; you may just be hearing the words of the Lord Jesus and taking steps out in faith that seem bizarre to others, but in reality it is the path He has set before you. Do not go to others to get confirmation of where you should be going. Go to the Source of Life, Christ Jesus Himself. If you know He is telling you something, do not hesitate to follow and obey it. He has and never will lead you astray.

August 19

"Should you then seek great things for yourself? Seek them not" - Jeremiah 45:5

I was just flipping through the pages of Jeremiah when I stumbled upon this verse of wisdom. I love the wording of what the Lord is saying, "Should you then seek great things for yourself? Seek them not." He speaks straight to the heart of mankind: seeking great things for themselves and trying to make themselves look better than everyone else. Paul speaks on this, telling the Roman believers to "not think of yourself more highly than you ought, but rather think of yourself with sober judgment, in accordance with the measure of faith God has given you" (Romans 12:3).

But we love thinking of ourselves greatly, sometimes at least, and if we are truly honest with ourselves, we think we are better than others in many areas of life. At least that is the case for me which I am trying to combat, the mindset of self-righteousness, that "I am not as bad as those Christians" mentality. That sense of pride is a huge struggle for me and I pray fervently for the Lord to remove it and bring me to a place of humility and meekness. It is a daily struggle that I have to remind myself about and let the Spirit move in my life.

The best way to battle this is to "seek first his kingdom and his righteousness" (Matthew 6:33) and to "seek his face always" (Psalm 105:4). It is only when we are looking to the perfect being of the Lord Jesus Christ, the Son of God, that we can truly take our eyes off ourselves and our selfish and petty matters and begin to accomplish wondrous things beyond our imagination. When you seek things only for yourself and your own gain, the only person it benefits is you and that is only temporarily, but when you seek things for the good of others and for Christ, numerous more people are being blessed, including yourself, and your Father in heaven is pleased with you. This is one of the reasons why Paul tells us to "Do nothing out of selfish ambition or vain conceit, but in humility consider others better than yourselves. Each of you should look not only to your own interests, but also to the interests of others" (Philippians 2:3-4). Friends in Christ, this is a serious matter that must be addressed in all of us. What are the motivations for the things that you do in this life? Are you doing things because of how they can help you out, or are you doing things because they help others out and you are thus representing the nature of Christ? Meditate on this today as I will.

"From everyone who has been given much, much will be demanded; and from the one who has been entrusted with much, much more will be asked" – Luke 12:48

There is the saying that "With great power comes great responsibility." That is a true statement for the followers of Christ as well. Each person has been blessed in different ways and some more than others. One person may receive more monetary blessings from the Lord while another may be the funniest person you have ever met and yet another may be a genius of the mind. Every one of those blessings has a purpose for the greater good and some may carry more weight than the other.

But I hear some of you saying "We are all one body in Christ. There are no parts greater than the other for we are equal." And this is true brothers, there are no parts greater than others, but there are some parts of the body that if they fail will carry a much heavier burden than others. For example, if a foot fails in being a foot and it decides to fall off, walking would be near impossible, but if a ring finger fails, the person could still function quite normally as a person and do everyday tasks. I hope this is more understood now.

Jesus uttered these words to His disciples while talking about watchfulness and the need to be ready for His second coming. He was telling them that they needed to obey their masters and do His bidding as good servants do before His return. The believers of that time only had the Old Testament, the teachings of Jesus and Jesus Himself with them. We have been entrusted with the whole Bible; we know Jesus and know how it is going to end. There are countless followers of Christ throughout the world who do not even have a Bible and still believe. Who do you think is to have borne more responsibility: us who have the entire Bible, or those without that revelation? I believe that is a no-brainer.

We who have been entrusted with so much, with more resources than most of the world, more avenues of technology to be able to reach others, more things tailored towards us in regards to evangelizing the nations, we have so much responsibility on our shoulders. Much is asked of us, yet there are so few of us who are doing anything with it. Yes, we may pray every now and then for the nations, or we may occasionally give to missions and may even go on a missions trip, but there is so much more. Ask the Lord today what you could be doing for His Kingdom's sake. Ask Him for strength to do the work commanded of you. Be ready, for whomever "knows his master's will and does not get ready or does not do what his master wants will be beaten with many blows" (12:47).

"Save yourselves from this corrupt generation" - Acts 2:40

This world that we live in is falling apart. There are more fatherless homes, more abortions, more divisions, more mass murderers, more wars, and there seems to be no end of it in sight. As I am scrolling through Netflix, I am seeing more and more TV shows that are rated TV-MA because of explicit sexual content and people are becoming more comfortable with watching them as well, both believers and non-believers alike. Shows like *Game of Thrones* and *House of Cards* to name a few.

My brothers, why are you allowing these sinful actions to creep into your lives and minds? Why are you willfully accepting these things as entertainment and nothing more? Do you not know that "The eye is the lamp of the body. If you eyes are good, your whole body will be full of light. But if your eyes are bad, your whole body will be full of darkness. If then the light within you is darkness, how great is that darkness!" (Matthew 6:22-23)? What you take in, will in one way or another, come out of you, whether in action or thought. It is a venom that poisons your very soul, eating away at you until there is nothing good left in you.

But there is more to saving yourselves from this crooked and depraved generation than merely avoiding certain activities and entertaining particular thoughts, you must repent and turn towards Christ. You could steer clear of all the sinful things that this world has to offer, do good things, and still end up going to hell because you never turned to Jesus Christ, who alone can and will mold you into His image and make you truly good. And when you do so, you will receive the gift of the Holy Spirit, which is Jesus Christ Himself living within you and every other believer that has ever lived.

So what will it be? Will you join in with those of this world, enlisting in their endeavors that are being led by the devil himself? Or will you be one who is willing to stand up and stand out for the sake of your Savior, upholding His values and commands because you know that He is making you holy and fit for His Kingdom in heaven? "For you have spent enough time in the past doing what pagans choose to do—living in debauchery, lust, drunkenness, orgies, carousing and detestable idolatry. They think it strange that you do not plunge with them into the same flood of dissipation, and they heap abuse on you. But they will have to give account to him who is ready to judge the living and the dead" (1 Peter 4:3-5). May that be so in our lives brothers, that we can be so bold to follow our Christ to the very end of all things and know that it is for Him that we are living and not for our own pleasure or other's approval. Stand out, or be thrown out.

"Do not believe every spirit, but test the spirits to see whether they are from God, because many false prophets have gone out into the world" – 1 John 4:1

We need to be able to read one another if we are to be useful for the Lord's service. What I mean by this is that each man has a spirit within him and we need to be able to distinguish what kind of spirit is within the man to best be able to minister to him. If we always tried to give the same prescription to everyone regardless of their illness, very few people, if any, would ever be healed. We must know man's spirit in order to know where they are at.

This is why Paul tells us to "Test everything" (1 Thessalonians 5:21) to what we know to be true in the Scriptures to determine if what we are hearing is from God or from the world or the devil. That is also why John is telling us to not believe every spirit because "Satan himself masquerades as an angel of light. It is not surprising then, if his servants masquerade as servants of righteousness" (2 Corinthians 11:14-15).

Each and every one of us has a spirit within us, whether that be the Spirit of God, or the spirit of pride or of jealousy or of stubbornness, we all bear a spirit of one sort or another. Please note however that if you have the Spirit of God within you, that is your normal spiritual condition. But your outer man can still display acts of pride and jealousy and thus clouding over the Spirit of God within you, hindering it from being displayed. This is when we need the Lord to break the outer man in those areas so that we would no longer be known by the spirit of pride or the spirit of jealousy, but we will be known by the Spirit of God because His characteristics are being manifested and not those of the flesh. When it is this way brothers, we are then better able to identify what type of spirit is within a man and thus we are better able to help them where they truly need and not where we think they need it.

"Distinguishing between spirits" (1 Corinthians 12:10) is indeed a gift of the Spirit that Paul mentions. When we can properly differentiate between the Spirit of God and the spirits of the world within someone, we can then suitably communicate and help them out and know more precisely what words to say so that we may "not let any unwholesome talk come out of [our] mouths, but only what is helpful for building others up according to their needs, that it may benefit those who listen" (Ephesians 4:29). When we can give someone a word of encouragement that they truly need and not just one that we think they may need, that can make all the difference in how their day is played out. Pray for this spirit of discernment so that you may bless others through it and give glory to God in heaven.

"Above all else, guard your heart, for it is the wellspring of life" - Proverbs 4:23

A lot of people that I know when they mention this verse, almost always refer to guarding one's heart in a relationship with someone of the opposite sex. But it is much bigger than that my friends. Why does Solomon, the wisest of all the men to have ever lived on this earth, tell us to guard our hearts above all else? What does it mean to guard our heart?

When you guard something, you protect it; you take care of it and treat it with special care and honor. You shield it from the elements of nature and anything else that may try to get to harm it or even just influence it. That is what Solomon is getting at here. He has understood that the heart is a fragile thing that needs to be guarded because from it flows the source of life, both physically and spiritually. When we are born again, our heart is being re-molded into the image of Christ Jesus because our old heart was corrupt and from it flowed wickedness. This is why we are told that "out of the overflow of the heart the mouth speaks" (Matthew 12:34) and surrounding our verse today, "listen closely to my words. Do not let them out of your sight, keep them within your heart; for they are life to those who find them and health to a man's whole body...Put away perversity from your mouth; keep corrupt talk far from your lips" (4:21-22, 24). Solomon knew that from our heart flowed harsh words and hatred, something that is not from the Lord.

And so it is true for us today. Our heart belongs to God and God alone. He has given us this heart and has told us to guard it because He knows that if we let the things of this world seep in; if we give our heart to earthly pleasures and gains, to things that do not bring satisfaction but destruction, then life will not flow from within us, the life that Christ is and came to give us. So much depends on the heart. If we let the grace of God cleanse us and make us new, our heart also shall be made new and we can begin to live as vessels of love and life for Christ! "The good man brings good things out of the good stored up in him, and the evil man brings evil things out of the evil stored up in him" (Matthew 12:35). What are you storing up within you? Are you protecting your heart from worldly influences and deceptions, or are you allowing the life of God to flow freely from it? Brothers, if you continue to let the things of the world enter your heart, things of the world will come from it. Safe keep it and may it only be given to the Lord.

"I am the Lord; that is my name! I will not give my glory to another or my praise to idols" – Isaiah 42:8

We are going to continue the topic of where we left off yesterday on being wary of what we let into our lives and what may be poisoning us slowly. We have a life force within us, a soul that is being etched into the very likeness of Jesus Christ day by day through the indwelling of the Holy Spirit. It brings life to our very being, a sanctifying life that only the Holy Spirit can produce in us and nothing of our own doing. This life is sacred and the things that we do are sacred because of Whom is inside of us and Whose we are, so why taint this body and soul and spirit that is becoming like Christ? Why hinder the work of the Spirit?

The Lord will not give His glory to another, or as He says later on, "I will not yield my glory to another" (48:11). How can He? He is the Lord and there is no other like Him. Some may claim that there are, but they are liars and they will be shown for what they are. "We belong to the Lord" (Romans 14:8) and "I am my lover's and my lover is mine" (Song of Songs 6:3), so why do we offer ourselves to others and not wholly to Christ? Why are we bouncing back and forth between earthly pleasures and heavenly pleasures, between what we know is wrong and what we know is right? Why are we receiving the grace of our Lord Jesus in vain? Why are we allowing our minds and hearts to wander away from the truth, to stroll the paths of darkness and take part in the toxin that is bringing about the slow demise of our very being?

My brothers, this should not be. We are giving the glory that is due to the Lord to idols, to women, to ourselves, to our businesses, to our governments, to our entertainments, to things that are not the Lord! Beloved, does this not pain you? Does this not cut you deeply, urging you to come to the Lord in repentance of your sins? Do you not desire to become like our Christ, holy and pleasing to our Father in heaven? Do you not long to have purified thoughts that are pleasant to our Lord? Do you not crave to have control over your emotions instead of being led by outbursts and feelings? Jesus Christ is Lord. He *will not* share His glory with anyone or anything else because He wants all of you, not only part of you a few hours a week, but *all of you!* The Lord will not stop working within us until we reach perfection, which will come when He returns for us. But until that time, He is sanctifying us into His likeness. Do not hinder it or get in the way. Make clear the way of the Lord to be at work in your lives.

"We wait for the blessed hope—the glorious appearing of our great God and Savior, Jesus Christ, who gave himself for us to redeem us from all wickedness and to purify for himself a people that are his very own, eager to do what is good" - Titus 2:13-14

To purify means to remove dirty or harmful substances that are contaminating something. It is the freeing of undesirable elements, those things that are causing imperfections. This is what it means to purify, to be in the process of being made perfect. This purification is what Jesus Christ desires of us, His people, His children, His church. The means of this purification is through the discipline of the Holy Spirit in our lives, molding us and reshaping us to live and move and breathe more like Christ.

We know that discipline does not always seem pleasant, if ever (Hebrews 12:11), but we also know that it is through this same discipline that we begin to see how small and weak and fragile we really are. Before said discipline, we may think that we are godly people given over to the Lord, but after the discipline hits us, we realize how much the things of the world really do affect our behaviors and mindsets. Paul reminds us that it is Christ Jesus who gave Himself for us to redeem us from all such wickedness and impurities, and to make us pure and holy. Peter calls us "a chosen people, a royal priesthood, a holy nation, a people belonging to God" (1 Peter 2:9). As the apostles of Christ wrote these letters through the Spirit's inspiration and as they walked throughout Asia, they did not label believers by what they once were, but by what they were becoming, which was holy and perfect through the sanctification of the Holy Spirit.

It is when Christ Jesus returns to us that we shall then be made perfect, but until that time, we are in the continual transformation into His image, removing all contaminants from within that encumber us from doing His will and from the liberating release of the Spirit within. These impurities that cause imperfections among us are just that, impure. We may not necessarily see them as impure because they are so natural to us, occurring with such regularity that we tend to look right past them until the Lord enlightens us to see the hindrance that they truly are. As pollutants in water need to be removed, so pollutants in our hearts and minds and lives need to be removed and burned. It is only when water is boiled that its impurities are eradicated and the same rings true for us; we need the heated and unpleasant discipline of the Holy Spirit working within us to remove the harmful substances that are poisoning us. Do not overlook the Lord's discipline brothers. See it, embrace it, endure it. He longs for us to be pure, so do not hinder His methods to purify His people. We belong to Him. Have your way Lord Jesus. Have your way.

"As a result, he does not live the rest of his earthly life for evil human desires, but rather for the will of God" - 1 Peter 4:2

I hope you have been noticing the trend the past couple of days, that of being wholly devoted to God through and through. We know that God does not merely want just our heart or just our brain or just a part of us, but He wants all of who we are, body, soul and spirit. He did not come to suffer, die and be raised to life so that He could only redeem a piece of us, but so He could deliver all of our being into the glorious freedom of His grace.

The apostle Peter is writing this in dealing with suffering "because he who has suffered in his body is done with sin" (4:1). When one is undergoing suffering, the trivial things of this life become just that, trivial, they are no longer seen as "necessities" as they are by some. Priorities are put in their proper place when one is suffering. They can see what matters and what does not. Please note that this suffering is in accordance with pain and distress for the sake of Christ and doing good, not for anything bad that you may have done, in which you would be deserving of such suffering. Suffering is only temporary, but in the moment, just like with discipline, we tend to forget that it is so and we get lost in the midst of it. Hence we must keep our eyes fixed on Jesus throughout it, as He comforts us and speaks to us words of wisdom and encouragement, whispering to us that He is eternal and the suffering is not.

Consequently, since when we undergo suffering for the Lord's sake, when we undergo His Spirit's discipline, we should not be living the rest of our lives for evil human desires. Pride, jealousy, envy, selfish ambition, adultery, immorality and more should not be the guide of our lives any longer. We shall not be slaves to sin anymore for "We died to sin; how can we live in it any longer?" (Romans 6:2). Those lifestyles, those choices, those frames of mind, they shall be on the forefront of our lives no more! But rather, the will of God shall be the focal point, the guiding force of our hearts and minds. When evil thoughts begin to creep in, dismiss them immediately and "put no confidence in the flesh" (Philippians 3:3), but instead set your heart and mind on Christ above, seated on His heavenly throne. We do not live for ourselves and the flesh; we live for Christ and His will to be done because it is worth the cost a hundred fold. His Spirit shall lead us, not fear or pain or the world, but the Holy Spirit Himself. Do heed His direction.

"They sought God eagerly, and he was found by them. So the Lord gave them rest on every side" – 2 Chronicles 15:15

King Asa of Judah was an interesting king. He started off his reign doing great things, depending on the Lord his God for military victories, obeyed Him, and reformed the land, but near the end of his life, he no longer relied on God for battles but on man. He was in endless wars the remainder of his life because of it. What was more significant with him was that his son Jehoshaphat, who succeeded him as king, started off and ended just like his father. Asa may not have known it at the time, but his son watched him more than he knew, and not for the better.

But King Asa had a wonderful moment throughout his reign when "He removed the detestable idols from the whole land of Judah and Benjamin and the towns he had captured in the hills of Ephraim" (15:8). The people then sacrificed to the Lord, seeking Him with all their heart and soul and made a covenant with Him. They worshiped Him. God in turn blessed them and gave them rest on every side.

Rest is a beautiful thing that is sometimes underappreciated. The nation of Judah has constantly been battling with Israel and other surrounding nations, fighting for years and never getting rest. But when King Asa entered into a covenant to seek the Lord and he and the people meant it wholeheartedly, God gave them rest. They did not have to fight anymore. They did not have to struggle and wonder if they were going to be dead tomorrow or not. They were at peace because the Lord was with them and the Lord Himself gave them this peace.

The only way for there to be rest on every side of your life is through the Lord God. You could tire endlessly and strive with every fiber of your being, becoming a busybody in hopes of obtaining rest and peace, but it would be to no avail. You will be burnt out, exhausted and wondering why that throughout you efforts you could not obtain it. Because there is only one way, and that is to let the Lord take care of things. "Cast your cares on the Lord and he will sustain you" (Psalm 55:22). As the people of Judah sought the Lord their God with everything, so must we. "Seek first his kingdom and his righteousness, and all these things will be given to you as well" (Matthew 6:33). I cannot emphasize this enough my friends; we must always be seeking the Lord, night and day through our work and play, never not seeking His face.

"For the word of God is living and active" - Hebrews 4:12

The Word of God is just that, words, whether they are spoken or written or whatever, they are the words of God. I hope we know by now that words carry a burden and a power with them, a sense of responsibility and of purpose. They are not to be used idly or willy-nilly, but for a specific reason to gain a particular result. Words are meant to achieve what they were sent out to do and we should always watch the words that we say.

The writer of Hebrews, most likely Apollos, tells us that the word of God is living and active. How can words be living? They are just words that are spoken or written on a page, so how can they be living? Living means to have life and not be dead, simple enough. Jesus Christ, who is the Living Word (John 1:14), was and is alive, so that is one way how the Word of God is living. Everything that God has ever said, everything that is written in the Holy Scriptures, it is all living because Jesus Christ is alive today. The words written in the pages of the Bible are not just words, they are power, they are God speaking to us still today, thousands of years later. They have carried the same weight and authority as they were spoken way back then. This Word is energetic and life flows from it because the Spirit of God is within these pages.

The Word of God is also active. The Greek for this word is *energés* which means to be effective, powerful and operative. That is what the Word of God is brothers. The words in this wonderful book are extremely operational, influential, and have changed countless lives over the centuries, and continue to do so today. Since it says that God's word is active, it always produces some sort of result to those who come in contact with it.

If we do not sense the livingness of God's word, it proves that we have not touched God's word. How can you come into contact with something that is living and not be changed? When you come into contact with another person, you *will* have an impact on them whether for bad or for good, but they will be impacted one way or another. People have read the Word of God, but have only read it for the words inside and not for the life that it gives off. If a man hears the Word and does not start living, he has not really heard the Word, just the sound of it. "So is my word that goes out from my mouth: It will not return to me empty, but will accomplish what I desire and achieve the purpose for which I sent it" (Isaiah 55:11). Is the Word of the Lord effective in your life, or are they just mere words?

"Sharper than any double-edged sword, it penetrates even to dividing soul and spirit, joints and marrow; it judges the thoughts and attitudes of the heart" - Hebrews 4:12

The Word of God is the sword of the Spirit as we know as part of God's armor from Ephesians 6:17, but here goes even further, declaring that it is sharper than any sword. Swords are strong pieces of steel that can cut through any part of the body because of the leverage and force that can be thrust upon them, so dividing joint and marrow would be no problem. But dividing soul and spirit? That is something more altogether. That is much deeper and more profound than anything we have yet seen.

The Word of God is so sharp, so penetrating, that it is able to divide the very soul and spirit of our being; even the sharpest of all swords is not able to do that. A surgical knife can delicately cut into anything within the human body with such precision, yet that cannot divide the soul from the spirit; it cannot make that distinction. Only God's word can do such a thing. Like we learned yesterday, God's word is living and active, and now we learn that it is also so sharp that it is able to separate the soul and the spirit, something that we ourselves cannot begin to fathom.

We wish we truly knew what was inside of us, what we are made of. We wish we knew the thoughts and the attitudes of our hearts and minds, but we do not. Only when we come in contact with the Word of God are we even able to catch a glimpse of the reality that is inside of us. It is because the light of Christ is able to shine on us, revealing to us our true nature, enlightening us with the knowledge that we are not as holy and righteous as we make ourselves out to be. The thoughts and the intentions of our heart are laid bare before the King of kings because of the revelation of the Word of God through the Holy Spirit. Our true thoughts and our true motives are visible before the Lord.

The closer we are to the Light of Life, the longer our shadow becomes because we see our darkness that much clearer because of the intensity of His purity and holiness. Now that the trueness of your heart lies naked before your King, what do you see? Have your intentions and attitudes been all for yourself, for your flesh, or have they been for the Lord your God? Are the things you thought were done for the Lord ultimately done for yourself? His light and word reveals all and it does not lie. Who does the light say you are living for?

"Command those who are rich in this present world not to be arrogant nor to put their hope in wealth, which is so uncertain, but to put their hope in God, who richly provides us with everything for our enjoyment" – 1 Timothy 6:17

Why is money such a problem within the church? Why has this portion of worldliness infiltrated our walls possibly more than any other thing? Maybe it is due to the fact that we believe that the more money we have, the more freedom we have to do things and the greater security and comfort we can have. Or perhaps it is that we do not want to be at a desperate point where we feel we *need* to have God come through in order for us to make it through.

And so it is a crutch, a tool of hope for the church that is in fact a false hope. Paul told Timothy that wealth is so uncertain because it is here today and gone tomorrow and that "the love of money is a root of all kinds of evil" (6:10). Money has corrupted so many good people, so much so that they have wandered from the faith. However, money itself is not evil, but it is a tool that God has given us to be used responsibly for the sake of His church and His world. Our hope should not be in money, as many people believe that if they have it, *then* they would be satisfied and free from care.

But our hope is to be put in God! If our hope is in anything else but God, our loyalty is divided and we are of no use to Him. "No one can serve two masters. Either he will hate the one and love the other, or he will be devoted to the one and despise the other. You cannot serve both God and Money" (Matthew 6:24). You *cannot* serve both God and money. And please make note of this brothers, that if you make money your master, it will be just that, your master! You will not be in control of it as you may think, but it will indeed control you and make you its slave.

Put your hope in God. It is only in Him that we are truly satisfied. Paul even told Timothy that it is God who richly provides us with everything for our enjoyment. He is the One that blesses us with food and shelter and friends and a job and everything else that He has chosen to bless us with. May we utter the words of David, "Find rest, O my soul, in God alone, my hope comes from him" (Psalm 62:5). Find rest my brothers in the truth that God will meet your every need, not money. It is God who cares for you and it is God in Whom you should put your hope and trust.

"Though the fig tree does not bud and there are no grapes on the vines, though the olive crop fails and the fields produce no food, though there are no sheep in the pen and no cattle in the stalls, yet I will rejoice in the Lord, I will rejoice in God my Savior" – Habakkuk 3:17-18

In some of the greatest movies of all time, like *The Lord of the Rings, Star Wars, Saving Private Ryan, Gladiator, Braveheart,* and many more, there are dark and trying times through the movie. There are moments when all hope seems to have faded and people are giving over to despair, but not the protagonists, they see that minuscule glimmer of light shinning in the distance, giving them enough hope to rally a few foolish troops to make a final stand for the sake of their people. They did not let the darkness shake them completely, but they found hope amidst the hopeless situation and that made all the difference.

And neither did the prophet Habakkuk, who most likely lived during the same time as Jeremiah. The Book of Habakkuk is much like the story of Israel's complaints with God with a grumble then a reply from God. It actually reminds me of some of the psalms where there is doubt in the voice of the work of the Lord, but in the end their faith is once again restored. The prophet is talking about a time when nothing seems to be going right, where the things they relied on previously for sustaining life are failing, where their crops are not producing and they do not have sheep in their pens. But that does not stop him from rejoicing in the Lord! He will not let those tragedies hinder his praise to the King of kings!

Paul tells us to "Rejoice in the Lord always. I will say it again: Rejoice!" (Philippians 4:4). Note how he does not say "Rejoice in the Lord only when everything is going right or when you feel like it and forget the Lord when darkness approaches." That would be preposterous, but he says to rejoice in the Lord always! Paul was imprisoned when he wrote that. Habakkuk wrote those words in the face of Babylon destroying his homeland. He knew that evil was on Israel's doorstep and that is why he said "Yet I will wait patiently for the day of calamity to come on the nation invading us" (3:16). When the faintest glimpse of hope was nowhere to be found, Habakkuk decided that He would rejoice in the Lord and be joyful in his Sovereign God! He would not be shaken by his outside circumstances and neither should we. We have a God who is closer to us than our own skin. Do not let despair creep its way into your life and heart, but remember Who is there before you and with you and rejoice!

"So that you may know the certainty of the things you have been taught" - Luke 1:4

This morning at church we talked about the short introduction to the Book of Luke and his character. He traveled with Paul for a majority of the Book of Acts, starting in his second missionary journey (Acts 16:10). They were close friends and some believe that Luke was Paul's most loyal friend while most others deserted him (2 Timothy 4:11) as he continued to suffer for the sake of Christ. Luke was a doctor, a thorough investigator for the knowledge of the truth so others may know the same. As he writes in the intro to his letter, "Many have undertaken to draw up an account of the things that have been fulfilled among us, just as they were handed down to us by those who from the first were eyewitnesses and servants of the word. Therefore, since I myself have *carefully investigated everything* from the beginning, it seemed good also to me to write an orderly account for you" (1:1-3, emphasis added).

Luke wanted Theophilus, who most likely was a Gentile believer who was a nobleman, to know more certainly the truth which had been taught to him; the truth that is contained in his Gospel account of Jesus Christ and later of the Holy Spirit's work in the early church in his second letter to him known as the Book of Acts. How blessed it is of Luke to care about his friend that he wants to investigate the stories of the man known as Jesus of Nazareth who changed the course of history! How great it was of him to not want his dear friend to have a blind faith, but one that he could be able to back up with real historical accounts as included in his books.

Do you know the certainty of the things you have been taught? Do you, like so many American Christians in this day and age, "know" what you believe just because it was how you were raised or are you merely following blindly? But there is no need for that my brothers! The accounts of the Bible are in fact historically accurate and reliable and there are scholars like Jospehus and others who can attest to that. Christ in no way asks you to follow Him blindly; He wants you to know what you are getting into (Matthew 16:24-26, Luke 14:25-33, John 6:53-58). I urge you to not walk around blindly in your faith, but to know the certainty of the things you have been taught concerning Christ Jesus and His church.

September 2

"With their mouths they express devotion, but their hearts are greedy for unjust gain"
– Ezekiel 33:31

Is this not how it is in the church today? Is this not the attitude of countless "believers" that I see walk among me day in and day out? I see so many people that I grew up with, people who went to church with me and still do, who go to Bible studies and worship concerts and fit what the "Christian model" looks like, but when you actually examine their lives, you see so clearly how far they really are from the Son of God, living for mere appearances to please their parents or even convince themselves that they did what they were supposed to do.

Surrounding our verse, Ezekiel mentions that "My people come to you, as they usually do, and sit before you to listen to your words, but they do not put them into practice...Indeed, to them you are nothing more than one who sings love songs with a beautiful voice and plays an instrument well, for they hear your words but do not put them into practice" (33:31-32). These people only want to be entertained; they do not want to live a life of integrity before the Lord. They believe that the things they do are good enough to be accepted as followers of Christ, but that is just it; they are not following Christ but themselves! How easily do we fall into this same trap of self-deception? Have we come to the point where everything that we do is so habitual that we no longer put any thinking into it whatsoever? As the common saying goes these days, "We are just going through the motions."

These motions are just that, motions; our hearts are not in them much like the people Ezekiel is referencing. Then where is our heart? Towards other objects of our desire and passion. It is misplaced and misguided, being led down a path to the pit where it rots until it realizes it is covered in muck and mire and needs to be delivered. It is easy to get sucked into this trap of doing religious motions for the sake of doing it and treating it all as if it is a show. Brothers, our hearts *have* to be in it, "For where your treasure is, there your heart will be also" (Matthew 6:21). So what does that mean for you? Is your life one of integrity and authenticity to the Lord your God, practicing what you preach? Is your heart where your mouth is?

"I hate your religious feasts; I cannot stand your assemblies. Even though you bring me burnt offerings and grain offerings, I will not accept them" – Amos 5:21-22

The Lord said these things to His people Israel, to those who were supposed to be His "church" before there was an actual church. He said this to worshipers of His house, the Jewish people who came into the synagogue every week as was their religious duty. They held feasts unto the Lord such as New Moon festivals, Passover, and Tabernacles. But the Lord God said that He hated these things. Why?

They were all just a show, much like what we talked about yesterday. They were a religious front that had no depth to them. Can you point this out in the church today? Do you see the mega-churches that have their own restaurants in them, that play loud and boisterous music to try and keep the youth's attention, that do not tackle controversial issues because they are afraid to offend someone who believes otherwise? It is not just the big churches that do this, there are numerous small congregations that are filled with emptiness and shallow waters as well. God is speaking to the church now! "Away with the noise of your songs! I will not listen to the music of your harps. But let justice roll on like a river, righteousness like a never-failing stream!" (5:23-24). "Stop bringing meaningless offerings! Your incense is detestable to me...When you spread out your hands in prayer, I will hide my eyes from you; even if you offer many prayers, I will not listen" (Isaiah 1:13, 15).

The Lord is sick of the show that we try and offer Him; He does not want a show from us, but He wants *us*. It is not religious activities that please our Father, it is the posture of our hearts that do. And we think it is our culture that has shaped the church this way, of making appearances look nice and appetizing but then there is death on the inside and no flow from the river of life, but it has been around since the days of the Prophets and before. Our hearts need to be for the Lord and the things He desires, not what we think is right. Jon Foreman wrote about this in a song, "You turned your back on the homeless. And the ones that don't fit in your plan. Quit playing religion games. There's blood on your hands." This all comes from these two passages in Isaiah and Amos. Instead of a show to the Lord, let our lives be a living sacrifice where we live a life of love which is pleasing to the Father, ushering forth His Kingdom.

"Therefore, there is now no condemnation for those who are in Christ Jesus" – Romans 8:1

No condemnation. None for those who are in Christ Jesus. This sounds like it is wonderful, but what does it mean? Condemnation is the sentencing of judgment upon a guilty person and administering just punishment. The Greek word here, *katakrima,* specifically refers to the punishing following condemnation, so that is why this verse is a wonderful verse for those who believe! It means that we will not suffer punishment for our sins if we are in Christ Jesus "because through Christ Jesus the law of the Spirit of life set me free from the law of sin and death" (8:2).

In other words, we will not undergo condemnation because Christ saved us from our sins and "though [our] sins are like scarlet, they shall be as white as snow; though they are red as crimson, they shall be like wool" (Isaiah 1:18). He makes them white because He says, "I will forgive their wickedness and will remember their sins no more" (Jeremiah 31:34). Jesus forgives our sins and He forgets our sins. "As far as the east is from the west, so far has he removed our transgressions from us" (Psalm 103:12). You want to know how far away that is? If you continue to go east, you will never start going west and vice versa. I thought that was pretty neat.

My brothers, I sure hope you know why this verse is one of the church's favorite verses, because it means that we have nothing to fear about death. We know that when Christ returns and if we are in Him, we do not have to fear being punished for the wickedness we have done in our lives; Christ paid the highest price and took our place on that cross on Calvary. His great love and sacrifice for us is enough to pay the penalty for our sins so that if we accept Him as Lord and Savior and King of our lives (as He truly is), we will have eternal life and not an eternal death.

So what say you? Are you one who is in Christ Jesus, free from condemnation when He returns? The Old Testament Law could produce no pardon for sin, but only condemned it, but through Christ, who "is the end of the law" (10:4) and its fulfillment, there is grace and mercy in abundance for you and for me. There is no end to it. And since there is now this pardon for sin through Christ, will you accept His gracious sacrifice for you so that you can be free from bondage and slavery? Will you then live your life for the One who gave up His for you?

"As God's fellow workers we urge you not to receive God's grace in vain" – 2 Corinthians 6:1

Just because there is no condemnation for you who are in Christ Jesus, that does not mean you can now go live your life however you want and not have to suffer for your stupidity and lack of obedience. If this is what you choose to do, you are indeed receiving the Lord's grace in vain, making light of Jesus' suffering and sacrifice for you to be saved and sanctified. Hearing the truth is simply not enough; it must be embraced and applied to one's life in order for it to become effective and transforming.

You know you are taking God's grace in vain when you hear the word of the Lord and do not do what it says (James 1:22). We must be of those whom Jesus said that "everyone who hears these words of mine and puts them into practice is like the wise man who builds his house on the rock" (Matthew 7:24). We are to be wise men, not foolish men who build their houses in the sand so when the storms of life come, everything they have built will be destroyed, but because our house is on the rock, it will stand strong and survive. Because there is no condemnation for us, our lives should exemplify that of our Savior, who urges us to live a holy and sanctified life and not one full of wickedness and disgrace.

When we receive this free gift of grace in vain, we are still living for ourselves. But Paul said of Christ that "he died for all, that those who live should no longer live for themselves but for him who died for them and was raised again" (5:15). Christ died so that we would no longer live for our own selfish and evil desires that permeate our inmost being and make us rotten and fit only to be trampled on by men. He died so that we may live for Him and Him alone, who removes our sins far away from us and breathes into us His very life, so that He Himself is living within.

Brothers, I know at times we have in fact taken God's grace in vain by sinning willfully because it was convenient and easy and simply because we wanted to avoid a momentary pain or gain a temporary pleasure, but I know we know the truth that it is wrong and displeases our Father in heaven. Father, forgive us for when we have taken your grace for granted, knowing you would forgive us because we are your children. But that is not how a child of the Living God acts, and for that we are sorry. Guide us with your Holy Spirit so that we can live for you and you alone in this dark world, graciously accepting your unending grace that teaches us to say no to the world and yes to you and holiness. Thank you for hearing your children's cries. We love you Father.

"Since we have these promises, dear friends, let us purify ourselves from everything that contaminates body and spirit, perfecting holiness out of reverence for God" – 2 Corinthians 7:1

We have been discussing how important purity in the Body of Christ and in our individual lives is and how easy it is to let the world poison us with its influences and mindsets. Jesus told us that "you do not belong to the world, but I have chosen you out of the world" (John 15:19), so why should we live as the world does? Why should we react to situations the same way the world reacts to them? The answer is that we should not! We are different! We are not of this world just as Jesus is not of this world, but we are chosen out of it.

So why should we sicken ourselves with the things of this world? Why do we let them infiltrate and contaminate our bodies and spirits? Why do we "give the devil a foothold" (Ephesians 4:27) into our lives? My friends, we *must* purify ourselves from this sick and decrepit world and begin to live for God and the things of God: for love, righteousness, justice, mercy, joy, peace, holiness, self-control, integrity, honesty, discipline, gentleness, respect, temperance, generosity, and many more.

The promises that Paul refers to here are that God said "I will live with them and walk among them, and I will be their God and they will be my people" (6:16). Since God has and will fulfill these wonderful promises, since He is in our midst and we are His people, we *have* to live holy lives before Him. God cannot have imperfection around Him. Yes, while we are still living on this earth we will not attain perfection, but it does not mean we should not strive for it; that would be taking the Lord's grace in vain. We have the power of the Holy Spirit within us, perfecting us every moment of every day if we will just heed to its pruning, to its cutting us back and molding us into the likeness of Christ so that we can best represent Him and be useful in His Kingdom.

So how would you describe yourselves in this regard? Would you say that you are perfecting holiness out of reverence for God? Or would you more likely say that you have been lackadaisical in your walk with Christ; merely sitting and watching life go by, letting the world influence you more than you are influencing the world? I pray beloved that we can indeed be influencing the world much more than they are us and that we would be leaving it a better place than it was before.

September 7

"A man reaps what he sows" - Galatians 6:7

If you steal a car and get caught by the police for it, you will be punished because you committed a crime that is against the law. If you murder your coworker and get caught once again, you will be punished as is fitting to the crime. But if you do a good deed for a neighbor, he may do something good for you in return (because of how something benefits you should in no way be an incentive for doing something good). If you sow corn into a field, from that field you shall reap corn. A simple enough concept.

Paul goes on to say more clearly that "The one who sows to please his sinful nature, from that nature will reap destruction; the one who sows to please the Spirit, from the Spirit will reap eternal life" (6:8). What you put into life is what you should expect to get out of it. If you are lazy in your work, why would you expect to get rewards and special accolades? If you do a bad job, why expect to get good grades or be promoted? It does not make sense does it?

If you are feeding into the sinful nature, if you are constantly doing activities that please the flesh, if you are always thinking of ways in which to better yourself at the expense of others, you shall reap what you sow: destruction. Want a more thorough example of what things of the flesh are? "The acts of the sinful nature are obvious: sexual immorality, impurity and debauchery; idolatry and witchcraft; hatred, discord, jealousy, fits of rage, selfish ambition, dissensions, factions and envy; drunkenness, orgies, and the like" (5:19-21). So if you are sowing into any of those activities or lifestyles, why would you expect good and plentiful things to happen? They are what they are: void and lifeless, leading to ruin.

But when you sow into the things of the Spirit which are "love, joy, peace, patience, kindness, goodness, faithfulness, gentleness and self-control" (5:22-23), then you should expect those types of fruit to emerge in your life. It is simple logic. What does your life consist of? Are you sowing to please your sinful and selfish nature, believing that this life is all there is, or are you sowing to please the Holy Spirit because you know there is life after death? Do not go through another day gratifying the desires of the flesh which lead to death, but gratify the desires of the Spirit which lead to life everlasting!

September 8

"Remember this: Whoever sows sparingly will also reap sparingly, and whoever sows generously will also reap generously" – 2 Corinthians 9:6

There was a farmer who put a few seeds into the ground. He watered them and took care of them and when the harvest came, he had a few stalks of corn he could call his own. There was also another farmer who planted a whole field full of seeds. He watered them and took care of them and when the harvest came, he had a whole field full of corn that he could call his own and sell most of it in the marketplace.

This gives us a simple glimpse into our verse today, that whoever sows sparingly will also reap sparingly and whoever sows generously will also reap generously. Should the farmer who only planted a few seeds expect to have a plethora of corn at harvest time? And should the farmer who sowed a whole field expect to have a small harvest? By no means. They both got what they deserved from the amount of work that they put into it. This truth is the same for our lives as followers of Christ. Solomon wrote that "One man gives freely, yet gains even more; another withholds unduly, but comes to poverty" (Proverbs 11:24). This biblical principle runs true for us in how we deal with our finances. We know that God is the giver of all things, so the money we have is not even ours in the first place. Yes, you may work with your hands and receive a paycheck, but it is God "who gives you the ability to produce wealth" (Deuteronomy 8:18).

So why do we try and make money our gods? Are we afraid of losing it? Why do we not take up the principle that Paul tells us? Are we afraid to help sow into other people's lives financially? Because I know firsthand that helping others out is a tremendous blessing that I have been able to do, and the Lord has greatly blessed me because of my willingness. Not necessarily blessing me back financially, but in other ways that have molded me more in the likeness of His image. Solomon also tells us in that same chapter that "Wealth is worthless in the day of wrath" (Proverbs 11:4), so once again, why pile it up? Why not give it away freely as we have been given freely? What makes us think that we are wiser with our finances than God is? I urge you brothers to not limit the work of God because of your selfishness and stubbornness, but to sow generously into the Kingdom of God because those are the things that will last and you will indeed be blessed. What is stopping you?

"And let us consider how we may spur one another on towards love and good deeds" -
Hebrews 10:24

I just recently got back from the other side of the state after visiting some dear friends of mine. It was extremely encouraging for me to go there, not only for me but for them as well because there are not many people their age around them there. We relaxed, ate food, and talked about life and theological issues, along with them continually trying to set me up with the wife's sister. It was a wonderful weekend that we desperately needed.

What does it mean to spur one another? In terms of cowboy spurs that they wear on their boots, those are pointed prongs that poke the horse to help it do what they want to do; it encourages them to go a certain way and urges them to take action. Maybe that is what the author of Hebrews was getting at here, which is that we need to be frequently thinking of how we can be encouraging one another on towards the things of Christ, towards love and good deeds. That is one of the reasons why I love hanging out with those friends because we are all urging one another towards oneness with Christ and helping each other out with issues that we are trying to work through. We can talk to each other about anything and spur one another in the direction of a deeper walk with Christ Jesus.

Following this verse, the writer continues, "Let us not give up meeting together, as some are in the habit of doing, but let us encourage one another—and all the more as you see the Day approaching" (10:25). And oddly enough, Judgment Day was one of the topics that we talked about and whether we would remember our life on earth when in heaven or if that day would be both painful and celebratory, or only celebratory. We were all in agreement that we long for the day of Christ's return to bring us home with Him. We see the wars and injustice and oppression and selfishness all around us and pray for Him to come back and make all things new. We need to be encouraging one another on towards love and good deeds as we see the Day approaching because people will need that love more than anything as hopefully it urges them to come to Christ in the midst of chaos and destruction. There is an Aramaic expression that was used amongst the apostles in the New Testament, *Marana tha,* which means "Come, O Lord." And that is our cry today, Come O Lord!

"The day of the Lord is near for all nations" – Obadiah 15

Judgment Day. The Day of the Lord. This last phrase is scattered throughout the prophetic writings of the Old Testament. As with many prophecies in the Bible, they had both a temporary meaning for the people receiving it at the time and a meaning for those further down the road, us today. Being the shortest book in the Old Testament, this prophecy is about Edom's destruction because of their hostility towards Israel, and Israel's deliverance because God is with them.

As we move towards the future significance of this prophesy, we notice how New Testament writers are also using this phrase, "the day of our Lord Jesus Christ" (1 Corinthians 1:8). I am sure you know that this expression signifies the end of time, the day when our Lord Jesus Christ returns to "judge the living and the dead" (2 Timothy 4:1). "For we must all appear before the judgment seat of Christ, that each one may receive what is due him for the things done while in the body, whether good or bad" (2 Corinthians 5:10).

That day is coming brothers. The day where we shall be judged for the things we have done. We will get to stand before the judgment seat of our Lord and Savior Jesus Christ, the Son of God, and our whole lives will be played before us. Many people fear the coming of this day, but for those of us who believe and are saved, "there is now no condemnation" (Romans 8:1) for us, so there is no need to worry or fear that day. But for those who are not saved, be afraid because there will be condemnation for you. For those who believe, there will be reward, but for those who do not, there will be punishment. If you are one who does not believe in the Lord Jesus Christ, what is stopping you? Your stubbornness? Your belief in science? Your friends and family? Open up your eyes and heart to the things unseen, the things that are eternal, the things that are right in front of you, the things you have been searching for all your life in your never-ending pursuits that always end up empty and found wanting.

Jesus Christ came down from heaven to become a man just like us, to bear all the weight of our sins and iniquities, to suffer and die and rise again so that we do not have to experience an eternal death, but rather an eternal life with Him! "To those who by persistence in doing good seek glory, honor and immortality, he will give eternal life. But for those who are self-seeking and who reject the truth and follow evil, there will be wrath and anger" (Romans 2:7-8). The day of the Lord is near my friends. Are you preparing for it? Are you looking forward to it or are you afraid of that day?

"You have heard that it was said, 'Love your neighbor and hate your enemy.' But I tell you: Love your enemies and pray for those who persecute you, that you may be sons of your Father in heaven" – Matthew 5:43-45

This day marks the 13th anniversary of the 9/11 terrorist attacks here in America. It was a day that will forever be embedded in the minds of every American as our national security was breached in such a way that we have not seen an attack on our soil since Pearl Harbor sixty years earlier. It was then that our people and government acted in fear of another attack that we made an offensive against the perpetrators. The ones who committed this act of terror were Muslim jihadists and since then, their numbers have grown and so has their hatred of the West.

Many Americans hated Muslims after this attack occurred, so much that even the Muslims in our own country were being watched and questioned, under suspicion that they potentially knew something of the attacks, much like what we did to the Japanese after Pearl Harbor, even though the Muslims responsible account for a minuscule portion of the Muslim population in the world. It was not right of us to act as we did; it was out of fear of our enemies that we created such prejudices and we still feel the effects to this day because many strongly still feel this way.

Jesus approaches this sort of thing in a different light; He tells us, no, *commands* us to love our enemies and to pray for them. Although all His fellow Jews hated on the Romans who were there enemies, Jesus goes against that mentality and tells them to pray for them. Even while Jesus hung on the cross, He said "Father, forgive them, for they do not know what they are doing" (Luke 23:34). He knew that "our struggle is not against flesh and blood, but against the rulers, against the authorities, against the powers of this dark world and against the spiritual forces of evil in the heavenly realms" (Ephesians 6:12).

We were also enemies of Christ before we believed (Romans 5:10), but that did not stop Christ from giving up His very life for us so we may be saved. Jesus loves His enemies and does not wish harm to them, but prays that they may be saved. And as followers of Christ, as imitators of God, we are called to do the same. Do you desire for the enemies in your life to come to the knowledge of Christ? Or do you wish death and destruction upon them? Follow the example of your Savior and pray that they may see the error of their ways and be saved just as you were lost and now are found.

September 12

"Turn to God" – Acts 3:19

While reading through *The Final Quest* by Rick Joyner, he was describing the judgment seat of Christ and the beauty of the throne room there. He was interacting with men and women of faith in this great hall, and after talking with them, he sees all the darkness and wrong that his life was full of, all the pride and jealousy that moved these people to the lowest ranks of heaven. It was at this time that those he was talking to told him to cast aside such thoughts and turn to the Lamb on the throne.

"Turn to God" says Peter. "Fix your thoughts on Jesus" (Hebrews 3:1) says the author of Hebrews. "Look to the Lord and his strength; seek his face always" (Psalm 105:4) says the Psalmist. Are you catching the pattern here? We *must* turn ourselves towards Christ if we ever want to be of good use to Him. When we keep our eyes fixed upon us, we see very little and all we want to do is please ourselves. When we keep our eyes fixed on the things around us or on other people, we become short-sighted and all we want to do is please them. When such things occur, we forget who we are and what on earth we are here for, which is to bring glory to God. How can we give God glory if we are turned away from Him? How can we please our Father in heaven if we are not looking to Him for everything in our lives?

Satan tries to deceive us into thinking that we can get by in this life with only turning to God every once and awhile. If he can steer our gaze away from Christ on His throne, he will have won the battle, if it even was a battle. But friends, we need to remember to fix our thoughts on Christ seated at the right hand of God the Father. When we are facing Him, all other things become so much clearer as His light shines and exposes those things hidden. When we are turned towards God, we see Him and what He has done and is doing for us; our perspective changes as we begin to see from an eternal viewpoint through His eyes.

What do you do when you are overridden with guilt and shame? Or when you grow in despair at the rising darkness in the world? Do you sulk away in your shame and mope around with no flicker of hope? Instead of immersing yourself, well, in yourself, turn to the Lord your God who takes away the sins of the world. Turn to the One who alone can show you the way to fulfillment and truth and give your life real meaning. Only when you are no longer looking at yourself can you truly see the Light of Life and are then able to serve Him without hindrance.

"Like a city whose walls are broken down is a man who lacks self-control" - Proverbs 25:28

That is quite the analogy eh? "Like a city whose walls are broken down is a man who lacks self-control." Let us try and imagine that for a moment. Cities in Bible times had walls surrounding them to protect them from their enemies and anyone else who was not wanted. It signified where exactly they had the greatest influence and what precisely they had direct control and jurisdiction over. Now picture it with no walls. The people are scared to walk about for fear of outsiders. They feel vulnerable and open to anything and everything with no guard to protect them from foes and bandits. They are defenseless.

And yet Solomon informs us that people who lack self-control are just like those cities without walls; they are defenseless. They are much more affected by the things around them than they should be. If there were a flood outside the city, they would be open to it and there would be nothing they could do about it. All things would come into the city and influence it in one way or another. So with a man who does not practice control of the self, outside powers will pressure him into doing whatever they want him to do. He is constantly in danger of being carried away by his desires and passions and pursuits, even though he may think he is always in control, yet he is being controlled.

He has no defense against sin and temptation because he has not learned the virtue of self-control that is taught by the Holy Spirit. He is a fool, "but a wise man keeps himself under control" (29:11). It is better for "a man who controls his temper than one who takes a city" (16:32). We are at war as long as we live in this body. And since we are at war, we need walls to protect ourselves against the enemy. These walls are the barriers that shield us from letting outside influences have an effect on us that we do not wish upon ourselves.

Can you think of a time when you lacked self-control? In hindsight, is it easy to realize how selfish and childish you were and how you let your circumstances get the best of you? God has called us to live self-controlled lives because he who lacks it is easily swayed by the wind and cannot be trusted since he has no temperance or moderation; at any moment his emotions or thoughts may take control and then no one knows where he will go from there. Nowhere good I am sure. Pray for self-control in your lives my brothers so that you may stand firm in the grace of God, knowing that you will not let the world nor yourself be taken off-guard.

"Praise the Lord, O my soul; all my inmost being, praise his holy name. Praise the Lord, O my soul" – Psalm 103:1-2

The Hebrew word for "praise" here is better translated "bless", and since it is in relation to God, some translators use the liberty and change it to praise, since I am sure that many of you (including myself) do not know what it means to bless the Lord. Some commentators mention that the praise signified in this passage implies a strong affection and gratitude to the Lord, hence David saying to praise the Lord will all of his inmost being, his entire self.

As followers of Christ, when we see the word "praise" we tend to jump straight to praising the Lord through the form of song, and nothing is wrong with that. But we cannot limit it strictly to music, for praise is so much more than that. When praising the Lord will all of ourselves, we recall the character of who God is and the works He has done, as David does here saying "Praise the Lord, O my soul, and forget not all his benefits—who forgives all your sins and heals all your diseases, who redeems your life from the pit and crowns you with love and compassion, who satisfies your desires with good things" (103:2-5). It is God who does all these wondrous things for us, all because of His great love for His children.

How often do we forget that it is the Lord who graciously forgives us, that it is the Lord who drew us out of the mud and mire to set our feet on solid ground, that it is the Lord who blesses us in abundance, who "does not treat us as our sins deserve or repay us according to our iniquities" (103:10)? And David is saying that *that* is why we praise the Lord will all of our inmost being, with all of our heart and all of our soul and all of our strength.

Throughout the Scriptures, it talks about giving God all that He deserves and is worthy of, which of course is everything and the entirety of what we have. Six times in Psalm 103 it repeats the phrase "Praise the Lord, O my soul." Are you beginning to understand what life with the Lord is all about? It is not about you, but it is entirely about Him! It does not say "Praise John, O my soul" or "Praise Kim, O my soul", but "Praise the Lord, O my soul; all my inmost being, praise his holy name." Do not forget to do this my friends; it is too easy to get caught up in the motions of being a Christian that we forget what being a Christian is actually about, which is to be like Christ! May the Holy Spirit guide you into all these truths so that you may be more like Him today.

September 15

"Fix these words of mine in your hearts and minds" – Deuteronomy 11:18

Lately, I have really been reminded on how important the Word of God is in our everyday lives. Of course I know how imperative it is that we are constantly immersing ourselves into His Word and finding ways to apply it to our lives, but sometimes we leave it just at that, as a guidebook for our earthly journey, to teach us good things to do. But I know it is much more than that and I hope you do too. It is the Living Word, Jesus Christ Himself, that we open up and soak in the words, and when we take it lightly, we take Him lightly.

This is why recently I have taken it upon myself to be memorizing Scripture on a consistent basis. We read the Word and that is it; we do not memorize it and have it be absorbed into our very being. It is a lost form of worship to the Lord that the Hebrew people excelled at and where Hebrew boys, by the age of 13, were able to recite the first five books of the Hebrew Bible by heart. And even some of them go on to memorize the rest of the Tanakh, which is our Old Testament. Now that is incredible and that is dedication. Why do we not do this glorious thing while those who do not follow Christ do?

The Jewish people understand how much we need to have the Word of God ingrained in the fiber of our being, to "not let the Book of the Law depart from your mouth; meditate on it day and night, so that you may be careful to do everything written in it" (Joshua 1:8). We need to grasp what it means to ingest the Word of God, to have it flowing freely within us so that when it is time for our instincts to kick in, it is God's Word that has become our instinct because it is all that is within us. Jeremiah wrote concerning this saying "When your words came, I ate them; they were my joy and my heart's delight, for I bear your name, O Lord God Almighty" (Jeremiah 15:16).

God's words need to become a part of us, assimilated into our hearts and minds, as Christ the Living Word is within us. And Scripture memorization is a great way for this to begin and a good foundation for us to be thinking about how we can please the Lord all day long. The movie, *The Book of Eli,* inspired me to know and commit to heart God's Word as it drove the main character's life to be guided by it wholeheartedly and he had the whole Bible memorized. May you be motivated to have the words of the Living God be a part of your soul and I challenge you to begin memorizing some Scripture, whether that be a verse or a passage or even a chapter or more. I know you will rise to the occasion brothers because you have a thirst for Christ Jesus.

"I planted the seed, Apollos watered it, but God made it grow. So neither he who plants nor he who waters is anything, but only God, who makes things grow" – 1 Corinthians 3:6-7

My roommate has been talking to me lately about his frustration with his job and how the state barely allows him to teach anything, but mostly just tracks data of the kids so that the school can get more funding from the state. It is irritating him to the point that wants to quit his job and he cannot see himself being satisfied working at a school where he cannot teach his true passion which is the Gospel. It is only his first year of teaching as well.

The verse does not really play along too cleanly with this story, but it runs somewhat along the same lines. I want to talk about how we as followers of Christ do not always get to see the fruit of our labors. Let us look at the situation with my roommate: he does not see any hope for these kids because their parents also see no hope for them and he can see no way how he can effectively reach them for their betterment. He has only been teaching for a month. Of course you are not going to see much result in a month of teaching middle schoolers! This is causing him to lose hope in his work, but he has never given it a chance to grow yet.

When you plant a seed, it does not magically grow overnight like *Jack and the Beanstalk*, but you have to water it and nurture it and take care of it for a long time. If it is a tree, then you have to wait even longer for you to see the results of your patient and enduring work. Farmers are some of the most patient people on the planet and I believe that is why farming and agriculture are mentioned all throughout the Bible because our life as Christ-followers is all about patience and waiting on the Lord to come through.

The great heroes of the faith mentioned in Hebrews 11 never saw the fruit of their labor while living. But they kept their eyes on Christ and that is what pushed them further. "The man who plants and the man who waters have one purpose, and each will be rewarded according to his own labor" (3:8). We have a job to do as servants of Christ; we are never promised that we will enjoy the rewards of it in this life, but we shall in the life to come. We may be impacting people for God's Kingdom without ever realizing it, touching lives that we never even knew of. When we make it to heaven, then and only then shall we see the true fruits of our toilsome labor. Do not give up in doing good my brothers. Stay the course.

September 17

"After he dismissed them, he went up on a mountainside by himself to pray" – Matthew 14:23

Fall is approaching. The leaves are beginning to change. Cool, crisp air is starting to arrive. Football watching, apple picking, cider drinking, flannel wearing season is upon us. The best season of the year is here, which means it is time to take a vacation to get away from all the hustle and bustle of work and the monotony of life. A time to wind down and reflect, to recharge my batteries and refocus on the only One I should ever be focused on. It is important to get away every once and awhile.

Jesus understood this full well. He just got done feeding the five thousand when He decided it was time to get away to pray, and to a beautiful mountain nonetheless. The Son of God, the Lord Almighty incarnate, needed a vacation from His work, how much more do we need it then? If the Creator of the entire universe needed to take time and retreat from the busyness of His everyday life, what right do we have to say we are better than Him and are "too busy" to get away? How dare we! On the seventh day of creation, God rested from all His work (Genesis 2:2).

Vacation and recreation are especially necessary when we are depleted of everything and are running on fumes. It brings a restoration to our souls, filling us up again so that we are able to pour ourselves out to the work of God for others once more. But sometimes we tend to forget that, we think that by constantly being busy, we are therefore being more productive, but that is just not the case. In his new book *Simplify*, Bill Hybels wrote, "Sometimes, people feel an undercurrent of guilt for taking time to do things that fill their buckets, as if someone will judge them for having fun or spending time doing something for *themselves* rather than for others...But this is backward thinking. When your tank is empty, you have nothing to offer anyone else. You can't give what you don't have."

When was the last time you took some time for yourself, to refill your bucket, to truly connect with God who can help fill your bucket to overflowing so you can give even more? I encourage you brothers to take a short vacation, or work on a hobby of yours, or read a favorite book in the garden or journal by the fireplace, to do something that helps you reconnect with the Source of Life who gives it away freely and satisfies your desires with good things. Jesus went away to pray, so I urge you to go and do likewise.

"There is a time for everything, and a season for every activity under heaven" – Ecclesiastes 3:1

How often we forget this simple statement, this truth that hits the heart of mankind where it hurts. The world in all its technological advancements and instant gratifications struggles to manipulate and control everything in its path because if they are not in control, then someone else is and they do not like that. Heck, we in the church do not like that. We like being in control and quite honestly, we enjoy going at a fast pace, becoming impatient when something takes longer than a few seconds to load or our food longer than five minutes to cook. Something we cannot recall to memory that often is that God is never in a hurry; He works on His own timetable and He knows what He is doing.

If God were in a hurry, why did He not make all of creation in just one day? Why did He wait for Jesus to become thirty years old before He began His earthly ministry? Why has He waited so long to send Christ back to us and usher in the new heaven and new earth? He understands the importance of taking one day in at a time. He knows there is much that can happen in a day and that our feeble minds can only take in so much. That is why Jesus told us to "not worry about tomorrow, for tomorrow will worry about itself. Each day has enough trouble of its own" (Matthew 6:34).

One day at a time. We need to be reminded of this, well, daily. It is so easy to get caught up in the planning and scheduling of the weeks and months ahead and then lose sight of where you are at right here in the present. We overlook the truth that God is in control of all those days to come, just as He is in control right now. As we are learning to follow in our Savior's footsteps, we have to be living as He was living, and that is in complete dependency and trust in God the Father, the Sovereign One.

God is never in a hurry, so why should we be? Why should we be what our Lord is not? Everything that is not of God is of the devil and the world. There is no need to be anxious about tomorrow, or even today for that matter; there is a time for everything under heaven. So why rush? That is why patience is one of the most prevalent themes in the whole Bible. Take time today and this week to slow down, to relax, to not be like the rest of the world and become more like Christ, who never hurries because He trusts in God's timing which is always perfect.

"A furious storm came up on the lake, so that the waves swept over the boat. But Jesus was sleeping" – Matthew 8:24

Jesus just got done with a day full of teaching and healing in Galilee and He dismissed the crowds so He could have some down time with His disciples. So they got in their boat and set out to the other side, enjoying a peaceful and relaxing cruise. Jesus fell asleep because it was a long and tiring day for Him. But then out of nowhere, a squall brewed on the Sea of Galilee, so much so that these fishermen who have lived here their whole lives did not see it coming and were afraid for their lives. And yet, Jesus was sleeping while those around Him were panicking.

I am sure many of you have had days like that, where you are so exhausted, you literally crash at home instantly after work. But then as you are trying to settle down and relax and finally fell asleep, someone wakes you up with something they deem as urgent but you obviously do not because all you want to do is sleep. It is frustrating when this happens, and I am certain that Jesus was also frustrated with His disciples for waking Him as He said, "You of little faith, why are you so afraid?" (8:26). In other words, "Why did you wake me up? Did you so easily forget that I am the Son of God?"

This also illustrates for us Jesus' humanity, seeing that He was fatigued to the point of sleeping in a storm, but He also was at such a peace during it because He knew that everything was in His Father's hands, so there was no need to be afraid. And if Jesus was calm and restful, trusting in God during horrific storms, then so we also should go and do likewise. We often use our humanity as a scapegoat for not trusting in the Lord during life's troubles. We tend to say things like "I am only human" or "How can you expect me not to act this way? I am just a man."

Are we sleeping in peace throughout the storms of this life? Are we resting in our Lord's hands when difficulties come our way? Or are we running around frightened and alarmed as if something strange were happening to us, as if this was the end? And what if it was? Did we forget Paul's words, "to live is Christ and to die is gain" (Philippians 1:21)? Should not we as followers of Christ be the most eager to embrace death when it comes because we have the blessed assurance that we shall see our Savior face to face? What is stopping you from snoozing throughout the storm in peace and quiet, in restful faith in your God, as our Savior did?

"I have come that they may have life, and have it to the full" – John 10:10

I cannot believe I have not written about this verse yet, it is one of my favorites. I know I have mentioned it a few times, but to not have it as the main verse baffles me. Jesus spoke these words to His disciples as He was teaching them that He was the Good Shepherd who takes care of His sheep. He compares Himself to "The thief [who] comes only to steal and kill and destroy" (10:10), while He brings life to His sheep and in abundance.

The thief's interests are only for himself and how he may better himself, while Christ's interests are for His sheep, His chosen people, His motley crew. His chief concern is unselfish and He desires that we His sheep have life to the fullest. What does it mean to have life in the fullest? Well, it does not mean that Christ gives us just enough to survive, the bare minimum for existence; He does not merely give us mercy and grace so that we are saved from eternal damnation, but He blesses us with joy and peace so that life can be full of it. He desires for our lives to be happy, He does not want us to be miserable and in the dumps, but He loves to bless His people like a father loves to bestow gifts upon his children.

Life gives birth to life. Jesus is Life, and He gives that life to us, and we in turn can bring life to others through the Holy Spirit that dwells within, making us more like Him. Jesus is the Living Word, as in, He is not dead, and as the Living Word, the Holy Scriptures in the flesh, that life is bound within the bindings of the Bible. And you should most definitely feel the effects of it, life flowing to you and through you to the world so the world can be full of life. Lately, the Bible has been extremely life-giving to me because I am once again realizing the power contained in its pages and I have indeed been more joyful in my everyday walk with the Lord, bringing joy to those at my job and walking in His comforting peace.

Brothers, what has been on your heart as of late? What has your spirit been itching at? This is what has been on mine recently, so what is on yours? Are you doubting a certain aspect of God? Are you desiring a deeper and more intimate relationship with Him? Or are you thinking about the future and you do not know what He has in store for you? Do not be afraid to come before His throne of grace with confidence and boldness. Come to Him right now and tell Him what is on your heart, and never forget that He is living within you, bringing you life, so there is no need to be among the walking dead.

"Dear friends, I urge you, as aliens and strangers in the world" – 1 Peter 2:11

I am taking a mini-vacation right now in Traverse City for a few days. The weather is not as I would have hoped: it is in the 50's and cloudy with a chance of rain later, but I am still able to enjoy it because I like the cool weather. The breakfast at the hotel is no full-line continental breakfast, but they had cereal so I feel right at home. It just feels good to get away from home and venture to somewhere I have not been in quite a few years, somewhere near the water and nearer to nature; a simpler place. And this lifestyle of living in a hotel is simpler with less baggage and only the necessities; maybe that is why I enjoy traveling, because I have less.

And should we not take pleasure in having less? After all, Jesus really had nothing on this earth except the Father's presence and His disciples. He was a poor carpenter from Nazareth who told His disciples to "not take along any gold or silver or copper in your belts; take no bag for the journey, or extra tunic, or sandals or a staff" (Matthew 10:9-10). So if Jesus and His disciples went around this world with barely anything, why should we think we are any better to have more than what we need? Why do we so quickly get caught in consumerism, eager to get more and more? Why do we find comfort and security and pleasure in that? Do we not know that more *does not* lead to happiness, despite what the world tells us?

The United States has the richest people and the highest incomes in the world, yet they are ranked as the 26th happiest country in the world. In fact, the world's top ten richest countries are not in the top ten of happiness (UN World Happiness Report). Look at the rich people. They are always striving to gain more and more of something because they are never satisfied with what they have. But what I have learned is that when I do have less, like when I am traveling or camping, I am fine with that because it is all I really need. All the other things are merely luxuries, necessities. I do not need a TV or internet, but I like having them. That is where we all get messed up; we think we need those luxuries and cannot live without them, but I pray that we begin learn otherwise.

Many of the things we acquire in life will not make it to the next, so why invest in them? Wow, as I am typing this, the Holy Spirit is convicting me regarding this subject. People are worth investing in, not things because people are eternal. Father, I pray that we may live with less, to live simpler as your Son did, to live out your will on this earth as you sanctify us to become more like you. Teach us that less is indeed more. We love you.

"And Jesus grew in wisdom and stature, and in favor with God and men" – Luke 2:52

As I was hiking the beautiful trails of Mission Point this morning, the Lord began speaking to me there in the calmness of the woods. He spoke to me on a great deal of things, ranging from what He wants me to see, to Him enlightening me to aspects of His character. But one thing that especially stuck out was that as He was explaining life and growth through the nature around me; He mentioned everything is in constant motion, whether we see it or not, and once it ceases to move, it dies, and that is what hell is like, motionless.

If you think about it, it is true. We are not living if we are sitting or standing still. Everything is moving, from trees to animals to human beings; all of these are alive and if they do not continue to move, they will die. And so will we if we do not move in our spiritual walk with Christ. Even Jesus, the Son of God, had to grow up in wisdom and stature. All of the saints of old did not just get to where they were in a blink of an eye; it took them a lifetime of experiences and revelations by the Holy Spirit to mold them into the people that we know them as today. They never settled for where they were at in their understanding and relationship with the Lord; they always longed for more because they discovered how ultimately fascinating God truly is and they could not remain being content with a mediocre affiliation with Him.

Life in the Scriptures is always seen as something moving, like the wind or a river. They never cease, but if a river failed to be a river, the body of water that it flows into would conclude to host life and it would become a rancid swamp. Is that what you want for your spiritual life? You want it to be so rank that nothing good can live in you and you repel everyone around you? I do not think you would want that.

Which means that you then want life in your body and spirit, and so you must be regularly growing. Like I have mentioned before, our walk with Christ is like we are on a downward escalator and if we just stand still, we will go to the bottom, but if we strive to make an effort, we can make it to the top. Where would you place yourself in your spiritual journey right now? Would you say that you are just getting by, not really putting forth the effort you know you should be and thus being motionless, living in a sort of hell? Or can you honestly say that you are steadily and surely making progress moving onward and upward towards Christ-likeness? I pray for the latter my brothers. Do not settle in your walk, but forever be in forward motion.

"You do not have, because you do not ask God. When you ask, you do not receive, because you ask with wrong motives, that you may spend what you get on your pleasures" – James 4:2-3

What are things that you have asked God for recently? Were they good and noble things for the sake of His glory and for others, or were they selfish things that were for your own devices, to make life easier for yourself? I try and ask this to myself as often as I can remember to and when I do, I often find that I am indeed asking the Lord for things with the wrong motives in mind, motives that make me look good or feel better in the face of others and myself.

It is so easy to ask selfishly because it comes quite naturally to ask things for yourself that only benefit you. And when asking the Lord, we cannot hide our true intent for the asking, even if we try and justify it in our own minds; we can deceive ourselves into thinking that we ask for His sake or for another's, but we can never deceive God because He knows all. "O Lord, you have searched me and you know me. You know when I sit and when I rise; you perceive my thoughts from afar" (Psalm 139:1-2). The Word of the Lord, which is Christ Himself, "judges the thoughts and attitudes of the heart" (Hebrews 4:12), knowing our very thoughts and motives.

I am guilty of this my friends, of asking things of the Lord with impure motives so that life may be easier for me, or that I may enjoy select comforts, even though I may say that it is for the Lord that I am doing these things. But why do we tend to do this? Why is it so hard to ask selflessly of the Lord for things in our life and the lives of others? It is a habit of ours, and habits can only be broken by consciously and deliberately choosing against it and replacing it with something better. I pray we may get into the habit of, before we ask something of the Lord, thinking whether God would want us to ask this the way we are and if it is honoring and pleasing to Him.

I do not think we have a problem in asking God because quite honestly, we love asking God for things, but where we do have the problem is in our listening and in our intention for the asking. Father, remove selfishness and pride far from us, that we do not think of ourselves when coming to you, but that we think of you and you alone, and you will purify our hearts and minds to become more like you, that your desires and reasons may become ours. Nothing bad ever comes from you and we yearn for that goodness Father. Thank you for hearing us, help us to take time to hear from you in return. We love you.

"In his heart a man plans his course, but the Lord determines his steps" – Proverbs 16:9

Yesterday, I went exploring throughout the Sleeping Bear Dunes. I enjoyed beautiful scenery, climbed a monstrous dune, ran into the same couple over and over, and hiked some fun trails. Yet on this one trail, I knew it was a loop, but I lost my bearings and I thought I already looped around to where it breaks off, but I was dead wrong. It brought me somewhere I did not even know existed, traversing through woods and ultimately bringing me back to where I wanted to go, which was the parking lot near my car, and not the trailhead where I thought it would be. So it worked out better than I imagined, even though I was not prepared for it.

Like Solomon said, a man plans the course he desires to go, but it is the Lord that determines how he gets there. I eventually wanted to get back to my car, but I did not know that it would be that easy. Just because we do not know where we are going, that does not mean we are going the wrong way. Many times in this life, we may think we know what we want or where we want ourselves to be in one, five, or ten years. And heck, we may even go there and do that job, thinking we will work there until we retire. But we cannot make that absolutely certain, leaving no room for the Lord to work His way if necessary.

Solomon writes later that "Many are the plans in a man's heart, but it is the Lord's purpose that prevails" (19:21). We may plan for things, and it is good to plan, but we must remain flexible if God decides for us to go a different direction later. We will never fully know His ways while we are living on this green and blue planet; our finite beings literally cannot handle them, but when we finally do see our Savior face to face, then we shall fully.

Friends, never make a claim that you know entirely the Lord's plans for you, for He may "change" them and throw your knowledge off-kilter. The Lord does not change (Malachi 3:6), so what may seem like a change in His plans for us, is just one chapter ending and another one beginning. Everything He does has a purpose, and who are we to think we are able to grasp the precise details of our lives? God is infinite and all-knowing and He says "Who has understood the mind of the Lord, or instructed him as his counselor?" (Isaiah 40:13). Leave room for the Lord to work in your lives brothers, and do not consider that you know everything; be open to Him taking your path where He pleases because He sees the end while you barely see five feet ahead of you.

"These have come so that your faith—of greater worth than gold, which perishes even though refined by fire—may be proved genuine and may result in praise, glory and honor when Jesus Christ is revealed" - 1 Peter 1:7

We know that "faith is being sure of what we hope for and certain of what we do not see" (Hebrews 11:1). This faith, which we know is only possible through the Lord Jesus Christ, permits us with a perspective of seeing things as Christ does and should be a driving force in our lives. This faith is invaluable, but even more so, Peter exclaims that it is the testing of our faith that is of greater worth than gold. Gold is proved to be more gold-like and more valuable once it is processed through fire, destroying all other impurities, and the same is true with our faith.

Faith begins as a mere belief with our words, declaring Christ as Lord and Savior who has taken away our sins, but through time and through trials, it becomes much more than that. We can say a great many things with our tongue, things that we mean and do not mean; things of great value and things of little value, but when we ask Jesus Christ into our lives, to dwell within us, this demands to be backed up by a lifestyle of change and transformation.

Our faith *needs* to be tested. Without it, how can it be proved to be genuine and authentic? It needs to go through the fire. Fire is a purifier; it removes impurities and other elements that contaminate whatever is inside of it so that we may know whether it is what it appears to be. Just as a man's work will be shown for what it is, being "revealed with fire, and the fire will test the quality of each man's work" (1 Corinthians 3:13), so our faith, after being tested through trials and tribulations, will be exposed as either legitimate or counterfeit.

Do not shy away from such trials brothers, for it is the Lord who is bestowing them upon you so that your love for Him may be shown for what it is, which is hopefully real and true. And when your faith has stood the test, it shall result in praise and glory and honor when Christ returns; you will be presented before Him and He shall have the pleasure in saying "Well done, good and faithful servant...Come and share your master's happiness! (Matthew 25:23). Do you believe that your faith is authentic? Have you undergone testing and trials from the Lord? If so, do not dismiss them or take them lightly, they are of great value and they are there to make you more like Christ. Is that not what you want after all?

"The rising sun will come to us from heaven to shine on those living in darkness and in the shadow of death, to guide our feet into the paths of peace" – Luke 1:78-79

This is from the end of Zechariah's song after he was filled with the Holy Spirit because of his joy that his son John the Baptist was born. The majority of this song of praise was for his newborn son and he prophesied the great things he would do for the lost people of Israel, but in these last few verses, he references the coming of the Messiah, the Christ who would save the world.

Of course we know that Jesus is the Christ he prophesied about, and here He is referred to as the rising sun. I love that picture it paints because sunrises are one of the most consistently beautiful moments in all of creation and it lets us know that a new day is here. A new day was indeed beginning for Israel which has now been extended to us the Gentiles as well. This new day, this rising sun, comes down to us from the heavens to shine out and expel the darkness of the night. Jesus Christ, the Rising Sun, came down from heaven to shine on those people who were living in darkness, who were lost in the shadow of death. The majority of Israel at this time was living in this shadowy valley and that is why Christ came, to show them where they were at because they thought they were in a good place, but since they were surrounded in shadow, they could not know for sure because the darkness is deceiving; it makes you think that something is there, when in fact it is not, and vice versa.

This same Light shines on those living in darkness today, showing them the error of their ways. It points out the true path that is set before them, which usually is not good since it leads to death. Christ came to lead people away from this death; "He himself bore our sins in his body on the tree, so that we might die to sins and live for righteousness" (1 Peter 2:24). His light shines on our lives to guide our feet in the paths of peace, paths that lead us away from death and towards Him who is Life. Do you know people who need this glorious light to shine in their lives? Are you one of these people? If so, what are you doing about it? Are you allowing the penetrating light of Christ to do just that, to pierce through your reality and expose you and your whereabouts for what they truly are? Do not be afraid of the light my friends; it takes faith and risk to enter into it, but I guarantee that you will not regret it whatsoever.

"The city does not need the sun or the moon to shine on it, for the glory of God gives it light, and the Lamb is its lamp" – Revelation 21:23

I have not really seen the sun for a few days because it has been quite rainy here. I like the clouds from time to time, especially massive cumulonimbus storm clouds and after I have been in the sun for awhile, but after not seeing it for a couple days, you begin to miss it; you miss its warmth and the splendor that it shines on all of creation and the light that reveals things hidden. It is a wonderful and necessary piece of creation, as it gives light and life wherever it rays touch.

Our verse is what John describes as he sees a vision of the New Jerusalem in heaven. He noticed that there was no more sun or moon to give light to the world during the day or the night, "for there will be no night there" (21:25) because the Lamb of God, Jesus Christ, is the Light that exudes light and life in every direction, never setting over the horizon. There will be no more night, no more darkness, because the Light of the world is here to stay to make all things visible and everything will be laid bare.

What I notice even more in this is that it indicates that we do not need to rely on created things in the world anymore while we are in heaven because we have the Source of Life and that is all we need! We do not need the sun to make us walk by day or the moon by night, for we have Christ, our lamp. The Psalmist said "Your word is a lamp to my feet and a light for my path" (Psalm 119:105). Jesus is the Living Word, the Lamb of God, the Lamp of the New Jerusalem, the city of God. Isaiah prophesied many years earlier saying the same thing as John, "The sun will no more be your light by day, nor will the brightness of the moon shine on you, for the Lord will be your everlasting light, and your God will be your glory. Your sun will never set again, and your moon will wane no more; the Lord will be your everlasting light, and your days of sorrow will end" (Isaiah 60:19-20).

Do you not just love the image this portrays? The Lamb at the center of the throne, His glory and splendor radiating throughout all that there is, brighter than the noonday sun ever shined. All darkness is expelled and nothing more is hidden from our eyes, "for we shall see him as he is" (1 John 3:2). Oh what a glorious day that will be! I cannot wait for it, but I must, and I will as long as I live. The world will be full of His holiness. It is wonderful that He is mentioned as the Lamb here, signifying the gloriousness of His work on the cross as a sheep before a slaughter that now gives light to all. I pray that you are all longing for that day and until then, to be reflecting the light that Christ is.

"I urge you, brothers, to watch out for those who cause divisions and put obstacles in your way that are contrary to the teaching you have learned" - Romans 16:17

At my work, there are obvious divisions among people on our own team and even in our relation to other teams. If someone does not have the same mindset on how things should be done or a group thinks that someone on the team is annoying or just helpful, they divide over that fact. It is sometimes hard not to get involved in this because it happens so delicately. I continue to pray that this will stop and that I will not join in because there should be no divisions among our team because it creates inefficiency and generates distrust.

Paul understood the harm that divisions can cost in the body of Christ and that is why he speaks against them quite often. But why are divisions destructive? They are so because things were never meant to be divided, so they are going against their very design. Think of the American Civil War, or any civil war for that matter, it is a battle against each other within their own country, killing their brothers and sisters because of some unnecessary trait and belief that they do not agree with. And that is what divisions do in the church; not necessarily killing each other, but destroying what God has brought together. That is one reason why God hates divorce, the separation of what was one in marriage.

We are told that those who take part in these divisions are acting like children and are worldly because they are reacting to these as men of the world would and not like men of God (see 1 Corinthians 3:1-4). Men of God work hard together to keep such partitioning from happening. Everything that the Lord God is, is one. Jesus said that "Any kingdom divided against itself will be ruined, and a house divided against itself will fall" (Luke 11:17). We are the body of Christ my brothers, we *cannot* be divided against ourselves. It would be destructive for the Church and for our very souls. Since division happens because people take things way too personally or have a completely different belief than another, we now have thousands of different denominations within the body of Christ, each having certain beliefs and traditions, some man-made and others ordained by Christ. These separations were never meant to be, but people had strong convictions that the religious system that they were a part of was not biblical in a particular part, so they decided to leave instead of trying to work things out and help out the church instead of leave it. That is acting worldly; that is not what Christ has called us to. Christ has called us to unity.

"Accept him whose faith is weak, without passing judgment on disputable matters" –
Romans 14:1

Continuing on division, this is where things get fishy. People differ on what they view as disputable matters and what they view as necessary for the faith. Disputable matters are just that, disputable; they are debatable and may differ from person to person, depending on how one was raised or their family history or their own personal convictions. Like how Paul explains later in this letter that "Each one should be fully convinced in his own mind. He who regards one day as special, does so to the Lord. He who eats meat, eats to the Lord, for he gives thanks to God; and he who abstains, does so to the Lord and gives thanks to God" (14:5-6).

Such things as those are disputable matters. They in no way need to divide you, for they are petty and childish and not of God. For example, I have a few friends who just do not drink any form of alcohol, not because they do not like the taste or think it is evil, but they have decided for themselves that it is not right because of their family's past problems with it and they do not want even the slightest chance of that happening for themselves. That is no reason for us not to be friends anymore; I respect their decision on the matter. But there are believers who divide over such things, such petty and trivial ideas like infant baptism and dedication. It is not mentioned explicitly in the Bible, but different early church traditions do one and some the other, but unfortunately they split because they could not agree on this because they saw it not as disputable, but as necessary for salvation and faith.

Paul encourages us time and time again to "make every effort to do what leads to peace and to mutual edification" (14:19). He goes on and tells us that "whatever you believe about these things keep between yourself and God" (14:22), and not force them on others as being necessary for their faith. God never acknowledges division and disunity because it goes against His very nature. Jesus prayed that all believers "may be one, Father, just as you are in me and I am in you...that they may be one as we are one...May they be brought to complete unity" (John 17:21-23). And I pray that same for us brothers, that we can truly act and live as the united body of Christ, that works together in unison with the Head for the advancement of His Kingdom and the glory of His name. May we not divide ourselves over trifling issues, but stand firm together on what we believe, that Christ suffered for our sake, died and rose again, ascended into heaven and will come back for His people.

"O Lord, you have searched me and you know me. You know when I sit and when I rise; you perceive my thoughts from afar. You discern my going out and my lying down; you are familiar with all my ways" – Psalm 139:1-3

My mind has been running lately, or swimming since its better than running; swimming with thoughts about my future and where it is heading. I do not know where particularly that is, but thoughts about becoming an officer in the Air Force has arisen once again, along with other government-type positions. Further thoughts have also been including finding a wife and starting a family because I would really like that. These desires and longings of mine have made me pray earnestly and think more than I normally do, seeing as I am in that point in my life where decisions like these "have" to be made.

But even in the midst of all this chaos in my mind, these different directions that I am being pulled, I hear David's comforting words concerning the Lord found in these verses. The Lord knows us and He knows when I move about and He is able to understand my disarray of thoughts. He knows me inside and out and is familiar with all of my habits and tendencies. "Before a word is on my tongue you know it completely, O Lord" (139:4). The Lord knows me much better than I know myself, probably because He "created me in my inmost being; [He] knit me together in my mother's womb" (139:13). It brings me great comfort knowing that the Lord of lords comprehends my confusing thoughts; He sees them and speaks truth into me, saying things like "Do not fret because you do not know, My son, it leads only to evil. You can only see so far in front of you, but I can see the whole length of time because I am outside of it and I created it. So trust in Me, your caring and loving Father, that I will make things known to you in its due time, and even if I do not, continue to trust Me because I have and never will lead you astray."

Are you in a place of confusion right now, or a position where you feel decisions have to be made soon in regards to your future? No need my friends. Give it all to the Lord your God and trust Him with your life and desires and needs. He knows what you are going through and He sees you and understands His beautiful creation perfectly. So "Cast your cares on the Lord and he will sustain you" (55:22). Do not get so caught up in the moment that you forget that God is right there with you, inside of you, pushing for you and speaking to you. He does not wish for you to be swallowed up with doubts and fears, but to turn and face Him and have Him gladly bear your burdens.

October 1

"In the beginning God" – Genesis 1:1

The very first words of the Bible, "In the beginning God"; such profound words with much weight. In the beginning of all things, which some believe to be 6-10,000 years ago, and others 13.8 billion years ago, God was there. He was at the start of everything, before there was even time, He was there. He sees the end from the beginning. "For a thousand years in your sight are like a day that has just gone by" (Psalm 90:4). "Through him all things were made; without him nothing was made that has been made" (John 1:3). He created everything that you see here today.

So what is the purpose of this? Why talk about the everlasting character of our God? Why emphasize that God was in the beginning before a single thing in the universe came to be, even though the author of Genesis (believed to be Moses), indicates that God was at the beginning of time and not before it? Most likely because it is nearly impossible for us to grasp anything being outside of time, so that is probably why it is worded that way. First off, if God was at the establishment of cosmos, then whether you believe in the Big Bang or a six-day creation as told in Genesis, you know that God orchestrated it because He was there before a solitary particle had ever existed.

Secondly, Paul wrote to the Colossians that "He is before all things, and in him all things hold together. And he is the head of the body, the church; he is the beginning and the firstborn from among the dead, so that in everything he might have supremacy" (Colossians 1:17-18). He is of course referring to Christ here, but we know from John 1:1-2 that Christ was with God in the beginning and is God, so we can reference to either and still be accurate. Because God is the head of everything and all things hold together through Him, this is important for us because we for surely know that God has the supremacy. If God did not have supremacy, then that means someone else does, which would then make our faith futile because we would believe in someone who is not the highest and most sovereign.

But praise be to God that He *is* supreme, that He *is* sovereign over all things! Do you know what this means? This means that our faith is not useless and that it is true as He says it is. We then know that His promises for us, of eternal life in heaven with Him, of no condemnation for those who believe, of everlasting joy in His presence and the wicked receiving their due, are all true and that should give us hope and encouragement brothers. Thank the Lord today that He is the supreme authority and that He was there before the start.

October 2

"We take captive every thought to make it obedient to Christ" – 2 Corinthians 10:5

When I try and fall asleep at night, my mind sometimes begins to race. I am sure you have been like that at times. You try and sleep but you are continually thinking about the events of the day and what has to be done tomorrow or what you could have done differently. But as a cure for this lately, I have been relaxing for an hour before bed, reading the Bible and praying, clearing my mind and giving everything to Christ, thanking Him for all that He is and all that He has done during the day.

Why did Paul choose these words? Maybe because he understood the power of the mind to take us places we know we should not be. He may have found out that if we do not take captive every single one of our thoughts, they may in fact hold us captive and we will be enslaved to them. That is why he adds on not only to take captive our own thoughts, but to make them obedient to Christ. You know how easily it is for a lone thought of committing a particular sin or thinking some evil to enter your mind; it takes only a millisecond for it to enter. You may not dwell on it long at all, recognizing its evil nature, but it enters nonetheless. But if this happens on an ongoing basis, it can begin to wear down the walls of your mind, making it easier yet for them to enter and perhaps stay a little longer and possibly even make a shelter in the periphery of your thoughts.

We cannot let our minds control us and get the best of us, but we must make our thoughts and wills be controlled by the will of Christ. Everything should be controlled by Him; our thoughts, emotions, actions, words, motives, the whole shebang. When we begin to let our thoughts have their way in us, we are their slaves and they become our master; Christ is no longer our leader because we dethroned Him in our minds and we are our own leader now.

My friends, this dark and dangerous road only leads to destruction. But the road that leads to life and joy and peace is the road where our thoughts are imprisoned to Christ, where He is what guides them and brings goodness to them, transforming and conforming them into His likeness so we may begin to think as He thinks. Is this what you want brothers, to have your thoughts be made more like Christ and obedient to Him? Or would you rather be disobedient to your King, carry out a mutiny and crown yourself? One choice leads to life, the other death. What will you choose? Will you choose to surrender yourself to the will of God and enter a land of prosperity and freedom or will you be carried away to a foreign land by your thoughts and emotions?

"These people come near to me with their mouth and honor me with their lips, but their hearts are far from me. Their worship of me is made up only of rules taught by men" – Isaiah 29:13

"These people." Note how it does not say "My people." If they were God's people, He would unmistakably call them His own, but He does not here. Why not? He is speaking to those who live in Jerusalem yes? Although the people of Jerusalem, and ultimately of Israel, have not swayed to practicing idolatry at this time like the surrounding areas, they have not necessarily been worshiping the Lord their God either. They have rather begun performing a lip service to God, walking in hypocrisy.

Israel's heart was far from the Lord says Isaiah. They are God's chosen people, His children whom He has guided all these years, but their very hearts were distant from Him. Even though Isaiah does not refer to these people as God's people, they technically are, but since they are deliberately running away from Him and focusing on themselves, they gave up their right to be called His people. God said later that "All day long I have held out my hands to an obstinate people, who walk in ways not good, pursuing their own imaginations" (65:2). Israel heard the voice of the Lord, but they openly rejected it and chose their own way instead. They determined that they knew what was really important and best for them, even though God continually reached out to them. Their hearts were hardened (see Romans 10-11 for more on this). They have heard the truth all their lives, they had the Word of God with them, even in the flesh, and yet they denied it because they did not have faith. This reminds me of people I grew up with; believers who "knew" the Lord and His Word, knew the commandments and what the Word said on how we should live our lives, and yet they knowingly disobey, deceiving themselves into thinking that they are living for God.

Jesus quotes this passage in Mark 7:6-7, relating it to the hypocritical Pharisees of His day. And this still rings true for many in our own day. They are numerous believers whose hearts are so far from the Lord, they do not even know it. They go to church, they pray, they maybe go to a Bible study, but that is just for appearances sake, to please their parents or even themselves. Little do they know they are living a lie, living in deception, pushing themselves further from the Lord than they think. And then they wonder why God does not answer their prayers. My brothers, this stops today. If this describes you at all, repent and turn to the Lord your God. He is waiting for you. Give your heart to Him, and not only your heart, but your mind and your soul as well, all of you, so that you may be wholly His and live the life He has for you to the full!

"Three times a day he got down on his knees and prayed, giving thanks to his God, just as he had done before" – Daniel 6:10

This topic has been on my heart for a few days now and I finally get to write about it. It is not going where you think it is, I assure you. I am not going to write about Daniel in particular, even though I would love to, seeing as he is a wonderful example of living a God-centered life in a pagan world and carrying tremendous influence in it. But I would like to talk a little bit about how there are a lot of people today who pray and want prayer, although they do not believe in God. The kicker is that they only desire it when a tragedy strikes and something terrible has happened, i.e. a school shooting or their mother got cancer. You get the idea.

This notion really irks me. I remember reading a post a few years back on the school shootings in Ohio and the schools and those affected were asking everybody for prayer in that horrible time. Do not get me wrong at all, it was indeed a horrific experience and I do not mean to belittle it in the slightest, but what I do belittle is the fact that people only want prayer *after* the episode occurs, never before. They ban prayer in public schools, something like this happens, *and now* they want prayer. So the question needs to be asked: how many school shootings did we have when we had prayer in schools? They do not allow prayer in school because a few people are offended and believe the school is pushing Christianity on them, but then a tragedy happens and they want it? Foolishness I tell you.

How does Daniel get mixed into all this? Well, our verse tells us that he prayed every day, three times a day, giving thanks to God for all He has done and is doing, *just as he had done before.* He did not wait until something bad happened to pray to God, but he prayed all the time because he loves talking to Him and it is what allows him to do his job effectively in a pagan world. He knows that without God, he is nothing. Even though distress came upon him multiple times in his life, he continued to live as he had been. The point I am trying to get to is this: prayer should not only come forth from our lips when the going gets down, but it should be a continuous lifestyle of praise to our Father, in the good and the bad. David is an excellent example of this, with half of his psalms being of praise and worship to the Lord and the other half petitioning to Him to save him from his misery and anguish. God *is* there for us brothers. I pray that we do pray for those affected by life's calamities, that they may know the grace and mercy and peace of Christ Jesus in the midst of their trial and see that His arms are wide open for them.

"But you will receive power when the Holy Spirit comes on you; and you will be my witnesses in Jerusalem, and in all Judea and Samaria, and to the ends of the earth" – Acts 1:7-8

Last night, I saw the latest installment in the Darren Wilson documentaries titled *Holy Ghost*. In this film, he had no set-in-stone plan, but was open to being led by the Holy Spirit during the whole shoot, going throughout the world and revealing to people that the Holy Spirit does exist and has come to bring freedom from captivity the people of the earth and that He loves them. The Spirit performed healings, went where no foreigner had gone before, and ushered forth freedom to those who desperately needed it.

"Now the Lord is the Spirit, and where the Spirit of the Lord is, there is freedom" (2 Corinthians 3:17). We know that the Holy Spirit fell upon the Lord's disciples and those who believed on Pentecost, resulting in speaking in tongues and prophesying and healings and miracles. The Spirit's power was made manifest on that day. Some of the faith have come to believe that the Holy Spirit no longer works miracles or healings or things of that sort today. This film blows that belief out of the water by doing just that, speaking truth into people's lives that no one else knows about them, healing their broken bodies after years of hurt, and giving them a glimpse of what the Holy Spirit's presence feels like and how peaceful it really is.

These were Jesus' last words to His disciples, those who followed Him for the last three years, before He ascended into heaven. That is a tremendous task that the Lord bestows to His disciples. Did He really say to the ends of the earth? Jerusalem and Judea was enough land for them to cover, but Jesus wants them to witness to the whole world? How do they expect to accomplish this monumental mission without their Guide and Lord Jesus Christ? That is why He left, so that He could send His Holy Spirit, who can be manifested into the heart of every single believer. While He was in the flesh, He could only be at one place at one time, but now that He ascended and sent His Spirit into the world, He can be everywhere and *that* is how the disciples are able to help fulfill this great undertaking; through the power and indwelling of the Holy Spirit, moving through them as a conduit for His purposes.

What do *you* think? Do you believe that the Spirit still works miracles and wonders in the world today? You might say "I never see or hear of anything, so the Spirit must not be." And how did you come to that conclusion I might ask? Did it come through observation and faith, or through stubbornness and blindness? Do not give way to doubt, but open up the floodgates of faith.

"The wind blows wherever it pleases. You hear its sound, but you cannot tell where it comes from or where it is going. So it is with everyone born of the Spirit" – John 3:8

I have been in that camp before (referring to yesterday's post) of not believing in the Holy Spirit's power in the world today. But when I was sixteen years old, I went on a mission trip and the group I was with, mostly youths, experienced an outpouring of the Holy Spirit, and there were prophesies and healings and worship of the Living God amongst us youngsters. This is one reason how I know that the Spirit still moves in power in today's world.

Jesus refers to the Holy Spirit like a wind, blowing wherever it pleases. And that may be why at Pentecost, there was "a sound like the blowing of a violent wind [that] came from heaven and filled the whole house where they were sitting" (Acts 2:2). The wind is everywhere throughout the earth, moving different directions and at different velocities, and thus having different effects in different places. The Spirit of Christ Himself lives within every believer at the moment of their conversion when they are born again. "Having believed, you were marked in him with a seal, the promised Holy Spirit, who is a deposit guaranteeing our inheritance" (Ephesians 1:13-14).

In the *Holy Ghost* film, the crew went up to strangers, people they have never met, and prayed for them. I have done that only a few times in my life. I believe it is a great way to spread the love of Christ to the world and to those who are lost and seeking something, but I have not done it anytime recently. Why is that? What has happened to my faith? I believe the power of prayer and in being led by the Spirit to go out and pray for strangers, but why do I not do it anymore? Have I become so consumed with living in comfort and not wanting to be in awkward situations? Have I let fear of rejection and looking foolish establish a foothold in my heart and mind? Am I letting doubt seep its way into my life?

"He who doubts is like a wave of the sea, blown and tossed by the wind. That man...is a double-minded man, unstable in all he does" (James 1:6-8). I do not know why I have doubt rule me and not my faith in Christ. I know the truth in Christ and so do you brothers. Father, forgive us of our doubts in proclaiming your name to those living in darkness. Remove them and replace them with the boldness that comes from your Holy Spirit. May we look to you and your disciples in their lives of faith and go out and do likewise because we are born of the Spirit; so may we be unfettered from doubt and move freely for you Kingdom's cause. Thank you for your grace Father, we love you.

"After the earthquake came a fire, but the Lord was not in the fire. And after the fire came a gentle whisper. When he heard it, he pulled his cloak over his face and went out and stood at the mouth of the cave" – 1 Kings 19:12-13

Before the earthquake happened to Elijah here, "a great and powerful wind tore the mountains apart and shattered the rocks before the Lord, but the Lord was not in the wind. After the wind there was an earthquake, but the Lord was not in the earthquake" (19:11). But after not appearing in the wind, quake, or the fire, the Lord decides to at last appear to the despairing prophet in a gentle whisper. You would think that God would pass by Elijah through some mighty and powerful demonstration, but instead He chooses to pass him by through a mild murmur.

We have heard the phrase these days, "Listen to the still, small voice of God." And this is a true saying; we *need* to listen to the gentle whisper of the great and Almighty God. Too many times when asking things of the Lord as Elijah was, we desire and try to listen for huge and obvious answers, like an earthquake or a fire. We say things like, "I will not move until I hear a clear and obvious reply to my question." This is foolishness on our parts in trying to tell God what to do and control Him.

There are many stories throughout the Bible of when God did in fact intervene in enormous ways, but the majority of the accounts are about normal, ordinary people who lived mundane lives, but their lives were full of righteous living before the Lord. Believers today think they need to do something great and wonderful for the Lord, like moving to Africa and teaching the natives about the Lord. Or going to seminary and becoming a preacher, or working for a non-profit and help rescue girls who are being sex trafficked. These are all good and noble pursuits, but we must not come to believe that other jobs are anything less.

God thrives in the common and humdrum things of life. We need to stop looking for the big and powerful answers to our questions and begin to understand that the Lord moves in the ordinary, in the gentle whisper. Have you only been looking for huge responses from the Lord and are failing to hear the still, small voice that is right in front of you? God is only one step away from you, which is why He tends to whisper because anything more would scare the crap out of you and would be unnecessary. So calm your heart and mind, rid yourself of distractions and go to your secret place where you and the Lord commune best, and be the child of God that He is molding you into, not what you wish He was molding you into.

"As you do not know the path of the wind, or how the body is formed in a mother's womb, so you cannot understand the work of God, the Maker of all things" – Ecclesiastes 11:5

Elijah was a man who was giving up on the Lord. He had been preaching to an obstinate and stubborn nation, with cold hearts that would not thaw out to the way of the Lord, even though they were the people of Israel. The king he was preaching to, Ahab and his wife Jezebel, were after him because of the display of the Lord's power on Mount Carmel. The Lord asks him what he is doing there on the mountain, and he responds "I have been very zealous for the Lord God Almighty. The Israelites have rejected your covenant, broken down your altars, and put your prophets to death with the sword. I am the only one left, and now they are trying to kill me too" (1 Kings 19:10).

He thought he knew everything. He had believed that he understood all that the Lord was doing in his life and in Israel. He thinks he is the only faithful follower of God left in all of Israel and that his life's work up to this point was utterly fruitless. And because of this, because of his limited perspective on the situations surrounding him, he supposed it was time for the Lord's judgment to come upon Israel. That is why he expected the Lord to be in the wind, earthquake and the fire (19:11-12), all of which are signs of judgment, but instead the Lord shows up in the mild and quiet voice of a caring and loving Father and Shepherd of His people.

The Lord ends this conversation declaring that "Yet I reserve seven thousand in Israel—all whose knees have not bowed down to Baal and all whose mouths have not kissed him" (19:18). Elijah was way off; here he was being selfish and thinking he was the only one left, that there was no one in all of Israel who was still faithful to the Lord besides him, and then God tells him that He has seven thousand who are still true to Him.

The point is this brothers: we do not and will not know the Lord's plan completely and how everything will come to be. Yes, we may know bits and pieces of it, but to know absolutely everything about how it will come to be is extremely unlikely. "A man's steps are directed by the Lord. How then can anyone understand his own way?" (Proverbs 20:24). Elijah thought it was time for the Lord's judgment, when in fact it was time for the people of Israel to step up and boldly declare His name. Do not think you know it all, for we are finite beings who only know in part and in the present. Be flexible in the Lord, having no future plans set in stone, but have faith in the Lord that He knows what He is doing and I guarantee you it is for the best.

"Lot looked up and saw that the whole plain of the Jordan was well watered, like the garden of the Lord, like the land of Egypt…So Lot chose for himself the whole plain" – Genesis 13:10-11

Abraham and Lot have been traveling together ever since they left their home in Ur. They lived in Egypt together and also in Bethel for a short while until we come to our verse. They both saw it best for them to go their separate ways now because "the land could not support them while they stayed together, for their possessions were so great" (12:6). The land only had so much water for their flocks and herds and so it would have been foolish to stay together, putting their livestock and livelihood at risk.

Abraham had always been a generous man, so he let Lot choose whatever land he wanted, and of course, he chose the best portion. But what is wrong with that? What is wrong with choosing the best for oneself? Lot could have been a man about it and split part of that luxurious plain with his uncle Abraham, being even a little bit generous like his uncle always has been with him, but he did not. He saw the best and he took it. They were both very rich men after their time in Egypt, but Lot wanted even more, and the land he chose, with its proximity to other cities of the plain, could help him do just that.

What I am getting at is greed. Greed is the selfish desire for more; more wealth, more power, just more, without thinking of what it may cost you in the end. Out of the entire plain, Lot decided to pitch "his tents near Sodom. Now the men of Sodom were wicked and were sinning greatly against the Lord" (13:12-13). Because of his greed, he was in extremely close proximity to sin city, flirting with temptation. And as the story goes, Lot eventually moves into Sodom and he is no longer the man he used to be, for the city has taken its toll on him. He became so perverted that he would even give up his own daughters to be raped by the men of Sodom (19:8).

Greed destroys you. Lot's greed removed all sense of morality from him and his family, as later when fleeing the city as it was being destroyed, his wife looked back and became a pillar of salt (19:26). Paul wrote Timothy saying "For the love of money is a root of all kinds of evil" (1 Timothy 6:10). Money is in fact a tool to be used for the glory of God, not for our own selfish gain and fame. Greed and covetousness destroyed the life of Lot and those near him and Abraham had to intercede to the Lord for his very life. Do not get to that point in your greed brothers. Repent from it and turn to Christ for forgiveness. Channel your desires towards Him and His Kingdom.

"Lift up your eyes from where you are and look north and south, east and west. All the land that you see I will give to you and your offspring forever" – Genesis 13:14-15

The opposite of greediness is generosity and that is what Abraham represents in these passages. He is in stark contrast to the covetousness of Lot. Abraham was a very wealthy man, but he did not indulge in his wealth and desire more as Lot did. Instead, he "gave a tenth of everything" (14:20) to Melchizedek, acknowledging his kingship, trusting that what he gave him was to be used for the Lord's bidding. Melchizedek blessed him prior to Abraham giving him the tenth.

As Abraham gave his nephew Lot the choice of the land, even though it looked the most promising at the time, the Lord told him to look in all directions and it would all be his. "I will make your offspring like the dust of the earth…Go, walk through the length and breadth of the land, for I am giving it to you" (13:16-17). He did not see the fruit of his decision for quite some time, since he yet had no children of his own. Abraham had absolute trust in the Lord for his family and possession because he gave Lot the choice of the land and what he got left with did not supply much vegetation and water for all his livestock. Abraham did not need to look out for himself because he had the Maker of heaven and earth looking out for him.

Are we able to be so bold as Abraham was for the Lord? Are we capable of trusting God with *all* of our possessions and money and family? Do we honestly believe that it is all the Lord's in the first place? Because if we do, then we know that none of it really belongs to us at all, but it is entirely a gift from God. And since it is a gift, then why not be generous with it as Abraham was, right? "A generous man will prosper; he who refreshes others will himself be refreshed…whoever trusts in his riches will fall" (Proverbs 11:25,28).

May your trust be in God and not in your riches because God gave them to you. Trust the Giver, not the gift itself. You may do as you wish with the wealth and blessings you have been given, but like Lot, you will have to suffer the consequences of your decisions sooner or later. You might as well be generous with it then; giving freely to those who need it, tithing at church, supporting missionaries and other organizations, using it on things that last and not on those that are here today and gone tomorrow because they have no eternal value. Do not be afraid to trust God with what He has given you; He is the King, and He knows how to use everything under His dominion.

"Submit yourselves for the Lord's sake to every authority instituted among men" - 1 Peter 2:13

This sounds like a mighty undertaking, to submit to every single authority that has been established on the earth; how can Peter present such a request? First off, it is not a request, but a command and commands need to be obeyed because John said that "This is love for God: to obey his commands" (1 John 5:3). So if we claim to love God, then we will be willing to obey what He commands of us, and here He commands us to submit to every authority among men.

Note here that this does not mean that we obey these earthly authorities if it means a blatant disobedience to the commands of God; His authority has the first and foremost say in our lives. We submit to the governing agencies appointed over us because "there is no authority except that which God has established. The authorities that exist have been established by God. Consequently, he who rebels against the authority is rebelling against what God has instituted" (Romans 13:1-2). What Paul is saying is that since God has ordained all the authorities that we see, we obey them because He put them there for our benefit. And indirectly, when we disobey a human authority, we disobey God who created that authority.

When Peter wrote this letter, Nero was emperor of Rome. He was perhaps the most ruthless tyrant there ever was, who killed his own mother and persecuted the church relentlessly. And yet, Peter commands the church to submit to his authority, as long as it is not in violation to God's law. That must have been extremely hard for the readers of this letter, to see their brothers and sisters being persecuted because of this man and to read that they must submit to his authority. But Peter continues, writing "For it is God's will that by doing good you should silence the ignorant talk of foolish men" (2:15).

Christians should honestly be the best citizens of any state, province or country because good citizenship is a fine counter to any false charges that a person may have against you, as in the case of Daniel 6. You may strongly dislike your president, or you boss, or your local law enforcement agency, but you must obey them and submit to their God-given authority over you. It will be a great example to non-believers to see you in your obedience to governing authorities, despite of whether you agree or not with their policies. We *are* salt and light my friends. Let us live as such.

"Let your eyes look straight ahead, fix your gaze directly before you...do not swerve to the right or the left; keep your foot from evil" - Proverbs 4:25,27

Think of the last time you went for a hike in the woods: you are walking down the path, enjoying the sounds, sights and smells of nature without a care in the world when all of sudden you are lost and you have no idea where you are. You do not have a trail map and it is overcast so you cannot use the sun for directional help. You try and use your phone to determine your location but there is no service. You are in the middle of nowhere and the only way to get out of nowhere is to keep on walking, not knowing where it will lead you.

Brothers, getting lost in the woods is one thing, but getting lost in this world is a completely different game. In fact, it is not a game but serious business. When hiking, it is incredibly easy to get lost without even recognizing it and the same is true when traversing through the spiritual life in your walk with Christ. You are on the path of life following in His footsteps, when for a brief moment, you notice something to the side of the road and you investigate further to determine what it is. Meanwhile, you look further and further, intrigued by the chase of what it might be, and then you realize that you are indeed lost and you do not know where the path of Christ is anymore. You got distracted.

Like I said, this happens easily, which is why we keep our eyes straight ahead of us, fixing our gaze directly on Christ and not swerving to either side, but walking firmly and keeping ourselves from evil. Moses told the Israelites long before this to "be careful to do what the Lord your God has commanded you; do not turn aside to the right or to the left. Walk in all the way that the Lord your God has commanded you" (Deuteronomy 5:32-33). These wise men knew the importance of staying directed and focused on the Lord and the path He has set before us.

Are these same things happening in your life? I admit, as I was writing this, I was distracted by a few things and the Spirit hit me good, warning me that I was not at all practicing what I was talking about. It is that easy to be led off the path of life. Do not let it happen to you brothers. Keep yourself fixed upon Christ, upon His commands and how He lived His life. Do not get distracted by the petty things that are lurking around every corner, craving for your attention. Ignore them, rebuke them, and keep on your merry way with the Lord, the King of kings who always leads His people in glory and victory.

"Be self-controlled and alert" – 1 Peter 5:8

This is going to follow much of the same lines as yesterday in dealing with being focused and direct in your walk with Christ in the world. Going through school growing up, they tried to teach us many subjects to become familiar with almost every field of study. I never really liked that because I wanted to learn what I liked learning about and other things I could not care less for. C. S. Lewis said that "the greatest service we can do to education today is to teach fewer subjects" because then we become mediocre in our studies and never find our niche in life. Look at those who graduate high school in Germany for example: they either go to a university, to a trade school, or to the military and become specialized in a particular field and are able to master it.

What are we masters of here in America? Being trivial and knowing the latest celebrity news or sports statistics? These things are all insignificant in the grand scheme of things and deep down we know that is the truth. That is why Peter wrote to us to be self-controlled and alert, because he was reminded of when he was with Jesus in the garden of Gethsemane and failed to keep watch and pray and instead fell asleep three times (see Matthew 26:26-46). Jesus wanted them to stay awake and pray, to be vigilant and wary of their surroundings so that they "will not fall into temptation. The spirit is willing, but the body is weak" (Matthew 26:41).

Peter practically used the same words as his Master did: "Your enemy the devil prowls around like a roaring lion looking for someone to devour. Resist him, standing firm in the faith, because you know that your brothers throughout the world are undergoing the same kind of suffering" (5:8-9). Like I have said before, it is quite simple to get side tracked and lose focus of what is really important, which is the Lord your God and every other importance stems from that single priority.

What is stealing your attention from the Lord? Where are your eyes and mind and heart wandering to, taking away your devotion and time from the One that matters most in this life? Is it your job, or hobbies, or friends, or television, or the internet or something more? Whatever it may be, do not let it keep you from remaining vigilant and keeping watch with the Lord for the enemy because the enemy is sly and knows how to infiltrate. "Be on your guard; stand firm in the faith; be men of courage; be strong. Do everything in love" (1 Corinthians 16:13-14).

"Wake up, O sleeper, rise from the dead, and Christ will shine on you" - Ephesians 5:14

When we suffer from the lack of physical sleep, our bodies tend to shut down quickly. We cannot think properly, we become irate and irritated at everyone and everything around us. So when we are driving and begin to nod off to sleep, we try everything we can to keep ourselves awake, whether that involves blaring music, rolling down the windows, singing or drinking coffee. But yet when we are spiritually asleep, we tend to let that slide as if it is no big deal, but it is much more vital than making sure we are physically awake.

That is a tendency I have been noticing a lot lately, that we have a propensity to care a great deal more about our physical well-being than our spiritual well-being. Like when Paul wrote to Timothy that "physical training is of some value, but godliness has value for all things, holding promise for both the present life and the life to come" (1 Timothy 4:8). The church has been falling asleep spiritually, in spite of its growth throughout the world and in countries where it is being persecuted. Here in America, church growth is down as more and more people are suffering from spiritual sleepiness. They are not caring about sharing the Gospel with others, there is a lack of sensitivity to sin in their lives and the lives of others, and they only speak of God's work in their lives in their past and not their present. I believe this is why Paul wrote these words to the Ephesian church because Jesus' words to this church in Revelation are to "Repent and do the things you did at first" (Revelation 2:5).

Those who are asleep are insensitive to any danger that may be lurking around them. Those who are asleep cannot see or hear of the truth that surrounds their existence or wonder at the beauty in the world because they are fast asleep and numb to everything else. Those who are dead and asleep have this in common: they are lying still. However, when someone is sleeping and the house around them is on fire, do we not do whatever we can to wake them up? How is it then that we are not doing whatever we can to wake our friends and family up, our coworkers and even ourselves up from our slumber? Danger is around the corner; judgment is at hand for those who do not belong to the Lord. We as the church are not to lie still, but to be watchful and attentive, not giving way to complacency, but being active in the church and in the world, illuminating it for the glory of Christ!

"It was not by their sword that they won the land, not did their arm bring them victory; it was your right hand, your arm, and the light of your face, for you loved them" – Psalm 44:3

Too often we get caught up in ourselves, forgetting the ultimate reality. Let me explain. We become so knowledgeable through our education system, so well-informed in our Bible studies, gaining so much wisdom and understanding, growing strong through our training and efforts, all the while believing that *we* made ourselves this way, that *we* built ourselves to be intelligent and resilient. This is what I mean by getting caught up in ourselves.

The Psalmist understood this full well. He grasped that it was not by the army's strength and training that they had won their battles, but that it was by the Lord's power and might. This is evident in many Old Testament stories: with Moses and the Exodus, with Jericho, with Gideon, Elijah, just to name a few. The numbers are always stacked in favor of the enemy until you put God in the equation, then whatever side He is on has the victory no matter what.

We work hard, we study long, we train day in and day out, all to make ourselves more money, become more intelligent and grow stronger. But it is not our knowledge nor our skills nor our power that gets us anywhere significant in life. Yes, they may bring us places, to the job that we love or the location we desire, but ultimately, it was all the Lord's doing. We may fight our hearts out in a vicious battle that we have trained years for, but the outcome does not lie in our strength, but in His. The Psalmist continues saying "I do not trust in my bow, my sword does not bring me victory; but you give us victory over our enemies, you put our adversaries to shame" (44:6-7).

Why do we put our trust in ourselves and our own abilities? Is it because we worked so hard to gain them and so we think we can trust them? Brothers, I guarantee you that your strength will falter, your knowledge will fade, that everything you have built up for yourself with fall with a thunderous crash. "My flesh and my heart may fail, but God is the strength of my heart and my portion forever" (73:26). When all of our being has failed us, God never will. Know that everything of importance, everything that comes your way is the Lord's bidding. Through Him and Him alone is the victory! Without the presence of the Lord in our lives, what would your life look like?

"When a prophet of the Lord is among you, I reveal myself to him in visions, I speak to him in dreams. But this is not true of my servant Moses; he is faithful in all my house. With him I speak face to face, clearly and not in riddles" – Numbers 12:7-8

How cool is that for Moses! With the prophets before him and those after him, we know from the Scriptures that the Lord came to them in visions and dreams, but with Moses, He came directly to him, face to face! That is one special relationship that we do not see again until the incarnation of the Son of God. And Moses was faithful with this extraordinary relationship, not taking advantage of it, but being "a very humble man, more humble than anyone else on the face of the earth" (12:3).

The Lord spoke these words in our text to Miriam and Aaron after they had complained about Moses because he married a Cushite, but behind this complaint was pure jealousy. "'Has the Lord spoken only through Moses?' they asked. 'Hasn't he also spoken through us?'" (12:2). They were jealous of their brother's special relationship with the Lord, even though the Lord also spoke through them and were part of God's gift to Israel. "I sent Moses to lead you, also Aaron and Miriam" (Micah 6:4). If they were not that important, then why would a prophet over hundreds of years later write about them being right there with Moses as he was leading the people of Israel? Their jealousy was uncalled for, as most jealousy is, feeling resentment towards their brother because he was chosen for this great task and they were not. Jealousy never leads anyone down a good road; it tends to spiral towards worse things, eating away at a person, which may be why "When the cloud lifted from above the Tent, there stood Miriam—leprous, like snow" (12:9).

The point of this writing today is not jealousy, but that the Lord speaks to all of us differently; there is no formula with God. With one, He may speak through movies and books. With another, He may speak through great vastness of nature and the weather. And yet another He may speak through dreams and visions or through another channel. But the common factor in all of these is this: it is the Holy Spirit that works differently in each of our lives. There is no need to be jealous that the Lord speaks to one person differently than He does you. Praise the Lord that He even speaks to you at all! Look at all He has done for you and give Him the glory. Stop looking at others and start looking to the Lord of lords and be thankful that He cares about you enough to want to speak with you.

"What if there are fifty righteous people in the city? Will you really sweep it away and not spare the place for the sake of the fifty righteous people in it?" – Genesis 18:24

This is Abraham's plea for the cities of Sodom and Gomorrah. He is of Middle-Eastern descent so he knows the art of haggling; he figured fifty would be a good low number to start with for two good size cities. I am sure he thought there would be at least fifty righteous people in those cities of sin that the Lord was about to destroy; after all, his nephew Lot lived there and so he must have led a few people to the Lord during those years there.

But the Lord could not find even fifty righteous people in Sodom and Gomorrah. So Abraham continues in his haggling, "what if the number of the righteous is five less than fifty...What if only forty are found there...What if only thirty can be found there...what if only twenty can be found there...What if only ten can be found there?" (18:28-32). Abraham knew the Lord was merciful but also that He was just, so He would not destroy the righteous with the unrighteous. But the Lord could not even find ten righteous people in the cities! Lot had a wife with two daughters who were pledged to be married, possibly sons and two more daughters, so maybe Abraham was thinking that if that number was ten, then the cities would be saved, but even most of them did not count, for the angels only saved Lot, his wife and two of their daughters.

Abraham knew that "The Lord is compassionate and gracious, slow to anger, abounding in love" (Psalm 103:8), so he decided to intercede for his nephew and family and potentially other righteous people in the city. This is the first act of intercession in the Bible; Abraham pleading with the Lord, continuously asking Him to be merciful and gracious, putting the Lord's nature to the test. He was bold, trusting in the Lord to hear his request for the sake of a few.

Intercession for the lost and even the saved is few and far between these days. Why do we not do it? Do we forget, or do we just not think about it? I think a little bit of both, but now that we have this reminder once more, there is no excuse. Father, help us to intercede for those who are lost and blind in our lives, knowing that you save the lost and give sight to the blind. May you use us as a conduit for your Spirit, bringing forth light and life wherever we go so that more may be brought into your glorious Kingdom. Be with those suffering for the sake of the Gospel; give them hope and joy in their sufferings, knowing that they get to share in them with you. Thank you for your grace Father and may your will be done. We love you.

"If one of you says to him, 'Go, I wish you well; keep warm and well fed', but does nothing about his physical needs, what good is it? In the same way, faith by itself, if not accompanied by action, is dead" – James 2:16-17

There are millions of people all throughout the world who are in need of our help. They need the basic necessities to life, such as clean water, food, clothes, along with more complex things like education, jobs, and a Bible. There are countless organizations through which you can help donate and assist in something bigger than yourself and your cozy American bubble, so there is no excuse why you should not pitch in and help your brothers and sisters all over the world.

James' letter never really prevaricates things, but tends to always lay it out bluntly, telling his readers that it is no good of them to wish well those people who are in need if they do not plan on helping them out themselves in one way or another. We Americans live in the most blessed nation that has ever existed upon the face of the earth, owning more possessions and wealth than the majority of the world. And what do we do with the bulk of it? Hoard it to ourselves so that we may live more comfortably, have a nice and relaxing retirement, and so life may be easier for us. The apostle John said that "If anyone has material possessions and sees his brother in need but has no pity on him, how can the love of God be in him? Dear children, let us not love with words or tongue but with actions and in truth" (1 John 3:17-18). Love moves not only through our words but more powerfully through our deeds, especially if we are in a position to help out.

Friends, most of us are in a stable enough position to help out. We may not necessarily think we are, but if you look at your budget and you look at what you have in your home, you are more than able I am sure. So are you going to do something about it then? Are you going to sponsor a child in need? Are you going to support a missionary who is helping build churches where there are none? Are you going to send Bibles oversees to people who have never had a chance to hear the good news of Jesus Christ and how much He loves them? Many believe that Christ will return when "this gospel of the kingdom will be preached in the whole world as a testimony to all nations, and then the end will come" (Matthew 24:14). "All men will know that you are my disciples, if you love one another" (John 13:35). So what are you going to do now? Pray about what the Lord wants you to do and then do not hesitate to do it. Be a blessing to the world that so desperately needs it.

"I will celebrate before the Lord. I will become even more undignified than this, and I will be humiliated in my own eyes" – 2 Samuel 6:21-22

As a church, we occasionally celebrate things such as Christmas, Thanksgiving, birthdays, and baptisms, among others. As a culture we love celebrating things as well, like sports events, award shows, and New Year's festivities. But we tend to limit it to just those things and to be quite honest we, more often than not, show more enthusiasm for football games than we do for church and the things of God. Why is that? Are we ashamed of how we will present ourselves? We are not afraid to make a fool of ourselves for our favorite sports team, looking rather childish at times, but when it comes to making a fool of ourselves for the sake of Christ, we hesitate.

David however, did not hesitate. He celebrated with the people of Israel after bringing the ark of the covenant to Jerusalem, to where he, "wearing a linen ephod, danced before the Lord with all his might, while he and the entire house of Israel brought up the ark of the Lord with shouts and the sound of trumpets" (6:14-15). Not only that, he even went on to bless the city, giving "a loaf of bread, a cake of dates and a cake of raisins to each person in the whole crowd of Israelites" (6:19). But his wife was despised with him for his celebrating and dancing, seeing as she does hold bitter feelings for him, after all, she is Saul's daughter.

And people will try and hinder your celebration for the Lord because they believe it is uncouth and barbaric for such a civilized person to act in a foolish way. They would rather have you be sulking and down in the dumps like they are. But do not let them get to you brothers; never let someone tell you that you cannot dance before the Lord your God! Even if in your church it is considered unholy or imprudent of you, do it anyways if the Spirit of the Living God is compelling you.

Do not hinder yourself from being free by the Holy Spirit. Do not say to yourself, "I bet these people behind me will think of I am weird" or "I feel silly for raising my hands and belting at the top of my lungs." If the Spirit of the Lord is making you want to do such things, do it! Be free before the Lord your God and dance if you have to. Follow the example of David who would rather be humiliated in his own eyes than to not celebrate the great things the Lord has done. We have reason to celebrate; we are breathing right now and have food to eat, we have the Scriptures before us and a roof over our heads. There is always a reason to rejoice in the Lord. What is yours?

October 20

"Bad company corrupts good character" – 1 Corinthians 15:33

While at work, it is unfortunately easy to have one person on the team's attitude or a passenger's demeanor affect everyone else around them. Someone could be angry and peeved off about something that happened outside of work and then they bring all their garbage in to work and try and drag everyone down with them. It really does have a negative impact on the whole team's performance and then the passenger's receive the effects of it for no other reason than being there.

It is quite simple to see how bad company corrupts good character, but what we do not normally look at is the inverse of this quotation that Paul took from the Greek comedy *Thais*, which is that good company influences bad character as well. And this is also true: for example, if someone is cheery and optimistic on their outlook for the day and then they come to work like that, I guarantee you that someone will benefit from it because they have had a bad day so far and all they needed was a little bit of laughter and cheer to make their day. In addition, if you smile at someone, whether or not they smile back does not matter because inside they are smiling since feel-good endorphins are released in their brain.

Look at the stories of Joseph or Daniel or Paul; the people they encountered on a daily basis were affected by their godly and honest character for their betterment. Those around them became believers of God and followers of Christ, not because of anything they may have said, but by looking at their lifestyle and how they approached every aspect of their life. Things may have gotten bad for them at times (and they do for us as well), but we have a choice to make: we can either let our situation control us and thus be swayed by our emotions in the moment, or we can stand on top of it all and know that God is in control and we think to ourselves on how Christ would act in that scenario. And so we choose joy, we choose hope, and we choose love to show the world the goodness of God.

Are you being easily affected by those around you? Are you allowing other's negative attitudes and posture to bring you to a pessimistic place where no one wants to be around you? Or are you having other people's days be blessed because you choose to try and help make their day better than what it was before? Bad company does corrupt good character, but do not let it; be the kind of company that people want to be around because there is much rejoicing and grace. Follow the footsteps of your Savior and bring the best out of people, not the worst.

"Do not be overawed when a man grows rich, when the splendor of his house increases; for he will take nothing with him when he dies, his splendor will not descend with him" - Psalm 49:16-17

Many go through life striving to accumulate wealth and riches at any cost, destroying themselves and others in the process, not looking at the outcomes of their actions because they are so fixated on becoming prosperous. Money is one of the most talked about subjects in the entire Bible, and so it is important to God, so it shall be important to us as well.

I have noticed some of my friends growing rich because they got nice high-paying jobs and they are buying newer and bigger things. I have envied them at times; envying the freedom that they have with their wealth, even though I knew it was wrong. James said that "where you have envy and selfish ambition, there you find disorder and every evil practice" (James 3:16). I was selfish in my envy of them because I had wished that I could have such an income so I could do things like that.

But what I failed to remember in those moments was that money is such a temporary tool that the Lord chooses to bestow on His people for His glory and praise, not for my selfish gain. We shall not look upon the rich and desire what they want because, like the Psalmist points out, they can take nothing with them when they die. Solomon echoes that saying that "Wealth is worthless in the day of wrath, but righteousness delivers from death" (Proverbs 11:4). Righteousness teaches us to live self-controlled lives, lives full of wisdom and generosity, not foolishness and egocentricity.

If we can come to truly realize that wealth is not all there is and that it does not buy us happiness, then we have made progress my friends. Do not look to the rich who will lose their wealth when they die, but look to Christ who died and rose again and is the King of all kings to whom we pay our due. What about you? How do you view your riches? Are you living in such a way that your finances are storing for you treasures in heaven that cannot be destroyed? Or are you storing them for the here and now, not knowing when you will die or the Lord return, and thus missing the point? Brothers, do not be afraid to trust the Lord with what He has given you. Invest in people because people matter and people are what makes it into eternity, not things.

"But a time is coming, and has come, when you will be scattered, each to his own home. You will leave me all alone. Yet I am not alone, for my Father is with me" – John 16:32

The disciples finally told Jesus that He was beginning to make sense in what He told them and not in parables and figures of speech. They at last believed that He came from God, giving them hope. But then Jesus uttered these words to them, words that indicate they will leave Him, dashing them again and that is when He then says, "I have told you these things, so that in me you will have peace. In this world you will have trouble. But take heart! I have overcome the world" (16:33).

Jesus Christ was alone as He said He would be, even before His death. As Jesus was being arrested in Gethsemane, we are told that "all the disciples deserted him and fled" (Matthew 26:56). After His death, they went into hiding "with the doors locked for fear of the Jews" (20:19). They had indeed left their Master, their King for the past three and a half years in the time when He perhaps needed them the most.

Times of trial are troubling to go through, although I may not have had some severe trials as several of you may have gone through. But I know that in times of need, how important it is to have those who care about you nearby to encourage you and keep you company, reminding you of the truth that you know that we tend to forget in tough times. However, we may not always have someone physically present to be there for us to help get us through our ordeal and that is when it gets harder. Like the old adage goes "When the going gets tough, the tough get going" and that is what the disciples did to their Savior in His darkest hour.

But brothers, the point of all this is clear: we are *never* alone. Although no one may be there presently for us, the Lord is *always* there with us to help get us through. That is one reason why He sent His Holy Spirit so that He could be in all believers everywhere at the same time, encouraging them to persevere and move forward. If Jesus, Lord of all was left alone, why should we expect anything less for ourselves? There are countless believers suffering persecution throughout the world at this very moment and many have no one with them but the Lord Jesus Christ, and that is sufficient for them. Christ said Himself that in the world we will have trouble, but only in Him may we have peace, for He is our peace. Are you undergoing distress and misery right now because you think no one is there to help you along the way? Take heart friends, and know that God is with you *right now!* Lean on Him as Christ did, giving Him the strength to continue on in the mission He was called to.

"Do not love the world or anything in the world. If anyone loves the world, the love of the Father is not in him" – 1 John 2:15

Last night I watched the WWII movie *Fury*. It took place during the last months of the war in Germany and it was about a tank crew that had gone through hell and back together. One of them quoted this verse and the two that follow during the last battle scene, which was the last time that the entire crew was together as they were facing insurmountable odds. After saying these three reflective verses, especially "but the man who does the will of God lives forever" (2:17), this gave them the hope to fight on, knowing they were doing the Father's will and that they would live forever so there is no need to fear death.

What is the world? Is it its people or the creation surrounding it? No, it is the realm of sin that encloses it, of which Satan is its master. John tells us to not the love this world, to not love sin and the devil which are utterly against God and righteousness. And if we do love this world of wickedness, then the love of the Father is not in us. For God's nature is pure and holy, and so sin and darkness can have no place anywhere near Him. I have said this many times before, "For what do righteousness and wickedness have in common? Or what fellowship can light have with darkness?" (2 Corinthians 6:14). They can have no place in the dwelling of a believer!

As followers of Christ, we should be doing just that, following Christ, not the ways of the world that are here today and gone tomorrow, that lead to pain and suffering and immorality. Christ's ways are not the world's ways; His ways lead to life and holiness and Christ-likeness. The world's ways lead to death, selfishness and devil-likeness. If we love the world, we cannot love the Father because they are polar opposites. "No one can serve two masters. Either he will hate the one and love the other, or he will be devoted to the one and despise the other" (Matthew 6:24).

What about yourself? Have you fallen in love with the world and its ways, or are you fully devoted to your Father in heaven? One loves you so much, and the other unreservedly could not care less about you. One leads you down a path of righteousness and peace, and the other down a path wickedness and pandemonium. The choice is always before you and you have to decide everyday whom you will love and serve; the world or the Lord. So who will it be?

"For everything in the world—the cravings of sinful man, the lust of his eyes and the boasting of what he has and does—comes not from the Father but from the world" – 1 John 2:16

There are three things that John describes as being in the world: the cravings of man, the lust of his eyes and the boasting of what he has and does. Or as the King James Version puts it (which I personally like): the lust of the flesh, the lust of the eyes and the pride of life. This word lust in the Greek is *epithumia*, which its root is *epithumeo*, which is the same word that Jesus used when He said "anyone who looks at a woman *lustfully* has already committed adultery with her in his heart" (Matthew 5:28, emphasis added).

This lust of the flesh, this lust of the eyes, it is an intense longing where one's heart is set upon obtaining something wholly, which may be why the NIV chose to translate the first lust to cravings, which gives it a connotation that one hungers after it. What the world longs for, what wets its appetite, what fulfills its mere animalistic hankerings, does not come from the Father in heaven, but from the world. The lust of man's eyes, the things that he looks upon and covets intensely such as clothes, cars, houses, people, wealth, and other materialistic stuff, these things belong to the world and not to the Lord.

And the pride of life, the boasting of what a man has and does, is a part of the world and should have no part in the life of a follower of Christ. They may have partaken in such things before they were saved, but now that they have been born again, they shall have no place in their lives. I have been a victim of this; I know that I am a strong man who is athletic and easy on the eyes, and I tend to take pride in that, but at the same time, I boast in the dwellings of my mind that I am better than others in certain areas, thinking things like "I am much better looking and funnier than that man. How come he got that beautiful woman instead of me?"

These thoughts are purely evil and must be rebuked at the sight of them. Even though I do not say these things, I think them, which is just as wicked. My friends, the lust of the flesh and the eyes and the pride of life, stay away from these worldly cravings that the world holds in high honor. These things that they take pride in doing will indeed one day fade away and they will realize that it was all such a waste; that they had wasted the vast majority of their lives on trivial pursuits and not things of true eternal value. My brothers, we know the truth and we know the way to life and we know that these worldly yearnings are all for naught. Take a careful examination of yourself and pray about this, and may the Lord lead you into works and possessions that will last for eternity.

"The world and its desires pass away, but the man who does the will of God lives forever" – 1 John 2:17

Is this not good news brothers? The man who does the will of God will live forever, but those things that the world puts all its efforts and time towards will merely pass away like the grass of the fields. What is the will of God? It is one of the most sought after questions in Christianity because people just want to know what it is. "Be joyful always; pray continually; give thanks in all circumstances, for *this is God's will for you* in Christ Jesus" (1 Thessalonians 5:16-18, emphasis added). That is a great place to start for trying to determine what God's will is for you right now; to be joyful and always praying while giving thanks no matter the situation.

We also know that Paul wrote earlier in that letter that "It is God's will that you should be sanctified" (1 Thessalonians 4:3). So in honesty I can say that anything that leads you towards sanctification and Christ-likeness is aligned with God's will for you. Along with this, we have Paul saying "Do not conform any longer to the pattern of this world, but be transformed by the renewing of your mind. *Then* you will be able to test and approve what God's will is—his good, pleasing and perfect will" (Romans 12:2, emphasis added). Therefore, when we no longer think and reason as the world does, or react the same as they do to circumstances, but instead are transformed and conformed to the likeness of Christ, then we will be able to distinguish the procession of what God's will is beyond what we have already discussed.

Are you being molded into a child of God? Are you becoming one who will indeed live forever? I sure hope so because if not, then you, like the world, will pass away. But the man who is always joyful, giving thanks, becoming holy and transformed into a son of God, he shall live forever, and this should give us hope. Hope that no matter what comes at us in this life, whether evil finds its way to our doorsteps and decides to end our earthly lives, or it passes us by the wayside and we must wait until our body gives up, that if we have lived our lives for the will of our great and glorious Father in heaven, we shall endure and live on forever. Friends, I urge you with all of my heart to not take these words lightly, as I am sure some of you have and even I have myself at times, but that we will meditate on such wondrous truth and decide to build and invest in the things that will last in the life to come. It is quite hard on occasion, but that should not hinder us from striving and persevering and doing what we know we must. I have faith in you, as you have faith in the Father.

"Offer hospitality to one another without grumbling"- 1 Peter 4:9

While watching the movie *Lone Survivor*, which may as well be one of the best modern warfare movies out there to date, the Pashtun people in a particular village of Afghanistan upheld a custom that has been around for ages called Pashtunwali; this particular portion of Pashtunwali refers to Nanawatai, which is when someone is seeking refuge and the host to who they come to will fight or die for the sake of that person, no matter what, and that is what happened to the Navy Seal who went there in his time of need.

That is a great example of hospitality that I wish would make itself here in the West, being willing to die for someone whom we welcome into our home. There are times when I do not even want to feed someone who comes in, let alone die for them. But the Lord has been convicting me of this lately as He is making me more like Him; nudging me to not care about myself as much and to care about others more, despite what it must cost me. Paul tells us that we should "Practice hospitality" (Romans 12:13) and in letters to Timothy and Titus, he says that men of God should be hospitable.

Hospitality is held in high regard throughout the Middle East and parts of Asia. It comes from the word *hospes*, which means host or guest. It has come to signify that we take care of the needs of the guests that come into our homes. It means that we feed them and provide for them, entertaining them, making them feel comfortable and right at home, just like Tom Bombadil in *The Fellowship of the Ring*. The root of such hospitality should spring forth from our love for one another, and especially as believers, it should be a wonderful opportunity for us to show the love and compassion of Christ to those who need it. "The alien living with you must be treated as one of your native-born. Love him as yourself, for you were aliens in Egypt" (Leviticus 19:34).

Have you been one to practice such hospitality, of which hospital is very close to the word, where the sick are healed and the weary are refreshed? What could you do the next time someone knocks at your door looking for help? Would you shoo them away because whatever they are asking is inconvenient for you, or would you think of these verses and cultures that take time out of their lives to take care of such people? Those Pashtun people in the movie (which actually happened), by living by the code to protect the Navy Seal, took their lives into their hands by painting targets on their backs for the Taliban because they counted him as one of their own. Is being hospitable to someone too much to ask, really?

"It does not fear when heat comes; its leaves are always green. It has no worries in a year of drought and never fails to bear fruit" - Jeremiah 17:8

Today was the first day that it snowed this season. It did not do so very long and it did not accumulate, but it snowed nonetheless. I do not always like snow, especially driving in it, but when I saw the flakes falling, I bore a grin on my face because it somehow made me happy. Maybe it was the change, or maybe it just me being thankful for different seasons or just because it was pretty. Whatever the reason, I was happy although it was cold, but I did not fear what the rest of this winter has to offer.

Many of the people at work were grumbling and complaining about it, and even angry, fearing what the winter season may bring. But the prophet Jeremiah exhorts us to be like the man whose trust and confidence is in the Lord so that we "will be like a tree planted by the water that sends out its roots by the stream" (17:7). As this tree, we shall not fear the heat that seeks to destroy us, to burn our leaves and kill them. In other words, we should not be afraid of the evil and sin that tries to hunt us down and demolish all the work that we put forth all those years, but instead we should have our faith and assurance on the Lord. If we try and only see what the world throws at us and panic about it, we will fail to notice the life that still flows because our roots are in the stream that is continually fed.

Droughts may come, dry seasons might linger about, and storms may attempt and shake the foundations on which our house is built, but if we are firmly planted in the confidence and dependence of the Lord, then we shall have no need to fear or worry about what may try and ruin our joy. Things may look dry on the outside of our lives, looking as if the drought and heat were affecting it, but what you do not see are the roots that are ever absorbing water and nutrients so that it may remain alive and well.

How would you describe yourself in accordance with these verses? Could you say that you are such a tree that does not dread or fear what the day or the next or the coming year may bring? Could you say that whatever the world decides to throw at you, you will remain strong in the Lord your God and continue to bear fruit all the years long? I pray this for you brothers, and for myself, that we will endure through the droughts and storms because our foundation is solid on Christ. Do not be anxious about anything.

"Religion that God our Father accepts as pure and faultless is this: to look after orphans and widows in their distress" – James 1:27

The other night at church, our pastor talked about orphans throughout the world and America and even Michigan. One fact that surprised me was that there are nearly 3,000 orphans in the state of Michigan and over 11,000 churches. The point of this was that the orphan problem in Michigan could be easily defeated if just one family from every church decided to adopt a child. He said that the orphan crisis in America is not a problem that should merely be solved by politics and the government, but that it is the church's responsibility to step up to the plate.

Now do not get me wrong, there are many Christ-following families who are doing just that, being led by the Holy Spirit to adopt and help children who have no families, but the church could do much more. I am not saying that everyone should adopt, because that is not what we are all called to, but we are called to look after them and help them out and there are ways to do that besides just adopting them.

But why does James write this? Why is this is such an important issue to God? It is because those who are orphaned feel unloved and rejected because they have no one there for them in their lives; no one to hold them close and tell them they are loved, no one to provide for them and cheer them on in their endeavors, no one to just be there for them, and God wants them to know that He loves them and they will know by our actions towards them. My pastor said that "Our move toward a life of holiness should go right along with an action-oriented faith." Action-oriented, meaning that something has to be done. This is dear to the Father so it should be dear to us as well. The prophet Isaiah told us to "Seek justice, encourage the oppressed. Defend the cause of the fatherless, plead the case of the widow" (Isaiah 1:17).

Some orphans move around from house to house and foster home to foster home because they are just too much for the family, and the adoption rate gets even lower as they hit the teenage years, but they are never too much for God. We too were adopted by God into His loving family; "For you did receive a spirit that makes you a slave again to fear, but you received the Spirit of sonship" (Romans 8:15). As adopted children, we have the same rights as the parent's children. Since we were adopted, so should we not also pray and be there for those who long to be adopted by earthy families as well? Pray about these things and discover what the Lord has for you in this matter.

"Yet I am not ashamed, because I know whom I have believed, and am convinced that he is able to guard what I have entrusted to him for that day" - 2 Timothy 1:12

Yesterday at work, my coworkers were talking about something and then they handed me a Gospel tract that a passenger gave them and they threw away, telling me that I need it because I am going to hell. I thought that quite strange, so I informed them that I knew precisely that I was in fact going to heaven. They laughingly said that they were going to hell and that another coworker was driving the bus. I am not sure if they were really joking about it, but it still made my heart ache for them because they kind of laughed the matter off.

I believe this laughter is a defense mechanism of theirs to avoid talking about the reality of their mortality and their final destination. I have seen it before and I am sure you have as well. People think they are immortal until a tragedy strikes them and reality begins to sink in. And they also see hell as a place they are destined for and where there will be one giant party that will never end, but little do they know that hell will be a "lake of burning sulfur...[where] They will be tormented day and night for ever and ever" (Revelation 20:10). But we know who we believe and that God is able to protect our inheritance in Him and avoid the second death.

I pray for more opportunities as this for me to let my coworkers know a little bit of what I believe and I pray for boldness and courage in doing so, so I may not be ashamed of the good news that I believe, but share it willingly and joyfully. The broken world around us, those you work with and live near, I bet the majority of them do not know where they will end up after their death, but you do. I pray for engagements in such conversations to get them to begin thinking about these things. We know, if we have the Spirit of the Living God within us, that we will join our Father in heaven when we pass on and that there will be much rejoicing and rest in the city of our Lord. Our coworkers and families and friends may not necessarily know and for that, they may be scared which is why they may laugh such occurrences off because they do not want to deal with it. I urge you to pray for them and to pray for the Holy Spirit to bring such a conviction upon them on the subject, one that burns their insides to where they are hit with the ultimate reality. These people need your prayers, your intercession, to break down the miles of walls they have built in defense of the truth. Father, be with them, tear down the walls in their minds and hearts to your truth, so that they may be open to receive your Son, or even to just talk about such things. You are good Father and we believe what we have asked for. Thank you for your grace.

"Endure hardship with us like a good soldier of Christ Jesus" – 2 Timothy 2:3

The *X-Men* saga has always been one of my favorites, especially those that deal with Wolverine, which is why last night I finally was able to watch *The Wolverine*. It takes place in Japan after *X-Men: The Last Stand*, when Wolverine no longer wants to be the killer and animal that he is used to being. He does well at it too, until circumstances that were outside of his control drew him back into the game because he could not stand for the injustices and evil he was witnessing. In the end, the girl that he came to like said to him, "Am I wrong to think you might visit me soon? Stay" and he responds, "I can't, Princess. I'm a soldier, and I've been hiding too long."

Powerful words. He tried to outrun and hide from who he was, but he could not and neither can we; we may think we can, but it will come back to us eventually. Like myself, I had wanted to be a police officer or in the military while growing up, but there were seasons where I shied away from it and so dismissed it. The years passed and it comes back to me yet again, the desire to help people and fight against injustice, like Wolverine, I cannot stand injustice. I tried to reason myself out of it in the past, but this time I cannot, for I know what I must do.

Paul advises Timothy, his son in the faith, to endure hardship like a good soldier of Christ. Why use that analogy? Because soldiers, especially the elitist of them, are trained to endure literally everything that mother nature and the world can throw at them: extreme cold and heat, starvation, exhaustion, isolation, destitution, and even death. And so we as good soldiers of Christ Jesus, should endure what the world throws at us and not think any of it strange or odd that it came to us, but we should expect it. If we try and hide from it, we will become more and more like the world and less and less like Christ and thus forget our purpose and actually go against ourselves and Christ.

Soldiers are willing to suffer for their country's sake; we must be willing to suffer for Christ's sake. Come out of hiding and live the life you are supposed to live for your King. Stop running from who you know you are because your family or friends are telling you otherwise. Listen to the Spirit, Christ Himself, within you and may He be your only guide for your life. Do not think you will live a life of ease because you are a follower of Christ; I have fallen under that spell too often and it is a lie. Welcome hardship, endure it, and expect it to happen as you walk day by day in the steps of your Commanding Officer. Oh Father, help us in this endeavor.

"Though my father and mother forsake me, the Lord will receive me" – Psalm 27:10

I began reading John Bunyan's *The Pilgrim's Progress*. It is a tough read because of the complexity of its language and it feels like I am reading Shakespeare half the time. But already, there is so much truth in this book as it has Scripture references in the margins for almost everything that happens to Christian, the main character in the story. Here in the beginning, he sets out without his wife and children, but has a neighbor with him for a short while until he gets discouraged and leaves, and in the margin it writes, "A man may have company when he sets out for Heaven, and yet go thither alone."

Oh, such truth! We may begin our journey of faith with a group of people or even just one other person; things are going great until something unexpected that cannot be explained happens and the other person becomes disheartened and goes back to where they came. Maybe you have experienced such desertion from someone you thought would never leave you and would never fall away from the faith, but they did. David tells us in the Psalms that though his own father and mother may abandon him, he knows that God never will.

"No one who puts his hand to the plow and looks back is fit for service in the kingdom of God" (Luke 9:62). You cannot look back to your old way of life, wishing you were there when things were easier and you did not have the responsibility to the Kingdom of God that you do now. You must heed Paul's instructions on "Forgetting what is behind and straining toward what is ahead" (Philippians 3:13). If your family leaves you because of your faith in Christ, if your friends desert you on account of your love for Christ, let it be. What is done is done.

"A man may have company when he sets out for Heaven, and yet go thither alone." Do not be discouraged if people walk out on you because of Christ, but continue on the journey heavenward. Jesus' own family and disciples abandoned Him when He needed them the most in His time of need, yet He continued on to complete the mission that the Father had assigned Him. "Do not be afraid or terrified because of them, for the Lord your God goes with you; he will never leave you nor forsake you" (Deuteronomy 31:6). Remember that beautiful promise if you ever feel like you are going through this world alone, brothers. You are never alone.

"Now choose life, so that you and your children may live and that you may love the Lord your God, listen to his voice, and hold fast to him. For the Lord is your life" – Deuteronomy 30:19-20

It is finally November. Most of the leaves on the trees are already gone due to those colder fall winds and there is even frost on the car every now and then. There is more brownness and darker tones than there were a few weeks ago, but the trees and nature are far from being dead. They may have given up their dead leaves, but the rest of the tree is full of life, storing and preparing for the harsh winter and waiting until the warm spring arrives so its patience was not in vain.

These are the words of the Lord through Moses to the people of Israel. He says, "See, I set before you today life and prosperity, death and destruction" (30:15). Those choices are before us today: life and death. Every choice that we make, every thought we think, every word we speak, is either moving us further along the path of life or further along the path of death. But who would not want to choose life? It seems like the obvious choice right? Yet every day, numerous amounts of people choose death because it is easier and more convenient than choosing life. The road that leads to life is lengthy and tiresome, full of hardships and long-suffering. The path that leads to death is wide and smooth, looks attractive but leaves you empty. Jesus tells us to "Enter through the narrow gate. For wide is the gate and broad is the road that leads to destruction and many enter through it. But small is the gate and narrow the road that leads to life, and only a few find it" (Matthew 7:13-14).

Why do you not choose life? Why do you not want to live for the Lord, to love Him, listen to His voice and hold fast to Him? When has He ever led you astray or did not fulfill what He said He would? I believe that many of those who can answer negatively to these questions put the blame on God instead of themselves and their choices when the road they chose does not go where they thought it would. What path are you traversing on? Does it involve smooth sailing and living the life of luxury, caring only for yourself and what affects you, or does it involve trials and adversity, in which you stumble every few steps but you keep on going the right direction? If you are on the wrong path, choose life today, and if you are on the right path, continue to choose life every day, for the Lord is your life and makes your life worth living.

"Do not take revenge, my friends, but leave room for God's wrath, for it is written: 'It is mind to avenge; I will repay,' says the Lord" – Romans 12:19

Revenge is an interesting topic because it is one that is so ingrained within our culture, in TV shows and movies, literature, and everyday life. We tend to praise those on our televisions where everything is based on revenge and getting back for the wrongs that were done to them. Why do we applaud these qualities when we see them? Is it because deep down we believe that those who did wrong to us should be repaid in the same way that they have hurt us?

This is not the way of the Spirit-filled life brothers, but the world-filled life. Paul explicitly tells us to not take revenge for the evils done to us. Why? Because God Himself will take the case and right the wrong, we do not need to take it into our own hands as many of us deem we have the right to. Jesus declared, "You have heard that it was said, 'Eye for eye, and tooth for tooth.' But I tell you, Do not resist an evil person. If someone strikes you on the right cheek, turn to him the other also" (Matthew 5:38-39). It cannot be more clearly stated than right there, in which we do not have the right to get back at someone for the hurt they have caused us.

"But I want to get at them. They caused me much pain and anguish" you might say. Ok fine, take revenge into your hands; disobey the orders of your Commanding Officer and lose your rank. Friends, why do you think God tells us to not take revenge? One reason is because He knows that it does not lead to a holy and righteous life, not that He wants to spoil our fun or make us seem soft, because He knows better. Another is that He knows that it will not bring satisfaction to us if we repay the wrong; it will not give us the feeling of justice and will not fill that area of hurt with contentment. Our God is Sovereign; He knows what He is doing and always plans the best for us, never the worst.

Is there someone in your life right now that you are plotting to get back at? I urge you not to, but rather to forgive them for the hurt they have caused you. But you say, "That drunk driver killed my family. How can I forgive him for taking everything from me?" The same way that the incarnate Son of God can forgive you for a lifetime of wickedness and disobedience to Him when He had done nothing wrong at all, but instead loved you so much that He took your rightful place on the cross, carrying your iniquities, and made you clean before the Father in heaven. It is as if you have never committed those sins; "they shall be as white as snow" (Isaiah 1:18). God will right all wrongs in the end my friends, so there is no need to take that upon yourself now.

November 3

"For the Lord is a God of justice" – Isaiah 30:18

Some people see justice as something that is relative, that is in flux, but we know that justice is absolute because God is absolute and He is a God of justice. Here in America, our judicial system is one that deals out a punishment that fits the crime. So if someone steals a car per say, they will not receive the death penalty, and some believe this is justice being served. But if someone committed mass murders, we believe that he should receive the death penalty and thus think that justice is being served.

For God, if someone commits a sin, no matter the type of sin, he is punishable by death because "the wages of sin is death" (Romans 6:23) and "whoever keeps the whole law and yet stumbles at just one point is guilty of breaking all of it" (James 2:10). So in essence, we all deserve death. God has every right and would be just in giving us the death penalty because that is what we are worthy of, and that is what we all got, but when He sent His only son Jesus, He took our place on death row, dying so we did not have to. It is in His very nature to be just, so He cannot act outside of justice.

But you say, "God is merciful, so He will extend mercy to me, not justice." And that is true; He will give you mercy, but you must not abuse the mercy He extends to you. When Christ died on the cross, it was the ultimate display of God's justice to the world because His wrath was poured out on His Son for our sake. "Since we have now been justified by his blood, how much more shall we be saved from God's wrath through him?" (Romans 5:9). We deserve some sort of justice, do we not? We deserve death because of the atrocities done in our lives, but "Our God, you have punished us less that our sins have deserved" (Ezra 9:13).

But justice does not only deal with punishment, but also rewarding. He does not overlook the good deeds and works you have done for His Kingdom. However, He does not reward you because you somehow deserve it by what you did, but because He promised to. "He rewards those who earnestly seek him" (Hebrews 11:6). Justice is both parties getting what both parties are owed. God is the standard of equity, so what He says goes; there is no changing His mind in the matter or trying to present your side of the case in order to get a lesser sentence. You have to play by His rules, and His rules tells us to love Him with all of our inmost being and to love others, to trust and depend on Him alone, and to believe in His son Jesus Christ.

"When he came to Jerusalem, he tried to join the disciples, but they were all afraid of him, not believing that he was really a disciple" – Acts 9:26

This is in reference to Paul. He was a Christian killer before the Lord Jesus visited him on the road to Damascus. The Followers of the Way, the first Christians, were afraid of this man because he was given "authority from the chief priests to arrest all who call on [Jesus'] name" (9:14). He was a Hebrew of Hebrews, one that Jews looked up to, but after he began persecuting Christians, not for the right reasons. The early church had every reason imaginable to not trust this man because of his past life, but Ananias and Barnabas gave him a chance because the Lord showed them he was no longer the man he used to be.

We are not who we used to be since we have received the Holy Spirit. "Neither the sexually immoral nor idolaters nor adulterers nor male prostitutes nor homosexual offenders nor thieves nor the greedy nor drunkards nor slanderers nor swindlers will inherit the kingdom of God. And that is what some of you were. But you were washed, you were sanctified, you were justified in the name of the Lord Jesus Christ and by the Spirit of our God" (1 Corinthians 6:9-11). We are not who we used to be; we have been changed by the indwelling of the Spirit of Christ.

Sometimes we will want to judge people by what they have done in the past, by their previous sins and failures and shortcomings, but what good does that do? Would we want them to judge us by those same standards? I sure hope not because I know I have done some bad things in my history that I would not want to be evaluated by. I know how far I have come by the grace of God and the sanctification of His Spirit within me and I know that I do not want to live as I have previously. So why should we look at people for what they did before and believe they have not changed while we hold ourselves to a different standard because we know we have changed? "For in the same way you judge others, you will be judged, and with the measure you use, it will be measured to you" (Matthew 7:2).

Is it hard to look at people in the light of the new life they have received in Christ, although you knew how they were before Christ and wonder how they could be different? "Think of what you were when you were called" (1 Corinthians 1:26). We have all been changed by the redeeming blood of Christ and His Holy Spirit. We are not what we once were, but we are new and unlike our previous selves, so stop judging others by who they were and begin to look at them for who they are now and who they are becoming.

"Do nothing out of selfish ambition or vain conceit, but in humility consider others better than yourselves" – Philippians 2:3

I think I may be able to say with sincerity that selfishness is the root cause of the many downfalls of our society. Think about it: there are abortions because the potential mothers are only looking out for themselves and not even thinking about the child (even if it was an accident they got pregnant or raped). Or there are many fatherless homes because fathers have been walking out on their families since it is not convenient for them or something else trivial. Selfishness is at the core and this is not good.

Yet we play it off way too easily, saying this person has the right to do this or that, which they do, but all they ever do, and even what our culture teaches us, is to look out for numero uno. Themselves. Paul gives us this word of advice, no, this command, to do *nothing* out of selfish ambition or vain conceit. How often do we as followers of Christ try to outdo each other in our indulgences? How often do we miss opportunities to show the love of Christ and bear fruit because we are too busy striving to do things that merely benefit ourselves? How often do we lose unity in the body of Christ because of someone's selfishness to make themselves look better than everyone else?

This is what Paul is getting at here. Immediately before this verse he writes, "make my joy complete by being like-minded, having the same love, being one in spirit and purpose" (2:2). He is saying that we must put aside such selfish and egocentric behaviors for the sake of church and the sake of Christ because it is first and foremost sinful and not of God and secondly, our Head and King never acted in such a way so neither should His body and servants. Jesus Himself said that "Greater love has no one than this, that he lay down his life for his friends" (John 15:13) and that is the exact opposite of selfishness which is Christ-centeredness, and ultimately selflessness as we are not constantly looking for ways to make ourselves look better in the eyes of others.

Jesus was a man who "was despised and rejected by men, a man of sorrows…like one from whom men hide their faces" (Isaiah 53:3). He was not one who went out to make a name for Himself, but for God, and so shall our motive be. Our culture says to make oneself look better than everyone else, especially in interviews where we are told to "sell ourselves". But that is not the way for us believers, if we truly are believers. We are to go out and make a name for Christ and to deem others worthy of greater respect than we even give to ourselves. This is not an easy task and it is easier said than done, but I am glad that our Sovereign Lord dwells in us to make us more selfless and humble like Him.

November 6

"Each of you should look not only to your own interests, but also to the interests of others" – Philippians 2:4

We are born to look after our own interests, and after that we are molded to do so. Our parents growing up tell us to "Do what you like doing and everything will fall into place", not "Go and help others in their pursuits." By no means am I asking you to cast aside all of your interests, but just to begin pondering about also thinking of the interests of the people in your life.

I am surrounded by coworkers at work who honestly only have one goal in mind for the day: to do what pleases them and makes them happy without looking at the expense it may have on others. I am constantly convicted of the same actions that I also use on the job because I prefer to be at one position over another. Paul's words come to mind when he says to "Do everything without complaining or arguing" (2:14), and this even applies to complaining on the inside although you may not display it but in your heart there is grumbling. Why is it so hard to look to the interests of others in situations? Why do we become so selfish and get this "tunnel vision" about us? Because ultimately, I believe we do not really care about others' well-being and what they are interested in, especially if it has no benefit to us.

But we know that is not how it is to be, but we do it anyways because we forget about what is supposed to be at the root of our lives and everything we do: love. And love *never* looks to ourselves first, but always to others because that is what God does because "God is love" (1 John 4:16). Paul is commanding us to break down our narrow vision that is embedded in selfishness and begin to live with a broader perspective that sees the things and people that are beyond ourselves. The context of this passage is in regard to unity in the church, and so we must consider the concerns and interests of other members of the church as our own and not so easily dismiss them as we would not want them to dismiss ours.

The church is called to be one because God is one. And where there is unity, there is strength and power, but when selfishness and self-centeredness are involved, it creates a strong sense of disunity and factions which God abhors. Brothers, we must repent of our selfish and childish behavior and embark on living a selfless, holy life because love "is not self-seeking" (1 Corinthians 13:5).

"Therefore, I urge you, brothers, in view of God's mercy, to offer your bodies as living sacrifices, holy and pleasing to God" – Romans 12:1

Sacrifice; something I have talked about every now and then throughout this book, and yet I have not talked about it enough. Sacrifice is the willingness to give up something you care deeply about for the sake of something else that you care even more for. It involves the utter removal of self: "[He] made himself nothing, taking the very nature of a servant...he humbled himself and became obedient to death" (Philippians 2:7-8). This is what Christ did, the personification of sacrifice and humility that we should follow.

Paul says that we should offer ourselves as sacrifices to the Lord *because* of the mercy He has shown us, not because a law requires it or it makes me feel better, but because of His compassion. Christ emptied himself of His glory that is rightfully His while He lived on earth. He did not have money or many possessions, was looked down upon and even "his own did not receive him" (John 1:11). He gave Himself so that the Father's will would be fulfilled and that should be our aim as well for our sacrificing. I like what J. Hampton Keathley III said of this, "The bottom line is this: Christ voluntarily emptied Himself of anything and everything that stood in the way of the glory and gain of His Father through Him."

Since Christ voluntarily made himself nothing and emptied Himself for the glory of the Lord, so we shall live in such a matter. We should always be in a state of willing abandonment, that is to say, we should be ready to give up possessions, people, status, rights, and mindsets if the Lord is requiring it of us for His fulfillment and our growth. Nothing should be off limits and if we deem it is, then it is an idol and must be removed because nothing ought to be above the Lord in our lives.

"Anyone who loves his father or mother more than me is not worthy of me; anyone who loves his son or daughter more than me is not worthy of me; and anyone who does not take his cross and follow me is not worthy of me" (Matthew 10:37-38). Christ calls for total commitment, not half-heartedness. You are either all in or all out, and your willingness to sacrifice the things of this life for the Lord's sake will help determine which side you are really standing on.

"He was despised and rejected by men, a man of sorrows, and familiar with suffering" –
Isaiah 53:3

For the past couple of weeks, the Lord has been speaking to me on this subject of suffering. I do not know if it has any correlation with what I have been watching on TV or stuff going on with work or me simply reading Isaiah 53 which is all about the sufferings of Christ, but nonetheless, He has something for me in this arena. God wants us to look at His Son and His life while on this earth and that is how He desires us to live ours out. Isaiah described Christ as being a man of sorrows, one who was rejected by men; these are characteristics of the Son of God. Are they also characteristics of us?

"If the world hates you, keep in mind that it hated me first…If they persecuted me, they will persecute you also" (John 15:18,20). They should be attributes of ours, especially if we long to be like Christ as we are called to be. So why do we strive to do whatever we can to make sure we are liked by the world? Why do we shy away from suffering as if it is some sort of disease that should not be a part of our lives? Do we so easily forget that our Christ's life was full of suffering and affliction, or that the name Israel, which stands for God's people, means *struggles or wrestles with God*? If you are a follower of Christ, your life should be difficult and if you come to a point when there is not some sort of strife, take a good look at your spiritual walk with the Lord.

God never promises us ease and comfort in this life, so why should we expect it? Did Jesus ever have it? He did not have a place to lay His head, He had no home, His friends deserted Him, He underwent ridicule and hatred from the religious leaders of the day, He was beaten up and crucified by the Romans and He carried all of our sins and iniquities that we would ever commit. It does not look like He did, seeing as He gave up the life of luxury in heaven for a time so that we might have a chance to go there with Him. Why do we run and hide from hardship and suffering? Why do we think it is strange when such things happen to us? We *should* expect them to happen.

Are you living the good life? Is your life easy and comfortable right now? Is it because you are afraid to go out and risk for the Lord, fearful of making a mistake? Or is it that you like where you are at and do not want anything to change? We are to find contentment wherever we are at (Philippians 4:12), but that does not mean we should settle. Life is supposed to be difficult, and it is in those times where our character is being molded and shaped into the man of God that He aches for us to be, stripping away everything that is not of Him.

"So we must fix our eyes not on what is seen, but on what is unseen. For what is seen is temporary, but what is unseen is eternal" – 2 Corinthians 4:18

Waiting for things used to be a part of life: we had to wait weeks to receive letters from loved ones, we had to be on a boat for months to travel to Europe, we had to actually grow our own food in the field, but now we can send and receive text messages in an instant, we can fly to Europe in ten hours, and we can go to the grocery store and pop our food in a microwave for one minute. And even the things now are too slow for us. We have grown so impatient in this society and we *need* instant gratification and if we do not get it, we go mad.

John Bunyan dubbed these two worlds as Passion and Patience in *The Pilgrim's Progress*. Passion is the instant and now while patience is just that, patient; the battle between the immediate and the eternal. We need to not let this poison of passion, of getting things and results now, infect us as the Church. What we see now, what is already right in front of us, is in fact temporary because it will fade away and not last. It will have to give way to what we cannot yet see, the things which are to come and to which nothing will come after them because they are eternal and will never fade. It is these things that we must fixate ourselves and our efforts upon, not the many toilsome things of this present life that are fleeting.

David sang, "Be still before the Lord and wait patiently for him...For evil men will be cut off, but those who hope in the Lord will inherit the land" (Psalm 37:7,9). Those who follow the Lord should be living lives of patience and waiting, knowing that what is yet to come is so much more than what is now. It is evil men who will fade away because it is evil men who have their hope in this world and not in the next, and they will see when their time is up that everything they invested in and entrusted themselves to was useless. The Hebrew word for hope in Psalm 37 is more rightly translated as wait. Waiting in the Lord describes the life of His followers, at least it should.

Does it describe your life? Do you live in such a way that you make a habit of saying no to many immediate things because you are willing to have patience and wait for them so they do not control you? Brothers, we do not need things now; sure we may *want* some things instantaneously, but more often than not, we do not *need* them right now. Exercise restraint as Christ and the saints before you have also done because they saw that which is unseen, that which is unending.

November 10

"Hate evil, love good" – Amos 5:15

Growing up in a Christian home, I was taught not to hate things or people, which is good advice since we are told to love everyone. But I was mainly taught this because it was not nice to hate, not necessarily because Christ wanted us to love. As I grew older, I discovered this verse along with "Hate what is evil; cling to what is good" (Romans 12:9) and I learned that hating evil is a mark of a believer of Christ. Note that I said hating evil itself, not the person who carries out such wickedness because we are advised to "Love your enemies, do good to those who hate you, bless those who curse you, pray for those who mistreat you" (Luke 6:27).

Do we actually *hate* evil? Can you honestly say that you hate evil itself, or are you like the majority of society who has become so tolerant and numb to the evil so close in proximity to them? Evil is rampant, right down the street and in your workplace, but do you hate it? Do you utterly despise the existence of evil and the trouble and chaos it causes, or are you deadened to its presence and indifferent to who it affects? "Let those who love the Lord hate evil" (Psalm 97:10). "To fear the Lord is to hate evil; I hate pride and arrogance, evil behavior and perverse speech" (Proverbs 8:13). Do we hate those qualities in ourselves and in others? I sure hope so, but that does not give us any ground to hate the person who bears them, only the behavior, "For our struggle is not against flesh and blood" (Ephesians 6:12).

The Lord hates evil way more than we ever could: "There are six things the Lord hates, seven that are detestable to him: haughty eyes, a lying tongue, hands that shed innocent blood, a heart that devises wicked schemes, feet that are quick to rush into evil, a false witness who pours out lies and a man who stirs up dissension among brothers" (Proverbs 6:16-19).

What is the evil in your life that you need to begin to hate? What is the evil that you have grown a tolerance for, seeing it as no big deal when in fact it is destroying countless lives because that is what evil does? Brothers, do not take evil lightly; keep your head on a swivel and do not be tolerant towards those things that the Lord abhors because they are toxic and could soon eat at you as well. "Seek good, not evil" (5:14). If you hate evil, you will no longer have any attraction to it and you will cease to seek it, and if you love good, you will seek it.

"Then we will no longer be infants, tossed back and forth by the waves, and blown here and there by every wind of teaching and by the cunning and craftiness of men in their deceitful scheming" – Ephesians 4:14

Today is actually my birthday and the first thing I did after having breakfast this morning was to thank the Lord for all the wonderful things that He had done through me this past year. There have been lots of changes, ups and downs, moving around, but through it all, He was right there with me, forming me to be more like Him. I have seen how I have grown and what I continually need to work on and let Him have His way in.

The imagery that Paul uses paints a simple picture of the life of a new believer who is not yet deeply rooted in their faith, so they are easily moved by the elements around them. I am in no way new to the faith (even though I am still young in years), but some of you are and all of us should always be in a state of learning from those who have more years under their belt because they (for the most part) have experienced more of life in its different seasons. Every year that passes is yet another year that hopefully your spiritual walk with the Lord has progressed and not regressed, moving onward and upward, not backward and downward.

"Instead, speaking the truth in love, we will in all things grow up into him who is the Head, that is, Christ" (4:15). Instead of being tossed back and forth by the wind and the waves, we will grow up into Christ, into His likeness. I hope that you are able to see advancements in your walk as you look back over the past few years, that you no longer think a certain way, or look at people with the lust you once did, or say the words that you used to breathe out. If you are on the path towards holiness and righteousness, you would know, and if you do not, that is troubling.

My friends, my family, look back over your life. Gaze into your past and take note of the present and pray there are differences, even subtle ones because some positive change is better than none. My growth has been a subtle, slow-moving one that I cannot really notice on a day to day basis, but only when I look back on the years as a whole. May we be of those who are not tossed back and forth, who do not follow the lies of wicked and deceitful men, who are not standing on a downward escalator, but are actively and persistently moving forward towards Christ heavenward.

November 12

"The one who calls you is faithful and he will do it" – 1 Thessalonians 5:24

As I move along in this life, I am constantly reminded that a lot of people just cannot be trusted. We may want to trust to them because they are our family or friends or coworkers, but time and time again they bring us disappointment in the trust department. And even when we think we have made some headway, one mistake on either party sets it back further than it was before, creating a larger barrier between us.

However, this should not hinder us from continually striving to trust one another because even Jesus' disciples who left everything to follow Him, repeatedly disappointed Him but since they were His friends and brothers, He continued to trust them and love them because "Love is patient...[it] always trusts" (1 Corinthians 13:4,7). And that is another great thing about God, that even though everyone we care about in this life will at a point fail us in one way or another, God is always, *always* faithful and we can forever trust Him. When the world around us fails and everything begins to crumble, when every other piece of dust that we have put our trust in besides Christ has proven to be futile, God is still that Solid Rock on which are able stand because He is always faithful. "He alone is my rock and my salvation; he is my fortress, I will never be shaken" (Psalm 62:2).

Where have you been disappointed by those you love lately? Have you entrusted them with something and they let you down time and time again? Have you given them second and third chances to make it better and they still fall short? My brothers, I know they cannot be trusted and I am sure you are utterly frustrated with them and just want to give up, but do not do it; persist on giving them chances as the Lord persists on giving you chances. The one who calls you is faithful and He will do it; He will make you more like Him, more merciful, more humble, more selfless, more trusting, more faithful, more just. Even if your loved ones are not proving faithful, that does not mean that you are to be faithless. If God was not faithful every time that you were unfaithful to Him, life would suck because we disappoint Him often, but yet He is faithful and so we also must be.

"While Paul was waiting for them in Athens, he was greatly distressed to see that the city was full of idols" – Acts 17:16

Today we had our first legit snowstorm of the season and it hit with a bang: extremely slippery roads, blinding snow and chilling temps on top of that. Flights are delayed, cars are driving extremely slow and schools are beginning to close. Luckily I do not have work the next few days so I can stay home and not travel. People are becoming troubled and concerned because of the dangerous conditions out there and they have a right to be.

But Paul was distressed about something of a different nature, something that affects people just as much, if not more than winter storms: idolatry. He came to the city of Athens to escape Jews from other cities who were persecuting him and as soon as he arrived there, he noticed how destructive the city was because of its fill of idolatry. Petronius, a writer of the time, said that in Athens, "it was easier to find a god than a man there." Idolatry was a huge problem there and it upset Paul to the point that "he reasoned in the synagogue with the Jews and the God-fearing Greeks, as well as in the marketplace day by day with those who happened to be there" (17:17).

And reason with them he did, informing them of an unknown God who is actually real, "who does not live in temples built by hands" (17:24). Paul was a very knowledgeable man who used things in their own culture to point them to Christ (v.23,28) and that should be a good example for us to do the same. That way, they can see the connection in a way that is clear to them. The Gospel message has and always will remain the same, but the means in which it is made known shall change and be adjusted to the crowd, as Jesus used parables to the Jews because they were a story-based culture.

There are then two things to take away from this: 1. We should be distressed by the idolatry and sin that is so rampant in our society and 2. We should do something about it, which is to talk to people about it and use things that they are familiar with to help get the point across. If we can do that, people's lives will be changed and they would no longer be lollygagging around, worshiping every little thing that brings them temporary satisfaction, but rather using that same energy to serve a real and great God who made everything that we see before us. Father, give us boldness and wisdom in making these things happen. Let us not become discouraged when they do not listen, but persevere and do the work you have sent us out to do. You are faithful God.

"In a little while I will once more shake the heavens and the earth, the sea and the dry land. I will shake all nations, and the desired of all nations will come, and I will fill this house with glory" – Haggai 2:6-7

Earthquakes shake the ground with such a force that buildings crumble and the earth splits because of them. The largest and most destructive earthquake ever recorded was the Chilean earthquake of 1960, with a magnitude of 9.5 and where it killed 1,655 people, 3,000 were injured, 2,000,000 were left homeless, and caused $550 million in damage, and this does not even include the tsunami it produced, impacting the U.S. and Southeast Asia.

When the Lord shakes the heavens and the earth however, the devastation will be even more horrendous, utterly obliterating everything that is not set to be in the new heavens and the new earth. He will shake the whole of humanity when He returns, to see what has eternal value and what does not, and the things that do not will crumble and fall. Haggai was referring to the second coming of Christ, in talking about the former and the new, declaring "The glory of this present house will be greater than the glory of the former house" (2:9). What he is saying is that the things that are shaken, the things of the former house, have been proven useless because they have a weak foundation, which is this life and not the life to come. Paul speaks on the subject, "If any man builds on this foundation using gold, silver, costly stones, wood, hay or straw, his work will be shown for what it is, because the Day will bring it to light" (1 Corinthians 3:12-13). If what we have built during our life on earth survives, then we know that we have been building up things for the life to come and we will not suffer loss. The world around us and the possessions we own may be destroyed, but we know we have better and lasting possessions that are preserved and awaiting us in the new heaven.

What you have set your life upon, the things you have worked and strived and sweated for, are they going to survive the great shaking of our God and King? Are they going to survive the coming of our Lord and Savior because they are eternal belongings, as Paul said, "they will lay up treasure for themselves as a firm foundation for the coming age" (1 Timothy 6:19)? My brothers, may we work and build towards things that are rich toward God, things that will not be shaken because they are rooted and established in Christ Jesus, the Rock and Horn of our salvation! Do not fall short when the time comes, but know where you stand so that you will not be shaken because of loss.

"Therefore, my dear brothers, stand firm. Let nothing move you. Always give yourselves fully to the work of the Lord, because you know that your labor in the Lord is not in vain" – 1 Corinthians 15:58

Every now and then, life is just plain hard. Things at work may be struggling, your relationships may be dwindling because you have less time for them, and your walk with the Lord may be taking a hiatus. But this *is* a part of life and it must not shake us or frighten us. This is why Paul encourages us to stand firm and let nothing move us because he knows how hard life can be and Christ for surely knows and we are allowed to stand firm because "He gives us the victory through our Lord Jesus Christ" (15:57). We cannot be shaken because of Christ's death and resurrection and this should give us hope! When our feet are planted in the Rock of Christ, we will not move.

Although we are standing firm in Christ, we can still become discouraged because of the outside circumstances affecting us. But ultimately, they should not be disturbing us because we are confident in the faith and the work that we are doing in the Lord. When people reject the message of Christ or reject our lifestyles because of Him, especially those people that we care about, it can be disheartening, but Paul cheers us up to continue giving everything that we have and are for the Lord's cause in spite of what else may be going on in our lives. We must "be prepared in season and out of season" (2 Timothy 4:2) to do His work and not only when it is convenient.

Our labors in the Lord are never in vain if we are doing them in Him and in His strength. Even though we may see no results and may come to think that it is all for naught, it is not. All the duties that are required of us Christians are involved in this command, not just work in ministry-related capacities. Such duties as: praying for our enemies, doing good, loving the Lord and others, walking by faith, giving generously, living selflessly, proclaiming truth, being thankful, knowing the Word, fearing God and keeping His commands, and the list goes on and on.

These labors should not feel arduous, but rather joyous because we have the opportunity to share in the labors of Christ and be a part of His Kingdom which will never end. Also, when we die, we know it is not the end, but rather the beginning of something greater still because we shall be resurrected and rewarded for our work in the Lord. Are you feeling discouraged and downcast? May it not be so my friends, but be ever so encouraged by the promises of the Word of God in your lives.

"Then the whole town went out to meet Jesus. And when they saw him, they pleaded with him to leave their region" - Matthew 8:34

This is what happened in the region of the Gadarenes (or Gerasenes) after Jesus had visited with a strong, demon-possessed man there. He released him from the demons that were possessing him and the demons begged for Jesus to send them into the herd of pigs that were nearby, so he did and then the pigs "rushed down the steep bank into the lake and were drowned" (Mark 5:13). The herders of the pigs went into town and told them what had happened to the man and their pigs, and that is when they asked him to leave "because they were overcome with fear" (Luke 8:37).

This demon-possessed man was a wild man who was living among the tombs naked, crying out day and night with substantial strength where no one could bind him up. And here comes Jesus who releases this immensely troubled man, giving him a freedom he has never felt before, and the people of the town want Jesus gone. Were they not excited for the man of their town to be released from possession? Or were they more worried about their financial loss from the two thousand pigs that just ran into the lake? Jesus performed a miracle in their very midst, yet all they cared about was their loss of money.

"Are you not much more valuable than they?" (6:26), Jesus said concerning birds. We are much more valuable than the birds of the air, the fish of the sea and the animals of the earth. We are not all equal as some world religions or philosophies tend to think we are. Just think for a moment: there are enormous fines for harming or killing certain animals or disturbing a part of nature, but there are no penalties or anything for killing babies via abortion. Our views are backwards my friends, and that is why we need to let the world know that people are more important, not animals, not things, not wealth, but people.

Humans are of much more value than pigs, but the townspeople could not grasp that because they were afraid Jesus would do more harm to their financial well-being. Are you getting more upset or frustrated over the loss of possessions versus the suffering of your brothers and sisters throughout the world? Are you more distraught over petty issues than real issues that determine the final destination of people after they die? Brothers, Jesus cares more about you than anything else in His creation. Do not be afraid to go and do likewise.

"If any of you lacks wisdom, he should ask God, who gives generously to all without finding fault, and it will be given to him. But when he asks, he must believe and not doubt" – James 1:5-6

James, brother of Jesus and servant to God Most High, writes this to us after immediately telling his brothers to be joyful when trials come upon them because it develops perseverance in their faith, and "Perseverance must finish its work so that you may be mature and complete, not lacking anything" (1:4). It is during these times of trials and testing where we need the Lord's wisdom the most to help give us the right perspective during it and how to best react to what comes our way.

Anybody can claim and believe anything they want to, but how do you react when troubles come knocking at your door? Whatever you believe, this will reveal the trueness of your faith and whether or not your faith is legitimate. We tend to think we can get ourselves out of certain trials because we think we know better, a certain book told us how to positively think our way out of it, or if we just take a vacation, the trial will magically diminish by the time we get back. But from experience we know this is not the case. We need to not be afraid to ask the Lord for wisdom during our testing because it is that wisdom that will grant us the vision to see that it is indeed from the Lord and that we must endure to the other side of it. This wisdom will help us bear through the trials in a proper manner that is expected of a man of God; one that does not let ordeals get the best of us and think that the Lord is against us, but rather that we can retain joy in spite of our suffering. "If you falter in times of trouble, how small is your strength!" (Proverbs 24:10).

C.S. Lewis was once asked, "Why do the righteous suffer?" He replied, "Why not? They're the only ones who can take it." This is true because of the wisdom that we can receive from God when we ask for it *and* believe we have received it. Brothers, how can we consider overcoming our times of testing without the Lord's wisdom? It cannot be done and we will be swallowed whole like the rest of the world without such wisdom. So when the next hardship comes your way, ask God for wisdom so that you may have the strength during those tough times. It is a defogger that clears your view in times of trial, allowing you to see things as they really are.

"The Lord detests lying lips, but he delights in men who are truthful" - Proverbs 12:22

I recently finished a TV series and throughout it, everyone is lying to everyone else close to them in order to protect them and keep them safe. It seemed like the best idea at the time, but eventually the truth broke out from another source and it hurt the person they cared about more than they could possibly imagine. They felt betrayed and lied to, not knowing who they could trust anymore. The lies that were supposed to protect their family members, in the end, tore the family apart, never being able to repair itself.

Something as small and innocent as a lie which you began because you did not want to hurt those closest to you, actually does more harm the longer the truth is being kept a secret. Lying does not protect, it only wounds because it is not from God but from the devil. What is so hard about telling the truth to someone, especially those who love and care for you? Yes, whatever news you may inform to them could perhaps produce immediate pain, but it would in no way be as great if they eventually found out later from someone other than you. But the truth does indeed hurt sometimes, but it is a good hurt for our betterment. For instance, if the doctors just discovered a cancerous tumor on your liver, would you not want to undergo surgery right away and remove it before it infects other parts of your body? Or would you wait a few years until it completely destroys all your internal organs and leaves you lifeless? There will be pain from the surgery to remove the tumor, but it would save you more immense pain than if you waited.

A lying tongue never does anyone any good, and it puts on a facade between you and everyone in your life. "A lying tongue hates those it hurts" (26:28). You read that correctly; when you lie you are not living a life of love, but of hatred and selfishness, neither of which come from God who is love and which is selfless. Like in *Veggie Tales: Larry- Boy and the Fib from Outer Space,* what starts off as a minute and innocuous lie, could eventually turn into something huge because you have to continue to lie and make them more extravagant in order to not get caught and in the end, you and those around you do not even recognize you. The Lord detests lips that lie, but instead He delights and loves those whose words are truthful. Be of those whom the Lord your God delights in.

"When tempted, no one should say, 'God is tempting me.' For God cannot be tempted by evil, nor does he tempt anyone; but each one is tempted when, by his own evil desire, he is dragged away and enticed" – James 1:13-14

The other day we talked about having wisdom when undergoing trials, but we also need the same wisdom when we run into temptations. God does not tempt people, even though many claim that He does. For example, some may say, "If God does not want me to have sex before marriage, then why did He put this awesome and beautiful person in my life and give me these intense desires to have sex with them?" Kind of like in the Garden where Eve must have thought, "Why would God put this tree of the knowledge of good and evil in the middle of Eden and make it pleasing to the eye, if it were not meant to be eaten from?" Brothers, it is not God who tempts, but we tempt ourselves because of our own evil desires.

The devil can never force you to do anything; he can only talk to you and try to manipulate your thinking and rationale, but he can never make you do something that you do not want to do. You are the one that makes the choice to give into temptation. You cannot say, "The devil made me do it" or "My friend put me up to it". No. You put yourself up to it because of the inclination within you to do it. Stop shifting the blame to someone else like your forefathers did and own up to your wrongs and confess them to your Heavenly Father. The apostle John writes that "If we claim to be without sin [shifting the blame], we deceive ourselves and the truth is not in us. If we confess our sins, he is faithful and just and will forgive us our sins and purify us from all unrighteousness. If we claim we have not sinned, we make him out to be a liar and his word has no place in our lives" (1 John 1:8-10).

The difference between temptation and testing is simple: we enjoy temptations but not testing. God forbids certain things not because He is holding out on us as Eve thought, but because He knows the pain that it will cause, because He loves us and has even better things for us than that. He knows that sex within the boundaries of marriage is so much more beautiful than outside. He knows that by denying yourself today, by resisting the devil and the lies he speaks to us, you can move deeper and further in your walk with Christ and enjoy true and wondrous things that will last. We are not victims of our circumstances, our upbringing, or our society because we are the ones making the choices. And a good way to help make the right choices is to confess your sins to the Lord, gaining a heavenly perspective and by filling your life with good and wholesome things, not objects that will induce you to sin.

"If I had cherished sin in my heart, the Lord would not have listened; but God has surely listened and heard my voice in prayer" – Psalm 66:18-19

We have all sinned. Even nonbelievers know they have sinned and made mistakes that were wrong and that they regret. But to see the iniquity that is within you, to have regard for the sins you have committed, to hold them in there as a keepsake because for some reason you are proud of it and are unwilling to let it go, that is where the error lies. To cherish sin is to not forsake all sin and not count it as evil and something that does not belong in a man of God.

The Psalmist was a man who fortunately did not cherish sin in his heart because he said that the Lord has heard his prayer; for if he had not been willing to abandon all sin in his life and become the holy man that God so desires, then the Lord would not have listened to his prayers and given him the encouragement he needed to move forward. James wrote that "When you ask, you do not receive, because you ask with the wrong motives, that you may spend what you get on your pleasures" (James 4:3). A wrong motive would include holding on to a past sin that you may not have necessarily seen as wicked and sinful because it felt good to do. Like with an ex of mine, there were times when I believe we got too physical for a non-marital relationship and it felt good of course, but I did not immediately recant of what I did because I was not thinking straight, so I never purposed to withhold from that again while I was with her because she liked it and I was a weak man. But now, thanks to the Lord's grace and His ever-increasing desire for me to be holy, I no longer cherished such a sin in my heart and was able to see its evil and be released from it.

My brothers, this is why the author of Hebrews encourages us to "throw off everything that hinders and the sin that so easily entangles, and let us run with perseverance the race marked out for us" (Hebrews 12:1). We should let nothing get in the way of our pursuit of holiness to the Lord because everything that we say and think and do should lead us to a deeper and greater holiness than we were before. There should be no love of evil in our hearts and we must leave behind all sin to the Lord if we ever want to have an effective prayer life. Is there a sin in your life that you have been cherishing in your heart that you have been unwilling to leave at the foot of the cross? Leave it to the Lord and be free from it and pray with the boldness that comes from being a released child of God.

"Give thanks to the Lord, for he is good; his love endures forever" - 1 Chronicles 16:34

Thanksgiving is just around the corner; a time of celebration and remembrance, of food, football and family, of recalling and giving praises to the Lord for all the great things He has done for us in the past year. At least that is what it is supposed to be, as has been practiced for years, but is that how it still is? Is it even a day where we give thanks anymore?

Why do we even celebrate Thanksgiving as a Christian community? Should we not be giving thanks to the Lord every day throughout the year? I have been thinking that we Americanized Christians like holidays such as Thanksgiving and Christmas because it permits us to only be thankful for the work of the Lord, to celebrate and remember Jesus' birth for only a few days out of the entire year and then the rest of the year we can live as we please, giving thanks to ourselves for the "hard work" we have done and the many things we may have accomplished. That is so pagan of us, so heathen and that is one way how our country has failed to recognize many of us as followers of Christ because we are doing just that, not following Christ and we are blending in too much.

Give thanks to the Lord, for he is good; his love endures forever. The Lord our God is good, He is always good and has never been anything but good. And we know His love endures forever because He is love and He endures forever. When we are grateful for what the Lord had done for us, it keeps us aware that He never leaves us. A spirit of gratefulness helps to keep our heads straight and facing the right direction, not getting sidetracked and distracted by every little thing that fights for our attention. Do not think that these are merely empty words; try them. When you are feeling down and lowly, if your day at work is in the crapshoot, take a moment or two and thank God for something, or a few somethings, and notice how your attitude and outlook has changed. I have used this on the worst of days and it makes a world of difference.

Give thanks to the Lord, for he is good; his love endures forever. Pound this verse into your memory bank. "These commandments that I give you today are to be upon your hearts. Impress them on your children. Talk about them when you sit at home and when you walk along the road, when you lie down and when you get up" (Deuteronomy 6:6-7). Thankfulness is a necessary part of the fruit of the Spirit and so it must be a part of our lives and not just one or two days of the year, but every day, just as we do not love only a few days of the year, but all the days of our lives. So what are you thankful for right now?

"Whoever loves money never has money enough; whoever loves wealth is never satisfied with his income. This too is meaningless. As goods increase, so do those who consume them. And what benefit are they to the owner except to feast his eyes on them?" – Ecclesiastes 5:10-11

The sad part about Thanksgiving is the day after it, Black Friday. It is the day where people become animals, where they forget any and all manners and what it means to be civilized, where they are exceptionally selfish and everyone sees it justified for the sake of a cheaply-priced good, where Christians are no longer Christians because they camp throughout the night for the sole purpose of buying something for themselves when the holidays should be a time of giving, not receiving. It is quite sad, especially since it is the day after, and lately even the day of Thanksgiving.

Solomon, the author of Ecclesiastes, who is believed to have been the richest person to have ever lived, enlightens us to the truth that he has learned that money does not buy happiness. Vanity he calls it, a parasite that is never satisfied and always craving for more. I love the words in verse 11, "what benefit are they to the owner except to feast his eyes on them?" We are being led by the things that bring our eyes pleasure, whether that is goods on Black Friday, or the lust of a woman, "the cravings of sinful man, the lust of his eyes and the boasting of what he has and does" (1 John 2:16). If the richest man who has ever walked this earth firmly believes that money does not make you happy, then why do we think we know better? Yes, money gives us stability, a security blanket in case something goes wrong, where we will still be ok and comfortable, but should we not rely on something, or Someone more stable than money and material possessions which are here today and tomorrow thrown into the fire, never to be seen of again?

My friends, do not put your trust in such belongings, do not treat Black Friday shopping as some sort of sacred pilgrimage because you are saving the most money at the expense of potentially losing your humanity and faith in the process. I have seen good men and women of God lose themselves because of their pursuit of such goods, sacrificing this one day out of the year, along with Cyber Monday, to allow themselves to splurge on buying things for themselves that will not last. Do not be one of them, but be one of God's beloved children that strive to put such effort towards holiness, sanctification and prayer, which result in lasting possessions that will never be destroyed. Do not be a flip-flopper that is "thankful" one day and completely unrecognizable the next, but be firm and solid in the Rock of your salvation who will stand throughout the ages.

"Make every effort to be found spotless, blameless and at peace with him" – 2 Peter 3:14

What is the one thing that you have tried the hardest on in order to achieve the highest goal? Did you tire day and night towards it, knowing that your demanding work would eventually pay off? For me, it might have been getting in shape and growing strong during high school in order that I may become a better football player. It was tiring and I hated it a lot of the time, but in the end, I was a much better player because I had set my mind to become one and worked vigorously towards it.

Just think if we put the same effort, the same determination and spirit of wanting the best in our walks with Christ; we would be unrecognizable I am sure. Peter writes these words after encouraging us to be looking ahead to the new heaven and the new earth that will come when Christ returns. To be found spotless we know is impossible but that does not mean that we should settle for anything less. If we came to a point in our lives where we say "I think I am holy enough, I am not going to try to cleanse myself from any more filth than I already have", that is foolishness brothers. If the Holy Spirit continually convicts us of particular sins in our life, it is folly to ignore it and think we have reached our place of rest. Note how Peter does not say "Make some effort to become spotless and blameless, then when you think you have reached a good point, you can stop trying to be more like Christ." That would be preposterous! But instead he tells us to make *every* effort to be found spotless and blameless and at peace with Him; to make it your life goal to be more holy and righteous because of the work of the Holy Spirit in your daily life. Peter pens earlier "You ought to live holy and godly lives as you look forward to the day of God and speed its coming" (3:11-12).

By becoming more like Christ in our holiness and blamelessness, the world will see more of it and how truly different we are from them and by so doing, we shall speed the Lord's return to us. Is that not what we want, for Christ to come back and make all things new? But until that time, "Be perfect, therefore, as your heavenly Father is perfect" (Matthew 5:48) so that others can see the Lord Jesus through your lifestyle and desire the peace and confidence that you walk with. Are you making every effort to be found spotless, blameless and at peace with Christ, working in unison with the Spirit to be the holy ambassadors we are called to be?

"But even if he does not" – Daniel 3:18

These are some of the most faith-filled words that can be spoken by a child of God in the valley of the shadow of death and even in the green pastures of life. They indicate a particular level of trust in the Sovereignty of the Most High God that His will shall be done no matter the circumstances they are in and whether or not they are rescued from trouble, as Shadrach, Meshach and Abednego knew full well. They had such a faith in the Lord and would not worship the idol of king Nebuchadnezzar that they were willing to be thrown into a blazing fire because of their sole desire to worship God and God alone, knowing that anything else is idolatry. They did not know that God would save them from being burned up alive. They may have hoped that He would, but it was not a requirement on God's end to do so; He did not make a deal with them saying, "If ever comes the chance for you to give your life for My sake, do not worry, I will not let it devour you."

No, God never promises these things. We may hope that He would indeed save us from such episodes, bearing a great testimony for His name that we were saved in the midst of our enemies, but He does not have to do anything. These three men of God knew that God did not have to and nor did they expect Him to, but were obedient to the truth they knew to be true, even to the point of death. They had their minds all made up and knew that they would never turn their back on God because He had never turned His back on them nor would He ever. They knew it was right to worship the one true God and nothing else and nothing in all the great earth could change their minds, regardless of whatever may happen to them because of it.

We may not have situations where we would be thrown into fires because of our dedication to the Lord, but there are still opportunities for us all the time to either say yes to the Lord or yes to self and pleasing others and saving face. I struggle with this because at times, I subtly choose the latter in order to be seen in a certain light by peers and coworkers and for that I need forgiveness. I need the courage and faith that these godly men had to stand firm in the face of evil and say yes with confidence in the Lord Almighty. Is your mind made up with what you would do in a similar situation? Would you be able to say that God is able to save you from it, but even if He does not, you will still stand faithfully despite what follows? I pray that all of our minds are made up right now beforehand so when the time comes, we may stand firm in the truth.

November 25

"He who is not with me is against me" – Matthew 12:30

One of the many attributes of God, if you can call it an attribute, is that there is no grey area in Him, no middle ground. You either believe or you do not believe; you either love Him or you do not love Him. We like to think there is an area of compromise so we can make ourselves feel better in particular events, such as watching television or movies that constantly contain sexual material as a staple in them; we then say it does not affect us, but it slowly implants itself into our minds and thinking processes, allowing us to think more sexually and look at people in that way and not like we normally would.

There is no grey with God and that is why Jesus tells His disciples that he who is not with Him is against Him. It may sound absolute to some, as in *Star Wars Episode III: Revenge of the Sith*, when Anakin told Obi-Wan, "If you're not with me, then you're my enemy." And that is exactly how it is; if you are not on God's side of the battle, then you are on the enemy's side, fighting against Him, which is why Jesus follows this up saying "And he who does not gather with me scatters" (12:30). In other words, if you are not helping, you are making things worse. There is no room for neutrality because you either are in support of the things of God and of His good or you are in support of the things of the devil and his good, no matter how you try to justify your actions. If you are not a child of God, then you are a child of the devil; you cannot be a child of both.

This all goes back to whom you serve and to whom you swear your allegiance, so when the going gets tough, which mindset do you refer to: the mindset and ways of Christ or the mindset and ways of the devil? "This is how we know who the children of God are and who the children of the devil are: Anyone who does not do what is right is not a child of God; nor is anyone who does not love his brother" (1 John 3:10).

Jesus' words to His disciples forces us to make a choice: we must either follow Jesus and resist the devil or we must follow the devil and resist Jesus. Neither party sees anyone as being on neutral territory, no matter how passive nor out of the way they try and make their lives be. There are many who think they are spiritually neutral because they neither follow God nor the devil, but are rather Hindu or Buddhist or Atheist or something else, yet that is not how God sees it because if they are not for Him, then they are against Him. It is a battle out there, one that has been going on since the beginning of time, so which side of the battle are you on? There is only one winning side and that side is the Lord's, so I hope you are on it. Choose to do God's good today and do not compromise your loyalties.

"But Ittai replied to the king, 'As surely as the Lord lives, and as my lord the king lives, wherever my lord the king may be, whether it means life or death, there will your servant be" – 2 Samuel 15:21

Loyalty is something hard to come by these days. People go and are led by their feelings or wallets or emotions and not by a deeper conviction based on principle and duty to a particular concept or group. For example, we are on teams at work and they change every year and unfortunately I do not want my team to change because I have grown quite loyal to them, I know how they operate and how best to communicate with them for the betterment of the team and the work we do. I would do almost anything for my team because I trust them and they me.

King David's servant, Ittai, spoke these beautiful words to him as they were fleeing from his son Absalom. It is like the stuff you see in the most epic of movies, when they are at the last battle and they inform their commander that they will never leave their side no matter how bad it gets and they will fight to the death. Ruth spoke similar words, "Don't urge me to leave you or to turn back from you. Where you go I will go, and where you stay I will stay. Your people will be my people and your God my God. Where you die I will die, and there I will be buried. May the Lord deal with me, be it ever so severely, if anything but death separates you and me" (Ruth 1:16-17). That is the essence of loyalty, of never leaving or compromising your trust to someone or something because you love them that much, kind of like a nice golden retriever who will never leave your side and they are easily satisfied and all they want is to please their master.

How about you? Are you someone who can be trusted with the riches and glories of the kingdom of heaven? Are you as loyal to God as He is to you? Because you know that "He will never leave you nor forsake you" (Deuteronomy 31:6), can the same be said of you towards Him? When the road ahead looks bleak and uninviting, when the present is full of darkness and despair all around you, when you think you are at your wits end, are you still loyal to your Lord and Savior, to your King? Do you stay faithful and devoted to the One who is always faithful and fulfills His promises to you? My brothers, God is not looking for people who will blindly do what He says, but He desires for His followers to be loyal to Him unto death which ultimately brings life because Christ was loyal to us unto death and brought us life. Can you with sincerity say the words of Ittai and Ruth to the Lord?

"Faithless is he that says farewell when the road darkens." – Gimli, The Fellowship of the Ring.

"It is more blessed to give than to receive" - Acts 20:35

This is one thing I love doing: giving gifts to those I care about. It grants me great joy to see their faces light up or be surprised because they did not know they were receiving a gift. Gift giving I guess you can say is one of my gifts, even though at times I am hesitant to do so because I see how much I spend on them and the devil tries to convince me to use that money on myself instead. Like with this visa gift card I have right now which expires in a month, I have been thinking and thinking on what I should buy myself, but as of this morning, I came to the conclusion that I could use it to buy some gifts for my friends and family and that is what I am going to do.

It is more blessed to give than to receive. Do we genuinely believe that? Especially during this holiday season with Christmas creeping up, can we honestly say that it is more blessed to give than to receive? We as human beings love receiving gifts, not only because it shows that people really do care about us, but that we can just have more. We make huge Christmas lists with every little thing that we want, mostly expensive, and expect others to rise to the occasion and buy them for us. Why? Do we not have enough already? We are so quick and eager to receive gifts from those whom we expect to receive them from, but are we as quick and eager to give the same quality and thought of gifts to them as well, not to even out the playing field, but because we love them and desire to show our appreciation for them? I hope we can come to that point in our giving, the point of sacrifice and selflessness.

When we give, we have the opportunity to bring happiness to others, along with happiness to ourselves. It can bring us peace that we were able to express love in such a way with a pure heart, with no ulterior motives in mind than to help make their day. God is the most selfless and giving being that has ever been or will be, giving without expecting anything in return, and He is also the most joyful because of it. Are you joyful in your giving of gifts, if you give at all? Do you believe that it is more blessed to give than to receive as your Savior said? This Christmas season, do not give heed to the voice of the devil and the world that has you only looking out for yourself, but pay attention to the voice of the Spirit that encourages a cheerful and giving heart.

"His divine power has given us everything we need for life and godliness through our knowledge of him who called us by his own glory and goodness" – 2 Peter 1:3

Christ's divine power, His very nature says Peter, has given us everything that we need for our spiritual formation and knowledge. We have all that we need to walk this life of faith through Christ because of His divine power, His indwelling Spirit; there is no "secret knowledge" that is necessary for our salvation, as the Gnostics of Peter's day claimed that there was. John stresses the same truth in his letter, "As for you, the anointing you received from him remains in you, and you do not need anyone to teach you. But as his anointing teaches you all things and as that anointing is real, not counterfeit—just as it has taught you, remain in him" (1 John 2:27).

It is Christ's divine nature which has anointed us with the real teaching and knowledge that leads to life because it leads us to Himself and not to some special knowledge that the Gnostics claimed to possess. It also gives us everything we need for living a godly life, which is necessary and arduous in this world full of sin and deceit and darkness. The godly nature of Christ is being instilled in us through His Spirit that is in the business of making us holy as He is holy. All this is possible because He has called us by His own glory and goodness; His excellence and righteousness. Christ's very essence, His being is excellent and magnificent and that being chose us to be vessels of His divine power and His Gospel. Not only is His essence full of glory, it is also good that reigns down promises from heaven to those on the earth. It is the Father's goodness that is exuded in the sending of His Son and His Spirit to the world, healing the sick and raising the dead, opening up the eyes of the blind and bringing light in the darkness of our lives.

Peter continues, "Through these he has given us his very great and precious promises, so that through them you may participate in the divine nature and escape the corruption in the world caused by evil desires" (1:4). We are becoming partakers of the divine nature, as we are being sanctified to become more like Christ, who also escaped the corruption in the world by remaining in the Father at all times and that is what His glory and goodness to us incites us to do, remain in Him. Brothers, we are given what we need; stop looking for more in worldly philosophies and sciences, but continue to look to Christ and His divine power through which we are called by His excellence and are given promises that shall be fulfilled to the full.

"When he has done this, then the Son himself will be made subject to him who put everything under him, so that God may be all in all" – 1 Corinthians 15:28

God the Father gave everything He had to His Son, so that He may rule for some time, but in the end, out of submission and not inferiority, Christ will give it all back to the Father so that He may reign supreme. Late nineteenth and early twentieth century pastor and author Andrew Murray said that "Sin consists in nothing but this, that man determined to be something and would not allow God to be everything." We as men do long to be something and we strive to figure out who we are and what we are made of and what our purpose is in this world.

We get so focused on this that we bring up God on the back burner and just ask Him to bless what we have already chosen in our hearts and minds instead of having Him take us where He wants us. But it is Christ, the Spirit and the Father who must be at the forefront of our lives, not ourselves; we are to be made subject to them, not they to us. Paul writes that "All things were created by him and for him. He is before all things, and in him all things hold together. And he is the head of the body, the church; he is the beginning and the firstborn from among the dead, so that in everything he might have the supremacy" (Colossians 1:16-18). Christ is the first in all things, so why should we even begin to dare to try and make something of ourselves when doing so would try and dethrone Christ from being all in our lives?

Christ made Himself subject to the will of the Father and so should we since Christ is our only example for living, not celebrities or family members, but Christ and Christ alone. Murray continues on saying, "The all of God is what we must seek. There should be no use of our time, no word on our lips, no motivation of our heart, no satisfying of the needs of our physical life that is not the expression of the will, the glory, and the power of God. God must not be merely something to us or even a lot, but all."

Are you willing to follow the example of your Savior, who "made himself nothing, taking the very nature of a servant" (Philippians 2:7), one who does not make demands of your God but subjects himself to His good, pleasing and perfect will? Will you let the Lord be your all in all, not just a lot, but all? Will you let Him have the supremacy in your life in all areas, allowing yourself to be a dutiful and faithful servant that pleases his Master?

"The man of integrity walks securely, but he who takes crooked paths will be found out"
– Proverbs 10:9

Today at work, we had some training, or more like a refresher, on how to be people of integrity in the workplace. And this is especially important in my line of work, being one of the most visible government workforces that the public interacts with, where we need a certain degree of trust in order to do our job most effectively. A saying we have is that "Each officer represents every other officer."

This is just as pertinent to followers of Christ as well. If a Christian somewhere does something incredibly stupid, the world will most likely know about it, especially in this day of instant news and social media, and then there are the people who will subsequently perceive other Christians as bearing the same type of stupidity, even though they themselves live a wise and righteous life. When you say yes to Jesus, you represent not only Him, but every other believer around you. I think my colleagues at work have a negative view of Christianity and thus a negative view of my life choices because they have encountered some bad eggs who claim to be Christians along their journey in life. Today I got a good chance to stand up for my faith and choices which is a good start to have the Holy Spirit begin to stir within their hearts and soften them.

The man of integrity walks securely. To walk with integrity means to be able to do the right thing, no matter how difficult it may be and how it affects you, even when no one else is watching. We should do what is right because it is right, not because of its outcome or because we are afraid of its repercussions, but because it is right to do it. There are choices every day that have to be made, choices to do good and something right and choices to do bad and something wrong. You know from the get go what choice needs to be made (the right one), but you look at what may happen because of your choice and you decided you did not want to go down that road and rather play your chances that nothing bad comes from your poor decision.

"The integrity of the upright guides them" (11:3). Is integrity guiding you and your decision-making process? Are you shedding a good light on your fellow brothers and on Christ by your lifestyle and choices? Is your conscience clear before yourself and the Lord, knowing that you do what is right and not just what is easy? If not, repent and turn towards Christ and begin to live the life you know you ought as a child of God.

December 1

"The Word became flesh and made his dwelling among us" - John 1:14

As we head into the final month of the year, with Christmas being a few weeks away, we once again turn our attention towards the birth of Jesus Christ. This is how the Father chose to bring His Son into the world, through being born as a helpless baby. He did not come down as a mighty god with sword and shield in hand like a Norse god ready for battle; His glory and brilliance were not shining like the stars in the sky, but He came down as a baby, vulnerable and real.

The King of kings, the Lord of lords, the One who was there at the creation of the universe, came down from His heavenly throne where He has reigned from the beginning of time, to be with His lowly people, us, His creation. Imagine that: think of a beloved king from medieval times who was always in his castle doing kingly things, and then one day decides to go out into the market where the peasants and common folk do their daily business and he decides to live and breathe and work like a normal man for a bit. Would the people not rejoice because their king shows his love and compassion for them, coming to them on their level, empathizing with them and becoming one of their own? That was the first thing I thought about when I read this verse and how much joy it brought to me, to see my King coming to be with His people; that is true leadership and true love.

"The virgin will be with child and will give birth to a son, and will call him Immanuel" (Isaiah 7:14), which means God with us and that is exactly what happened. When John wrote that Christ made His dwelling among them, he is referring to a tent or tabernacle, like the Tent of Meeting which was filled with the glory of God with the Israelites during their time in the wilderness. By using the words for a tent, it signifies that those within that same tent were of one family and regularly acquainted with one another and so John's following words are true, "We have seen his glory, the glory of the One and Only, who came from the Father, full of grace and truth" (1:14).

We also have seen His glory, and yet "He came to that which was his own, but his own did not receive him" (1:11). The King of all kings has come off His throne to be with you, so that you may love and receive Him and have fellowship with Him that is unhindered by cultural or economic barriers. The Word became flesh for you and sacrificed much, including His life so that you may be with Him and enjoy what He enjoys. What are you going to do with this?

"But the pot he was shaping from the clay was marred in his hands; so the potter formed it into another pot, shaping it as seemed best to him" - Jeremiah 18:4

He has got the whole world in His hands; the simple yet truthful song that we tend to forget about when it relates to us. "We are the clay, you are the potter; we are all the work of your hand" (Isaiah 64:8). Our Father in heaven is our maker; He is the One who forms us in all different shapes and sizes and for different uses and functions. Who are we to say what is superior and which is better? "Does not the potter have the right to make out of the same lump of clay some pottery for noble purposes and some for common use?" (Romans 9:21).

We are the marred pot that the Potter began forming into another pot, a better one, one without flaws or blemishes. Do note that the fault of the pot references to the clay, not the skill of the Potter. "Like clay in the hand of the potter, so are you in my hand, O house of Israel" (18:6). God will mold us according to His purposes, not to our own. He can change anything that He wants and has the right to do as He wishes, as Jeremiah continues saying, "If at any time I announce that a nation or kingdom is to be uprooted, torn down and destroyed, and if that nation I warned repents of its evil, then I will relent and not inflict on it the disaster I had planned. And if at another time I announce that a nation or kingdom is to be built up and planted, and if it does evil in my sight and does not obey me, then I will reconsider the good I had intended to do for it" (18:7-10).

Once the clay becomes baked in a kiln with extreme heat, it cannot be made into clay again. It is solid and free from moisture and will last for ages unless prepared improperly or smashed. This is why the potter reshaped the clay as he was still molding it because if he went through the entire process and then found out it was ruined, he would have to break it and start with new clay.

But the Lord wants to remold you into His perfect and holy image, free from sin and darkness and made firm and beautiful in accordance to His liking. Brothers, do not fight against the work of the Potter in your life; heed His hand of healing and direction, shaping and forming you as He sees fit. We know that the Lord is perfect, so why not trust Him with our hearts and lives? Since He made us, He knows us better than anyone else. Trust Him as the Maker and Molder of our lives and of the whole world.

"Or take ships as an example. Although they are so large and are driven by strong winds, they are steered by a very small rudder wherever the pilot wants to go. Likewise, the tongue is a small part of the body, but it makes great boasts" – James 3:4-5

Yesterday I was running outside, improperly dressed most likely, and it was one of my better running days and I hate running and am awful at it. I was making good pace but I had to stop earlier than I would have liked because my fingers were absolutely frozen. The rest of my body was not near as cold, but my fingers had just had enough and forced my body to stop. I was mad because I still had plenty of fuel left in the tank, but because my fingers were telling me otherwise, I stopped and made it no further.

The fingers are such a small part of the body, much like a tongue or a foot or an eye, but if something happens to these small parts, it can have devastating effects on our entire being. And that is what James is getting at here, pointing out how something as small as a ships rudder, or a small spark or a tongue can make something much larger than itself do as it pleases. Sin in our lives can have that same impact on us; a "small" sin (no sin is small in God's eyes by the way) may bring detrimental consequences on our whole body, although we may see it as insignificant and non-threatening because of its size. Jesus said that "If your right eye causes you to sin, gouge it out and throw it away...if your right hand causes you to sin, cut it off and throw it away. It is better for you to lose one part of your body than for your whole body to go into hell" (Matthew 5:29-30).

My brothers, is there a sin in your life that you are potentially overlooking because it occurs in such small doses? Is there something you are doing that you know is wrong but you hide it in the back of your mind and even convince yourself it is not there? Are you slowly injecting yourself with porn, poisoning your mind and soul, or every day at work making a prideful statement so that you can look good in front of your coworkers or allowing some lie to create a foothold in your life and you have to keep on covering it up, even to those you love and care about? Do not be led by these sins, these evils any longer. If Christ is the Savior of your life and you trust Him for that, then bring these transgressions to Him and He will gladly relieve you of those, as He already has on the cross. Although they may seem small, they can take control of your life. Do not let them; cut them off of you as Jesus declares and throw them into the fire to be done away with. Be led by the Holy Spirit who is your Guide that will lead you to pastures of goodness and mercy.

"Give generously to him and do so without a grudging heart; then because of this the Lord your God will bless you in all your work and in everything you put your hand to" - Deuteronomy 15:10

Generosity should be a staple in the believer's diet, something that we should never have a debate about whether or not it should be included. Moses is speaking to the Israelite people about cancelling debts, which would be done every seven years so that there would be no poor people among the blessedness of the Israelites in the Holy Land, giving them another chance. But as always, "if only you fully obey the Lord your God and are careful to follow all these commands I am giving you today" (15:5).

"There will always be poor people in the land" (15:11), and so we must not be hesitant to help out our brothers among us who are in need. "God loves a cheerful giver" (2 Corinthians 9:7), not someone who grudgingly gives because he is forced to, but who actually delights in having the ability to be able to bless their brothers, not only because the Lord commands it, but because he has been given so much by the Lord so he is compelled to have the same heart towards the poor. Even though the Lord promises rewards to those who are generous to the poor, that should not be our incentive, but rather to obey and please our Father and King in heaven. Jesus tells us, "For I was hungry and you gave me something to eat, I was thirsty and you gave me something to drink, I was a stranger and you invited me in, I needed clothes and you clothed me, I was sick and you looked after me, I was in prison and you came to visit me" (Matthew 25:35-36). These are simple ways in which we can be generous toward the needy; it does not just have to be helping them pay rent or fixing their car, it can be anything in which you give of yourself so that they may be better in one way or another.

One of the best things to keep in mind during all this is this: "Whatever you did for one of the least of these brothers of mine, you did for me" (Matthew 25:40). In other words, when you give to the poor, you are ultimately giving to Christ Jesus. That is a great way in which we can touch our Father's heart, by giving to those He has put in our lives, by exuding selfless love and helping those who need it. You are blessed to be a blessing; do not waste what you have been given.

"For God did not appoint us to suffer wrath but to receive salvation through our Lord Jesus Christ" – 1 Thessalonians 5:9

Wrath is something that no one ever wants thrust upon them, but it is what everyone is destined for who does not believe in the name of Jesus Christ. And this is not something that God chose to give us either; rather it is the choices that we make that bring such wrath upon us. It is God who is finally giving the people who did not choose Him what they really want, which is nothing to do with Him and everything to do with their wickedness.

All of this is in accordance with the end times, the coming of the Lord. For those who do believe in the Lord Jesus Christ, God appoints for them to receive the salvation that they have waited all their lives for, and this salvation is not only the sanctification and perfection of their being, but also the culmination of the promises that they will get to see the Lord face to face. "He died for us so that, whether we are awake or asleep, we may live together with him" (5:10). These words should give us hope! Hope that all the labor and toil we have been doing for the Lord is not in vain because He appointed us to receive salvation and what God appoints, no one can oppose. We are given certainty of God's success and that should propel us to continue on all the more in His work, as Paul continues, "Therefore encourage one another and build each other up, just as in fact you are doing" (5:11).

God appointed us to receive salvation. He did not appoint us because of some good works we may have done or because we believe a right doctrine; no, he appointed us salvation because of His generous mercy because He does not want us to suffer wrath like those who do not believe will. This salvation will be ours soon, friends. The time is coming for the Lord to return.

So we must be awake and alert, living a life of holiness and righteousness at all times because we do not know when He will return, only that He will. And when He does, the final salvation will be fulfilled and we shall be like Him as He is, no longer plagued by the ills and woes of our earthy body. Do not live as those who are asleep and in the dark, but as those who are wide awake and in the day, seeing all around them, patiently awaiting the Lord's return and His salvation.

"To him who is able to keep you from falling and to present you before his glorious presence without fault and with great joy" – Jude 24

You do not know this or even care, but I have not actually written in a few weeks. I have been so good and working hard and trying to keep up to date with this, but just over the last few weeks, I have been either busy or instead of writing, have been solely reading the Scripture and praying more and it has been rejuvenating to my soul. Even though I love writing, it felt good not to be at my computer. But I believe this hiatus was necessary and even vital for finishing up this book strongly, as I feel I may have slipped in some of my writings over the past couple of months. Forgive me for not writing and relying on the Lord more wholly as I should have.

As we finish out this last stretch, it is a beautiful reminder that Jude presents to us in the closing of his letter, that God and God alone is able to keep us from falling to the world of darkness which is constantly striving to take us down with it. It is God who allows us to persevere amidst the wickedness and ungodliness because it is He who is right there with us through it all. Is this not great and encouraging news for those who are in fear of potentially falling away from the faith or failing the mission that Christ set them out for, that God is more than able to keep them from completely falling away from Him? It might seem that for a season that God is not there with you, as He may be testing the quality and strength of your faith, but know without a doubt that He has never left you if you are one who believes in Him, for He never abandons His children, those who trust in Him.

Not only is God able to keep you from diminishing downward, He is also able to dress you up in heavenly garments to be presentable before His throne. Jesus mentioned the concept of wedding garments in a parable in Matthew 22, and the idea behind that is that everyone wears them and they are all the same, so there was no distinction between rich and poor, no embarrassment or pride or anything of that sort. That is how it will be for those who overcome: "They will walk with me, dressed in white, for they are worthy" (Revelation 3:4). My brothers, my friends, "to the only God our Savior be glory, majesty, power and authority, through Jesus Christ our Lord, before all ages, now and forevermore" (25) as we live out our days with great joy as we await the coming of our Lord and being presented to Him blameless and without fault. Be strong.

December 7

"Bless those who persecute you; bless and do not curse" - Romans 12:14

At my work, there are occasional passengers who are just angry people and want nothing more than to make everyone else angry as they are. Then they come up to you at the podium, frustrated about flying and the process they have to go through so they are able to fly, accusing you for everything they have to do because you are wearing that uniform. And yet, we cannot react as they do; we must be better than they because people are always watching and we must act professionally if we want to keep the public's trust.

If we could respond to individuals like that in our human, emotional way, of sinking down to their level, we become no better than them. But we must be better if we desire to be good witnesses for Christ and for His kingdom and that is why Paul said what he said, that we must bless those who persecute us. Although a person may bash the work that I do, I must still respond cordially and continue doing my work. We know that it is hard to bless someone who wants nothing to do with you, to bid them good tidings and goodwill when all they want is to have you suffer. It is tough to do so, but it must be done seeing that it is in our job description as followers of Christ; we signed up for it when we made the choice to believe in the Lord Jesus Christ and having Him be our Master and Commander.

There are times still when our old nature, our flesh, tries to repay others as they have done to us; they tear us down so we then tear them down even further. Brothers, this shall not be how we live and we know this. But how can we silence our sinful nature, considering it dead, so that we may bless our enemies and those opposed to our mission? You can do so by believing in Christ as you already are, but walking in the belief that He has put your flesh to death, that He is sanctifying you by His precious blood, that He dwells within your very being. We must live lives of absolute trust in Him and His ways, that He will accomplish what He said He would and that His covenant and promises will indeed be fulfilled. He says, "I am the Lord, and there is no other; apart from me there is no God" (Isaiah 45:5).

No one can do what our God can do; ultimately which is changing a wretched and depraved human soul as we used to be into a godly and useful vessel for His glory as we go about this life blessing people who do not deserve it because we have been blessed by God although we did not deserve it. "I will strengthen you, though you have not acknowledged me" (Isaiah 45:5). Stand above reproach my friends and continue on in the call of Christ Jesus which leads you heavenward.

"But we also rejoice in our sufferings, because we know that suffering produces perseverance; perseverance, character; and character, hope" - Romans 5:3-4

Why does the topic of suffering continuously find its way into these pages? Why does the Spirit of the Lord decide to indulge me with suffering when I am in the quiet and meditative moments of my work day? Honestly, I was just sitting on the exit this morning at work and out of nowhere, that is what the Lord did; He had me think of those who undergo suffering in life, like colleagues of mine, random passengers, and ultimately Christ and the pain they may have had to go through. They may not have chosen the way of pain; it could have been thrust upon them, yet they potentially have found ways in which to deal with such pain, whether good or bad.

The apostle Paul in his letter to the Roman church not only tells the followers to rejoice in their sufferings, but shows them how their suffering for the Lord is not in vain and without fruit. Look at the people of Israel for example: if they had not been in slavery for four hundred years, if they had not wandered through the wilderness for forty years, if they had not fought countless battles in order to claim the Promised Land, and if they had not have been brought into captivity, they may not have had the opportunity to produce in themselves the perseverance and character and hope that the Lord desired for them. Without suffering, what do we need to persevere from? How can we attain character if we had not suffered some great injustice and persevered through it, proving that we will not allow such circumstances to turn us into something we are not? How can we have hope if we have already attained everything that we could ever want and dream of? "But hope that is seen is no hope at all. Who hopes for what he already has?" (8:24).

So you see brothers, suffering is necessary if we want to bear the fruit of perseverance, character and hope in our lives. When undergoing suffering, our true priorities should come to light and we can then hope that the promises made to us shall be fulfilled because in those promises, there is "no more death or mourning or crying or pain" (Revelation 21:4). Do not be the one who shies away from suffering and pain, bringing on a spirit of complaining and criticism, but rather embrace it, knowing that the Lord your God already underwent the most dreadful of afflictions for your sake and that you may join in "the fellowship of sharing in his sufferings" (Philippians 3:10). Instead of listing the negatives that come along with your pain and anguish, record the fruit that may be bore when done in the right spirit, in the Spirit of Christ. Pain and suffering produce in you what nothing else can.

"I waited patiently for the Lord; he turned to me and heard my cry. He lifted me out of the slimy pit, out of the mud and mire; he set my feet on a rock and gave me a firm place to stand" – Psalm 40:1-2

A few weeks ago, I went up to the U.P. with some college friends of mine to Cedar Campus to relax and have a good time. It finally snowed up there one night and the next day I went for a hike. I trekked off the trail thinking I knew my way back to camp, but in the snow and the woods, I apparently had no idea. I ended up being lost for over four hours, hiking over ten miles in unfamiliar territory, stamping through bogs and brush, yelling at the top of my lungs for someone to hear me, until I finally made it back to camp by the grace of God just before nightfall with the early stages of hypothermia.

This was not one of the highest moments of my life; I was fine at first, not worrying about hiking a few extra miles, but once I got more wet and continuously found my same set of tracks, I came to the point of discouragement and despair that I have never felt before in my entire life. I literally cried out to the Lord there in the woods out of pure exhaustion, thinking I might have to spend the night out there and might not wake up. All I wanted was the smallest glimpse of hope to move on, since I could not hear any traffic or water or find any other trails. I have never been more grateful to the Lord for honestly lifting me out of that pit of despair and finding me, even though I was never lost to Him.

The good and gracious Lord heard my cry as I am sure that He has heard your cry to Him. I was no longer trotting through the marshes, having to poke my stick with every step to make sure I would not sink in, but I was now standing on the solid ground of surety and trust, knowing that I could stand securely and need not worry. I was able to "put a new song in my mouth, a hymn of praise to our God" (40:3) because He has done a new thing and delivered me as He has delivered His people for thousands of years.

I was lost and then was found by Him. Being lost is scary because you do not know where you are or where you are going, but when you are at a place of certainty in the Lord and are found, you know where you are going and that is towards Him. Brothers, are you lost on your way back home? Do you think you know the way, although by looking at your surroundings, you apparently have misplaced your bearings and are coming closer and closer to nowhere? Come to the Lord, who longs for you to come to Him in faith and humility, and reclaim your heading and walk closer and closer to Him!

December 10

"All the people answered, 'Let his blood be on us and our children!'" – Matthew 27:25

The Jews in Jerusalem, the chief priests and the elders of the people, shouted these fateful words to Pilate as they had decided to crucify Jesus, the so-called King of the Jews. It is one thing to say, "Let his blood be on us", signifying full responsibility for the actions that were taking place, but it is a completely absurd notion to involve ones children and their children in the matter, and that is exactly what these stubborn and obstinate people did. Little did they know the weight that their words would carry for generations to come.

It is such a rash thing to say, especially since Pilate "knew it was out of envy that they handed Jesus over to him" (27:18). And this my friends is why you need to be careful of what you say, particularly when your actions follow through with it and it is obviously the wrong choice. The words will come back to bite you as they have the Jewish people. They have been scattered, killed, banished, looked down upon and treated more poorly than any other people in the world. They finally received their own land in 1948 and not without cost, and where they are continues to be the epicenter of many battles and wars. I do not see this as some mere coincidence for how they treated the Savior of the world, for I do not believe in coincidences, but in divine intervention.

The words you utter, when linked closely with you actions, may haunt you with guilt because you know you have done wrong. Jesus predicted that Peter would deny him three times before the rooster crows and Peter of course said, "Even if I have to die with you, I will never disown you" (26:35). Just a mere forty verses later did Peter recall the words of his Master after they were fulfilled and he was overcome with grief. Judas also, after betraying Jesus with his words and actions, and "saw that Jesus was condemned, he was seized with remorse and returned the thirty silver coins...then he went away and hanged himself" (27:3,5).

Words carry a weight that are indeed a burden to bear, so why not speak such words that are light and cheery, encouraging and life-giving? Words that are expressed in emotion and not patient, wise thinking are foolish because they are not said in the proper mindset, a mind set on the principles of God. "Reckless words pierce like a sword, but the tongue of the wise brings healing" (Proverbs 12:18). Do not be like the Jewish people of Jesus' day, foolish in speech and rash in action, but be like Christ Himself, who although was being accused by His own people, He remained quiet, "as a sheep before her shearers is silent, so he did not open his mouth" (Isaiah 53:7). Be like your Master in all ways.

"For a long time now—to this very day—you have not deserted your brothers but have carried out the mission the Lord your God gave you" - Joshua 22:3

Joshua said this to the Reubenites, Gadites, and the half-tribe of Manasseh, all of which were tribes settled on the east side of the Jordan River (present-day Jordan and Syria). These two and a half tribes were separate from the rest and that is how they liked it, being on the other side of the Jordan opposite the remaining nine tribes. They originally did not want to get involved in war conquering the Promised Land, but they made a promise to Moses, that if they aided in the fight for Israel, they would claim the land east of the Jordan. "Your servants will do what the Lord has said. We will cross over before the Lord into Canaan armed, but the property we inherit will be on this side of the Jordan" (Numbers 32:32). And if they failed to keep their promise, they would have to live on the west side of the Jordan.

These two and a half tribes have kept their promise; they have done everything they were commanded and fought faithfully and now they were finally able to return home. Although the land in which they were fighting for they would not attain, they were helping out their brothers so they could attain what was promised to them. They did not desert their brothers during the conquest, even though the odds looked bleak at times, but instead they carried out their mission to completion because they were a people of their word; they wanted to back home to their families and live their life of pastoralism, the raising of livestock.

Joshua also urged them to "love the Lord your God, to walk in his ways, to obey his commands, to hold fast to him and to serve him with all your heart and all your soul" (22:5). This return to their homeland reminds me of when the hobbits returned to the Shire at the end of *The Return of the King*. They were so happy to be back, to be in their comfy homes and simple lifestyles, but because of their journey and the adventures they had been on, they had not returned as the same people.

We also are not the same people we once were because of the experiences we have gone through in the Lord during our life of faith. Whether or not we have carried out our mission as faithfully as these tribes had, are you in a position where you can say that you have not deserted those you swore to protect and care for, to love and serve? My brothers, it is only through the Lord that we can faithfully carry out our mission, which is to serve Him, give Him the glory and have the whole world know that He is King. And then, we shall return to our home in heaven, perfected in His holiness.

December 12

"You know how I lived the whole time I was with you" - Acts 20:18

The apostle Paul had always seemed to have been a bold man, one who would not hide or cower behind another or not take responsibility for his actions. Even before he believed in Jesus Christ, he was this way but now all his boldness and efforts were being directed towards saving people for the Lord's sake instead of destroying them, preaching the Gospel to those who have yet to hear it.

His words in this verse, "you know how I lived the whole time I was with you", indicate that he was a man of transparency, a man of integrity who did not hide anything he said or did, but was completely vulnerable and open to the people around him so they may see the awesome work that the Lord God has been doing in his life. He did not live one way in his public teaching and then live another, a sinful way, in his private life because his whole life was on display for the Ephesians to see. And even if it was not all on display, I doubt that his private life would show much difference in his interactions with the Lord and with others.

Friends, such transparency of our lives is essential for our impact in the world for Christ's sake and for those we encounter. If our non-Christian friends see us living one way while at work and then a totally different, unholy way while at home or around town, what must they think of other Christians if this one that they call their friend cannot live their own life in unity and integrity? How do we expect to show others the greatness and beauty and love and peace of Jesus Christ if our lives are not transparent, if our actions are not following our words, if we are living in two different worlds? If our lives are not whole in Christ, if there is disunity within our own being, how does that attract others to becoming a follower of Christ as we are?

Integrity. Our lives should not be hiding things that we are ashamed of, for we should not be ashamed of anything we say or do if we are living the lives that Christ wants us to live and commands us to. Do people know how you live your life in all arenas? Is there someone who knows you better than you know yourself, so even if you are unintentionally hiding something from yourself, they will see it and point it out to you? Pray that we may lives of clarity and simplicity, lives of honesty, truth and reliability as we walk this earth for the praise and glory of our Father in heaven who sees and knows all.

"Here is a boy with five small barley loaves and two small fish, but how far will they go among so many?" – John 6:9

Jesus had tried to get to a solitary place after a long day's work, but the people found him and so he healed their sick. They loved being around Him and would not even leave although night was approaching and they seemed to be hungry. And so a young boy came to the disciples with some barley bread and fish; barley bread which was cheap and less healthy than wheat bread, and also being the bread of the poor and of horses and donkeys. Yet Jesus was going to use this insignificant amount of food offered by a boy to feed over five thousand people.

The boy did not have much at all, but even what little he had, he gave to Jesus to be used more effectively than he could have ever thought possible. He did not wait until he was a millionaire with plenty to spare before he offered Jesus some food, nor did he wait until tomorrow so he could take some more with him and offer even more. No, right there in the present, he went to Jesus and gave Him what he had at that moment in time and that is all that Jesus needed to perform one of the greatest miracles recorded in Scripture.

All you have to do is give Jesus what you have right now and that is enough for Him to work wonders in you and among those in your life for His glory. Let us take a quick look at Shamgar, a judge in the Bible you may have never heard of because he is only mentioned in one verse. "After Ehud came Shamgar son of Anath, who struck down six hundred Philistines with an oxgoad. He too saved Israel" (Judges 3:31). He most likely was a farmer and all he had was a goad that he used to guide his oxen, and with it he killed six hundred of his enemies, saving Israel. He did not have a sword or an army at his side, but he had a goad and that was all the Lord needed.

Friends, do not wait until you have an excess before you offer it to the Lord for His work; He does not need much in order to do something great, for little is much with the Lord. Are you in a state of waiting until tomorrow, until you have this job or that spouse or this car or that house before you offer what you have to the Lord Most High? Because people are in need now! Do not hesitate and do not wait until you get somewhere else; you are already where the Lord needs you to be to offer yourself to Him.

December 14

"We have different gifts, according to the grace given us" – Romans 12:6

The other night I watched *Divergent*, and what I learned from that movie is not that we must go against the system in order to achieve the results that we want, but that we need to embrace who we are and the abilities that we have been given. Tris, the protagonist in the movie, was a divergent, which means that she did not fit into any particular faction in the city, but rather a few of them, making her dangerous in the eyes of leadership because she was different and did not conform to their system just because of how she was.

God has made each one of us unique, not one the same as the other; we are not mass produced like bricks but are rather select stones that are cut out of the rock, chosen for particular purposes. We have all been given certain qualities and attributes that are particular to us, all of which are to be used for the glory of God. When we deny ourselves one of these traits, trying to hide it because we are ashamed of it or afraid of how other will perceive us, we are denying a gift that the Lord has given us and thus bringing Him displeasure.

Do not be ashamed my brothers of how God has made you. Do not hide the beautiful masterpiece that you are. "For we are God's workmanship, created in Christ Jesus to do good works, which God prepared in advance for us to do" (Ephesians 2:10). God wants you to do good things with the good things He has blessed you with through Christ Jesus for His glory. You were not made the way you are by accident or happenchance, but by divine purpose and ordination.

"With this in mind, we constantly pray for you, that our God may count you worthy of his calling, and that by his power he may fulfill every good purpose of yours and every act prompted by your faith" (2 Thessalonians 1:11). We know that God is with us and for us my friends, so what is there to be ashamed or fearful of? All those things do is limit the work of God in our lives and we will have none of that. Father, work in us as you worked in your Son Jesus Christ, to use the characteristics you have bestowed upon us to the best of our abilities through the strength of your Spirit within us, to do your good will to all we encounter without hindrance and prejudice, to the praise and glory of your holy name. Amen.

December 15

"Does this offend you?" – John 6:61

When we accidentally offend people, we sometimes feel bad, depending on what we did to offend them. For example, if you point the soles of your feet towards someone of Arab decent, you disrespect them because the soles are considered the dirtiest part of the body and when directed to them, it is quite impolite and shows how you feel about them. And if you were ignorant about that fact, you could apologize and all should be forgiven, but if you did it again with you newfound knowledge, it is a true offense.

We will offend people throughout our lives, whether we mean to or not, it will happen. And in our walk with Christ, we will most definitely offend people if we are living out our Christian mandate to be salt and light to a dying and dark world. If we are living as we should, people will be offended by our actions, our words, our thought processes, our attitudes, ourselves. They will try to attack the very things we believe in, calling us narrow-minded, legalistic, naive, foolish. They do not necessarily think about what they are doing because "the way of the wicked is like deep darkness; they do not know what makes them stumble" (Proverbs 4:19). They do not have the Light of Life in them, so how can they see that the way they are going is the right one? They cannot, but we can because "The path of the righteous is like the first gleam of dawn, shining ever brighter till the full light of day" (Proverbs 4:18).

Jesus offended many people, mainly the religious and community leaders of His day because He did not abide by their standards which were merely rules taught by men and not the rules of heaven as taught by the Father. Do not be afraid to offend someone when talking about your faith in Christ Jesus, but "Be wise in the way you act towards outsiders; make the most of every opportunity. Let your conversation be always full of grace, seasoned with salt" (Colossians 4:5-6), along with being "completely humble and gentle; be patient, bearing with one another in love" (Ephesians 4:2).

If you have not offended someone because of your faith in Christ, are you sure that you are indeed walking with Him day by day, being led by the Spirit of truth? I am not asking you to go out and blatantly offend your neighbor, but the conduct of your life and demeanor should bring offense to those who are lost; potentially convicting them of any guilt and turning to the Lord for a way to remove it and replace it with freedom and joy and peace. Be the light and salt that you already are, embracing the change that comes with being a child of God.

"Teach us to number our days aright, that we may gain a heart of wisdom" - Psalm 90:12

Many youths, including myself at times, think that we are invincible; that nothing can touch us or hurt us and that we will be forever that way. This causes us to do some stupid things at times, things that only later in life we will regret after we have grown wiser and seen how foolish we were.

This is why the Psalmist is trying to teach us that we should number our days aright because we do not know what will happen tomorrow or a year from now or even an hour from now. All of our days are in the palm of the Lord Most High and He will deal with them as He well pleases. "Show me, O Lord, my life's end and the number of my days; let me know how fleeting is my life. You have made my days a mere handbreadth; the span of my years is as nothing before you. Each man's life is but a breath" (39:4-5). It is only when we can begin to understand this truth, that we are here today and gone tomorrow, that we can gain the heart of wisdom that the Lord wants us to bear and be of actual use in His kingdom's service.

Our days are numbered and they are but nothing to the Lord; "For a thousand years in your sight are like a day that has just gone by" (90:4). So why not make the most of our time here on earth, since our days are fleeting like a wisp of smoke? Why do we so easily get entrenched into the foolish trivialities of our days and our culture, actually caring about what our favorite celebrities' cherished pastime is or when an artist comes out with their latest album? Do we so effortlessly forget that life is but nothing and that "The grass withers and the flowers fall, but the word of our God stands forever" (Isaiah 40:8)? So why not do things that last and make a difference in the kingdom of God? Why not give away more money than you ever have before to the church or to help fund someone? Why not take more time to pray and thank God for everything He has given you and more? Why not have real conversations with friends and family that go beyond surface level? Why not go for a long walk by yourself and sing and pray to the Lord your God like you never have before? Why not make the decision to read through the whole Bible in a year and memorize some verses along the way? Why not volunteer at church and help the body of Christ and the surrounding community? My brothers, I am in no way perfect as I hope you have discovered by now and I need these things just as much if not more than you. Father in heaven, help us in this endeavor, to be wise in how we spend what little time we have in this life and get to know you more and more and make a difference while doing so. We love you Father. Thank you for hearing our cries. Amen.

"I will give you a new heart and put a new spirit in you; I will remove from you your heart of stone and give you a heart of flesh. And I will put my Spirit in you and move you to follow my decrees and be careful to keep my laws" - Ezekiel 36:26-27

This is the Lord speaking to the house of Israel about the New Covenant that Christ Jesus will usher in. No longer will the people of God be under the burden of the Old Covenant where they had to keep their part of the covenant as God held up His part. The Old says, "Obey me and do everything I command you, and you will be my people, and I will be your God" (Jeremiah 11:4).

There are two parties in a covenant, and the premise behind them is that both parties will be faithful on their part and if one fails, then the covenant is broken, as in the case with Israel. They did not come through on their side, aka, obeying all that the Lord commands of them, and thus the covenant was broken, although God held up His part. But in the New Covenant that is being presented in Ezekiel, God steps in and takes responsibilities for both parties because He is the one who gives us a new heart and spirit; a heart of flesh that is open to Him and a spirit of obedience that *will* follow His laws and commands. It is a total transformation from the Old Covenant because it is no longer dependent on man's faithfulness but on God's promise to put in us a new heart and spirit that will obey and follow Him. The old heart of stone and the old spirit of disobedience are being removed not by our own doing but by the Lord God who alone can replace them with something much better and more able to follow His decrees and do His will.

"Before this faith came, we were held prisoners by the law, locked up until faith should be revealed. So the law was put in charge to lead us to Christ that we might be justified by faith. Now that faith has come, we are no longer under the supervision of the law" (Galatians 3:23-25). Under this New Covenant, it is the Lord's Spirit that He puts within us that allows us to walk and live in a way pleasing to Him, not by observing the law or by doing good works, but through living by faith. Author and pastor Andrew Murray said that the Galatian church "cannot understand that it is not to the law but to a Living Person that we are now bound, and that our obedience and holiness are only possible by the unceasing faith in His power constantly working in us. It is only when this is seen that we are prepared truly to live in the New Covenant."

Does this knowledge not give you peace in your life, knowing that it is Christ within you who helps you keep your end of the covenant, the covenant that says, "you *will* be my people, and I *will* be your God...My dwelling place *will* be with them" (36:28, 37:27, emphasis added)? I hope it does my friends.

December 18

"Teach me to do your will, for you are my God; may your good Spirit lead me on level ground" – Psalm 143:10

Our purpose in lives is to do the will of the Father in heaven, just as it was for Jesus who said, "For I have come down from heaven not to do my will but to do the will of him who sent me" (John 6:38). The Father has sent us into the world to do His will, and He does not leave us on our own to do it, but causes and moves us to do it with the new heart and spirit He has given us. And He also gives us the written Word of God, along with the Living Word of God, through whom we must abide in order to live the life worthy of the calling we have received, which is to do His will.

We are being taught day by day to do the Lord's will as we grow and remain established in His Word and in prayer. Andrew Murray wrote that "As the Word abides in you, the Spirit will reveal to you the will of God in every circumstance of your life." That simple connection is seen in our verse, as it connects doing the Lord's will with being led by the Spirit. If someone is lost in their life of faith, they need not look further than to the Word of God, as they will read centuries of writings including people from all walks of life and how God worked and spoke to each of them all in different ways so that His will may be done on earth. Jesus prayed, "your kingdom come, your will be done on earth as it is in heaven" (Matthew 6:10). And that should always be our prayer as well because in heaven, it is always the Lord's will being done and we should desire that same submission to His will here on earth.

He is our God and we should yearn to please our God and do as He says, for He has created us and knows us better than anyone else ever will. His Spirit is right there with us, leading us onto level ground, ground that is smoother to walk on and where there is less chance of danger and falling. How can we be led by the Spirit if we do not have the Spirit within us? How can we get to such a place? By knowing the Word of God and what it means to have the life-giving Spirit within us; "The Spirit gives life; the flesh counts for nothing. The words I have spoken to you are spirit and they are life" (John 6:63).

Jesus' words are that life as He is the Life and gives life through His Spirit to all who believe in Him and the Father who sent Him. And it is through knowing this person of Jesus, through communion in His Word and through prayer that we can be taught and discern what the good, pleasing and perfect will of the Lord is.

"After that, we who are still alive and are left will be caught up together with them in the clouds to meet the Lord in the air. And so we will be with the Lord forever" – 1 Thessalonians 4:17

Yesterday I watched a few shows and in two of them, they talked about the belief that when you die, you become the like the stars in the night sky, literally. Both of these were totally unrelated and that is why I pondered about it, wondering why the Lord will bring this to me that day and it quite possibly might be for the very reason to tell you that we do not become stars in the sky when we die; no, we will have eternal life with the Lord Jesus Christ in heaven, not the night sky. We will be alive, unlike those balls of gas millions of light-years away; more alive than we ever have been before.

"But we know that when he appears, we shall be like him, for we shall see him as he is" (1 John 3:2). And our Lord is seated on His throne in the city of our God, the New Jerusalem with which the River of Life flows throughout. Paul told the Corinthians that "We will not all sleep, but we will all be changed—in a flash, in the twinkling of an eye, at the last trumpet. For the trumpet will sound, the dead will be raised imperishable, and we will be changed. For the perishable must clothe itself with the imperishable, and the mortal with immortality...then the saying that is written will come true: 'Death has been swallowed up in victory'" (1 Corinthians 15:51-54).

And death has been swallowed up in the victory of Christ on the cross and life given by His resurrection! And that life is extended to us who believe and follow Him by faith. Are you not glad that we do not become like stars, even though at first thought it may sound nice to be shining down on the world? But being alive with our Savior and King in the most beautiful place ever created with the most beautiful Person there ever was, praising His Holy Name, worshiping Him and enjoying unceasing fellowship with Him and countless others who believe for all eternity sounds so much better!

A place where there will endless joy and peace, nothing dark and nothing hurting there; a place of fulfillment and satisfaction beyond reckoning and understanding and there will be no end to any of it. Think of the most beautiful thing you have ever seen or encountered and this will be infinitely more beautiful as our God is infinite. I cannot wait for that day when I will see His face and be with Him forever. I pray the same for you, that we do not get choked up by "the worries of this life, the deceitfulness of wealth and the desires of other things" (Mark 4:19) but are focused on the things to come.

"Those who carried materials did their work with one hand and held a weapon in the other, and each of the builders wore his sword at his side as he worked" – Nehemiah 4:17-18

The Jewish people as they were rebuilding the walls of Jerusalem had to be vigilant and careful as the text shows, working as well as defending the city against invaders who want nothing more than to continually see the city of God's people in ruins. That would be a pain, having to fight when you are trying to work; it seems as if it would take much longer to complete the job because your whole focus is not in it, but also in protecting the city from being run over again.

And yet the same is true for us today. We have our own jobs to do, our own way of living in which we do our work but at the same time, we also have to remain vigilant against the powers of darkness that are at work in our world. Peter warns us to "Be self-controlled and alert. Your enemy the devil prowls around like a roaring lion looking for someone to devour" (1 Peter 5:8). He and his servants may be lurking around every corner, waiting to trip us up, but we cannot let that happen; there is work to be done in spreading the good news of Christ Jesus and in building one another up in love and humility, just as the Jewish people had to repair the walls so they could return to their homeland for good.

Paul also encourages us to "Be on your guard; stand firm in the faith; be men of courage; be strong. Do everything in love" (1 Corinthians 16:13-14). Paul was a great example of someone who did work (he was a tentmaker) and someone who also fought back the forces of darkness and brought forth light. Paul, along with the Jews who were helping rebuild the wall with Nehemiah, had to be well-prepared for either working nonstop on the wall so they could rest easier because it was finished, or for fighting for their lives and those of families and their people. It can be discouraging to know that your enemy is surrounding you, waiting to pounce when you least expect it, but Nehemiah encourages his people saying "Don't be afraid of them. Remember the Lord, who is great and awesome...Our God will fight for us! (4:14,20).

Our God will fight for us! God's grace is with us if we are persistently abiding in Him and walking in His will, eager to do what is good and right and just. We have to be prepared for anything the enemy may throw at us, and this can only be accomplished by unrelenting prayer, reading of Scripture and the power of the Holy Spirit within us and the church. "Therefore, my dear brothers, stand firm. Let nothing move you. Always give yourselves fully to the work of the Lord, because you know that your labor in the Lord is not in vain" (1 Corinthians 15:58).

"Such a high priest meets our needs—one who is holy, blameless, pure, set apart from sinners, exalted above the heavens" - Hebrews 7:26

Christ Jesus is that High Priest who meets our needs! He is "the mediator of the new covenant" (9:15), the one who "is able to save completely those who come to God through him, because he always lives to intercede for them" (7:25). As the Mediator of the New Covenant, Christ is always standing there between us and the Father, and as Andrew Murray puts it, "He is ceaselessly engaged in watching [our] needs and presenting them to the Father, in receiving His answer and imparting its blessing."

Now that is a High Priest that meets our needs; that speaks for both God and for us in both of our best interests. Just think of what Christ being our Mediator, our High Priest, means: it means that He helps make us look presentable before the Father on the throne in heaven, He makes our aches and groans and requests sound somewhat respectable to the God of the universe. And then He responds back to us what the Father had said, much like what the high priests of the Old Covenant did, except this High Priest, "he does not need to offer sacrifices day after day, first for his own sins, and then for the sins of the people. He sacrificed for their sins once for all when he offered himself" (7:27).

Our High Priest is perfect. He is set apart from sinners, meaning that He Himself had never sinned, making him blameless and pure, the faultless sacrifice that was needed in order to take away the sins of the world once and for all. He is able to save completely those who come to Him through faith by the Holy Spirit. To save completely not only means that we have gained salvation and pardon from our sins, allowing us to possess eternal life with God in heaven, but moreover it signifies that Christ is able to make us holy and blameless as He is holy and blameless, sanctifying us day after day to be more like Him.

Apollos later writes that "by one sacrifice he has made perfect forever those who are being made holy" (10:14). We are those who are being made holy because we have a High Priest who is holy and who meets the needs of His people once and for all. Because we are being made holy and perfect, we should not be choosing to do things that bring displeasure to our Lord and thus spoil the gift He has given. Thank you Father that we have a great High Priest who speaks on behalf of His people and whose sacrifice was enough for us all. May we live under such truth, knowing that it is Christ who makes us holy and not our efforts.

"When they saw the courage of Peter and John and realized that they were unschooled, ordinary men, they were astonished and they took note that these men had been with Jesus" – Acts 4:13

Major evangelists such as D.L. Moody and Billy Sunday of the 19th and early 20th century were not educated men as you think of preachers who have gone through years of seminary; Moody was a shoe salesman and Sunday was a baseball player, both who later became popular and effective, reaching hundreds of thousands, possibly millions of people for the sake of Christ. And yet these were just ordinary men who had a passion for preaching the good news of Jesus Christ to those in all levels of society, speaking in unconventional ways and using familiar language and not that of scholars.

The same was said of Peter and John and the rest of Jesus' disciples; they had no proper schooling or education in the art of preaching pastoral sermons, but it is noted that these men had been with Jesus, as I am certain that Moody and Sunday had been as well. Now I am not bashing the idea of those who are going to seminary to learn Hebrew and Greek and systematic theology and those academic venues so they can study and preach better, but what I am saying is do not think it is necessary that you have to go there in order to preach the Gospel of Christ; you can preach Christ right now! If you are being led by the Holy Spirit to preach, by all means, preach! Do not wait until you have "educated" yourself on the properness and the "right way" to preach about Christ; there is no right way to do so as long as you are speaking the truth of the Word of God in love.

The only ingredient that you need is that you must be with Jesus. How can you imagine preaching about Christ if you do not personally know Christ on an intimate level? It is absurd. What the first century apostles knew was that by their being with Christ and they having the Holy Spirit of Christ dwelling within them and seeing the transformation that He has performed in their lives, they had all they needed in order to proclaim His good news. They did not need anyone else to teach them because they had Christ's anointing teaching them (1 John 2:27) and that "the Holy Spirit, whom the Father will send in my name, will teach you all things and remind you of everything I have said to you" (John 14:26). We are also ordinary men and women, children of God in this world; we need to practice unhindered communion with Christ throughout our days so that nothing distracts us from our mission which is to glorify His Holy Name!

"Taking the five loaves and the two fish and looking up to heaven, he gave thanks and broke the loaves. Then he gave them to his disciples to set before the people" – Mark 6:41

Feeding the five thousand is one of the few events of Jesus' life and ministry that is recorded in all four Gospels and I have never really known why. There were many other miraculous and awe-inspiring stories like when He walked on water or raised Lazarus from the dead or calmed the storm with His voice that seem just as marvelous as His feeding of the five thousand, so why is this one of them that made the cut to be in all four?

Jesus said that "I am the bread of life. He who comes to me will never go hungry" (John 6:35). Jesus, as being the bread of life that gives life to those who come and believe in Him, was also the Lamb of God, whose body was beaten and bruised, "his appearance was so disfigured beyond that of any man and his form marred beyond human likeness...he was pierced for our transgressions, he was crushed for our iniquities" (Isaiah 52:14, 53:5). His own body was broken, although none of His bones were as prophesied in Psalm 34:20. During the Last Supper Jesus said of the bread that He broke, "This is my body given for you" (Luke 22:19). He gave Himself for us in order that we may have eternal life in Him.

What is more is that Mark tells how Jesus then gave the broken pieces of bread to His disciples to give to the people there. This is Jesus' giving of the Holy Spirit after His death and resurrection to His disciples as they "will receive power when the Holy Spirit comes on you; and you will be my witnesses in Jerusalem, and in all Judea and Samaria, and to the ends to the earth" (Acts 1:8). Jesus broke and then He blessed.

This is why this story is mentioned in all four Gospels, along with the Last Supper, the crucifixion and the resurrection of Jesus Christ because it is all about how His body was given for us to bless the multitudes through the work of the Holy Spirit who is now at work in those who believe. All of this is possible because Christ was looking towards heaven, bearing the godly perspective needed to live a holy and righteous life. Not only so, but it gives us the example to follow Christ who said along these same lines, "If anyone would come after me, he must deny himself and take up his cross and follow me" (8:34). That is what it means to be broken, to break the outer self and allow the Spirit to be released to destroy the works of the flesh. That is self-denial to the point of death to self and then following the One who made it all possible. Be broken, let His life reign in you and you shall be a blessing because of it.

"Saul died because he was unfaithful to the Lord; he did not keep the word of the Lord and even consulted a medium for guidance, and did not inquire of the Lord. So the Lord put him to death and turned the kingdom over to David son of Jesse" – 1 Chronicles 10:13-14

Saul was God's anointed king of Israel (1 Samuel 9-10). He led Israel well at first, but then he started slipping and began only obeying the Lord half-heartedly (which is technically not obeying at all). He then made rash excuses for such instances and even fought against the notion that the Lord had chosen someone else to replace him as king of Israel who was not his son, as was the custom.

Saul died because he was unfaithful to the Lord. It does not say that he died because he committed suicide by falling on his sword as it did earlier (10:4), but because he was unfaithful, foreshadowing what happens to those who are unfaithful to the Lord and reject Him; they die. Those who are faithful to the Lord do not die, but they live eternally with Him who is Life. Saul was also unfaithful in that he did not keep the word of the Lord, having disregard for His laws and statutes. And like many of today's leaders and followers in the world, they do not first consult God when they are in need of help and in trouble, but they go everywhere else first to see what their opinions are and potentially heal their ailment by themselves. People do go to mediums; they do go to gurus; they do take medications and drown themselves in alcohol; they do turn to the latest fad or what Dr. Phil or Oprah has to say on the matter; they do turn to pornography; they do turn to abuse; they do turn to all these things and more when they should be turning to the Lord first and foremost.

We are guilty of this brothers. We are guilty of forsaking our Lord who has never forsaken us because we are afraid of the truth and what that may bring. Our God is truth, but that should never frighten us, but give us relief that we do not need to hide because He knows us, including how we feel on the subject. It should usher freedom within us. When we are unfaithful to the Lord our God, when we abandon the first commandment, "You shall have no other gods before me" (Exodus 20:3) and to "Love the Lord your God with all your heart and with all your soul and with all your strength" (Deuteronomy 6:5), we are not living as we ought and thus bring a form of death to ourselves and those around us. We must bring life in our spheres of influence as David did, as his lineage did, as Jesus was born of it. Inquire of the Lord. Come to Him when you are in need and come to Him first, for He is infinitely better than anywhere else you could go and He is the only one who can truly deliver you.

"While they were there, the time came for the baby to be born, and she gave birth to her firstborn, a son. She wrapped him in cloths and placed him in a manger, because there was no room for them in the inn" – Luke 2:6-7

The time that the Jewish people have been waiting thousands of years for has come; the Savior of the whole world has been born into it. There was much rejoicing from the angels, "Glory to God in the highest, and on earth to men on whom his favor rests" (2:14). And yet, the baby Jesus was born in the most humblest of circumstances, to a virgin in the town of Bethlehem as the son of a carpenter. Nothing special about this other than it was foretold hundreds of years before by the prophets.

"But you, Bethlehem Ephrathah, though you are small among the clans of Judah, out of you will come for me one who will be ruler over Israel, whose origins are from of old, from ancient times" (Micah 5:2). "Therefore the Lord himself will give you a sign: The virgin will be with child and will give birth to a son, and he will be called Immanuel" (Isaiah 7:14).

That is one of the beauties of Jesus' birth: we were told about it before it happened, and it all came true! In Matthew 2-4, there were already five prophesies about Jesus from the Old Testament that were being fulfilled. Jesus, the Messiah, the Christ, the Redeemer of the world, has come at last and it was all predicted beforehand. This could only have happened if God, the One who created the heavens and the earth, was truly Sovereign and in control of all that happens in the universe, and He is! His Son being born is one example and so are countless other events in the Bible and in the life and ministry of Jesus and His disciples.

Christmas is more than a time of remembrance of Jesus' birth and what that ushered in for the world, but it is also a time of celebration because everything else that was predicted can now come to fruition because we have been redeemed of our sins, which is necessary for us to carry on the work of the kingdom of heaven. Friends, this is not just another Christmas to celebrate with friends and family, as that is all well and good, but it is a Christmas for newness with you and a chance for you to praise the Lord for His Sovereignty in that this world is not all there is, that when He says, "if I go and prepare a place for you, I will come back and take you to be with me that you also may be where I am" (John 14:3). This also will come to fruition as His birth and death and resurrection did. Be joyful because of it and wait patiently in expectation!

"But now in Christ Jesus you who once were far away have been brought near through the blood of Christ" - Ephesians 2:13

In one of Denzel Washington's best movies, *Man on Fire*, he was a burnt out CIA operative who has killed many in his day. He asks his former coworker, "Do you think God will forgive us for what we have done?" "No" was his response. And he goes on to be a bodyguard for a young girl in Mexico City. He is a drunk and he tried to kill himself, but the bullet misfired. So from that point on, he strived to be a friend to the young girl, who became infatuated by him and gave him a pendant of St. Jude, the saint of lost causes, showing to him that he was not a lost cause at all. And he was not, for she got kidnapped and he tore the city apart looking for her and in the end, gave the enemies his life in exchange for hers, being the example of love that she craved.

No one is too far away for Christ to save them. No one has committed too many or too horrendous of sins that Christ's redeeming work on the cross could not cover. Paul says that those who were once far away have been brought near through the blood of Christ. Look at the story of the woman at the well. She has had five husbands and is currently living with her boyfriend and in those days, she would be considered an outcast because of such nonsensical living, which is why she was drawing water at the heat of the day because people usually did so in the cool of the morning and evening. Nevertheless, Christ offered her living water and "whoever drinks the water I give him will never thirst. Indeed, the water I give him will become in him a spring of water welling up to eternal life" (John 4:14). She was someone who was deemed too far away to be saved, but in the eyes of Christ and His truth, she was not and neither are any of you.

There are no lost causes in Christ Jesus. "Christ Jesus came into the world to save sinners—of whom I am the worst. But for that very reason I was shown mercy so that in me, the worst of sinners, Christ Jesus might display his unlimited patience as an example for those who would believe on him and receive eternal life" (1 Timothy 1:15-16). That was His mission while on earth, to save sinners and not just a few of them who only committed "minor" sins, but all sinners. "He is patient with you, not wanting anyone to perish, but everyone to come to repentance" (2 Peter 3:9). So in response to what Denzel's character said earlier, do you think God will forgive you for what you have done? Do you think He is able to cleanse you from the muckiness of your past and present and put white robes on you, making you clean? He *can* forgive you for what you have done. You only have to "confess with your mouth, 'Jesus is Lord,' and believe in your heart that God raised him from the dead, you will be saved" (Romans 10:9).

"So I say, live by the Spirit, and you will not gratify the desires of the sinful nature" – Galatians 5:16

The sinful nature, otherwise known as the flesh, is what we are born into. We are born sinful; we are born being selfish which is at the root of the flesh. Selfishness comes naturally and you can see that with almost any child that screams, "Mine!" And much of that same attitude stays with many adults, thinking that the whole world still revolves around them and they honestly throw a hissy fit every time something does not go their way. It is quite sad to watch.

All of this behavior is the nature of the flesh, the nature of selfishness and pride that is rooted in the world and in the devil. The nature of the Spirit however, is one of selflessness and humility and is rooted in God and His love. We all were at one point gratifying the desires of the sinful nature (or may still be) and we will always gratify it unless we have the Spirit of God dwelling within us. There is no other way to get that pure selfishness expelled from you unless you are born of the Spirit. You may strive to do good, humanitarian deeds like working in your local community or volunteering at the homeless shelter and convince yourself that you are doing good for the other's sake, but ultimately you are doing it to make yourself feel and look good if you do not have the Spirit of the Living God within you.

This does involve self-examination and God-examination. It is very easy to deceive yourself in your motives, as I have recently deceived myself in my pursuit of a girlfriend, merely looking for one to fulfill my own selfish desires of feeling wanted instead of fulfilling her desires and loving her and glorifying God together with her. "Those who belong to Christ Jesus have crucified the sinful nature with its passions and desires. Since we live by the Spirit, let us keep in step with the Spirit" (5:24-25).

If we belong to Christ and have His Spirit, we no longer have to live selfishly and of the flesh because it has been crucified. "If anyone would come after me, he must deny himself and take up his cross daily and follow me" (Luke 9:23). We have to die to the flesh in order to live by the Spirit and that involves a daily death to self, denying ourselves and instead looking to how we may bring glory to the Father and help others out for their sake and not our own. You are not alone in this battle; remember the glory of the New Covenant where God says that *He will give you* a new heart and spirit and *He will cause you* to follow His commands (Ezekiel 36:26-27). The Lord will help you in this. Walk in faith.

"Whoever wants to become great among you must be your servant, and whoever wants to be first must be slave of all. For even the Son of Man did not come to be served, but to serve, and to give his life as a ransom for many" – Mark 10:43-45

As the year is coming to a close, I want us to make sure we know what our lives as followers of Jesus Christ entails, which is to do just that, *to follow Christ.* He did not come down to earth to reign, to lord His authority over people and make them subject to Him. No, He came down as a servant, living the life of the greatest love of sacrifice, and "humbled himself and became obedient to death—even death on a cross!" (Philippians 2:8). And because of this selfless obedience to the One who sent Him, "God exalted him to the highest place and gave him the name that is above every name" (Philippians 2:9).

Christ did not go out and seek to be exalted and to receive the highest name award, but He went out to serve His fellow brothers, to show them the insurmountable love that the Father has for them. We are told to follow in those same footsteps, not seeking greatness, but seeking lowliness and servant hood, living a life of humility and selflessness as our Master did before us. "Be imitators of God, therefore, as dearly loved children and live a life of love, just as Christ loved us and gave himself up for us" (Ephesians 5:1-2) said Paul to the church in Ephesus. He understood what it meant to serve others, for he gave up his cushy life as a Pharisee to live life as a pilgrim, traveling around Asia and preaching the good news of Christ. He urges us to use our freedom to "serve one another in love" (Galatians 5:13).

Why do we try and seek greatness for ourselves? Why we do ask what James and John asked, "Let one of us sit at your right and the other at your left in your glory" (10:37)? They were in the presence of the Son of God and they had the audacity to ask Him that, which is of course a request out of pure selfishness and for their own glory and not that of the Lord's. But how often do we do the same thing? The Holy Spirit, God Himself, lives within you and is everywhere present, and yet we ask childish and self-centered things of Him all the time. We need to shift our mindset in our prayer life and our lifestyles, to be more God-focused and others-focused, that we may serve them faithfully as our Savior has and is serving us ever more faithfully. He made the way for us and showed us how to live the God-centered life. Do not seek greatness, but seek Him. Go and do likewise. Andrew Murray wrote, "Do we think we can go by any other road than that which the Master trod?" We cannot.

"So he said he would destroy them—had not Moses, his chosen one, stood in the breach before him to keep his wrath from destroying them" – Psalm 106:23

Intercession is vital to our lives as followers of Christ. Without the intercession of the saints (that is us), what hope does the world have to hear of the glorious news of Jesus Christ and be saved? Without intercession, darkness will continue to rule in the corners of the earth where millions are yet unreached, never to have heard of the saving power of Christ.

We have talked about intercession before. This is a reminder for me and hopefully for you as well to continue in it because I have failed in this. I have failed to pray more fervently for the lost around me and have continuously prayed selfishly which bears no fruit and displeases our Savior. This verse speaks wonders of the power of intercessory prayer and the impact it can have on those in darkness. God would have destroyed the people for their wicked ways if Moses had not stood in the breach and prayed for them and for the Lord to show mercy. The same can be true for those around us at our jobs and in our communities; they are on the path that leads to destruction unless we stand in the breach and pray to our Father in heaven for them that they may be saved.

Isaiah wrote, "I have posted watchmen on your walls, O Jerusalem; they will never be silent day or night. You who call on the Lord, give yourselves no rest, and give him no rest till he establishes Jerusalem and makes her the praise of the earth" (Isaiah 62:6-7). Watchmen are those who are attentive to their surroundings, looking for dangers while others are sleeping. It is not their time to rest while others are, but to keep watch over the people they are protecting. Watchmen are the intercessors that are working vigilantly day and night for the people under their watch; we are those watchmen and the world is under our watch. We have to pray on their behalf for their betterment day and night without ceasing because we do not know the day or the hour of the Lord's return.

God's judgment is coming my friends and we should long for people to be on the right side of that judgment, the side of glory and not condemnation. So will you pray to the Lord for the lost and the misguided, the prodigal sons and the rebels? We were one of them once, but now we have seen the marvelous light of Christ, and we should desire for them to be where we are. So will you deliberately intercede for the world as Christ intercedes for us? May there be an outpouring of the Spirit of intercession upon the church; the world desperately needs it.

"So I will always remind you of these things, even though you know them and are firmly established in the truth you now have. I think it is right to refresh your memory as long as I live in the tent of this body" – 2 Peter 1:12-13

If you have not noticed by now, I talk about the same things over and over and that is not without reason as I am sure you know. Repetition is a beautiful thing when it is done in the Spirit of the Lord, which is why people like to get into the habit of having a devotional first thing in the morning so they can have the Word of God ingrained into the fibers of their being as they go about their day. This is why I have made it my goal to memorize a portion of Scripture while I am at work and continually reciting myself the verses I had previously learned so they will all be stuck in my mind and heart forever.

And this is why Peter says these words to the church, because he desires for them to remember the things that they know to be true. As humans, we so easily forget things and that is why there are a myriad of verses on remembering the Lord and what He said; we just plainly fail to remember certain truths because we get focused on other ones. I do not always read the Bible to learn something new, even though I continuously do, but rather to remember the truth I have been told and the different characteristics of a godly man after Christ. As long as we live in the tent of this body, in other words, as long as we are living on earth, our memories need to be refreshed, otherwise we forget.

"Love the Lord your God with all your heart and with all your soul and with all your mind...Love your neighbor as yourself" (Matthew 22:37,39). "For everyone who exalts himself will be humbled, and he who humbles himself will be exalted" (Luke 14:11). "He who belongs to God hears what God says. The reason you do not hear is that you do not belong to God" (John 8:47). "Believe in the Lord Jesus, and you will be saved" (Acts 16:31). "Love never fails" (1 Corinthians 13:8). "And whatever you do, whether in word or deed, do it all in the name of the Lord Jesus, giving thanks to God the Father through him" (Colossians 3:17). "Without holiness no one will see the Lord" (Hebrews 12:14). "He will wipe every tear from their eyes" (Revelation 21:4).

These are but a few of the truths we may have forgotten, but with the help of the Holy Spirit, we shall be reminded of them as we commune with God daily with anticipation and praise, knowing that we are closer to our Savior and Lord than we were the day before. May we always be advancing in the Kingdom of God, taking new territory and remembering the Lord, who He is and what He is doing.

"The Spirit and the bride say, 'Come!' And let him who hears say, 'Come!' Whoever is thirsty let him come; and whoever wishes, let him take the free gift of the water of life" – Revelation 22:17

So we have made it to the end of our journey; 365 days of devotions with the Lord and our expedition comes to its close with the last chapter of the Bible. John had just received his last revelation that the Lord had given him; of heaven, of the end times and the glorious return of Jesus Christ. I cannot imagine what it must have felt like for John to experience these wondrous visions and then have to come back to reality, and that is when he wrote these words. The Holy Spirit, the New Jerusalem and the hearers all say "Come!" How can you not after reading of the marvels that are to come and the magnificence of heaven and the return of Christ?

This is the deepest cry of our hearts and some of us truly know it. "Come, Lord Jesus" (22:20). We pray for Him to come back, to make right the things that are wrong, to usher forth the perfection and fellowship that was in Eden in the beginning, and to make us whole as we were meant to be. Jesus encourages us saying, "Yes, I am coming soon" (22:20). And since He is coming soon, although His meaning of soon is different than ours, it should still give us a sense of urgency in our everyday lives, throwing off the trivial things that do not seem to matter and putting more effort towards those that will last in eternity.

Since Christ Jesus is coming back and we long for Him to do so, what does that mean to you? How are you living your life differently because of this truth that brings the whole of the book of Revelation and the Bible in its entirety to life and fulfillment? Jesus did not only come so that we may be pardoned from our sins and live the rest of our lives with that knowledge. No, He came so that we may have life! (John 10:10) and that life in its fullness shall be seen when He returns to bring us home with Him and His Father where there are many rooms that He is preparing for us. "I will come back and take you to be with me that you also may be where I am" (John 14:3).

The Spirit and the bride say "Come!" We say "Come!" Come Lord Jesus, return to us like you promised. Help us to advance your cause on earth by your Spirit you have given and help hasten the day of your return. We love you Lord and we will serve you faithfully till the end of our days. *Marana tha,* "Come, O Lord!"